World Yearbook of Education 2006

This volume considers the ways in which educational research is being shaped by policy, across the globe. Policy effects on research are increasingly influential, as policies in and beyond education drive the formation of a knowledge-based economy by supporting increased international competitiveness through more effective, evidence-based interventions in schooling, education and training systems.

What consequences does this increased steering have for research in education? How do trans-national agencies make their influence felt on educational research? How do national systems and traditions of educational research – and relations with policy – respond to these new pressures? What effects does it have on the quality of research and on the freedom of researchers to pursue their own agendas?

The 2006 volume of the *World Yearbook of Education* explores these issues, focusing on three key themes:

*   Globalising policy and research in education
*   Steering education research in national contexts
*   Global–local politics of education research

The 2006 volume has a truly global reach, incorporating transnational policy perspectives from the OECD and the European Commission, alongside national 'cases' from across the world in contrasting contexts that include North and South America, Canada, France, Singapore, China, Russia and New Zealand. The range of contributions reflects how pervasive these developments are, how much is new in this situation, and to what extent evidence-based policy pressures on research in education build on past relationships between education and policy.

Education Research and Policy considers the impact of the steering processes on the work and identities of individual researchers, and considers how research can be organised to play a more active role in the politics of the knowledge economy and learning society.

Jenny Ozga is Professor of Educational Research and Director of the Centre for Educational Sociology (CES) at the University of Edinburgh, Scotland. Her research interests include education policy, teachers' work and teacher professionalism, and the transfer of research knowledge into policy.
Terri Seddon is Professor of Education at Monash University, Australia and Director of the Centre for Work and Learning Studies. She is currently researching the educational impact of changes in work and society, especially the drive to a knowledge economy and learning society.
Thomas S. Popkewitz is Professor of Curriculum and Instruction, University of Wisconsin-Madison, USA. His studies are concerned with the knowledge or systems of reason that govern educational policy and research in teaching, teacher education and curriculum.

World Yearbook of Education Series

World Yearbook of Education 2006

Education research and policy:
steering the knowledge-based
economy

**Edited by Jenny Ozga,
Terri Seddon and
Thomas S. Popkewitz**

Routledge
Taylor & Francis Group

LONDON AND NEW YORK

First published 2006
by Routledge
2 Park Square, Milton Park, Abingdon, Oxon, OX14 4RN

Simultaneously published in the USA and Canada
by Routledge
270 Madison Ave, New York, NY 10016

Routledge is an imprint of the Taylor & Francis Group

© 2006 selection and editorial matter Jenny Ozga, Terri Seddon and
Thomas S. Popkewitz; individual chapters, the contributors

Typeset in Times by
HWA Text and Data Management Ltd, Tunbridge Wells
Printed and bound in Great Britain by
The Cromwell Press, Trowbridge, Wiltshire

British Library Cataloguing in Publication Data
A catalogue record for this book is available from the British Library

Library of Congress Cataloging-in-Publication Data
A catalog record for this book has been requested

ISBN10: 0–415–35934–1
ISBN13: 978–0–415–35934–4

Contents

Figures and tables

Figures

Tables

Contributors

Angelos Agalianos received his PhD from the University of London in 1997. His research in the sociology and politics of educational innovation combined ideas from the sociology and politics of education, the social studies of technology and from cultural studies. Since 1998, he has worked in the DG-Research of the European Commission in Brussels. He is currently working in the unit that supports European research in the social sciences and humanities. His duties include contributing to the development of European research policy for the social sciences, the management of several research projects supported under the fifth and sixth EU Framework Programmes for research, and the dissemination of results from EU-supported research in the social sciences and in the field of education in particular.

Elizabeth Bullen is a Research Associate in the Faculty of Education at Monash University, Victoria, Australia. She has a PhD in Australian literature from Flinders University, South Australia. Her research interests include gender, globalisation, and consumption practices. She is co-author with Jane Kenway of *Consuming Children: Education-Advertising-Entertainment* (Open University Press, 2001), and co-editor with Jane Kenway and Simon Robb of *Innovation and Tradition: The Arts, Humanities and the Knowledge Economy* (Peter Lang, 2004). She is currently co-authoring, with Jane Kenway, Simon Robb and Johannah Fahey, *Haunting the Knowledge Economy* (International Library of Sociology, Routledge).

Kari Dehli is Associate Professor at the Ontario Institute for Studies in Education, University of Toronto, Canada, where she teaches in areas of cultural studies, feminist poststructuralism, governance and state formation. Her research and publications trace the organisation and effects of power and difference in schooling through investigations of education policy and governance. Her current research follows the terms and effects of 'improvement' from nineteenth-century schooling to contemporary schemes that seek to transform schools, communities, families and selves.

Ana M. Donini is Professor of Education and Director of the MA Program in Educational Management at the National University of San Martin Argentina. She has an MA from the State University of California (Stanislaus) and an EdD from University of the Pacific, Stockton, California. She was Coordinator of the Area of International Cooperation in the Argentine Ministry of Education, Science and Technology. Her research interests include educational reform and educational policies in higher education in Argentina. Current projects include teacher education in Argentina. She is author of *Nuevo siglo, nueva escuela?* (Santillana,1998) and several articles in the field of educational policies.

Johannah Fahey is a freelance writer and a Research Associate in the Faculty of Education at Monash University, Victoria, Australia. She has a PhD in cultural studies from Macquarie University, Sydney. Her research interests include post-structuralism, post-colonialism, contemporary Australian visual arts, and globalisation. She is author of the art monograph *David Noonan: Before and Now* (Thames and Hudson, 2005). She is currently co-authoring *Haunting the Knowledge Economy* (International Library of Sociology, Routledge).

Mark B. Ginsburg is Professor of the Department of Administrative and Policy Studies (Education) and Department of Sociology (Faculty of Arts and Sciences) and Co-Director of the Institute for International Studies in Education, University of Pittsburgh. His main interests are in the field of comparative sociology of education and he focuses on social class, race/ethnicity, and gender in relation to the politics of education, teacher education, and educators' work and lives. Current projects include: a longitudinal, ethnographic study of political socialisation of educators in Mexico; the second phase of a ten-year, USAID-funded action-research project on 'improving educational quality' in developing countries; an edited volume *Cuban in the Special Period: Cuban Perspectives*; a comparative historical study *Construction of Citizen-Workers in/through Teacher Education in Canada, Mexico, and the United States*; and a book series for Garland Publishing on 'Studies in Education/Politics'.

Jorge Gorostiaga is Associate Professor of Education at the School of Graduate Studies, Universidad Nacional de San Martín (Argentina). He obtained his PhD in comparative education at the University of Pittsburgh (2003). He is the co-editor (with Mark Ginsburg) of *Limitations and Possibilities of Dialogue among Researchers, Policy-makers and Practitioners* (RoutledgeFalmer, 2003). His research focuses on the reform of school governance in Latin America.

David Hogan is Professor and Vice-Dean at the Centre for Research in Pedagogy and Practice (CRPP) at the National Institute of Education, Nanyang Technological University, Singapore. Prior to that, he was Professor of Education at the University of Tasmania, and before that, an Assistant Professor and Associate Professor at the Graduate School of Education, University of Pennsylvania. Professor Hogan has written extensively about the history of education in the US and has received the American Educational Research Association Outstanding Book Award (1986), the Henry Barnard Prize, and the History of Education Society Award. His publications include 'The social economy of education and the contract state', in G. Davis and A. Yeatman (eds), *The State and the New Contractualism* (Macmillan,1997) and 'The logic of protection: citizenship, justice and political community', in K. Kennedy (ed.) *Citizenship Education and the Modern State* (Falmer Press, 1997).

Irina Isaakyan is a PhD student in the Moray House School of Education at the University of Edinburgh. Her thesis is on academic careers of Russian academic emigrants. Before that she completed an MA in educational administration at the University of Minnesota. In 2000, under the auspices of the Freedom Support Act, she had worked as an English instructor at the Ryazan State Pedagogical University, Ryazan, Russia. Her research interests at the moment include globalisation, academic careers, gender construction and migration.

Eric M. Johnson is a PhD student in comparative education and political science, Teachers College, Columbia University, New York. His research interests include outside-school supplementary education, or 'shadow education', and competing theoretical explanations of its global expansion. His region of specialisation is the former Soviet Union, specifically Central Asia. He is a recipient of the Foreign Language and Area Studies (FLAS) Fellowship for the study of Russian and Uzbek and a Social Science Research Council (SSRC) grant for the study of Kyrgyz.

Cynthia Joseph is a lecturer at Monash University. She researches, publishes and teaches in the areas of socio-cultural studies in education and international education. Her areas of specialisation are postcolonial and feminist theorisations of identity and difference. She uses these lenses to research identity, ethnicity, and education; and cultural differences and globalisation within an international context. She is also interested in the paradigms of research methodologies. Her new area of specialisation is ethnicity, religion and transnational identities. She has had experience within the education sectors in Malaysia. She completed her PhD at Monash University in the area of gender, ethnicity and schooling. She was awarded the 2004 Mollie Holman Medal for Excellence for her doctoral thesis 'Theorisations of identity and difference: Ways of being Malay, Chinese and Indian schoolgirls in a Malaysian secondary school'.

Jane Kenway is Professor of Global Education Studies in the Faculty of Education at Monash University, Australia. She is currently co-authoring *Haunting the Knowledge Economy* (International Library of Sociology, Routledge) which deploys alternative theories of economy (risk, gift, libidinal and survival) in order to explain some of the social, political and cultural aspects of the global knowledge economy that are excluded by its dominant discourses.

Zack Kertcher is a PhD student at the Department of Sociology at the University of Chicago. His research is broadly concerned with the linkages between social psychology and institutional change. He is currently constructing an analytical bridge between the theories of action of Blumer, Habermas and Giddens for the study of computer-mediated interaction. In addition, he is studying identity conflict, emotional attachment, and degree of embeddedness of high-tech professionals in the context of contract employment.

Kenneth King is Director of the Centre of African Studies and Professor of International and Comparative Education. His research interests include comparative and international education; analysis of inter-relations of science, technology and education; non-formal education and informal sector employment in Third World countries; educational planning in the Third World; historical aspects of education in Africa; research on educational quality; vocational education and training, including in OECD countries; analysis of aid policies in education. He has just completed books on the informal economy in Kenya, higher education in the developing world and education in South Africa, and his recent publications include *Jua Kali Kenya: Change and Development in Kenya's Informal Economy, 1970–1995* (James Currey, 1996).

Sverker Lindblad is Professor of Education at Göteborg University where he is acting as Head of Research. He is a member of different boards and committees, including the Centre of European Studies at Göteborg University, the trans-university Committee for 'A Safer City', and the board for 'The Centre for Educational Science in Teacher Education'. He is currently researching 'pedagogy and politics', where, for example, political aspects of pedagogical interaction are in focus. In addition, he is now initiating a study on international university rankings. Recent publications include: *Educational Restructuring: International Perspectives on Travelling Policies* (co-edited with Thomas S. Popkewitz, Information Age Publishing, 2004) and 'OECD Examiners' Report on Educational Research and Development in England' (with S. Wolter, E. Keiner and D. Palomba, *European Educational Research Journal*, 2004).

Ingrid Lohmann is Professor of Education at Hamburg University where she was appointed in 1992 to the Chair of Theory and Social History of Education. Her main interests are in the origins and purposes of public education, Jewish educational history and the privatisation and commercialisation of education and science. She is author of 'Commercialism in education: Historical perspectives, global dimensions and European educational research fields of interest' (*European Educational Research Journal*, 2002), editor of the series *Jewish Educational History in Germany* (with B. L. Behm and U. Lohmann) and heads the project on 'A core curriculum in educational sciences – content development and evaluation' (KC-EDU) for the e-Learning Consortium Hamburg (ELCH). Her current research focuses on the inter-relations between economical and pedagogical discourses in modern times.

Allan Luke is Foundation Dean, Centre for Research in Pedagogy and Practice, National Institute of Education, Nanyang Technological University, Singapore. Before joining CRPP in 2003, Professor Luke was Dean at the University of Queensland in Australia and Chief Advisor to the Queensland Minister of Education. Professor Luke is author and editor of fifteen books including, most recently, *Struggles Over Difference: Texts, Curriculum and Pedagogy in the Asia Pacific* (State University of New York Press). He is currently co-editor of *Teaching Education* (Routledge), *Review of Research in Education* (AERA), *Asia Pacific Journal of Education* (Routledge) and *Pedagogies: An International Journal* (Lawrence Erlbaum).

Erica McWilliam is Professor of Education and Assistant Dean Research in the Faculty of Education at the Queensland University of Technology. The first two decades of her career in education were spent in Queensland secondary schools in both the government and the private sectors. Her educational publications cover a wide spectrum, as is evidenced in her numerous publications on innovative teaching and learning, research methodology and training and leadership and management. She is currently series editor of 'Eruptions: New Thinking across the Disciplines', an academic series for Peter Lang Publishing, New York. Erica is also an author and social commentator on some of the charming absurdities of corporate practice.

Shira Offer is a doctoral candidate in sociology at the University of Chicago and a research associate at the Alfred P. Sloan Center on Parents, Children, and Work. Her research interests include familial and community processes in the urban context, patterns of immigrants' integration, and welfare and social policy. She has published several articles about the well-being of low-income families in the USA and about the Ethiopian community in Israel. In her dissertation, she examines the disparities in social support systems of families living in disadvantaged communities by race and ethnicity and their impact on the educational aspirations and achievements of adolescents.

Jenny Ozga is Professor of Educational Research and Director of the Centre for Educational Sociology at the Moray House School of Education, University of Edinburgh. Her main research interest is in education policy and her current research includes work on social inclusion policies, on education and youth transitions throughout the UK and on knowledge transfer in higher education in Scotland. Her recent publications include: *Policy Research in Educational Settings: Contested Terrain* (Open University Press, 2000); 'Researching Education Policy: Interpreting the Evidence' in B. Davies and J. West-Burnham (eds) *Handbook of Educational Leadership and Management* (Pearson Collins); 'Research and Practice' (with P. Munn) in T. Bryce and W. Humes (eds) *Scottish Education: Post-Devolution* (2nd edn, Edinburgh University Press); 'Modernising the education workforce: a perspective from Scotland' (*Educational Review*) and 'Travelling and embedded policy: the case of post-devolution Scotland within the UK' in E. Zambeta and D. Coulby (eds) *World Year Book on Globalisation and Nationalism in Education* (Routledge, 2005). She is series editor (with Thomas S. Popkewitz and Terri Seddon) of the *World Yearbook of Education*.

Mónica Pini holds a Master of Science in public administration from the University of Buenos Aires, Argentina and PhD in educational thought and sociocultural studies from the University of New Mexico. Her areas of interest are politics and administration of education and critical discourse analysis. She has worked as a teacher in elementary, middle and high schools, and as a professor in universities and institutes for teacher preparation in Argentina. She has participated in several education research projects in Buenos Aires, and in the National Program of Management of Teacher Training at the Argentine Ministry of Education. She has published several articles, chapters and a book, *Escuelas chartery empresas: Un discurso que vende*, (Miño y Dávila). Currently she is Associate Professor, Director of the Graduate Program in Education, Language and Media, and Coordinator of the Research, Development and Assistance Program in Education at the Graduate School of the Universidad Nacional de San Martín.

Thomas S. Popkewitz is Professor of Education in the Department of Curriculum and Instruction at the University of Wisconsin-Madison, USA . His studies are concerned with the knowledge or systems of reason that govern educational policy and research in teaching, teacher education, and curriculum. He has also served as a research consultant to European countries on educational policy in issues of equity and justice. His most recent books are: *Educational Restructuring: International Perspectives on Traveling Policies* (edited with Sverker Lindblad, Information Age Publishers, 2004); *New Perspectives in the Politics of Education: The Changing Terrain of Knowledge and Research* (with B. Franklin and M. Bloch, Athens: Atrapos Editions, 2003, in Greek); *Educational Partnerships: The Paradoxes of Governing Schools, Children, and Families* (edited with M. Bloch, K. Holmlund and L. Moqvist, Macmillan Palgrave, 2003); *Governing Children, Families, and Education: Restructuring the Welfare State* (with B. Franklin and M. Pereyra, Macmillan Palgrave, 2001); *Cultural History and Education: Critical Studies on Knowledge and Schooling* (Routledge); and *Educational Knowledge: Changing Relationships Between the State, Civil Society, and the Educational Eommunity* (edited with L. Fendler, SUNY Press, 1999).

Xavier Rambla is an Associate Professor in the Department of Sociology, at the Autonomous University of Barcelona (UAB). Before that he was a lecturer at University of Vic (Barcelona) as well as a researcher at the Anti-Sexist Education Program (Institute of Education, UAB). Currently, he is a member of the Seminar for the Analysis of Social Policy (at the Department of Sociology, UAB) and collaborates with the Globalisation and Europeanisation Network in Europe. His main research areas are the analysis of social inequalities, sociology of education and educational policy.

Simon Robb is a writer and a Research Associate in the Faculty of Education at Monash University, Victoria, Australia. His research interests include textual theory, aesthetics and sustainability. He has published with the Electronic Writing Research Ensemble and is author of the experimental history *The Hulk* (Post Taste, 2003); he is also co-editor of *Innovation and Tradition: The Arts, Humanities and the Knowledge Economy* (Peter Lang, 2004). He is currently co-authoring *Haunting the Knowledge Economy* (International Library of Sociology, Routledge).

Peter Roberts is an Associate Professor in the Faculty of Education at the University of Auckland. He teaches philosophy of education and educational policy studies. He has published widely in international journals. His books include *Education, Literacy and Humanization: Exploring the Work of Paulo Freire* (Bergin and Garvey, 2000); *University Futures and the Politics of Reform in New Zealand* (with Michael Peters, Dunmore Press, 1999); and *Digital Developments in Higher Education* (edited with Mark Chambers, Taylor Graham Publishing, 2001).

Barbara Schneider was Professor of Sociology and Human Development at the University of Chicago until 2005 when she joined the faculty at Michigan State University as the John A. Hannah Chair in the College of Education. She currently directs the Data Research and Development Center, and co-directs the Alfred P. Sloan Center on Parents, Children, and Work. Interested in the lives of adolescents and their families and schools, she has written widely on these topics. Her most recent publications include: *The Ambitious Generation: America's Teenagers, Motivated but Directionless* (with David Stevenson, Yale University Press); *Becoming Adult:*

How Teenagers Prepare for the World of Work (with Mihaly Csikszentmihalyi, Basic Books); and *Trust in Schools, A Core Resource for Improvement* (with Anthony Bryk, Russell Sage Foundation). She and Linda Waite have recently completed a book based on findings from the 'Sloan 500 Family Study' exploring the lives of working families entitled *Being Together, Working Apart: Dual-Career Families and the Work-Life Balance* (Cambridge University Press). She is currently conducting a new random assignment project, TEACH Research that is designed to improve adolescents' transition to post-secondary education. She serves on a number of advisory boards including the AERA Grants Board. Recently, she was selected by the American Sociological Association as the new editor of *Sociology of Education*.

Tom Schuller is Head of the Centre for Educational Research and Innovation (CERI), OECD, Paris. Formerly Dean of the Faculty of Continuing Education and Professor of Lifelong Learning at Birkbeck, University of London, from 1999 to 2003, he has also worked at the Universities of Edinburgh, Glasgow and Warwick, at the Institute for Community Studies and, in the 1970s, for four years at OECD. He has been an adviser to the government on numerous issues, especially on lifelong learning. Recent publications include: *The Benefits of Learning: The Impact of Education on Health, Family Life and Social Capital* (with John Preston *et al.*, RoutledgeFalmer, 2004); *International Perspectives on Lifelong Learning* (edited with David Istance and Hans Schuetze, Open University Press, 2002); *Social Capital: Critical Perspectives* (edited with Stephen Baron and John Field, OUP, 2000); *Part-time Higher Education in Scotland* (with David Raffe *et al.*, Jessica Kingsley, 1998); *Life After Work* (with Michael Young, HarperCollins, 1991).

Terri Seddon is Professor of Education at Monash University and was Associate Dean Research from 2002–05 in the Faculty of Education. She is also Director of the Centre for Work and Learning Studies. She was Director of Research Degrees at Monash University from 2001–02. She has longstanding interests in continuity and change in education and is currently researching the educational impact of changes in work and society, especially the drive to a knowledge economy and learning society. Her most recent book (with Lawrie Angus) is *Beyond Nostalgia: Reshaping Australian Education* (Australian Council for Educational Research, 2000). She is currently a member of the Australian Research Council College of Experts. Her other publications include: 'Research Education: Whose Space for Learning?' (with B. Doecke, *Australian Education Researcher*, 2002); 'What is doctoral in doctoral education?' in B. Green, T.W. Maxwell and P. Shanahan (eds) *Doctoral Education and Professional Practice: The Next Generation?* (A Kardoorair Press, 1999); 'Research, recommendations and realpolitik: Implications for consolidating the EdD' (*Australian Educational Researcher*, 1996); *Pay, Professionalism and Politics: Reforming Teachers, Reforming Education* (as editor, *Australian Education Review*, 1996); and *Context and Beyond: Reframing the Theory and Practice of Education* (Falmer Press, 1994).

Iveta Silova holds a PhD from the Graduate School of Arts and Sciences, Columbia University. She works in the Centre for Educational Innovations in Baku, Azerbaijan, and as an adjunct professor at Teachers College, Columbia University, where she co-teaches an online course on international education policy. She is the author of *From Sites of Occupation to Symbols of Multiculturalism: Re-conceptualizing Minority Education in post-Soviet Latvia* (information Age Publishing, 2005). Her most recent book project is entitled *Dealing with the Post-Socialist Education Reform Package: From Baku to Ulaanbaatar* (with Gita Steiner-Khamsi, Kumarian Press, forthcoming), which examines the role of NGOs in education reform in Central Asia and the Caucasus. Research interests include globalisation, democratisation, and educational borrowing in Eastern and Central Europe and the former Soviet Union.

Noah W. Sobe is Assistant Professor in the Cultural and Educational Policy Studies programme at Loyola University in Chicago. His primary areas of scholarship are in the history of education and comparative education, with a geographic focus on Europe and the USA. His work has appeared in *Educational Theory* and *Paedagogica Historica*. He is currently at work on a history of the international emergence of the problematic of the child's attention as a pedagogical and educational research concern.

Gita Steiner-Khamsi, PhD, is Professor of Education in the programs of comparative and international education and international development at Teachers College Columbia University, New York. Her research is situated in education policy studies, globalisation studies, and in particular policy borrowing/lending research. She is involved in school and teacher education reform projects in European and Central Asian countries. Her most recent monograph (with Ines Stolpe) is entitled *Educational Import in Mongolia: Local Encounters with Global Forces* (Palgrave Macmillan, 2006). Recently published edited volumes include *The Global Politics of Educational Borrowing and Lending* (Teachers College Press, 2004); and *New Paradigms and Recurring Paradoxes in Education for Citizenship: An International Comparison* (with Judith Torney-Purta and John Schwille, Elsevier Science, 2002).

Alison Taylor is an Associate Professor in the Department of Educational Policy Studies at the University of Alberta, Canada. She is the author of *The Politics of Educational Reform in Alberta* (University of Toronto Press, 2001). Her current research projects focus on policies and practices related to school-to-work transition and school choice.

Patricia Thomson is Professor of Education in the School of Education, University of Nottingham and is the school's Director of Research. Before coming to the University of Nottingham in May 2003, she directed the professional doctorate in education and an offshore PhD programme at the University of South Australia. She was Deputy Director of the Centre for Studies in Literacy, Policy and Learning Cultures. She remains an Adjunct Professor in the School of Education (UNISA). She previously managed strategic planning in the state education department and before that she was a school principal and has represented Australian principals on national policy-making bodies and at international conferences, and was President of the South Australian Secondary Principals Association. She was a member of national and state policy-making bodies and has extensive experience in equity policy development. Her recent publications include: *Schooling the Rustbelt Kids: Making the Difference in Changing*

Times (Allen and Unwin (Australia) and Trentham (UK), 2002); and *Rethinking Public Education: Towards a Public Curriculum* (edited with Alan Reid, Postpressed, 2003).

Rui Yang is a Senior Lecturer at the Faculty of Education, Monash University in Australia. He received his PhD in comparative studies in education policy from the University of Sydney. He has taught and researched in Guangdong and Hong Kong in China, and New South Wales, Western Australia and Victoria in Australia. An expert on Chinese higher education, and internationalisation of Chinese universities, he has published widely in these areas and has established an international reputation. His current interests are in the fields of comparative and international studies in education, higher education and education policy. His recent book *Internationalisation of Higher Education in China: A Study of Guangzhou* (Routledge, 2002), appeared as part of the series 'East Asia: History, Politics, Sociology, Culture'.

Agnès van Zanten is a Senior Researcher at the Centre National de la Recherche Scientifique (CNRS) in France. She works at the Observatoire Sociologique du Changement which is a research centre of Sciences-Po Paris, where she also teaches sociology of education to master and doctoral students. She is also the Director of RAPPE (Réseau d'Analyse Pluridisciplinaire des Politiques Educatives), an international network on educational policy. Her main research areas are the reproduction and transformation of social advantage in education, the organisational and professional dynamics of schools and local public action in education. She is also interested in qualitative research methods and in international comparisons. Her most recent publications are *Les politiques d'éducation* ('Que sais-je' series, PUF, 2004) and *Sociologie de l'école* (with M. Duru-Bellat, Armand Colin, 3rd edn, 2005).

Series editors' introduction

This volume on *Education Research and Policy* picks up one of the major themes of the 2005 volume on *Globalization and Nationalism in Education*, that is globalisation and its impacts on education. It develops this theme through a focus on educational research, in particular on how policy for educational research is shaping research processes and practices around the globe. There have been very considerable changes in the steering of educational research since the publication of the *1986 World Yearbook* on this topic, and this volume offers an updating of the global picture of research in education in a context in which research is seen to be central to the building of new knowledge economies through its contribution to increased international competitiveness and its support for more effective, evidence-based interventions in schooling, education and training systems.

The volume does not adopt a perspective on globalisation that takes its trajectory for granted and reads off its effects. Rather it seeks to keep in play a dynamic tension between the homogenising global agendas for policy steering that seek to shape knowledge-based economies and the impact on those agendas of different national and local practices and cultures of educational research. A key concern of the volume is to explore the ways in which educational researchers in different regional/national contexts respond to and mediate international and national pressure to steer research, and to identify the cultural and political resources that they recognise and deploy in such processes of mediation, at the same time as exploring the workings of the different systems of funding and recognition that are in play within and across systems. The volume takes the opportunity presented by the global reach of the *World Yearbook* to bring together material from across the globe in order to explore and illustrate the many different ways in which international/supra-national pressures on research play out at local/national/institutional level, and thus offers the possibility of some assessment of the capacity of education research in different contexts to respond to, mediate or rework global agendas for research steering. The global reach of the volume also enables an assessment of how pervasive these developments are, how much is new in this situation and the extent to which evidence-based policy pressures on research in education build on past relationships between education and policy.

The steering of research is a policy area of increased significance but it has not received much attention as a significant emergent policy area that seeks to create particular forms of education research identity and research practice in globalising conditions. This volume seeks to capture some of these developments, to highlight their significance and to foster debate about education research in these conditions, by bringing together a wide range of contributions, that link globalising developments through supra-national and transnational agencies such as the European Commission or the Organisation for Economic Co-operation and Development (OECD), to contrasting national contexts and to individual social and cultural practices of research.

Jenny Ozga, Terri Seddon and Evie Zambeta
Edinburgh, Melbourne and Athens, 2005

Introduction

Education research and policy – steering the knowledge-based economy

Jenny Ozga, Terri Seddon and Thomas S. Popkewitz

The focus of the 2006 volume of the *World Yearbook of Education* is contemporary changes and challenges in education research. Specifically, it focuses on the way policies in and beyond education drive the formation of a knowledge-based economy by supporting increased international competitiveness through more effective, evidence-based interventions in schooling/education/training systems. The book is grouped around three key themes that take the focus on policy steering and apply it to educational research. The first theme explores the nature of the steering processes themselves, which include the activities of supra-national agencies in sponsoring particular kinds of research, in commercialising research and in shaping and codifying educational research to address key policy priorities. The second theme is that of national contexts for educational research and the interaction of globalising influences with national traditions and assumptions about research and about the relationship between research and policy. One of our key aims in this volume is to illustrate the diversity of research steering processes and the relationships between these processes and assumptions – that may be more or less implicit – about the purposes and direction of educational research in different contexts. The third theme is that of research in education as a political process, and here we include contributions from researchers that discuss ways of responding to steering pressures on research that acknowledge and interrogate the complexities of globalising processes. In this regard we are seeking to respond to Appadurai's call for debates on globalisation and research to move beyond the parochial and challenge current discourses of expertise in order to engage with social forms and forces beyond the Academy as well as within it, in ways that transform research and support the transfer of knowledge (Appadurai 2003: 3).

These themes each shape a section of the volume. *Part 1: Globalising Policy and Research in Education* is concerned to discuss the nature and workings of globalising policy and research in education, through supra-national and transnational agencies such as the European Union (EU), the Organisation for Economic Co-operation and Development (OECD) and the World Bank, as well as information and communication technologies (and their sponsors) and international research associations. *Part 2: Steering Research in National Contexts* looks at how education research is being steered in different and contrasting national contexts, exploring the different kinds of resources available to researchers in shaping responses to research steering in education. *Part 3: Global–local Politics of Education Research* looks at how a politics of educational research might emerge, in the interaction of global-local politics of education research. Together these sections combine to offer consideration of the inter-relations between global, national and local developments in education research and policy, and thus support a sharper understanding of the way research is implicated within, and mediates, the trajectory towards a knowledge economy and 'learning society' across the globe.

The initial impulse for this topic arose from our own changing experiences as education researchers. It seemed that our work in education research had changed over time. We could remember times when doing research entailed extensive reading of literature; having relatively unpressured time to think, write and conceptualise; and the capacity to exercise considerable autonomy and discretion in terms of what we researched and how. Publication was important but its nature was different: there was little requirement to produce on demand, to write to specific research users, or to privilege the utility of our research over the representation of its intrinsic research logic. We acknowledge that we are able to retain some of these research practices, at least some of the time. Yet, our sense is that the rhythm and pace of research has speeded up. The business aspects of research – getting funds, employing and managing staff, building networks with research users, attending to their research needs and ensuring the timely preparation of relevant research products – seem to constitute the foreground of research, displacing day-to-day research practices and passions. In addition, agencies outside the research community seem to be increasingly intrusive, having a growing influence in both the regulation and conduct of research.

The sense of education research sitting at the confluence of many different expectations and pressures is illustrated by a snapshot of the world of Australian education researchers in the first week of July 2005. Early July is the middle of the academic year in Australia, the mid-winter break when many conferences are held and when researchers look forward to actually getting some research done.

In that week, many researchers with current applications to the Australian Research Council (ARC) must have been preparing their rejoinders to assessors' appraisals of their applications. They have up to five assessors' reports to consider and respond to, and, by the end of the week, must have up-loaded their considered one-page response to these assessments onto the ARC website. These rejoinders are important because they can make or break a successful funding application. The Australian Research Council is the premier research funding body in Australia. Success rates are around 20 per cent. Education wins around 3 per cent of total ARC funding. Success brings prestige to researchers but it also means that it gets universities, desperate for funds and for research prestige, off their backs.

In that same week, they would have been able to read the headline 'Education research irrelevant' (*Age*, 2 July 2005: 5). A Professor of Education at Melbourne University had gone to the press arguing that education research has no impact on schools and is ignored by policy makers. The Australian Research Council, he stated, was 'grossly unreliable' with unaccountable assessors who are not experts in the field and who lack international standing in the field. The main point of this critique was to argue for the formation of a 'national network of researchers, policy makers, teachers, principals and parents to decide what should be researched'. The Professor had gone to the press with his views before presenting them at a focus conference on research quality, run by the Australian Association for Education Research (AARE). AARE is the major professional association of education researchers. It had organised the conference on research quality because the Commonwealth government was designing and implementing a new regulatory framework to govern research and Commonwealth research funding allocations, like the UK's Research Assessment Exercise. AARE was concerned that the conceptual models informing the Research Quality Framework would disadvantage education research. The conference was intended to inform members about the research quality agenda, engage with the policy process so that the policy design would accommodate features of education research, and encourage dialogue among researchers in order to share ideas and resources about ways of addressing the quality framework within education research, research education and research management.

The Wednesday press offered a new headline, 'Research Council in Nelson's (the Minister for Education) firing line' (*Australian*, 6 July 2005: 31). The article indicated that the Australian Research Council could be abolished and more control over research grants handed to the Commonwealth Minister. This possibility was being debated in the context of recommendations in the Uhrig Review urging Commonwealth Ministers and departments to review the statutory authorities in their portfolios against two organisational templates: an executive management model and a board model. The Commonwealth had already agreed that the board model should only be used where they could be given full power to act. The ARC currently has a board, but does not have full power to act because the Minister retains a veto power on grants – a power he used in 2004 to stop funding to three social sciences and humanities projects that had been recommended for funding by the ARC. The article indicated that this scenario meant that the ARC could be wound back towards an executive management model, with only an advisory board and a chief executive officer who reports directly to the Minister.

This 'week in the life of Australian education research' could be a parochial story, except that it is being replayed across the globe. The pressure on researchers to win research funding is a common theme across countries. It is driven by universities' quest for funding and prestige, and by national and regional policy agenda that argue for competitive advantage in the emerging knowledge-based economy. Intrinsic curiosity that might motivate the investigation of a research issue or question is being displaced by inter-institutional and international competition for research business. This fiercely fought competition embraces universities and long-established foundations and research centres but it also increasingly involves small and large consultancies, accounting firms, dedicated research businesses, start-up companies and hybrid networked organisations based in public and private agencies. The competition for funds is backed up by policy hype and increasingly professionalised research proposal development units within universities and private companies. We see a new research division of labour emerging, global in scale.

The Australian Research Quality Framework is a late arrival in the global landscape which is already populated by the UK's Research Assessment Exercise, New Zealand's Performance-Based Research Framework and similar schemes in Hong Kong, the Netherlands, and elsewhere. It joins a range of other regulatory and legislative developments that places demands and constraints on research and researchers. Protocols around ethics and intellectual property formalise rules and processes that bind the way research is done. Funding bodies define the way reports must be submitted and the kinds of dissemination activities that researchers must engage in. In the USA, Congress passed the Educational Sciences Reform Act (H.R. 3801). The bill created the Institute of Education Sciences and established rules that privileged particular approaches to education research, requiring researchers to emphasise 'evidence' and 'scientific validity' in research. Greater control of research is another common feature around the world, although the resort to direct ministerial control broached in Australia seems anachronistic compared to other governance regimes that operate through management of information, risk and choice.

Our parochial stories are, then, also global stories about contemporary education research and the construction of research business. This global-local dialectic prompted questions:

• How do researchers experience contemporary education research and its changing context?
• How is education research being re-regulated? And how is it driven – globally, regionally, nationally and locally?
• What scenarios are emerging from these changing formations and practices of education research?
• In what ways, and to what ends, are individuals, groups, networks and nations engaging with these developments?
• What counts as practical politics in the emerging world of education research and research business?

These broad questions have informed the *World Yearbook of Education, 2006*. They have shaped its conceptualisation, the selection of contributors and the themes that they address. In the next section we outline the way we have approached these questions, before turning to a more detailed discussion of the structure and content of the volume.

Approaching the issues

Globalisation

Globalisation haunts our discussion of education research and its changing formations and practices. Our simple, starting-point defines 'globalisation' as: 'the increasing interconnection between economic and social life' resulting from the particular interaction between technological innovation and the development of capitalism (Gray 2000: 32–3). But, as we indicate, this is a complex phenomenon with many layers.

Globalisation was a key theme in the 2005 *World Yearbook of Education*. This volume considered the relationship between globalisation and nationalism (Coulby and Zambeta 2005). As the 2005 volume suggests, globalisation is usually discussed and understood in relation to its capacity to dissolve distinctions between the international and the domestic, the global and the local. Its effects are evidenced in core economic activities (where multinationals operate across continents and capital flows across nation states) and in media and electronic communications (which make the flows of capital possible). These effects play out in financial markets, the internationalisation of corporate strategies/ management, the spread of worldwide patterns of consumption, the internationalisation of nation states and the diminished capacity of national governments.

Accompanying social and cultural consequences are evident in terms of accelerated people mobility as individuals pursue jobs across the globe, seek economic advantage through migration, adventure as tourists, and flee as refugees and displaced persons from places disrupted by the destabilisation of international relations and the established frameworks of nation-states and nationalisms. These experiences mean that, more and more, difference is encountered on a day-to-day basis, through the people we see and talk to, and the media images that flow through their lives.

These cultural effects of globalisation shift the horizons of the everyday, opening people's eyes not just to developments on the world stage but also to features of the local that were previously obscured. Global processes and flows, and the proliferation of sub-national discourses that dispute the authority of nation-states, disrupt commonplace understandings of the nation-state as the natural scale of politics. The national scale continues to provide a particular set of cultural scripts, albeit authoritative and authorised in ways that give them particular power and legitimacy, but they exist alongside other scripts of greater or lesser power emanating from other discursive contexts operating at different scales (Prakash and Hart 1999, Djelic and Quack 2003). These alternative 'interpretive frames' provide other ways for understanding the relations of power-knowledge-organisation within different spatial registers – global, regional, local (Gibson-Graham 2003).

The co-presence of these different cultural scripts intensifies the politics of scale within which policy and practice are asserted and enacted. These politics of scale are significant because they are intimately connected to governance and the configuration of politics as a capacity to shape praxis. While the state has been problematised in the context of globalisation, it remains a powerful and critical locus for institutional design – the way agency is shaped and enacted in and across space, and how actors produce spaces through their praxis. The effect is to fuel practical politics that dispute locii of decision making, jurisdictions and decisions, and define empowered and unempowered constituencies across spatial registers.

Giddens captures this complexity of globalisation in his well-known definition:

> Globalisation can thus be defined as the intensification of worldwide social relations which link distant localities in such a way that local happenings are shaped by events occurring many miles away and vice-versa. This is a dialectical process because such local happenings may move in an obverse direction from the very distanciated relations that shape them. *Local transformation* is as much a part of gloablisation as the lateral extension of social connections across time and space (Giddens 1990: 64 emphasis in original).

From this perspective, as Appadurai argues, it is possible to identify 'vernacular globalisation' in which there is change and reconfiguration in global, national and local interrelationships but mediated by local and national history and politics (Appadurai 1996). Old notions of 'centre' and 'periphery' are collapsed in communities that are overlapping, complex and disjunctive. Disorganised capitalism creates fundamental disjunctures between the economy, culture and politics (Appadurai 1990). Globalisation produces rebalancing of national and global functions; in Sassen's words:

> Globalisation is partly endogenous to the national and is in this regard produced through a dynamic of denationalising what has been constructed as the national. And it is partly embedded in the national ... and in this regard requires that the state regulate specific aspects of its role in the national.
>
> (Sassen 2003: 177)

Knowledge and education

Knowledge has particular significance in the context of contemporary globalisation. On the one hand, knowledge is privileged as a critical resource within late capitalism, a resource that must be harnessed to underpin profitability. On the other hand, the lived experience of globalisation, in and beyond employment, encourages active knowing. The politics of scale and shifts in cultural horizons means that traditional ways of understanding are questioned and alternative processes of meaning making develop. Creative thinking, innovation and problem-solving are valued over and above the consolidation of static knowledge stocks. Yet this dispersed production of knowledge, so valuable in economic contexts, presents serious challenges to traditional social and political arrangements.

Castells (1996: 17) argues, for example, that we are moving from an industrial economy in which productivity depended upon energy sources and their innovative applications, to an informational economy in which the 'source of productivity lies in the technology of knowledge generation, information processing, and symbol communication'. The kind of knowledge that is important is not just the regular knowledge and information that has always informed economic production. Rather, he argues, what is distinctive in contemporary global economic development is 'the action of knowledge on itself as the main source of productivity'.

Active knowing sits at the heart of the innovation economy. Stehr (2002: 27) defines knowledge as a 'capacity for social action'. He argues that knowledge is activated in situations that are not fully regulated or defined through routine processes. Such situations, where there is some freedom in the course of action that might be chosen, support creative problem-solving that lead to increases in 'how-to-do-it' capacities (or 'incremental capacities') that can provide a competitive edge in economic and social development. Active knowing rests upon individual and collective learning. It develops through applied learning in practical contexts (Lave 1998, Wenger 1998). Moving knowledge to work can occur through everyday participation in work and social situations (Billett, 2001). It is optimised when applied learning is supported through actively designed pedagogic processes that enable the co-production of new knowledge and incremental capacities, which can be implemented in action (Lusted 1996). Supporting such applied learning involves the skilful integration of specific occupational and disciplinary knowledges, cross-cultural awareness and communication, and global networking. It rests upon sophisticated pedagogical skills and capabilities that are attuned to innovation and creative problem-solving yet are embedded within relevant occupational and disciplinary knowledges.

Knowledge-in-action is seen to be critical to economic growth and social well-being by governments and global agencies around the world. In this way, globalisation foregrounds education as a key instrument in economic and social development. It encourages attempts to harness education systems to the rapid and competitive growth and transmission of technologies and knowledge, and also to drive lifelong learning agenda outside (and where possible inside) the established institutions of education and training (i.e. schools, universities and vocational colleges). For example, the World Bank identifies the human capital requirements of adaptability, creativity, flexibility and innovation as those to be delivered by education and asserts that such qualities are best delivered in deregulated education systems in which competition is maximised and business is embedded.

Education policy-makers promote the attractiveness of their local products in the global marketplace; attempting to tie roving capital into long-term relationships based on the satisfaction of the needs of the new knowledge economy. Those needs require that public institutions, as well as business, become attuned to continuous change, as

UK Prime Minister Tony Blair argues,[1] we must have constant improvement to cope with change:

> The modern world is swept by change. New technologies emerge constantly, new markets are opening up. There are new competitors but also great new opportunities ... This world challenges business to be innovative and creative, to improve performance continuously, to build new alliances and ventures ... In government, in business, in our universities and throughout society we must do more to foster a new entrepreneurial spirit: equipping ourselves for the long term, prepared to seize opportunities, committed to constant innovation and improved performance.

This is a policy trajectory that is preoccupied with the construction of a 'knowledge economy' and 'learning society'. The OECD and the World Bank stress that education and training provide the entry requirements to participation in the new knowledge economy. Education and Training dominate policy agendas focused on up-skilling new knowledge workers and developing research and thus the knowledge that will secure success. Productive knowledge is believed to be the basis for national competitive advantage within the international marketplace. And this is echoed by governments at the national and regional level, for example in the Lisbon Declaration of the European Union. The constituent nations of the EU all declare that they are attempting to become 'knowledge economies'. As the Australian state of Victoria's government stresses, 'What people know and can do, their creativity, their ability to adjust to change, and to innovate' makes a difference to the economic and social success of individuals, regions, states and nations (Kosky 2002: 1).

Within this trajectory schooling/education/training systems are acknowledged to be significant instruments for economic and social change: for building intellectual capital and capacity for innovation; for enhancing workforce development in ways that realise economic and, to a considerably lesser extent, social and civic outcomes; and for managing communities in ways that seek to minimise alienation and exclusion, and that promote self-reliance, and resourcefulness. This policy discourse promotes a wide range of activity and justifies major shifts in national, institutional and individual practices and processes. Enterprising selves are promoted (in all senses of the word) in schooling and work, including research work.

Yet enterprising selves never exist in a vacuum. They are placed and embodied in particular ways and these locations play out in spatial scales centred on the body, family, community and other movements. They exercise their active knowing in many ways, in and beyond schooling and work. Economically acceptable innovation is accompanied by other kinds of knowledge production, active knowing and change. Graffiti, weblogs and different kinds of social mobilisations are a consequence. Knowledge, unlike other commodities, is not containable. It can be used but not used up. Its use generates more knowledge so that value is not contingent upon scarcity. Intellectual property protocols seek to fix active knowing in commodified knowledge but, once fixed, the knowledge loses value (Jessop, 2000). The challenge for governments driving towards knowledge-based economies, and for education systems repositioned and reconfigured as their instrument, is not just to promote active knowing as an economic resource but to trammel knowing, and the knowledge it generates as a collective (community) resource, within acceptable guidelines.

Policy and research

Our approach to the 2006 *World Yearbook of Education* acknowledges that the nexus of globalisation and knowledge has created a relatively coherent set of policy themes and processes through which policy makers (at national, international and trans-national levels) are reshaping education systems. Yet we are also concerned to recognise and explore the ways in which these policy agendas and processes interact with traditions, ideologies, institutions and politics that have developed on national terrains. To move beyond the very general statements that make up the knowledge economy and learning society policy rhetoric, and to capture the dynamic of de- and re-nationalising that Sassen identifies, we are drawing on Alexiadou and Jones' (2001) discussion of the relationship between 'travelling' and 'embedded' policy.

Alexiadou and Jones take travelling policy to refer to supra- and trans-national agency activity, as well as to common agendas (e.g. for the reshaping of educational purposes to develop human capital for the information age). Embedded policy is to be found in 'local' spaces (which may be national, regional or local) where global policy agendas come up against existing priorities and practices. Embedded policies include traditions, ideologies, forms of organisation, ways of working and patterns of social movement. They may have developed on the national terrain or at sub-national levels. And these national and sub-national practices may have also been inflected by wider international contexts and influences (such as, e.g., the cultural consequences of Canada's geographic proximity to the USA, the significance of Confucianism within South East Asia and the impact of diasporic Chinese culture, or the influence of longstanding Russian colonisation of Central Asia and the long prior history of migration and cultural exchange in this world of the Silk Road). This perspective allows for recognition that, while policy choices may be narrowing, national and local assumptions and practices remain significant and mediate or translate global policy in distinctive ways. For example, the reception of travelling policy varies within national policy elites, and there are differing degrees of local 'policy inflection' in which various forces (local policy communities, trade unions, social movements) have forced adaptation of global agendas, or in which local policy elites have integrated travelling policy with national agendas (Alexiadou and Jones 2001: 2).

In mapping this process of interaction between travelling policy and embedded local policy and practice, Alexiadou and Jones highlight the way that particular agenda generated by organisations, such as the World Bank, WTO and OECD, provide a reference point for national policy development in many different countries and also act as a legitimation for national level changes whose implementation may be controversial. However, they also affirm that these global policy discourses are not simply implemented in target nations. Rather, local communities at national, regional or local level interact with and negotiate these travelling policies, sometimes indigenise them, and sometimes contest and resist them.

There is, of course, a good deal of debate about how the conduits of travelling policy operate and a need for further enquiry into exactly how the design and delivery of national policy agendas respond to pressure from supra-national organisations and agencies (Lingard 2000, Dale 1998). We are seeking in this volume to contribute to discussion of these issues, with particular attention to the relatively neglected issue of the steering of educational research, and the equally neglected area of what might be called national cultures and practices of educational research.

Alexiadou and Jones (2001) indicate that travelling policy has certain features because of the common concern of governments and global agencies with reshaping education and education systems, and conceptualising educational purposes in ways that correspond to current shifts in the wider global economy. These features are:

(a) a focus on economic need which is seen in terms of developing a knowledge economy for which education must provide human capital;
(b) an insistence that the process of reform must be rapid – time horizons are short – and that it must penetrate deeply into education cultures among both teachers and students, with an emphasis on the development of strong management cultures – the creation of a leadership cadre and a workforce accustomed to directive leadership;
(c) an insistence that the national education system should become 'world-class', that is, it must continually improve not just in relation to the national past but also to international comparators. 'World-classness' is defined in terms of indicators that highlight exam-oriented success and measured by international league tables, such as PISA;
(d) a belief in the benefits of direct business involvement in state schooling – both in the interests of emerging private sector edu-business, and in conforming schooling to business agenda; and
(e) declining interest in equality of opportunity and outcomes, and a focus on promoting diversity and differentiation. This is achieved through the re-regulation of education within national contexts, reducing the emphasis on macro-action by government (e.g. through resource provision or income distribution) and expanded government intervention through a range of different regulatory mechanisms to ensure that the new policy priorities are privileged and that participation in policy debate is restricted so that 'undesirable' groups or interests are excluded from decision making.

The broad features of this travelling policy agenda are evident in the field of education research. In many countries, for example, there is evidence of increased trends towards commercialisation and competition, tighter specification of research processes and identification of approved research questions and topics. But while these trends are shared, they enter distinctive national terrains with their own traditions, ideologies, institutions and politics of education that continue to have meaning and relevance. While travelling policy seeks to steer education research, local and national systems and institutions have the capacity to mediate or interact with globalising, economising education policy for research by drawing on distinctive resources, and cultural and political practices of research. This makes education research a particular contested terrain in which specific contradictory challenges are confronted.

In the context of research, knowledge is *internal* to (i.e. part of), rather than *external* to and distinct from, the economic process. The new knowledge that research generates is a foundation for innovation and its activation by knowledge workers is the basis for the productivity of knowledge resources. National systems seek to ensure competitive advantage through the commercial exploitation and application of such knowledge. Knowledge production is brought into close relationship with economic policy – what matters is what works for the economy. Universities and their research are significant players in this policy frame. The centrality of research to the knowledge economy helps to explain the evidence of enhanced research steering practices across different national systems, with attention to the impact of supra-national agencies and pressures (e.g. the World Bank, OECD), and to the impact of emergent regional blocs (e.g. the European Research Area) that is apparent throughout this volume. Across the globe there is a trend towards prioritising techno-scientific research and its modes of operation and organisation.

Education research has its own significance because it informs learning, and produces knowledges that legitimise certain practices and policies advanced by government and global agencies. Such knowledge production is distributed across the spectrum between instrumental and critical rationalities. It can enhance understandings of knowledge work and the preparation of knowledge workers necessary for the knowledge economy, and also helps to inform wider practices of active knowing that are necessary for living productive lives and citizenship, and how such capacities for active knowing can be built and developed. These features mean that pressures for research steering in education are partly explained by the sensitivities around this education knowledge production and its role in developing and shaping the praxis of active knowing.

What we see is education research being framed by the desire of governments for clear and reliable evidence that can inform and support policy. Such steering places a premium on scientific inquiry, systematic (preferably quantitative) evidence and objective findings. Educational research, which has been weakened by criticism from powerful sources within and beyond national governments, is not securely positioned within the Academy and this positioning encourages the scientising of education research and the separate delineation of researchers as objective experts and research users. The reconfiguration of this relationship into a provider-consumer model that underpins research service provision provides a viable basis for research-industry partnerships that can support preferred approaches to active knowing. It is preferable to the more unpredictable praxis of active knowing that is sustained by the hybrid professional practitioner premised upon the model of the teacher-researcher. Where such teacher-researcher hybrids persist, they will continue to struggle to be recognised as serious researchers who produce serious knowledge. The generation of data in preference to more interpretivist understandings provides the basis for new regulatory regimes in which practices of governance depend upon self-regulating researcher assessments of opportunity, risk and choice, as already occurs in ethics procedures.

These features of education research point towards the contradiction of knowledge within the knowledge economy. This contradiction hinges on the nature of knowledge as a collective resource or as intellectual property where knowledge is treated as a fictitious commodity. Questions about what knowledge is produced and legitimised, how it can be mobilised and used, and whose resource it is (i.e. for which communities it can be a collective resource) are critical not just because they sit at the heart of education research steering but also because they are fundamental to the practical politics of education research.

About the volume

The volume thus seeks to foreground educational research as an object of policy steering within a knowledge economy. In so doing, it also seeks to reveal and explore the nature of educational research, its defining attributes, qualities and characteristics, in different 'local' settings, and consider the interaction of these global and local trends and trajectories in educational research. In mapping this territory, we have identified the following questions that have been raised by the various contributions, and that seem to us to be important in thinking further about policy steering of educational research:

- What impact does the pursuit of the 'knowledge economy' have on educational research globally?
- What steering mechanisms (improving, monitoring and management of performance; competitive funding etc) are in evidence globally?
- To what extent are these practices producing globalised/homogenous research, or do national/contextual differences remain? If so, what resources are in play that help to mediate steering pressures?
- Are researchers becoming more entrepreneurial? Does this differ in different contexts?
- What agencies are involved in research management/funding/and in doing research? To what extent are commercial/public-private agents active in research in different contexts?
- How does research relate to teaching in different contexts?
- In what ways are researchers able to pursue traditional research practice through and within these steering mechanisms? How do traditional practices meet the challenges of steering?
- In what ways and to what ends can research mediate wider processes of global steering?
- How can research be organised to play a more active role in the politics of knowledge production, distribution and use?

Within the chapters that follow, the questions are addressed to a degree, but this is not a comprehensive or complete guide to all the possible issues that demand attention in relation to this topic. What the volume does is to offer a snapshot of developments across the world in relation to the steering of education, and how it may be understood, and engaged with by education researchers.

Part 1: Globalising policy and research in education offers both policy and critical perspectives on the relationships between policy and education research. Chapters by policy actors (Aglianos, Schuller) provide insights into the globalised policy agencies and their rationales for steering research in education in the context of knowledge economies and learning societies. Both contributors signal the need for change in educational research, including change in how research is conceptualised and in how researchers position themselves in relation to policy. Chapters by academic commentators identify the influence of particular steering pressures and processes, for example accountability as a strategy of governance of research (Sobe); the operation of the global education market, supported by the internet (Lohmann) and trends in research publication, in relation to performance measurement through citation indices (Lindblad). These discussions identify key global players and consider the operation of networks of influence, they identify instances of policy transfer and borrowing, and of national and international trends in research in education. The chapters in this section provide a good overview of steering mechanisms and processes, of trends in the identification of sponsored research themes and preferred methodologies, of the policy discourse around research quality; and of the discursive structuring of possibilities and parameters for research and research practices.

Part 2: Steering education research in national contexts documents the way travelling policies have impinged upon national systems of education research and the institutions and researchers that work within those systems. Contributors to this section have responded to the idea that research steering is producing a global agenda for education research, and they each address the extent to which established and embedded practices and priorities are affected by strengthened policy agendas for research in their specific national context. They have each, to a greater or lesser extent, addressed the following themes:

- national traditions and established practices in education research;
- national policy trends towards knowledge economy and learning society – who sets the agenda and how?
- steering mechanisms and their operations;
- implications of policy steering for research in education;
- impact on the preparation of researchers and research training;
- dilemmas in education research and researchers' work.

The chapters document the tensions between internationally competitive elite institutional agendas and national/local/community education research issues; contradictory priorities between competition and capacity building; research agenda and national research priority setting; and implications for researcher-practitioner relationships. Contributors from a range of national contexts, including Canada, Argentina, Russia, Malaysia, South Africa, Singapore, New Zealand, the USA, Central Asia, Spain, France and China chart the emergence of shared trends, such as the criticism of research quality in educational research; the pressure to shift from supply-driven to demand-driven research priorities and to adopt 'scientific' forms of enquiry that are open to scrutiny and evaluation. The chapters document change from a wide variety of national perspectives, and while there is persuasive evidence of shared trends and indeed of policy borrowing across national contexts, it is also apparent that different contexts and resources produce different emphases and that particular configurations and locations produce particular convergences: for example in the juxtaposition of scientisation and fundamentalism in the USA or in the foregrounding of ethical concerns and more managerial versions of accountability in the management of research in Canada. It is apparent that the history and traditions of research have considerable continued significance in this new context. Insecure locations of researchers in relation to policy, and the associated issues of autonomy and disciplinary formation, have widespread continuing resonance, and this is perhaps most apparent in the contributions that look at the modernising, marketising contexts of research in Russia and China, or in post-colonial Malaysia, while the consideration of tensions between research and state knowledge in France provides some interesting contrasts. In all of these differing contexts, there are imperatives that drive education researchers to confront questions about positioning, about autonomy and about definitions of research in education. Looking at these chapters in more detail, in Canada (Dehli and Taylor) the intersection of accountability and the formal promotion of ethical conduct in research produces a dissonance that has to be negotiated and managed by researchers, who become implicated in the processes of production of calculative knowledges. In Argentina, (Gorostiaga *et al.*), neo-liberal restructuring and painful adjustment to the demands of the global economy have increased the steering of research.

Research steering in Russia is shaped by rapid modernisation but is also influenced by Soviet practices and assumptions about the planning of research, while the research community is severely under-resourced and continually depleted by emigration (Issakyan). The intersection of postcolonialism, nationalism and education is explored in Malaysia (Joseph), where the uniqueness and complexity of the multi-ethnic context provide resources for new forms of educational research. In the context of sub-Saharan Africa the growth and impact of consultancy is assessed (King), with particular attention to its detrimental effects on the University as the laboratory for the production and fostering of new talent and knowledge. Singapore provides a further source of comparison of specific research steering policies (Luke and Hogan). The focus in New Zealand (Roberts) is the system of performance measurement of research, and its effects on researchers' work and identities. A significant element in the steering of research has been the emphasis on more objective 'scientific' methods, and we look at the peculiar tension in the USA between such imperatives and the revival of religious fundamentalism (Schneider *et al.*). The next chapter (Steiner-Khamsi *et al.*) focuses on the degree of policy borrowing that can be traced in the travels of outcomes based education into Central Asia, with particular attention to what this tells us about the balance between travelling and embedded policy in education. Policy remains the focus in the chapter on Spain (Rambla) which takes as its focus the extent to which policy drives research activity, and shapes and sets limits to enquiry. Discussion of the relationship between different forms of knowledge – state knowledge and research knowledge – in France (van Zanten) highlights the significance of history and institutional and disciplinary formation in creating the landscape within which increased steering is being attempted. This section concludes with a return to a focus on policy, but in the context of China, and considers the impact on education policy researchers there of external pressures (including the influx of Western knowledges) with local struggles to create new knowledges and power.

This section of the volume provides a very rich and diverse contextualisation of the steering of educational research. The picture is not one of uniformly negative consequences for indigenous research of steering processes, although considerable concerns are identified. However, it is important to note that steering has sharpened the focus on research purposes, on the role and nature of knowledge within and beyond the academy, and on epistemological and methodological issues that are critical of 'traditional' research practices while cautioning against some of the trends documented here.

Part 3: Global–local politics of education research. This section takes up some of the questions raised in the documentation of travelling and embedded research policy in order to focus explicitly on the ways in which researchers are actively engaging with and contesting these emerging policy directions. The weaknesses of current knowledge economy constructs and their effects on university research are revealed through illumination of the importance of the aesthetic and the cultural work of the academy (Fahey *et al.*). Responses to steering pressures that produce epistemological engagement and development are considered (McWilliam), as are the possibilities of developing policy scholarship that works with the grain of research practices and defining qualities that are often claimed by the Academy but require to be returned to and reclaimed (Thomson). This section seeks to support a more active politics of educational research through its consideration of the implications of current changes for the conceptualisation of research, for its organisation and for the patterns of production, distribution and exchange of research knowledge.

Notes

1   Department of Trade and Industry *Our Competitive Future: Building the Knowledge Driven Economy* (foreword by Tony Blair) Cm. 4176 (London: The Stationery Office, 1998).

References

The Age (2005) 'Education research "irrelevant"', Saturday, 2 July: 5.

Alexiadou, N. and Jones, K. (2001) *Travelling Policy/Local Spaces*, paper to the Congrès Marx International 111 Paris, September 2001.

Appadurai A. (1996) *Modernity at Large: Cultural Dimensions of Globalisation*, Minneapolis, MN: University of Minnesota Press.

Appadurai, A. (ed.) (2003) *Globalization*, Durham, NC and London: Duke University Press

The Australian (2005) 'Research council in Nelson's firing line', Wednesday, 6 July: 31.

Billett, S. (2001) *Learning in the Workplace: Strategies for Effective Practice*, Sydney: Allen and Unwin.

Castells, M. (1996) *The Rise of the Network Society*, Oxford: Blackwell.

Coulby, D. and Zambeta, E. (2005) *Globalisation and Nationalism in Education* (*World Yearbook of Education 2005*), London: RoutledgeFalmer.

Dale, R. (1999) 'Specifying globalization effects on national policy: a focus on the mechanisms', *Journal of Education Policy*, 14(1): 1–17.

Department of Trade and Industry (DTI) (1998) *Our Competitive Future: Building the Knowledge-Driven Economy*, Cm. 4176, London: The Stationery Office.

Djelic, M.-L. and Quack, S. (2003) *Globalization and Institutions: Redefining the Rules of the Economic Game*, Cheltenham: Edward Elgar.

European Council (2000) 'Presidency conclusions', Lisbon European Council, 23–24 March 2000 http://ue.eu.int/ueDocs/cms_Data/docs/pressData/en/ec/00100-r1.en0.htm (Accessed, 4/6/04), 63–78.

Gibson-Graham, J.K. (2003) 'Enabling ethical economies', *Critical Sociology*, 29(2): 123–61.

Giddens, A. (1990) *The Consequences of Modernity*, Cambridge: Polity Press.

Gray, J. (2000) *False Dawn: The Delusions of Global Capitalism*, London: Granta Books.

Jessop, B. (2000) 'The state and the contradictions of the knowledge-driven economy', in J. Bryson, P.W. Daniels, N. Henry and J. Pollard (eds), *Knowledge, Space, Economy*, London: Routledge.

Kosky, Hon. Lyn (2002) *Knowledge and Skills for the Innovation Economy*, Melbourne: Department of Education and Training.

Lave, J. (1988) *Cognition in Practice: Mind, Mathematics, and Culture in Everyday Life*, Cambridge: Cambridge University Press.

Lingard, B. (2000) 'It is and it isn't: vernacular globalisation, education policy and restructuring', in N. Burbules and C. Torres (eds) *Globalisation and Education: Critical Perspectives*, New York: Routledge.

Lusted, D. (1986) 'Introduction – Why pedagogy?' *Screen*, 27: 2–15.

Prakash, A. and Hart, J.A. (1999) (eds) *Globalization and Governance*, London and New York: Routledge.

Sassen S. (2003) 'Spatialities and temporalities of the global: elements for a theorization', in Appadurai A. (ed.) *Globalization*, Durham, SC and London: Duke University Press.

Stehr, N. (2002) *Knowledge and Economic Conduct: The Social Foundations of the Modern Economy*, Toronto: University of Toronto Press.

Wenger, E. (1998) *Communities of Practice: Learning, Meaning and Identity*, Cambridge: Cambridge University Press.

Part I

Globalising policy and research in education

1 Universities, the internet and the global education market

Ingrid Lohmann

Privatizing educational services in an unstable marketplace raises a number of troubling issues. It does not require a leap into science fiction to foresee the development of a government-financed education industry complex that is ultimately as unaccountable as the military-industrial complex. To whom, other than their investors and share-holders, might the bearers of these new technologies be accountable?

(Michael Barker 2000: 114)

A few years ago, an observer of the e-learning scene in the USA noted that the most ambitious amongst the various newly emerging educational service providers were those 'that want to create via the internet a learning environment that might actually dispense with the teacher – at least in the conventional, classroom sense of the word' (Barker 2000: 107). He saw the education industry as the perfect example of the way the internet transformed the US economy by generating companies that would not have existed otherwise. As of yet, nobody could imagine a world where learners were actually taught by intelligent machines but it would be easy to envision how information and communication technologies (ICT) and the internet would one day change the nature of teaching. The pioneering spirit of the late 1990s is characterised by a then much publicised remark from John Chambers, CEO of Cisco Systems, a US manufacturer of network technologies and co-founder of Internet2: 'The next big killer application for the internet is going to be education. Education over the internet is going to be so big it is going to make e-mail usage look like a rounding error' (as quoted in Barker 2000: 108).

Since then, the euphoria of those years has somewhat subsided. Nevertheless, there is hardly a decline in product developments in the e-learning and online content sectors and even less an end to the transformations that drive the privatisation and commercialisation of education and science worldwide. In the educational and academic sectors, there are enormous profits to be made from a commercialised internet. This situation is by no means the cause of the global privatisation of public educational and academic systems. The profitability of the internet, however, which has been structured accordingly, is a factor that very much accelerates these transformations. Subject to these are not only the actual processes of acquiring an education that are a part of an individual's existential provisions, but also the normative ideal of education as a public good and a human right (cf. Lohmann 2002). When this basic right succumbs to the innovation rhetoric, there are indeed no more arguments as to why people should not pay for their individual education themselves. For the university sector that is at the centre of this article, I take:

- *privatisation* to mean all measures that are aimed at the elimination of the universities' public duties in favour of virtually changing them into extended workbenches of commercial companies; measures like changing the universities' legal form into private-law foundations, for instance; or installing university councils consisting of representatives from the commercial sector in management positions; the (short-term) acquisition of funds on the capital market through university-owned real estate; the assignment of research results (that have still been financed with public money) to commercial businesses etc.
- *commercialisation* to mean the orientation of courses, diplomas and course contents towards the market; the elimination of academic disciplines, topics and research subjects that are not market-compatible; the introduction of performance-related pay for university staff; the setting up of access restrictions to the internet by technical means and the submission of content development to the increasingly strict regulations of intellectual property rights; the elevation of 'successful operation on the global education market' to the most important maxim of academic policy (cf. BDA/HRK 2003).

In the university sector it is particularly obvious at the moment how educational processes are being transformed into *property operations with knowledge as commodity*.[1] German universities have long been involved in far-reaching restructuring processes, where the imperative of 'competitiveness on the global education market' has played a crucial role, as will be shown in the course of this article. One of the countless problems in the process is that, according to analysts, there is a critical mass for the ability to compete on the global e-learning market, so that universities have been forced to merge. In Great Britain, for example, there will be an estimated decrease of 10 per cent in the number of universities by the year 2010 (Sommerich 2002). Not surprisingly, there has been an increase in warnings against undesirable side-effects of the transformations lately. An astonishing number of 88 private universities have been closed by the Mexican government in the years 2001–3, due to the fact that the providers did not even meet the most basic of quality standards (cf. World Bank 2003). On the other hand, the closures are also part of regulation measures that are hardly in line with market conditions and have been taken by the Vicente Fox government in order to intervene in the mushrooming segment of private universities for the sake of more competitive suppliers. But first things first. Here are some figures relating particularly to the market segment of *studies abroad*:

- According to estimates from investment bank and financial consultants *Merrill Lynch*, the financial volume of the global knowledge enterprise industry amounts to about 2200 billion US$ per annum.[2]
- 85 per cent of all students abroad enrol in educational institutions in OECD countries.
- Student mobility into OECD countries has doubled over the last two decades; in these countries, and between 1995 and 1999 alone, the number of students from non-OECD countries rose by almost double the rate than that of students from OECD countries themselves.
- In 1999, 30 billion US$ were accounted for by around 1.5 million students from abroad, particularly from Asia, who were enrolled in tertiary-sector educational institutions in OECD countries – that is roughly the same as the international financial service industry's annual turnover.[3]

Out of the five segments of the educational sector according to WTO classification (primary education services; secondary education services; higher education services; adult education; and other education services like testing, external experts and others), higher education and 'other services' are the two areas where international trade has already become an important factor. Within the higher education sector, distance learning as well as consumption abroad have become the fastest growing segments (EUA 2001: 1 *et seq.*). In view of this growing market for education export,[4] the OECD countries are striving to meet the demand with lucrative commercial offers. At the same time, they point out that the *public* budgets at their disposal for the tertiary education sector are decreasing. It is being argued that privatisation and commercialisation of the education sector are inevitable, should the growing demand for higher education be satisfied.

The share of public budgets available for the tertiary educational sector varies considerably across OECD countries. It seems that only in Korea, Japan and the USA, native students are obliged to raise more than 30 per cent of the real costs for their studies privately. For the remaining OECD countries there are no reliable data concerning the costs to be borne by the students themselves. Nevertheless, there seems to be considerable leeway to pass costs back on to the demand side, i.e. the students. A statement from Ron Perkinson, Senior Education Specialist with the World Bank's *International Finance Corporation*, given at the *World Education Market* in Lisbon in 2002 applies to all of them: 'It is not a question of *if* but *when*. What is happening around the globe is that the larger traditional markets are being challenged through the globalisation of education. Britain and its fantastic tradition has so much to offer. It is certain politicians and government officials are going to look for better use of their education pounds' (as quoted in Sommerich 2002).

Contradictory utilisation of the internet

In this process, the internet is being utilised in a contradictory manner. On the one hand, rising prices for users are being legitimised with rising costs for the service providers – costs for technological infrastructure, networking, data transmission, content development etc. The providers argue that the introduction of break-even prices and/or the raising of fees are inevitable, as the costs for technological equipment as well as hard and software development in the technological and content areas could not be borne otherwise in the long term. Moreover, it is argued, the raised salaries expectations for the higher qualified would justify them bearing their share of the costs.

On the other hand, certain expenses can be avoided with the help of the internet. Both the suppliers and the demand side face high costs through travel, accommodation and the cost of living in a foreign country on the one hand, and the actual provision of properties with libraries, computer learning centres and full-time academic staff on the other. In order to minimise these costs for studies abroad in particular, a growing number of students especially from non-OECD countries are striving for enrolment in educational institutions they can access via the internet and e-learning from their own homes. They do have to pay tuition fees, of course, but the remaining costs are considerably lower. While certain categories of educational service providers in a wider sense – i.e. providers of accommodation for foreign students – are falling behind here, providers in the quickly growing market segments of e-learning, online teaching and e-content are coming onto the scene, often in co-operation with regional, private educational institutions.

It was an environment like this that generated well-known structures like the University of Phoenix in Arizona that, in the course of a few years, became the largest private university in the USA. It operates practically without any full-time staff or libraries; most tutors are teaching part-time and most students get large parts of the tuition fees reimbursed from the companies that employ them. The UoPX is a prime example for the new quality of educational processes as property transactions with knowledge as commodity: all of the participants are creditors and debtors at the same time – the university as a tax-paying business; the companies that finance their employees' qualification processes; the company specialists and consultants teaching part-time; and the students that need to make up for the costs invested in their qualification.

Technological infrastructure – the state of the art

Economic, legal and ideological dimensions aside, the internet also provides a new technological and infrastructural basis for the transformation of traditional educational processes into property operations with knowledge as commodity. This new basis facilitates and even generates the fastest-growing segments of the global education market and creates wholly new categories of protagonists. Not much is known about the technological infrastructure of the 'knowledge society', however, nor do we know much about the steering committees co-ordinating its development or about the economic interest behind them. Here is my attempt at a crash course:

At the beginning there was the Internet2®, launched in April 1998 by the then US Vice President Al Gore, a consortium consisting of:

- the US government;
- 206 US universities, from Arizona State to Yale under the direction of the University Corporation for Advanced Internet Development (UCAID);
- several dozens of leading global corporations as members, partners or sponsors, among them many companies from the IT industry as well as the research and learning industries; to name but a few: Apple Computer Inc., Cisco Systems, Ford Motor Company, IBM, Japan Telecom, Microsoft Research, Sun Microsystems, the Thomson Corporation,[5]
- as well as, for example, the Association for Communications Technology Professionals in Higher Education (ACUTA) as associated member and a good three dozen affiliated members, among them research institutes, companies in the education industry, and the World Bank (cf. Internet2).

This consortium develops and uses the most advanced electronic network technology. Its acknowledged aim is the creation of the 'Internet of the Future' that, among other things, differs from the conventional internet in the fact that it is not generally and publicly available.[6] The framework for its extremely fast data transmission is Abilene – Advanced Networking for Leading-Edge Research and Education. At the moment, Abilene provides a transmission speed of 10 gigabits per second with its cross-US backbone. The access to at least 100 megabits per second for every connected desktop is the next short-term aim (cf. Abilene 2005). In 1999, the University of Indiana received 10 million US$ for establishing the connection of the *Next Generation Internet* with

Japan, Korea, Singapore and Australia and the University of Tennessee collected 4 million US$ for the connection to Moscow and St Petersburg.

In this respect, though, Europe is hardly trailing behind the USA. At the European Council meeting in Lisbon in March 2000, the declared aim was to make Europe 'the most competitive and dynamic knowledge-based economy in the world' by the year 2010 (as quoted in European Commission 2002: 29). The internet in particular was to be harnessed to meet this objective. The most important instrument for this purpose is the EU Commission's *Sixth Research and Development Framework Programme* with its central strategic aim of strengthening the scientific and technological bases of the European industry and encouraging it to become more competitive at the international level (cf. ibid., European Commission 2002–6). As will be shown below, the development of German universities has been completely subordinated to this aim. To cite but one example that is symptomatic for the situation: in the area of e-learning and e-content development in Germany, there is no approval of funds that would not at the same time be tied to the proviso of a subsequent commercialisation of the product (as opposed to making it freely available on the internet, for example). This marks a departure and a qualitative difference from the earlier funds granting practice, at least for the humanities, and the social, educational and cultural sciences.

About 3,000 educational and research institutions in 32 countries belong to the present generation of the European research network Géant, connected via roughly 30 national and regional education and research networks. The European research network is financed by the affiliated states and for about 40 per cent by the European Commission. On behalf of the national research networks, it is planned and co-ordinated by Dante, the Delivery of Advanced Network Technology to Europe Ltd, a company with its head-quarters in Cambridge, UK (cf. Dante 2003).

Supporting Dante as an associated organisation is the Trans-European Research and Education Networking Association (TERENA); it organises the collaboration between the national research networks during the development and testing of new technologies. Terena has an observer status at Dante and at the European Group for Policy Coordination of Academic and Research Networks (ENPG). Moreover, Terena is a member of the Internet Society (ISOC) as well as an associated member of the US University Corporation for Advanced Internet Development (UCAID) which, in turn, operates Internet2. One of the main tasks of Terena is the carrying out of strategic studies about the future development and utilisation of the net infrastructure. ENPG on the other hand, co-operates with the EU's Community Research and Development Information Service (CORDIS), the central co-ordination and information service for research financed by the European Union, as well as with the EU Commission's Information Society Website (IS).

It is unnecessary, of course, to memorise these facts in detail, but one should nevertheless be aware of the newly changed environment one is operating in as member of a university.

In Germany, the research network WiN was founded in 1985 by 11 universities, some industry representatives and the federal ministry for research and technology (BMFT). In 1989 there was a first backbone network, in 1995 a first broadband research network (B-WiN) and since the year 2000, there is the gigabit research network (G-WiN) with a national backbone and central access nodes, comparable to Abilene. G-WiN is co-ordinated by the Association for the Promotion of a German Research Network (DFN-Verein) with its headquarters in Berlin. This association 'links universities and research institutions and promotes the development and the testing of new applications within the Internet2 community in Germany' (DFN-Verein 2005). An estimated 500 institutions and more than 1.5 million users are affiliated to G-WiN, which is connected to Abilene as well as the networks in the Asia-Pacific area via Géant in Internet2. Contracts and peering agreements integrate G-WiN into the global internet (cf. ibid.).

At present, three 2.5 gbit/s data lines connect Géant with the central North-American networks Abilene, Esnet and Canarie[7]: cables at the bottom of the sea mark the beginning of the transatlantic Global Terabit Research Network (GTRN) – a partnership between the US-American Internet2, the Canadian Canarie and the European Géant. A 155 Mbit/s connection from London to Tokyo already exists. In the meantime, special powerful networks are being provided and co-ordinated by the respective national organisations in many countries: in Asia including Australia and New Zealand, in Central and South America (but barely in Africa).

Among the African countries, it has so far been mainly those bordering on the Mediterranean – from Morocco to Egypt (and probably including Libya soon) – that have participated in the development of a network infrastructure covering the Mediterranean up to and including Syria and Turkey. In addition, the EU Commission is striving to link up the Republic of South Africa with Géant (cf. Martin 2002). A further 18 Central and South American countries – from Argentina to Venezuela (including Cuba) – will become Europe's potential partners on the global education market through ALICE, the programme America Latina Interconectada Con Europa that has been co-financed by the EU. A further development programme, South-Eastern European Research and Education Networking (SEEREN), is geared towards the south-east European region, including several EU membership candidates. There seems to be a lot of evidence, therefore, to support the EU's self-proclaimed world leadership in this area that it attributes to Géant's success and that puts Europe ahead of the USA – at least as far as the running of 'intraregional research networks' is concerned (cf. Dante 2003).

This could be part of the explanation why the EU Commission is very well inclined to agree to the USA's request, placed into the current GATS negotiations, for further market openings in the higher education sector. In other words, with regard to Europe's highly developed interconnectivity there is no need for her to shy away from competition on the global education market.

The campus between internationalisation and McDonaldisation

University campuses are important areas for the development and application of the branched-out programmes that the EU Commission and national governments, in co-operation with companies and trusts, use to control the formation and development of the 'European knowledge society'. On the one hand, there is a double focus on *inter-nationalisation* and *quality ensurance*. Apart from being desirable and feasible (cf. EUA 2001: 3 *et seq.*; ESIB/EUA2002: 2 *et seq.*), these two objectives are also part of the standard rhetoric surrounding the present structural reforms of the German university system. On the other hand and more importantly, it is about generating profits on the hard-fought global education markets:

•   In countries like Brazil, India, Columbia, Indonesia, South Korea and the Philippines, the share of tertiary-sector students pursuing their studies at private institutions is

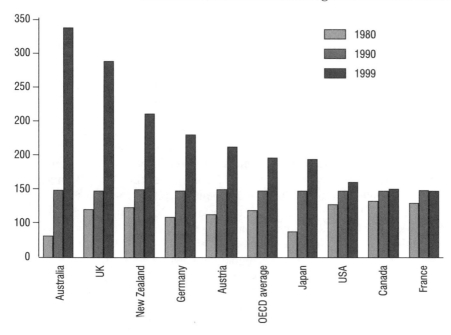

Figure 1.1 Students from abroad in selected OECD countries 1980–99

between 60 and 85 per cent; in India, for example, 75 per cent of all colleges are privately owned.

* In China alone, with its 1,274 private institutions and 4 million students (in 2000), 500 private institutions have emerged in the tertiary education sector between 1995 and 1999, many of them in co-operation with providers from OECD and/or EU countries.[8]

In these countries, the investment possibilities can only be called favourable. An ever-increasing share of the education market is dedicated to ICT, and this not only applies to the rocketing market of private educational institutions but to state-run public ones as well; particularly since, in the university sector most of all, the borders between 'public' and 'private' are becoming increasingly blurred and are destined to become even more obscure through international trade agreements like the General Agreement on Trade in Services (GATS) (cf. EUA 2001: 4).

All in all, two trends dominate the global education market at present: a fast growth in trade with educational services within the OECD as well as a substantial rise in exports of educational services from leading OECD countries into third countries, particularly threshold countries. The export rates for telecommunication equipment from OECD countries into OECD countries (1991–97: +116 per cent) and into non-OECD countries (+164 per cent) mirror this development – at least until the Asia crisis at the end of the 1990s and the year 2000's new economy slump at the international stock exchanges and financial markets (OECD 2003: 236, 238 *et seq.*).

To give just one example: One of the most competitive education exporters is Australia. Compared with the total number of students from abroad at Australian educational institutions, the number of those who have enrolled offshore (i.e. who live in their respective countries and frequent local subsidiaries) has risen from 24 per cent to 37 per cent between 1996 and 2001. Nine per cent of the Australian educational service providers' foreign students follow internet-based distance learning courses and the figures point upwards. More than half of all students from Singapore, Hong Kong and China using Australian educational institutions are enrolled offshore (cf. Patrinos 2000, Larsen *et al.* 2002).

The online service provider Universitas 21 Global with its headquarters in Singapore is exemplary for the Asian-Pacific developments. Its launch was announced in the spring of 2003 by global media and publishing giant Thomson Learning. U21 Global is a subsidiary of Universitas 21, a consortium of 17 universities (including Birmingham, Lund, Singapore, Melbourne and Freiburg) in 10 countries and the Thomson Corporation; the 50 million US$ alliance wants to secure a substantial share in the global electronic education market. For U21 Global, now, Thomson Learning has assembled a consortium of 16 universities, among them the universities of New South Wales, Queensland, Melbourne, Hong Kong as well as the National University of Singapore. U21 Global will start operations, a Master of Business Administration (MBA) degree course, with 800 students to begin with. Already in 2004, the number of students was meant to rise to about 5,000, most of them from the Asia-Pacific region. Optimistic forecasts are part of the business and so U21 Global's CEO expects a rapid growth in demand for educational services in the Far East and particularly in the online segment. He estimates the market volume to be around 111 billion US$ per year (Thomson Learning 2003).

It is a well-known fact that German providers have long been represented with university subsidiaries, like the RWTH Aachen in Bangkok and Munich Polytechnic in Singapore, on the quickly growing Asian market.

> Only behind closed doors it is being speculated about the impulses for German universities that could come from the establishment of those subsidiaries: the close co-ordination of courses on the market, the break-even principle, i.e. course fees, choosing the students – this means the opportunity to try something out off-shore that German university boards at home are still being prevented from by law.
>
> (Heinemann 2003)

While the German Federal Minister for Research and Education still speaks up for tuition-free first grade studies, this situation has meanwhile changed. Since the Federal Constitutional Court's decision from January 2005 the German federal states are allowed to raise tuition fees at their universities.

ETS and Thomson – note on a neighbouring market segment

Only one of the five educational sectors named at the beginning, namely the segment 'other education services', is still awaiting further liberalisation in the WTO-GATS negotiations. Accordingly, economies that are strong education exporters, and the leading Anglo-Saxon countries in particular, are pressing for an opening of the market. Among other topics, educational testing is on the agenda. If the international exchange of students continues as planned this would seem to require language and qualification tests and entrance exams. If, at the same time, the universities that are being re-equipped for competition were able to choose their students themselves and would gratefully fall back on external service providers, then educational testing would become an even bigger business than it is today. Indeed, there would then be not only a 'rapidly expanding market for the [test providing] institutes', but also for the implementation of global standards, although the USA and other GATS proponents continue to assure that 'by opening the market for testing services, they would not want to question the right to the national setting of standards' (GEW 2003: 32 *et seq*.).

Thomson Learning is a division of consultancy firm and electronic publishing giant Thomson Corporation (NYSE: TOC) with its headquarters in Toronto. A segment of Thomson Learning, again, is Thomson Prometric with its headquarters in Baltimore, Maryland. In January 2000, Thomson Corp. bought up Sylvan Prometric for 775 million US$, a division of the US educational service provider Sylvan Learning Systems that, amongst other things, runs charter schools (cf. ACI 2000). Since 1992, however, there have been close business ties between Thomson Learning and the Educational Testing Service (ETS) with its international headquarters in Princeton, New Jersey, and its European headquarters in Utrecht, Netherlands. Jointly, Thomson Prometric and ETS run the well-known brands Test of English as a Foreign Language (TOEFL), Graduate Record Examinations (GRE), Graduate Management Admission Test (GMAT), The Praxis Series (for teacher training) and others. In April 2002, both of them announced the reorganisation of their computer-based testing (CBT) operations that led to the closure of 84 testing centres worldwide – in locations as diverse as Abidjan (Ivory Coast) and Zurich; it was declared that the possibility of using hybrid testing models, computers and/or pen and paper, was in the students' interest (cf. Thomson Prometric 2002).

Founded in 1947, ETS is the largest educational testing service provider worldwide. 12 million of its self-developed tests are carried out in 181 countries every year and it would really be worth taking a closer look at the philosophy and the idea of the man behind those tests. ETS sees itself as a 'nonprofit company' at the service of customers 'in education, government and business'. Kurt Landgraf, a former leading manager of the pharmaceutical company DuPont and an avid supporter of US President George W. Bush's educational policies, has been ETS's president and CEO since August 2000. He has good connections to the US congress that occasionally gives him the opportunity to expound on his thoughts on the future of education, on the reform of teacher training and the importance of education testing in particular (Landgraf 2001, 2002).

Part of ETS as 'supporting companies' are the profit-making Chauncey Group International (development and running of programmes and certifications in vocational training), ETS Technologies (development and promotion of technology for online learning) as well as, until recently, ETS K-12 Works (testing services in US primary and secondary schools). Chauncey, on the other hand, merged with two other companies (Experior Assessments, iLearning) in March 2003 to form Capstar, which now puts its joint expertise at the service of 'corporations, government agencies, academic institutions and licensure and certification organizations', so that the customer 'now will be able to work with a single company that can assess training needs, develop and deliver the training electronically, assess the effectiveness of the training, and provide certification and licensure examinations' (Chauncey 2003). ETS boss Landgraf figures as CEO of the new company – right at the centre of the global education market, where it is most profitable. This is just one example from the Thomson empire with its widely branched-out connections which makes this company one of the biggest among the slim dozen of big players on the world education market (cf. Stokes 2001: 2; Sommerich 2002).[9]

World education market – entrance Germany

The common use of the English language promotes and strengthens the competitive advantage of the strong education exporters: USA, Great Britain, Australia, Canada and New Zealand. At present, these countries strive for further liberalisation of the global education market in the WTO's GATS negotiations. They are faced, however, with a growing number of political associations and bodies from EU countries and regions, the Third World and from the Anglo-American countries themselves, who warn against cultural deformation, the loss of cultural and linguistic diversity and against a 'McDonaldisation' of educational institutions. 'Think trade negotiations, and bananas, beef or steel might come to mind. But probably not education', a US observer commented recently. 'Yet today, with education emerging as one of the world's most vibrant and growing businesses, a number of countries are putting the classroom on the agenda of the World Trade Organization' (Fuller 2003: 15).

In 2003, the WTO received applications from the USA, Australia and New Zealand for further liberalisations of trade in education services within the framework of GATS. Amongst the trade restrictions that should be lifted in the opinion of these countries are, for example, restrictions on the electronic transmission of course materials; local, economical tests to ascertain the need for external education service suppliers; services that require a local partner; the refusal to grant private service providers permission to enter into or discontinue business relations with local and external partners at any time; protection agreements for local employees who are seen as the cause for less profitability. Those far-reaching deregulation attempts could transform even the education systems of rich countries into supermarket chains with special offers and bargain bins. In view of this situation, the European University Association (the association of European universities and university rectors' conferences) has warned for quite some time against a further trade liberalisation in the post-secondary education sector, among other things in joint statements with US-American and Canadian university associations as well as ESIB, the union of European students (cf. AUCC *et al.* 2001; ESIB/EUA 2002).

The development of the German university landscape shows, however, that further liberalisation will go ahead *with or without* a further expansion of the GATS agreement: Federal Education and Research Minister Bulmahn has hailed the last few years as the beginning of a new era. In a short space of time, course offers from German universities had been developed worldwide, from China to South America. The opening of the German University in Cairo (GUC) on 4 October 2003 'could be seen as a symbol for the new dimension in international university co-operation' (BMBF 2003b). Internet portals like Gate Germany, Campus Germany and HiPotentials that aim to promote Germany as an educational and research location have come to bear fruit, both in Germany itself and abroad. The World Education Market (WEM) 2002, one of the bigger recent trade fairs for the global education market, saw the participation of Otto-Friedrich-Universität Bamberg, FernUniversität-Gesamthochschule Hagen, Westfälische Wilhelms-Universität Münster, Rheinisch-Westfälische Technische Hochschule Aachen, Technische Universität Carolo Wilhelmina zu Braunschweig, Technische Universität Dresden, as well as

Technische Universität München. Although WEM was held for the last time in Lisbon in 2003, the organisers from media and publishing giant Reed Elsevier are planning future trade fairs for the faster growing education market in Asia. Campus Germany, too, have already travelled there for a promotional tour.

Preliminary conclusions

So what are the conclusions we can come to at present as far as the internet and the global education market are concerned? There seems to be a largely agreed, global technological and infrastructural basis that is being dominated by the US administration. In addition, however, there are partly overlapping *and* contradictory economic and political interests and strategies, at times in the same associations or in the same ministries (cf. Bulmahn 2002; BMBF 2003a, 2003b), with the contradictory part mostly on the side of non-governmental organisations, of course. One strategy is aimed at lifting all remaining international trade barriers, another one at the preservation of national development opportunities and regional diversity (cf. AUCC *et al.* 2001; AER 2002), a third one particularly endeavours the protection of *public* education (cf. European Education Forum 2004), a fourth one stresses the needs of the poorer countries (cf. Hartmann 2003; WEED *et al.* 2003) that have not had much of a say so far in the debate outlined above.

To a certain extent, the Union des Industries de la Communauté européenne (UNICE), 'the Voice of Business in Europe', also supports the strategy of diversity protection.[10] Therefore, this strategy does not offer enough distinct criteria in the search for allies against the triumphal procession of neoliberalism in higher education. The EU Constitution, in the end, included a kind of exception clause for the treatment of education (cf. AER 2004); we will see how much of a help this will be. It will probably not make defenders of the idea of public education or globalisation critics that oppose the sellout of the public sector in general – the Fórum Social Mundial, ATTAC or WEED[11] – sink back into their easy chairs.

The most powerful strategy variants, at least at the time, are both aiming at the worldwide commercialisation and privatisation of the education and research sectors. Not without a reason does Per Nyborg, Chairman of the Commission for Higher Education and Research of the European Council, point out the frictions that arise because the Bologna process (cf. 2003) is being pursued parallel to the ongoing GATS negotiations: 'Can the Bologna process based on co-operation and GATS based on competition co-exist in the sector of higher education?' (Nyborg 2002: 1). Nevertheless, in view of the number of protagonists and the diversity of their interests they will probably have to, in one way or another.

Certain previously rather arcane matters like *copyright* and *intellectual property rights* have become the most explosive topics on the campus (cf. Noble 1998, 2002; Bok 2003: 79–98). One possible scenario would be that 'in the future, there will only be the user who – individually, in a personalised way, independent of location and according to demand and possibilities – utilises communication technology' (Quandel 2001: 23). And who, let's not forget, in a manner that is equally individual, personalised, independent of location and according to demand and possibilities, will be asked to pay up. On the other hand, the necessarily worldwide battle about the preservation of public education, public research and free access to knowledge and information has only just started.

With regard to the role of education policy and research in the globalisation process, my findings imply one thing in particular, namely that the globalisation of *and* through education policy and research are two movements that today can only be separated analytically. As a matter of fact, they seem to converge at present – much more rapidly than the academe's insistence on self-reliance would have us think and much more rapidly, too, than the reproach of a lack in practice-orientation would have us believe (an accusation that is being raised with particular vigour in Germany at the moment). This convergence might be less of an evil than it is a clear and new challenge; not only insofar as education research self-reflexively asks for its historical place but also to the extent that it does not want to have the constitution of its subjects and research questions taken out of its hand.

Education policy and education research are equally moving towards the centre of events now, where national and international economic competition, commercial and trade policy are happening. Traditionally, these kinds of topics were hardly among the subjects of education research. Today, however, education policy and education research are part of the worldwide battle for and against the liberalisation of educational markets, in the current round of GATS negotiations as well as the OECD's PISA studies (including the way they are received nationally), or in the debate over the extent of national autonomy in education matters (as it is currently being discussed in the EU member countries within the context of the EU Constitution). In Germany, the anticipated federal reform was thwarted at the beginning of 2005 by the question of competencies in education policy; the dividing line, however, does not run simply between a Federal Government that wants to secure more scope for action and the 16 federal state governments that fear the loss of their cultural sovereignty guaranteed to them by the Basic Constitutional Law. The debate is rather about the main point of controversy, about liberalisation and globalisation in an educational sector that has become part of international economic policy and competition regulations.

How closely education policy and education research are intertwined today is demonstrated by the World Bank's online discussions, for example. One of them – the sixty-first the World Bank has carried out and neatly archived since June 2001 – is currently concerned with the question 'Does contracting out education services improve delivery?' (cf. World Bank 2005). Whereas the OECD has been quite successful so far in keeping up the impression that education research is independent of economic policy and competition regimes, the World Bank, also with the air of a fairly neutral observer, in reality is a propagator of what they presume to be an historical trend: the worldwide privatisation or rather abolishment of public educational institutions. GATS/ WTO, the World Bank, the OECD, the EU Commission – Hegel's motto 'what is rational is real, and what is real is rational' seems to be their common motto today. Education research, however, still can raise questions.

Notes

1   I take *property operations* to refer to actions aimed at any kind of economic utilisation for which proprietors' rights must be asserted: contract conclusions, purchase and sale, hiring and leasing, bequeathing and taking and giving out of mortgages or credits.

2   This figure is often circulated by propagators of the global education market, cf. World Bank's Harry A. Patrinos (2000), Cisco Systems (2002), World Bank's Ron Perkinson (2003) in his speech at the World Education Market, or Germany's Federal Minister for Education

and Research, Edelgard Bulmahn (BMBF 2003), at the conference 'Exportartikel Bildung' (*education as an export article*).

3 Figures quoted from Patrinos 2000, Larsen and Vincent-Lancrin 2003, Perkinson 2003.

4 According to WTO classification, foreign students' expenditures for course fees and cost of living are classified as education service exports from the country where the students are enrolled in educational institutions; they count as imports for the students' country of origin, however; cf. Larsen, Martin and Morris 2002, 4.

5 cf. Internet2 as of January 2005; for the beginnings cf. CNN 1998.

6 But also through the fact that downloading the *The Matrix* DVD, for instance, takes more than 74.7 hours via ISDN, whereas it only takes 0.011 hour in the 'Internet of the future' – UCAID president Douglas Van Houweling's example, 2001/2003, slide 20.

7 Energy Sciences Network, the US Department of Energy's highspeed network; Canadian Network for the Advancement of Research, Industry, and Education.

8 Figures from Patrinos 2000, Larsen and Vincent-Lancrin 2003, Perkinson 2003.

9 For further business associations between ETS and Thomson, cf. Chauncey 2000, 2001, Thomson Learning 2003, for both also AIRS 2003.

10 'Life-long learning requires co-operation and partnership between all stakeholders and is a shared responsibility between individuals, companies and governments. Life-long learning means building a solid basis for continuous learning throughout an individual's working life, underpinned by effective strategies and flexible systems and arrangements. Strategies and systems vary from one member state to another, depending on the different traditions and legal contexts in place. This diversity needs to be respected' (UNICE 2000, 2).

11 ATTAC: Association pour la Taxation des Transactions financières pour l'Aide aux Citoyens, originally an initiative for the implementation of the Tobin tax on speculative profits from financial transactions; WEED: World Economy, Ecology and Development, a critical voice in north-south and ecology politics, for GATS, cf. WEED *et al.* 2003.

References

Abilene (2005) *Advanced Networking for Leading-Edge Research and Education*. Online. Available HTTP: http://abilene.internet2.edu/.

ACI (2000) *The Thomson Corporation to Acquire Sylvan Prometric from Sylvan Learning Systems for US$ 775 million*, Paris: The Financial Markets Association. Online. Available HTTP: http://www.aciforex.com/new13b-02-00.htm.

AIRS Human Capital Solutions (2003) *News, Mergers/IPOs*, 4 April. Online. Available HTTP: http://www.airsdirectory.com/news/mergersipos/20030404.html.

Assembly of European Regions (AER) (2002) *Brixen/Bressanone Erklärung zur Kulturellen Vielfalt und GATS*, 18 October (Summary). Online. Available HTTP: http://www.are-regions-europe.org/PDF/CD-Main_Texts/Brixen-Declaration-def-D.pdf.

Assembly of European Regions (AER) (2004) *The AER Campaign Saves Culture, Education, Health and Social Services from being Mere Commercial Commodities*. Press release, 21 June (copy). Online. Available HTTP: http://www.erzwiss.uni-hamburg.de/Personal/Lohmann/ Materialien/ Stummann-6-2004.dot.

Association of Universities and Colleges of Canada (AUCC) (2001) American Council on Education (ACE), European University Association (EUA), [US] Council for Higher Education Accreditation (CHEA) *Joint Declaration on Higher Education and the General Agreement on Trade in Services*. Online. Available HTTP: http://www.aucc.ca/_pdf/english/statements/ 2001/gats_10_25_e.pdf.

Barker, M. (2000) 'E-Education Is the New New Thing', *Strategy + Business*, 18 (first quarter), 107–14.

BDA, Bundesvereinigung der deutschen Arbeitgeberverbände/ HRK, Hochschulrektoren-konferenz: Wegweiser der Wissensgesellschaft. Zur Zukunfts- und Wettbewerbsfähigkeit unserer Hochschulen. Berlin, Juli 2003, Online. Available HTTP: http://www.hrk.de/ publikationen/WegweiserWissensgesellschaft.pdf.

BMBF, Bundesministerium für Bildung und Forschung: Pressemitteilung Nr. 121/03 vom 02.07.2003 (2003a) Bulmahn: Berufliche Aus- und Weiterbildung 'Made in Germany' muss wirksamer als bisher weltweit vermarktet werden. Internationale Konferenz zu Bildungsdienstleistungen in Berlin. Online. Available HTTP: http://www.bmbf.de/press/894.php.

BMBF, Bundesministerium für Bildung und Forschung: Bulmahn: Präsenz der deutschen Hochschulen auf dem internationalen Bildungsmarkt wird ausgebaut, Pressemitteilung vom 17. Juli 2003 (2003b). Online. Available HTTP: http://www.innovations-report.de/html/ berichte/bildung_wissenschaft/bericht-20016.html.

Bok, Derek (2003) *Universities in the Marketplace. The Commercialization of Higher Education*, Princeton, NJ and Oxford: Princeton University Press.

Bologna Process (2003) *Realising the European Higher Education Area*. Communiqué of the Conference of Ministers responsible for Higher Education in Berlin on 19 September 2003. Online. Available HTTP: http://www.bmbf.de/pub/communique_ bologna-berlin_2003.pdf.

Bulmahn, Edelgard (2002) Wir dürfen Bildung nicht als Ware dem Handel überlassen. Die Welthandelsorganisation berät über den Import und Export von Hochschul-Dienstleistungen, in Frankfurter Rundschau, 8 July 2002, Dokumentation.

Chauncey Group International (2000) Press release, 11 October 11. Online. Available HTTP: http://www.amenglish.com/press/chaunceypress2.cfm.

Chauncey Group International (2001) Press release, 29 May. Online. Available HTTP: http:// www.chauncey.com/PDF/pressrelease05_29_01.pdf.

Chauncey Group International (2003) Press release, 31 March. Online. Available HTTP: http:// www.chauncey.com/PDF/CAPSTAR_Press_Release.pdf.

Cisco Systems (2002) 'Higher education market background'. Online. Available HTTP: http:// www.cisco.com/warp/public/779/edu/commitment/edu_internet_economy/higher_edu_ market.html.

CNN, Cable News Network (1998) 'Gore unveils "Internet2" for universities – private sector to help build super-fast network', 14 April, Online. Available HTTP: http://www.cnn.com/TECH/ computing/9804/14/i2/.

DANTE, Delivery of Advanced Network Technology to Europe Ltd (2003) Brochure. Online. Available HTTP: http://www.dante.net/about/DANTEbrochure6ppMay 2003.pdf.

DFN-Verein (2005) Homepage. Online. Available HTTP: http://www.dfn.de/index.jsp.

Die Zeit (2003) 27 February, N10. Online. Available HTTP: http://zeus.zeit.de/text/2003/10/T-Digital_Rights_Management.

ESIB, The National Unions of Students in Europe/ EUA, European University Association: Students and universities (2002) *An Academic Community on the Move*. EUA and ESIB Joint Declaration, Paris, 6 March. Online. Available HTTP: http://www.esib.org/news/ EUAESIBjointdeclarat.pdf.

ETS, Educational Testing Service (2001) *CEO Kurt Landgraf Praises President Bush*, Congress. Online. Available HTTP: http://www.ets.org/aboutets/statement.html.

ETS (2003) *Complete Test Directory*. Online. Available HTTP: http://www.ets.org/tests/atest.html.

ETS (2005) Homepage. Online. Available HTTP: http://www.ets.org/.

EUA (European University Association) (2001) *Memo on GATS (WTO) and the Implications for Higher Education in Europe*. Geneva: EUB.

European Commission (2002) *Research Networking in Europe – Striving for Global Leadership*, Brussels, September. Online. Available HTTP: http://www.dante.net/pubs/ECbrochure.html.

European Commission (2002–2006) *The Sixth Framework Programme*. Online. Available HTTP: http://europa.eu.int/comm/research/fp6/index_en.html.

European Education Forum (2004) Homepage. Online. Available HTTP: http://www. education-is-not-for-sale.org/.

Fòrum Social Mundial / World Social Forum (2004). Homepage. Online. Available HTTP: http:/ /www.forumsocialmundial.org.br/.

Fòrum Social Mundial / World Social Forum (2005). Homepage. Online. Available HTTP: http://www.wsfindia.org/.

Fuller, Thomas (2003) 'Education exporters take case to WTO', in: *International Herald Tribune*, Tuesday, 18 February 2003, Special Report. Online. Available HTTP: http://www.globalexchange.org/campaigns/wto/605.html.

GEW, Gewerkschaft Erziehung und Wissenschaft (2003) 'Globaler Bildungshandel – Eine neue "Bildungsphilosophie"', Frankfurt a M: GEW.

Hartmann, Eva (2003) 'The transnationalization of tertiary education in a global civil society', in: links-netz, January. Online. Available HTTP: http://www.links-netz.de/K_texte/K_hartmann_edu.html [also in Heidi Schelhowe, Gabriele Kreutzner (Hrsg.) (2003) 'Agents of change. Virtuality, gender, and the challenge to traditional university', Opladen].

Heinemann, Karl-Heinz (2003) 'Brückenköpfe – Uni-Dependancen im Ausland', *Frankfurter Rundschau*, 9 July: 11.

Houweling, Douglas van (2001/2003) *Internet2 Directions*. Chinese-American Networking Symposium. Online. Available HTTP: http://www.internet2.edu/presentations/20010312-Internet2Future-DVH.ppt.

Internet2. Homepage. Online. Available HTTP: http://www.internet2.edu/.

IS, [EU] Information Society. Homepage. Online. Available HTTP: http://europa.eu.int/information_society/index_en.htm.

Landgraf, Kurt M. (2001) *Measuring Success: Using Assessments and Accountability to Raise Student Achievement*. Online. Available HTTP: http://edworkforce.house.gov/hearings/107th/edr/account3801/landgraf.htm.

Landgraf, Kurt M. (2002) *Training Tomorrow's Teachers – Providing a Quality Postsecondary Education*. Online. Available HTTP: http://www.house.gov/ed_workforce/hearings/107th/21st/teachtrain10902/landgraf.htm.

Larsen, Kurt, Martin, John P. and Morris, Rosemary (2002) *Trade in Educational Services: Trends and Emerging Issues*. OECD Working Paper, revised version, May. Online. Available HTTP: http://www.oecd.org/dataoecd/54/44/2538356.pdf.

Larsen, Kurt and Vincent-Lancrin, Stéphan (2003) 'The learning business. Can trade in international education work?', *OECD-Observer*, 6 March. Online. Available HTTP: http://www.oecdobserver.org/news/printpage.php/aid/872/The_learning_business.html.

Lohmann, Ingrid (2002) 'Commercialism in education – historical perspectives, global dimensions and European educational research fields of interest' *European Educational Research Journal*, 1(3): 550–65. Online. Available HTTP: http://www.wwwords.co.uk/EERJ, (copy) http://www.erzwiss.uni-hamburg.de/Personal/Lohmann/Publik/ecer2002.htm.

Martin, Duncan H. (2002) *Global Research Networking*, September. Online. Available HTTP: http://www.tenet.ac.za/Publications/GlobalResearchNetworking.pdf.

Noble, David F. (1998) *Digital Diploma Mills, Part II. The Coming Battle over Online Instruction*. Online. Available HTTP: http://www.uwo.ca/uwofa/articles/di_dip_2. html.

Noble, David F. (2002) 'Technology and the commodicication of higher education', *Monthly Review*, 53(10). Online. Available HTTP: http://www.monthlyreview.org/0302noble. htm.

Nyborg, Per (2002) *European Co-operation in the Light of GATS – Quality Assurance and Recognition: The Importance of the Lisbon Convention*, Presentation, UNESCO Global Forum 17–18 October. Online. Available HTTP: http://www.see-educoop.net/portal/id_bologna.htm.

OECD, Organisation for Economic Cooperation and Development (2003) *Information and Communication Technologies – Communications Outlook*, Paris. Online. Available HTTP: http://www1.oecd.org/publications/e-book/9303021E.pdf.

Patrinos, Harry A.(2000) *Global Market for Education*, AUCC International Conference, Montreal, Canada, 31 October – 2 November. Online. Available HTTP: http://www1.worldbank.org/education/tertiary/ppt/aucc.ppt.

Perkinson, Ron (2003) *Global Education Market*, Presentation to World Education Market, Lisbon. Online. Available HTTP: http://www.ifc.org/ifcext/che.nsf/Content/Events.

Quandel, Gudrun (2001) 'Wissenschaftsnetze – Herausforderung Infrastruktur'. Online. Available HTTP: http://www.uni-muenster.de/PeaCon/medkomp/cd/thema3/frameset_quandel.htm.

Sommerich, Phil (2002) 'Universities learn the lexicon of business – new global demands could mean a big harvest in the groves of academe', *The Guardian*, 3 June. Online. Available HTTP: http://www.mail-archive.com/pen-l@galaxy.csuchico.edu/msg69395.html.

Stokes, Peter (2001) *A Global Education Market?* Eduventures Inc. White Paper. Online. Available HTTP: http://www.eduventures.com/pdf/Global_Education_Market.pdf.

TERENA, Trans-European Research and Education Networking Association. Homepage. Online. Available HTTP: http://www.terena.nl/.

Thomson Corporation. Homepage. Online. Available HTTP: http://www.thomson.com/corp/about/ab_home.jsp, http://www.thomson.com/index.jsp.

Thomson Learning (2003) Press release, 29 May. Online. Available HTTP: http://www.thomson.com/common/view_news_release.jsp?body_include=press_room/news_releases/learning/u21global_052903&section=learning&secondary=pr_market_group&tertiary=learning&subsection=pressroom.

Thomson Prometric (2002) *Prometric and Educational Testing Service Sign 3-Year Agreement*. Online. Available HTTP: http://www.prometric.com/PressRoom/ETSAgreement.htm.

UNICE, Union des Industries de la Communauté européenne/ Union of Industrial and Employers' Confederations of Europe (2000) *For Education and Training Policies Which Foster Competitiveness and Employment. UNICE's Seven Priorities*. Online. Available HTTP: http://www.mennt.net/files/%7B650d150a-2872-45ee-b830-572c90d13f6a%7D_unice%20sk%C3%BDsla%20um%20menntam%C3%A1l% 202000.pdf [Homepage: Online. Available HTTP: http://www.unice.org/].

UoPX, University of Phoenix Online. Homepage. Online. Available HTTP: http://www.uopxonline.com/.

US (2000) *Communication from the United States: Higher (Tertiary) Education, Adult Education, and Training, 18 December* (00-5552) Council for Trade in Services, WTO S/CSS/W23. Online. Available HTTP: http://www.wto.org/english/tratop_e/serv_e/s_propnewnegs_e.htm (!Sectoral Proposals!Education Services).

WEED *et al.* (2003) Wessen Entwicklungsagenda? Eine Analyse der GATS-Forderungen der Europäischen Union an die Entwicklungsländer. Stuttgart/ Bonn/ Berlin'. Online. Available HTTP: http://www2.weed-online.org/uploads/Broschuere_wessen_ Entwicklungsagenda.pdf.

World Bank/International Finance Corporation (2003) *EdInvest Newsletter*, June. Online. Available HTTP: http://www.ifc.org/edinvest/index.htm.

World Bank/EdInvest (2005) *Does Contracting Out Education Services Improve Delivery?* Online Discussion, March/April. Online. Available HTTP: http://rru.worldbank.org/Discussions/Topics/Topic61.aspx.

All hyperlinks were checked in April 2005.

2 Accountability in US educational research and the travels of governance

Noah W. Sobe

Since the end of the nineteenth century, educational research in the USA has been linked to the political rationalities of liberal democracy, specifically assumptions about society and the nature of social control, order and responsibility (Popkewitz 1991, 1998). Beyond the overt management of researchers' activities through professional associations, trends in the availability of funding and mechanisms such as Institutional Review Boards,[1] the governing that travels through US educational research is inscribed in the principles that divide and order the actions and objects of schooling. Educational research has inscribed a particular idea of progress in which the salvation of the individual can be delivered by saving or rescuing the child/student. Though 'an elusive science' in terms of its normative development (Lagemann 2000), the science of education in its many guises has historically tended to embody notions of redemption. Science was to rescue modern society from its unique predicaments. As Popkewitz (1998) has argued, it has been conventionally assumed since the nineteenth century that 'scientific knowledge' serves democratic ideals. This can be seen to occur as scientific inquiry brings a coherence and a rationalisation to the activities of governments, and as it equips a democratic populace with the tools and knowledge necessary for effective public participation and responsible individual self-management.

Such assumptions about the democratising and liberalising potential of social science research have formed the backdrop to much of what has historically occurred in the name of 'educational research' in the USA and they continue to be felt today in connection with the notion of 'accountability'. As a concern of educational research, 'accountability', as I will show below, has been problematised in a way that links it to the social administration of the individual and the design of salvational collective narratives. 'Accountability' – viewed both as the defining characteristic of an era (e.g. the 'age of accountability') and as an empirically researchable object – is currently one of the central concerns travelling through US educational research and in this chapter I focus on the governing that occurs as notions of accountability help to order the reason of individuals and communities.

As for other contributions to this volume, a key analytic point of this chapter is the intersection of research and policy making. In looking at the interplay between 'research-based policy' and 'policy effects on research', the question that I tackle is not whether the tail-wags-the-dog or the dog-its-tail but the question of how certain objects of reflection, action and intervention are fabricated across the domains of educational research and educational policy. The strategies of governance that I examine here are not the levers or control mechanisms that 'steer' US educational research in an instrumental manner. I am attempting to direct attention to the strategies of governance that create and are created by the relations between educational research and the ordering of the reason of individuals and communities. This analytic emphasis, of course, is not to deny the actuality of institutional arrangements and networks of actors through which the agendas of US educational research are formed, contested and reshaped. It is instead to shift attention to discourses that occupy a central position within contemporary educational research in the USA, discourses that can be seen as cultural practices structuring the possibilities and parameters for collective and individual agency as well as for what is considered 'reasonable'. Here, I focus on 'accountability' as an analytic strategy for investigating systems of reasoning that travel through contemporary US educational research conversations and interrogating cultural practices of social science research and policy making that are locally embedded at the same time as they may be globally converging.

In certain respects, the apparent contemporary emphasis on accountableness closely accords with the American exceptionalism that is alleged to have culturally imbued a continent and a nation with the global salvational mission of rescuing the individual and redeeming the social domain (Greene 1993, Ferguson 1997). Defined as one component of democratic governance, 'accountability' would seem to come ready-packaged for the US export market. At the same time, there are longstanding assertions of American exceptionalism in the arena of social policy, both in the social science models used to analyse the historical development of health and social welfare provision in the USA and in the explanatory frameworks that look at the ostensibly dispersed and decentralised character of US public administration (cf. Skocpol 1992). As a feature of US social policy, 'accountability' would seem to be linked to the wide distribution of administrative powers and the devolution of social welfare responsibilities to local levels. A claim of exceptionalism might also be levied with regards to the federal/national role when it comes to research steering in the USA (even given the recent revamping of the Federal-level Department of Education and reorganisation of some of the mechanisms through which US educational research is to inform policy making that will be discussed below). Thus, the standard story would be that there is such a dispersion of public agencies (on state and national levels), sources of funding (through a range of governmental agencies and private foundations), institutional arrangements and distribution networks that the USA cannot be said to have a national policy programme for researching education on a par with other parts of the world. This story of dispersion, variety and absence makes an odd companion for another story, the story of the global hegemony of US education research. Yet, an examination of 'accountability' reveals a set of coherent organising principles and allows for a discussion of the governance that does in fact travel through education research in the USA. Whether this is exceptional or simultaneously a global governance is a question outside the scope of this particular study, though this is certainly an issue that warrants additional research attention.

Concerns with accountableness have historically provided one of the rationales for harnessing the social sciences to the provision of public schooling in the USA. In the 'accountability' surge of the early 1970s, which I discuss below, the accountableness of governments (federal, state and local) was tied to a social engineering and a 'scientific' planning for a future – a deferred future of equality and justice in the Great Society to come. The use of social science research in US President Lyndon B. Johnson's War on Poverty, for example, held the promise of making governments better accountable *to* their citizens and better accountable *for* the ameliorative social projects being undertaken in the name of progress. To an extent, these employments of technological expertise and social planning can be seen as a continuance of New Deal government social interventions as well as of the planning models connected with the Second World War, yet they were also marked by greater sets of distinctions and different technologies than existed previously. 'Accountability' of the early twenty-first century overlaps with these previous notions but in its present forms has been linked to a reconfiguration of social governance that places more responsibility on communities; has been recast as a technical problem of actuarial expertise and data management; and, concurrently, has been attached to the political rationalities of liberal democracy as much through the specification of what is proper for governments as through the governance of the reason and actions of the individual.

The 'new era' of accountability

The centrality of 'accountability' on the contemporary American educational research landscape is underscored by its appearance in the themes of recent annual meetings of the American Educational Research Association (AERA), with the theme of the 2003 meeting '*Accountability for Educational Quality: Shared Responsibility*' and the 2005 meeting taking up '*Demography and Democracy in the Era of Accountability*'. With this last – the notion of 'the Era of Accountability' – it has achieved the level of a proposed label for our times, the chief defining characteristic of the times in which we live. In this section I discuss travelling strategies of governance within US educational research by looking at the notion that accountability is an appropriate label for the era. However, to begin with, it is worth noting that US education and research on it are not alone in appearing presently to reside in an accountability-time. Homologous discussions about accountability as our 'new era' can be found across multiple domains, notably within business and industry where this new epoch also appears to be acutely felt.

In 2002 the US Congress passed the Sarbanes-Oxley Act, officially titled the 'Public Company Accounting Reform and Investor Protection Act', legislation that restructured securities and corporate governance regulations on a scale not seen since the New Deal of the 1930s (Cohen and Qaimmaqami 2005). Coming on the heels of the Enron and WorldCom scandals, the Sarbanes-Oxley legislation requires increased public disclosure requirements, notably of the activities of corporate boards of directors. These new regulative provisions were advanced in the name of increasing accountableness and have certain implications in other areas, for example in the management of US-based non-profit organisations to which some of the audit and disclosure provisions apply. As in the spheres of education and educational research, accountability in these circuits is being increasingly viewed as a key feature 'of the times'. Accountability has created a 'brave new era', an article in *Business Week* magazine recently declared, in which 'professionals can no longer automatically sanitize everything they do ... nor can they barricade themselves behind a wall of ignorance' (France *et al.* 2004). The teleology of this periodisation, particularly the suggestion of an antecedent era without accountability, suggests that academics ought not unquestioningly to accept such political slogans and concepts as the critical tools and analytic frames of scholarship. In the 'new climate', the 'post-Enron' world of which Sarbanes-Oxley is only one part, declarations of accountability-time are frequently seen to represent a progressive evolution of the social, cultural (and financial/commercial) arrangements we inhabit. To bastardise a familiar Kantian formulation – but hopefully to capture its logic – it could be said that while we may not live in an accountable age, if it is an age of accountability that we live in, we are one step closer to freeing ourselves from our self-imposed immaturity.

Nonetheless, while caution is warranted with regard to both triumphant and despairing declarations of accountability-time, there are noteworthy features of the current state of cultural arrangements in the USA that accountability-related notions seem accurately to describe. Increased reporting requirements are the main contributions that Sarbanes-Oxley has made to the 'era of accountability'; however, what we are witnessing is much more than a restructuring of the legal provisions that apply to corporate governance. There is a larger social governance at play, a governance which means that the reporting/ dissemination and consumption of educational research assumes new imperatives and configurations. It is not only corporate executives who are no longer permitted to barricade themselves behind walls of ignorance. The responsibility to take responsibility for disclosing and being disclosed is becoming ever more widely dispersed.

The governing strategies that are connected with accountability, reporting and disclosure come into high resolution when we examine how this plays out with regard to community notification statues, laws which in the USA are often collectively discussed as 'Megan's Law'. This first appeared as 1994 New Jersey legislation requiring community notification when individuals identified by the state as potential sexual predators moved into an area. Such provisions have since been enacted as federal legislation (signed into law by President Clinton) and continue to generate attention in national and local politics. On the one hand, community notification provisions make governments 'accountable' in new ways to their citizens, yet with these statutes it can be argued that there is a net transfer of responsibility for ensuring public safety away from governments and onto individuals and their communities – a conundrum that nicely demonstrates how even within an accountability-time, what makes for 'accountability' is anything but straightforward. Ron Levi (2000) has argued that 'Megan's Law' disclosure provisions create a 'preventative state' that can be shielded from criticism on the basis of having undertaken risk management measures by deploying an actuarial expertise that is then translated into community-level actions. The dissemination of information by the state becomes central to a community's ability to protect and manage itself; it necessitates that community members act and not act in certain ways. Similar forms of what Nik Rose and others have termed 'responsibilisation' (Rose 1999) are now appearing in the mechanisms that the US government is presently employing when it comes to disseminating and shaping the use of educational research.

In the spring of 2002 the US Congress passed the Educational Sciences Reform Act (H.R. 3801), a bill which overhauled the Office of Educational Research and Improvement (OERI) and created in its place the Institute of Education Sciences within the federal Department of Education. Other features connected with these legislative changes, specifically an increased emphasis on 'evidence' and 'scientifically valid research' can be explored as strategies of governance traveling through US educational research in similar manner as the present examination of accountability (see e.g. Lather 2004, Popkewitz 2004). In terms of the government's role in the diffusion of educational research, H.R. 3801 is significant for helping bring the What Works Clearinghouse

(WWC) into existence. As an education research dissemination vehicle, the WWC operates along many of the same lines as community notification statutes. The clearing-house presents itself as a 'decision-making tool' that 'helps the education community locate and recognize credible and reliable evidence to make informed decisions.' Similar to the government's actuarial computations that assign certain individuals to sexual predator risk pools, the WWC uses an evaluative calculus that is designed to provide a community (the 'education community') with reliable resources for managing itself. As of late spring 2005 WWC had presented its reviews only of middle school math research – bestowing a green light double-checkmark upon a study that 'Meets Evidence Standards'; a yellow light single-checkmark on research that 'Meets Evidence Standards with Reservations'; and a red light 'X' on research that 'Does Not Meet Evidence Screens'. Particular 'interventions' are not endorsed by the WWC, rather information is coded according to these 'reliability' ratings and is transmitted for the purposes of informed decision making and the differentiation of, in their words, 'high-quality research from weaker research and promotional claims'. As the notion of meeting 'evidence screens' clearly suggests, the WWC is operating in an actuarial world of risk-level and confidence-level assessments. Despite the ambition of serving as a cut-and-dry 'trusted source of scientific evidence', the organisation's own statements hint at the probabilistic nature of these reviews and the research they present as matters entailing 'credibility' and 'reliability'. This is something, it could be argued, that comes with the territory of any such endeavour, yet what is of special significance for present purposes is that these strategies for disseminating and structuring the uses of education research constitute forms of social governance that reflect the responsiblisation we see also occurring across other domains in the accountability-time of our present.[2]

What Works constructs an 'educational community' that can putatively demonstrate its 'reasonableness' by basing its decisions on research findings that have been established to present less risk. (As a rule, qualitative research fails to pass the WWC evidence screen as allegedly being epistemologically incommensurable with the 'outcome evaluation'.[3]) The WWC's traffic-light icons fabricate a 'common-sense' around its procedures, for who in their right mind would run a red light! These become the new accountability provisions that govern educational research. The responsibility for equitable, quality educational provision is shifted over to communities of researchers and decision makers who must conduct themselves with prudence and be ever-mindful of the actuarial expertise that the preventative state provides in the course of discharging its duties. Researchers play a key role in this governance: to quote the presidential address of the 2003 AERA President, 'researchers too need to share responsibility' (Linn 2003). Walls of ignorance are no longer to serve as exculpatory barricades, which of course is something that can be welcomed for a host of reasons. However, we should also note that in advancing the spread of enlightened reason (thanks in part to the tri-colored illumination of the traffic signal), the accountability of our time is bringing a certain high stakes logic to US educational research itself and widely dispersing the responsibilities for managing successful educational provision. What Works works into a collective salvation narrative that has been recast to include actuarial expertise, disclosure and reporting as the keys to social hope.

Accountability as an empirical object

To say that within our accountability-time 'accountability' exists as a thing in the world is not the redundancy that it might seem on first blush. My intent here is to discuss how an analytic and theoretical concept can be transmuted into an apparent empirical reality – how accountability has become an object that is reasoned about in particular ways, as well as acted upon, and how educational research is drawn into these transformations. From the previous section it should be clear that the 'accountability' presently under examination pertains to much more than a pattern of relations between 'the elected' and 'the people'. We are dealing with a phenomenon of governance much more expansive and diffuse than the *Federalist Papers* style of concern for designing the democratic systems of government best able to be held 'accountable' to constituents. This notion of designing appropriate systems is, however, relevant, for it is common to find accountability analysed in US education research literature as a systems-management problem, e.g. in terms of 'accountability systems' (Linn 2003). Another congruent approach is to conduct research on 'accountability policies' (Spillane, Diamond, *et al.* 2002), e.g. as a bundle of mechanisms and inititatives sharing certain family resemblances. A focus on management systems and policy implementation might appear to skirt the notion of accountability as an empirical reality, however we will see that the sciences of education research themselves help to call this accountability-entity into existence. As a thing in the world, accountability takes a place on the landscape, affecting the social positions of subjects and structuring the social administration of the individual.

Forms of accountableness have appeared in various landscapes for some time now – as the above reference to the *Federalist Papers* hints at. In many of these instances, the emphasis has been on a relationship, a someone/something being 'accountable' to or for another someone/something. US educational research literature from the early 1970s evidences a burst of interest in accountableness. Notable in this respect is the work of Leon Lessinger (Lessinger 1970, Lessinger and Tyler 1971, Lessinger and Sabine 1973), as well as a progressive vision of the connections between public policy and social science research, a mode of thinking that, for example, played into making programme evaluation such a key feature of the 1965 Title I legislation (Lagemann 2000). In 1971 the National Council of Teachers of English (NCTE) felt compelled to adopt a position statement on accountability. This statement critiqued behaviourist evaluation paradigms and spoke of the multi-directional accountability relations that bound English teachers to students, colleagues, parents, administrators, the local community and vice-versa.[4] That we find a 1972 article in the *Journal of Higher Education* referring with evident exhaustion to the 'current "accountability" craze' (Cooper 1972) should be further cause for tempering present day claims about the absolute novelty of our 'new era'. The accountability movement of the 1970s attracted the critical attention of Thomas S. Popkewitz and Gary G. Wehlage (1973) who criticised the then-conventional concept of accountability as a technological mode of thought that rigidified thinking about schooling by installing behaviourist evaluative criteria, disregarding the diverse ways that people give meaning to experience, and considering schooling only to be a problem of bureaucratic management. Such critiques may still be quite relevant 35 years later, however, for my purposes here, returning to the early 1970s has its most value for pointing to features of 'accountability' that have been somewhat obscured with the accretions of time.

It will be illustrative to turn specifically to a November 1971 editorial from the *Journal of Higher Education*, as a way of tracking some transformations in 'what' accountability can be. This particular piece of commentary emerged in the context of a series of articles and discussions of accountability in US colleges and universities. In June of that year, for example, the journal had published an article on 'Autonomy and Accountability', a piece self-consciously written in the shadow of the Kent State shootings of the previous year and in the general context of 'turmoil and disruption on college campuses' (McConnell 1971). 'Autonomy' and 'accountability' were here problematised as relational descriptors that existed in a contentious, uneasy tension, something that the November editorial addressed by speaking to colleges and universities not as conforming to one or another ideal-type model but as political systems with 'complex interactions'. However, seemingly increasingly figuring in these interactions was 'accountability' (quotation marks in the original), in regards to which the *Journal of Higher Education*'s editor, Robert J. Silverman, noted: 'those who control information, those who utilize, manipulate, and evaluate data on university processes influence the definition of situations to which others respond,' adding 'in essence, they create the reality on which all are dependent' (1971). The shift from 'accountable' as descriptive (or not) of a relationship to accountability understood as a process is, I think, a key one. Quite evident and accessible in this 1971 statement is the acknowledgement that 'accountability' processes and systems *make up* part of our reality: they structure how individuals become positioned in relation to flows of data and information ('reporting' and 'disclosure', to use the terms I discussed in the previous section). Pointing to an historical instance in which 'accountability' is seen in terms of cultural/social processes and is acknowledged to be part and parcel of the construction of realities will, I hope, help to unsettle the brute force of its current, taken-for-granted prevalence. This contemporary 'presence' has the potential of making 'accountability' seem natural and necessary, and not a made and historically contingent part of the landscape (or edu-scape).[5] The empirical object 'accountability' that appears before US education researchers today is the flows of data and their management reified. This object is also one that owes some of its visibility to their work.

A study recently published in the *American Educational Research Journal* will nicely illustrate how the apparent empirical realities of 'accountability' have become problems of educational research. Samuel Stringfield and Mary Yakimowski-Srebnick (2005) present data from a longitudinal study of Baltimore public schools, organising their study according to what they define as 'three phases of accountability'. In one sense this harkens back to the above conversation of accountability-time, for the authors discuss the early implementation of standards in the period after the *A Nation at Risk* report (National Commission on Excellence in Education 1983), followed by a series of reforms connected with 1997 state legislation, and finally the implementation of initiatives connected with the No Child Left Behind federal legislation. Nonetheless, in looking at these phases, the researchers rely on accountability as the unifying theme, the object that took slightly different yet consistently recognisable shapes during this 15- to 20-year period. Stringfield and Yakimowski-Srebnick note that in recent years education researchers have had profound concerns about the narrowness of data measures and 'America's current testing regimen'. All the same, they remark that 'aggregated scores on various states' designated achievement measures have become key components of accountability for America's public schools' (Stringfield and Yakimowski-Srebnick 2005). The concept of accountability deployed in this study – as in other recent US education research – is one directly lifted from the contemporary political context with the result that as it circulates in scholarship, accountability has become the collection and reporting of data. In the transit from theoretical concept to object in the world and back to analytic construct 'accountability' now describes not the qualities of a relationship but constructs a social reality that, for example, makes the research problem for Stringfield and Yakimowski-Srebnick's study one of what works and what doesn't in 'accountability-driven reform'. This is, of course, not to point to any flaws in their study, rather it is to point to the way that it has become possible for 'accountability' to travel as an accepted empirical reality.

Conclusion

Accountability, as it moves within US educational research both as a thing in the world and as the defining characteristic of our era embodies strategies for the social administration of the individual. The common understanding of accountability as a problem of educational research, I have maintained, furthers a general social trend of increased responsibilisation that requires education professionals to act in accordance with a set of norms of reasonableness. As an empirical object, accountability can be seen as 'too little' or 'too much' present, part of the apparent reality that researchers and policymakers grapple with. We can note, for example, that 'Standards, testing and accountability' (in one breath) are among the research topics (others are 'School reform', 'Teacher retention') that the *Harvard Education Letter* includes when 'summarizing the latest education research and synthesizing it with practical suggestions you can put to daily use in your classrooms and schools'.[6] As we have seen above, accountability travels not in isolation but commonly in conjunction with 'standards and testing'. In US educational research, 'accountability' has, to considerable extent, come to represent the reification of flows of information and their management.

While such bureaucratisation and technicalisation takes us some distance from accountability as description of the qualities of a relationship between the governed and the governing, there is still a liberal-democratic political rationality embedded in the strategy of governance we have been examining here. Similar to 'Megan's Law' community notification statues, educational accountability generates a 'proper' social control. Government and its representatives are prevented from being overly intrusive, true to the liberal spirit; and in their stead, the maintenance of social order is entrusted to individuals as members of communities. The social science knowledge that educational researchers produce furthers this arrangement through studies of 'accountability-driven reforms' that rationalise and bring a coherence to the actions of governments. The social science knowledge that educational researchers produce also supports individuals as members of communities by giving them 'accountability data' to use in their decision making. 'Accountability' thus offers a salvation narrative for our times in which the properly informed (and properly reasoning) individual becomes proof of science's democratising potential and become the agent of a progress that offers social hope for redemption. This social redemption of the early twenty-first century is not the late nineteenth-century secularised saving of a soul but a redemption that rights past wrongs through the attainment of educational equity with no child no longer left behind.

Notes

1 Often referred to as IRB, these are university committees charged with ensuring the ethical treatment of human subject.
2 The quoted material in this paragraph is drawn from What Works Clearinghouse pamphlets and website. See http://www.whatworks.ed.gov/whatwedo/overview.html [accessed 12 March 2005].
3 http://www.whatworks.ed.gov/info/disclaimer.html [accessed 4 April 2005].
4 http://www.ncte.org/about/gov/reports/03annrpt/stcommit/107344.htm.
5 An analogous argument about social objects and subject positions could also be elaborated along the lines suggested by Arjun Appadurai's work on '-scapes' (Appadurai 1990).
6 http://www.edletter.org [accessed 10 March 2005].

References

Appadurai, A. (1990) 'Disjuncture and difference in the global cultural economy', *Public Culture* 2(2): 1–24.
Cohen, A.F. and Qaimmaqami, D.J. (2005) 'The US Sarbanes-Oxley Act of 2002', *International Journal of Disclosure and Governance*, 2(1).
Cooper, L.G. (1972) 'Decision ability, not accountability', *Journal of Higher Education*, 43(8): 655–60.
Ferguson, R.A. (1997) *The American Enlightenment, 1750 1820*, Cambridge, MA: Harvard University Press.
France, M., Lavelle, L. *et al.* (2004) 'The new accountability', *Business Week*, 3893: 30–3.
Greene, J. P. (1993) *The Intellectual Construction of America: Exceptionalism and Identity from 1492 to 1800*, Chapel Hill, NC: University of North Carolina Press.
Lagemann, E.C. (2000) *An Elusive Science: The Troubling History of Education Research*, Chicago, IL: University of Chicago Press.
Lather, P. (2004) 'This IS your father's paradigm: government intrusion and the case of qualitative research in education', *Qualitative Inquiry*, 10(1): 15–34.
Lessinger, L.M. (1970) *Every Kid a Winner: Accountability in Education*, Palo Alto, CA: Science Research Associates College Division.
Lessinger, L.M. and Sabine, C.D. (1973) *Accountability: Systems Planning in Education*, Homewood, IL: ETC Publications.
Lessinger, L.M. and Tyler, R.W. (1971) *Accountability in Education*, Worthington, OH: CA. Jones Pub. Co.
Levi, R. (2000) 'The mutuality of risk and community: the adjudication of community notification statutes', *Economy and Society*, 29(4): 578–601.
Linn, R.L. (2003) 'Accountability: responsibility and reasonable expectations', *Educational Researcher*, 32(7): 3–13.
McConnell, T.R. (1971) 'Accountability and autonomy', *Journal of Higher Education*, 42(6): 446–63.
National Commission on Excellence in Education (1983) *A Nation at Risk*, Washington, DC: Government Printing Office (Also available online http://www.ed.gov/pubs/NatAtRisk/risk.html).
Popkewitz, T.S. (1991) *A Political Sociology of Educational Reform: Power/Knowledge in Teaching, Teacher Education, and Research*, New York: Teachers College Press.
Popkewitz, T.S. (1998) 'The culture of redemption and the administration of freedom as research', *Review of Educational Research*, 68(1): 1–34.
Popkewitz, T.S. (2004) 'Is the National Research Council Committee's Report on Scientific Research in Education Scientific? On trusting the manifesto', *Qualitative Inquiry*, 10(1): 62–78.

Popkewitz, T.S. and Wehlage, G.G. (1973) 'Accountability: critique and alternative perspective', *Interchange*, 4(4): 48–62.

Rose, N.S. (1999) *Powers of Freedom: Reframing Political Thought*. Cambridge, United Kingdom; New York: Cambridge University Press.

Silverman, R.J. (1971) 'Editorial: accountability', *Journal of Higher Education*, 42(8): 692–3.

Skocpol, T. (1992) *Protecting Soldiers and Mothers: The Political Origins of Social Policy in the United States*, Cambridge, MA: Belknap Press of Harvard University Press.

Spillane, J.P., Diamond, J.B. *et al.* (2002) 'Managing in the middle: school leaders and the enactment of accountability policy', *Educational Policy*, 16(5): 731–62.

Stringfield, S.C. and Yakimowski-Srebnick, M. (2005) 'Promise, progress, problems, and paradoxes of three phases of accountability: a longitudinal case study of the Baltimore City Public School', *American Educational Research Journal*, 42(1): 43–75.

3 Crossing borders

The European dimension in educational and social science research

Angelos Agalianos[1]

Introduction

Europe is confronted by major societal challenges and opportunities such as social and regional cohesion, unemployment, migration, interactions between different cultures, poverty and inequalities, enlargement, demographic change, security and global interdependence. There is a need on the part of society in general and policy makers in particular for a deeper knowledge and understanding of such issues, of their driving forces and consequences, and of how best to tackle them. A need for significantly improved understanding of how social, economic and environmental objectives might be successfully combined, of how the key social, political, cultural and economic issues in an enlarged EU can be faced.

Generating in-depth, shared understanding of such complex challenges and providing an improved knowledge base for decisions on relevant strategies and policies, requires a strong collaborative research effort across the social and human sciences in all their strength and variety across Europe. The social and human sciences do not only contribute to current social, economic, political and cultural development processes, but also build the intellectual foundations and resources for dealing with future challenges, foreseen as well as unexpected. A vibrant research scene in the social and human sciences is an essential component of a dynamic Europe.

The activities of the European Commission in this field aim to provide a coherent and interlinked understanding of the challenges contemporary European societies are faced with and to support policy, thereby enabling Europe better to understand itself and face its future. This essentially descriptive chapter argues that these activities provide a new exciting arena where new interpretations and new practices of research have been generated that foster the interaction of *policy relevance*, *transnationality* and *multidisciplinarity* and stimulate innovative social and educational research. The argument of this chapter is that, especially after 1995, European social science research programmes have become a powerful way of beginning to draw together and understand the complex dimensions of contemporary social and educational change in Europe and beyond.

The chapter provides an insider's account of the development of educational research supported by the Directorate-General for Research of the European Commission since 1995. When and how did EU-supported educational research begin? What is its wider research policy context? What are some landmarks in its development? What are the key players involved? Why support educational research at a European level? What kind of research is it? What makes it different? Which research topics have been supported to date? What are some key conclusions from European research in this field? What are some major challenges for European educational research? These are some of the questions asked in this chapter.

Educational research matters

Education structures and processes are of foremost importance for Europe and are inextricably linked to core social, political and economic policy areas and concerns such as employment, housing, health, welfare, youth, migration, citizenship, social cohesion and social justice. At a time of major societal changes and challenges within Europe and internationally, research on learning and learning institutions, on education practices and policies, and on their interaction with other policies is a necessity.

In March 2000, the conclusions of the Lisbon Council confirmed learning as a basic component both for the development of the European economy *and* as a core driver of a European social model.[2] In doing so, it confirmed the need to study the shifting processes and practices of learning, and to relate these to wider aspects of contemporary social change in Europe and beyond.

Like in all other social science fields, the intuition that there is something common between those who study issues in the wider field of learning hides a great deal of variety and diversity in terms of subjects of study, perspectives and methodologies, as well as differences in links developed with some established professions. Researchers working in the field of learning in Europe draw on a wide range of experiences, disciplinary approaches, value commitments and methodological paradigms. This diversity generates some innovative work and is, in many ways, a considerable strength. Such influences also structure our understanding of issues, framing of research questions and interpretation of results.

However, the bulk of 'educational research' in Europe has for very long remained nationally congealed, narrowly focused, overly specialised, compartmentalised within foundational disciplinary boundaries, and poorly connected to policy and practice. It has formed a fragmented landscape inhabited by semi-isolated academic tribes leading a 'rural lifestyle' (Nowotny 2005, Becher and Trowler 2001). Most commonly found within stagnant academic institutions that often obstruct research innovations, this kind of education research has largely failed to add knowledge and value in the broader social science agenda and help resolve social, political, cultural, economic and environmental questions other than those experienced within the confines of formal education and training systems:

> Much educational research, as well as education policy, remains stubbornly one-dimensional, uncritical and decontextualised … failing to explore the relationship of specific practices to wider social and cultural constructions and political and economic interests.
>
> (Whitty 2002: 13)

How, for example, has educational research contributed to learning and thinking about *social and regional cohesion* – especially in regions of economic transition and social/ economic polarisation? How has it contributed to our understanding of and progress towards economic achievement, at an individual, workplace/firm, and local/regional level and how can we understand better how learning influences regional *economic disparities or convergence*? How much do we understand about the contribution of educational actors and actions of all kinds in developing and sustaining *political engagement* and of an *education for pluralism, complexity and creativity* (Montuori 2005); how has educational research contributed to tolerance, democratic participation, human rights and social justice? How has it contributed to building *better health* and *consumer protection*, especially for those most at risk, minimising the negative impact of globalisation and economic trends on *access to work, education, social and community services*? How has educational research helped to *improve safety and security* issues at a human and technical level, helped to improve the quality of research and achievement of innovation, supported good practice and new policies in *global governance* and *socially equitable trade*, or contributed to efficient, effective and equitable *public services* and *sustainable development*? How has educational research advanced our understanding of the *synergies* that can be achieved between economic, social and environmental objectives in Europe and in the world as well as of the trade-offs involved?

Ronald Sultana, a contemporary sociologist of education is asking:

> How have we tended to construct Europe in educational discourse? ... rather superficially and inadequately – largely because we have generally failed to engage the profound debates that have evolved in other areas and disciplines, including those of political economy, public policy-making and diplomacy.
>
> (Sultana 2002: 118)

While on the other side of the Atlantic, Michael Apple, a highly regarded theorist and activist of education, finds that:

> Too many of 'our' [educational researchers'] efforts amount to well-paid fiddling while Rome burns. Too many of them are not about anything of public importance.
>
> (Apple 1996: 118)

Moreover, the national, disciplinary and theory-practice fragmentation of education research has traditionally nurtured and defended myopic conceptualisations and methods of 'comparative' study:

> But it is striking ... how removed comparative education has been from some of the main currents in comparative history and social science. It is hard not to conclude that comparative education has been at times somewhat insular; sometimes too preoccupied with self-referential internal debates ...
>
> (Green 2002: 26).

There is currently a need to re-conceive the value and potential contribution of education research and in doing so require of those working in this domain to present fresh, coordinated proposals to demonstrate why and how they might participate in the decision-making processes of the European integration. *There is also a need for the wider social science research community to engage seriously with education.*

Without losing sight of the enormous importance of what happens (or not happens) inside and around schools, colleges and universities, of the driving forces behind particular policies and practices (or their absence) and of their consequences for individuals and social groups in the education arena, there is an urgent need to recognise that 'educational theory and educational policy that ignore wider social issues can be not only blind but positively harmful' (Whitty 2002: 139).

A pragmatic research agenda would include investigation into *the aims, ends and purposes of learning* as well as the search for better means and methods of education (Biesta and Burbules 2003). It would also question the current managerialist fascination with social darwinist notions of standards and competition observed in some countries (Frade forthcoming). A pragmatic research agenda would also help us understand the possibilities and limits of what can be reasonably expected from research in, on and for education, as well as of the kind of support that education needs. It would help understand what policy makers often tend to forget, that education cannot tackle all the issues alone, that 'education cannot compensate for society' (Bernstein 1970); that there is a need for 'joined up' strategies for 'joined up' problems (Armstrong 2000).

In the quest for such *combined* educational and social strategies, there is a need for the development of stronger links between researchers in the field of learning and researchers working on other policy fields. There is a need for *integration* and cross-fertilisation of disciplinary perspectives that will enable a more adequate response to the challenges contemporary European societies are faced with. There is also a need for the development of sustainable research capacities through opportunities for *interdisciplinary research training* and viable *interdisciplinary research careers* (Sperber 2003, Weingart and Stehr 2000).

While efforts to advance theoretical understanding and scholarship are indispensable, there is at the same time a need for research that will provide insights useful for policy formulation. Without denying the value of basic research, or declaring the search for policy recipes as the ultimate objective in the conduct of educational research in Europe, there is a need to reconcile the norms and cultures of basic research with those of *policy-relevant* enquiry that can inform policy making at different levels with trustworthy knowledge about the role education and learning may play in contemporary European societies, in connection and synergy with other policy fields.

The EU programmes for social science research

The EU does not have a separate programme for education research; research in relation to education challenges in Europe has been an integral part of the EU programme for research in the social sciences.

While some EU support to social science research existed before 1995 through activities like COST, 'Europe+30' and FAST (1978–82, 4.4 MECU), FAST II (1983–7, 8.5 MECU) and MONITOR (1988–92, 25 MECU)[2], it was in the Fourth EU Framework Programme for research (FP4, 1995–8) that the EU started supporting substantially research in the social sciences. The *Targeted Socio-Economic Research Programme* (TSER, 115 MECU) was one of the several 'specific programmes' comprising FP4. It expanded the research agenda to themes outside the realm of science and technology policy, and initiated the links of Community research in the social sciences and humanities with other policies of the Community. The programme was founded on the idea that the fragmentation of social science research communities was a major impediment in the development of social science research of European policy relevance and focused on three themes:

- science, technology and innovation in the economy and society;
- education and training;
- social exclusion and social integration.

From the beginning, the TSER Programme was problem-oriented, policy-relevant and multidisciplinary where possible, and this approach was also maintained in subsequent programmes. It supported 162 research projects and thematic networks.

The TSER was followed by a more ambitious effort in the *Fifth EU Framework Programme* for research (1999–2002) to broaden the audiences and themes addressed through the development of a mainstream European socio-economic research programme, the first programme that set objectives for the social sciences as a whole. Under FP5, the Key Action *Improving the socio-economic knowledge base* (165 MEURO) set out to cover many more, different but interrelated, research themes and topics. The scope was far less linked to social aspects of science and technology and was greatly broadened to include key institutional issues like governance, European integration and identity, and welfare systems. While the three fields of study previously supported under the TSER continued to receive some support, the programme shifted its focus to include most of social science areas and even some of the humanities. It addressed broader societal issues such as societal trends and structural changes, challenges from European enlargement, European socio-economic models and challenges, social cohesion, migration, welfare, governance and citizenship, employment and changes in work, and new development models aiming at multiple objectives. In doing so, it began to raise the issue of quality of life and started to work on a richer notion of development, preceding Lisbon. Growth and employment questions were addressed from several sides. For the first time, the Key Action brought in political science in a substantial and explicit manner. A major and conscious effort was made to address complex societal questions in a many-sided way.

Under the *Sixth EU Framework Programme* (2002–06), Priority 7 'Governance and citizenship in a knowledge-based society' (225 MEURO) used the multiple Lisbon objectives as an overarching framework and had two major sub-areas that were nevertheless linked:

- knowledge-based society and social cohesion;
- citizens, democracy and new forms of governance.

The humanities were expressly introduced, often related to a stronger explicit reference to culture than had previously been present. A major expansion of the effort devoted to the governance and related areas was undertaken. The research focus became slowly but increasingly more international, addressing issues such as global governance, and emerging growth regions (e.g. China, India) and their role in the world economy. There were also increasing efforts to relate politics to the other social science disciplines, with topics such as economic governance, regulation and services of general interest.

In FP6, new and larger types of research projects and networks have been introduced alongside the existing smaller ones, and typically have around 20 to 40 partners. The total FP6 budget for research in the social sciences and humanities was €225 million and the number of projects supported is expected to exceed 140.

The results from the projects in FP4 and FP5 have been published in the form of books, journal articles, as project final reports, state-of-the-art reports and sometimes specific reports on issues or sectors, and are all available on the web in a searchable database and on the projects' own websites. New indicators and databases resulting from surveys are also available. Project dissemination is mainly done within the projects, though considerable efforts have been undertaken at an EU level also. Many workshops and conferences have been held, at the national, European and sometimes regional levels. At the EU level, specific dissemination/valorisation efforts, each involving multiple projects in a given field, are being carried out through research-policy dialogue workshops, project clustering actions, and a set of reviews of the research findings in 20 different policy fields (see http://www.cordis.lu/citizens/).

At least 70 of these projects address directly issues of education and training. The total EU contribution to these learning-related research activities in FP4, FP5 and FP6 borders €60 million. These collaborative endeavours address a wide range of issues related to learning and learning institutions and involve a large number of research teams from across Europe and beyond. In bringing together research teams from several countries, these activities have laid the foundations for significant research cooperation in this field in Europe. Information on these activities can be found at: http://www.cordis.lu/citizens/.

Educational research in FP4 and in FP5

The TSER Programme attached a lot of importance to educational research; *education and training* was one of the three TSER thematic areas. Both the TSER and the Key Action were implemented through three different Calls for Proposals.[3] In all three TSER Calls and in the first and second key action Calls for Proposals, learning-related research topics were distinct and clearly visible (see Appendices 1–5 to this chapter) show the learning-related research topics available to the social science research community in each of these five Calls (between 1995 and 2000). At least 38 of the 162 projects supported under the TSER of FP4 and at least 20 of the 185 projects supported under the Key Action 'Improving' of FP5 addressed directly issues of learning. In addition to these, a number of smaller supporting activities (like book publications, workshops, conferences, studies, project clusters, reviews of research results and dissemination activities) related to learning were supported under FP4 and FP5.

Importantly, in the third (and last) Call for Proposals of the Key Action 'Improving' (2001), opportunities for learning-related research were not to be found under separate/ distinct headings, they were not offered as separate research topics. Rather, the education and training aspect was included as *a cross-cutting dimension*, as an aspect that was relevant to several of the other research topics available to the broader social science research community. The following example of a research topic shows that the education and learning dimension was linked to several other social science concerns:

> Research may be undertaken to identify social and institutional conditions that are
> especially favourable to learning and innovation in a 'learning society', the relation

to conditions in Europe, taking into account broad notions of innovation including social innovation. This may include issues of knowledge dissemination, social capital, trust, social networks, increasingly multicultural societies, ageing, etc. The role of formal education and training and of other forms of learning in this context may be addressed, including comparative, political economy, socio-cultural and critical perspectives more generally on education and learning; both macro and micro level research is encouraged.

(European Commission 2001: 12)

In another research topic of the same call, the education and training aspect was linked to concerns about the intergenerational inheritance of inequalities:

Research may address and clarify issues of cultural and social capital in relation to the quality of life. Of particular interest is how to reduce the intergenerational 'inheritance' of inequalities between individuals and socio-economic groups. This requires an improved understanding of the mechanisms of such inheritance and comparative research on why its importance seems to vary across European countries. The results of this work should also assist education and training policies and systems to reduce such inequalities.

(European Commission 2001: 13)

The decision to embed education and learning aspects as a cross-cutting dimension in European social science research rather than offer education as a free-standing research topic was not an accident. It was a conscious decision of the Commission that was meant to send a clear message to the research community: that education research should be an essential complement to social science research in other domains; that researchers working in the wider field of education should join forces and work together with researchers from other fields of the social sciences; and – very importantly – that the wider social science research community should overcome its reluctance to engage seriously with education and no longer look upon education and training as the Cinderella within the social sciences.

Transnationality, multidisciplinary, policy relevance and the new meaning of comparative research

Like all social science research projects supported by DG-Research under FP4, FP5 and FP6, all learning-related research activities have the following characteristics:

First, the projects are *transnational*, collaborative endeavours that bring together research teams from several different countries from within but also from beyond the EU. Evidence suggests that transnational research can be conceptualised and practised in different ways in European social science projects and carries with it a number of inherent difficulties that include methodological, communication and interaction challenges in multinational research teams (Kuhn and Weidemann 2005). This raises issues of quality. Different national perspectives and cultural traditions have produced very different approaches to educational research in the past. These differences create the potential for strong complementarities, synergy and mutual learning within cross-national research teams. However, they may also on occasion lead to misunderstandings, tensions and variations in research quality and create a risk that, instead of exploiting the strengths of each partner, some projects may end up with lowest common denominator solutions.

Secondly, many of the projects are *multidisciplinary*, in that they bring together representatives of different disciplines and enable the combination of different disciplinary perspectives. Research partners are able to approach the topic under investigation from several, different but complementary, disciplinary or sub-disciplinary angles – which widens the scope of understanding. Recently completed research on the ways in which multidisciplinarity is interpreted and put into practice in EU-supported social science research projects shows some of the benefits that accrue from the combination of different disciplinary perspectives in such a research project. According to this study, one of the benefits is the opportunity that many researchers find in these projects to escape from the limitations of discipline-based structures that predominate in their national research environments:

> For many coordinators, EU projects were seen as freeing researchers from the stifling character of national structures, not only by opening up new channels of communication and exchange among different disciplinary specialists, but also by providing research opportunities that transcended the concerns and agendas of powerful members of national academies.
>
> (Benavot *et al.* 2005: 124)

Thirdly, EU-supported social science research projects are based on a genuinely *'European' research agenda*, in that they address issues and concerns which are experienced differently but shared at a European level. They are centred around questions whose relevance and importance transcend single geographical boundaries, around supra-national challenges that different societies face differently as well as jointly.

Fourthly, EU-supported activities in this field are problem-oriented and policy-relevant. In addition to the expectation for high quality research that will advance knowledge and scholarship on a topic, projects are expected to focus on issues of relevance to European integration and to produce insights useful for policy formulation. This does not mean that the EU programme for research in the social sciences puts pressure on the research community for quick evidence-based solutions to the educational challenges of Europe. In the context of the programme, policy relevance is not synonymous to 'false expectations' for detailed policy recipes (Hammersley, 2002) for the short to medium term. Rather, the objective is to produce a deep scientific understanding of the various issues and challenges as well as improved understanding of the implications of alternative policy directions that could be ultimately useful for policy formulation.

Learning-related projects supported under FP4, FP5 and FP6 vary considerably in the degree and nature of 'policy relevance' they display. Depending largely on the nature of the research topic, as well as on the disciplinary and methodological angles from which the research consortium chooses to approach an issue, the type of 'policy relevance' pursued may range from a direct engagement with specific policies aiming to arrive at policy lessons and recommendations for specific measures at a European, national and/or regional level, to work that is more concerned with enhancing our understanding of broad policy directions or of the policy process itself rather than with finding solutions to specific problems.

The two types are not water-tight. The reality of many projects shows that there are significant crossovers between describing, comparing, understanding and evaluating and that 'policy relevant research' means different things to different researchers. Not surprisingly, in EU-supported social science and education research – like in any other arena of social science research – workers conceptualise 'policy relevance' and translate it into practice in different ways, confirming the view that policy research in education is a 'contested terrain', that conceptualisations of 'policy' and 'policy relevance' are continually struggled over (Ozga 2000: 4).

Evidence suggests that the policy orientation of EU-supported research in this field opens up new opportunities for education researchers and for social scientists in general. It gives researchers the opportunity to participate actively in social, political, ethical and other related debates that may influence or contribute to policy decision-making, mainly in two ways: (a) directly, through the policy relevant conclusions of their research; and (b) indirectly, through their opportunity to contribute to the debate on a specific topic and the way in which it is dealt with (Greco *et al.* 2005: 226–7).

A question that arises is whether – or to what extent– the desire for European research funding pushes researchers to compromise their interest for basic research in favour of policy-oriented research. A recent study on how participants in EU-supported social science research projects interpret and practise 'policy relevance' concluded that:

> Researchers who participated in the Framework projects were not simply opportunistically adjusting their research interests to fit the Commission's Call. At least some were already committed to this type of policy-relevant research.
>
> (Greco *et al.* 2005: 190)

Finally, European collaborative social science research has a strong *comparative* dimension. Most often, rigorous and systematic comparison is an integral part of such a project. By its very nature, European transnational collaborative research challenges traditional conceptualisations of 'comparative' educational enquiry. It is not only a methodological challenge that it brings in but, rather, a challenge to the very nature of comparative analysis. As early as in 1996 (in the very early days of EU-supported social and educational research), Jacky Brine was writing:

> … European social and educational research can, and hopefully will be, more than simply comparative studies of Member States. TSER … has the ability to enable research which will focus on the differences within and across Member States rather than simply between them. It can fund research into the structures and processes of power and agency and of opportunity across the Member States. It offers exciting possibilities for international rather than simply comparative social justice research.
>
> (Brine 1996: 13)

Almost 10 years later, a study that systematically documented the experiences of researchers engaged in EU-supported social science research projects showed that Brine's early excitement had become a reality. The study concluded that, in the framework of

European transnational collaborative projects, comparative research takes on a new dimension:

> By breaking down the traditional division between pure and applied research and by overcoming the limitations of observation in different national environments, European socio-economic research starts with an assumption of joint practical challenges for joint research projects. Research topics are viewed as a response to joint socio-political challenges emerging out of distinctive national socio-economic environments. European socio-economic research may be perceived as a collaborative social learning mode.
>
> (Kuhn and Remoe 2005: 6)

Thematic coverage and some key conclusions from FP4 and FP5 projects

A careful reading of the research topics available to the research community in each Call for Proposals of FP4 and FP5 (see Appendices 1–5 to this chapter) shows that the research agenda of both the TSER and the Key Action 'Improving' were permeated by an explicit *'bottom-up' rationale*. In all Calls for Proposals, the research tasks were largely open-ended, providing broad frameworks for research rather than tightly prescribed or narrowly focused topics. This was not an accident; it was a choice of DG-Research that aimed to allow researchers to develop their own interpretations of the research topics and decide on the angle from which they would choose to address them.

As a result of this openness of the research topics, the Commission received a very diverse set of education-related research proposals as a response to each Call for Proposals and supported a very heterogeneous set of research projects. The projects address a wide range of issues that include:

* the dynamics of education and employment;
* issues of teacher education;
* issues of higher education;
* the use of ICTs in learning;
* issues of education for citizenship;
* issues of quality and relevance of learning opportunities;
* lifelong learning strategies;
* issues of competence development and learning in organisations;
* innovative pedagogies and school improvement;
* issues of children, education, and migration; and
* issues of intercultural education.

It can be fairly stated that most of the education research projects supported under FP4 were thematically narrow and to some extent reflected the multiple fragmentation of a research community that was for the first time experimenting with European transnational collaborative research of this kind and scale. The spectrum of projects funded by FP4 (1995–8) lent strong emphasis to economic and employment-linked aspects of education and training (un/employment and [youth] transitions; funding and investment/return; skills/competence gaps and company-based training). Quality issues (evaluation, effectiveness and assessment; early learning; competence development) were also well represented. Studies focusing on the higher education sector were prominent. Some attention was given to access and integration issues (mobility, migration, older workers and adult learners). Small attention was also given to issues of education governance, school improvement and teacher training. There was also a small cluster of ICT-related projects together with a few on science education.

In comparison, the work funded under FP5 (1999–2002) placed greater emphasis on learning in and through work-based environments, and also introduced non-formal/informal learning through learning for active citizenship via participation. It placed a strong emphasis on governance, regulation and reform questions, with a view to the EU's internal and global future. Projects focused rather less on the higher education sector and gave a strengthened profile to vocational education and training (VET). Research on minority and migrant groups became more prominent and gender topics appeared (in relation to employment).

Projects in FP5 tended to be thematically wider than in FP4, with a tendency to address some of the links between aspects of education with other policies. In this effort, many of the projects involved a greater mix of social science disciplines in their work.

Research on Higher Education shows that the transformation of national HE systems is on the political agenda of every country in Europe. The HE sector is urged to 'modernise', 'adapt', 'diversify' and 'marketise'. It is expected to become 'entrepreneurial', 'competitive', more 'efficient' and more 'effective', more 'service oriented', and more 'societally relevant'. It is also asked to improve the 'quality of its processes and products', its 'relationship with the labour market', and the 'governance and management' of its institutions.

Research shows that the socio-political demands and expectations with respect to higher education have grown – especially concerning its economic role – whilst at the same time in most countries the level of public funding of higher education is stagnating or decreasing. This has led to an imbalance between the demands many stakeholders make on higher education, expecting a rapid reaction, and the capacity of higher education institutions to respond adequately to these demands.

Research on the transition of young people from education to work shows that the young people at the bottom of the qualification ladder encounter substantial difficulties in entering the labour market and are the most vulnerable to economic swings. They have higher unemployment risks and tend to end up in low-skilled or temporary jobs, facing a future of state-funded training programmes interspersed with insecure low paid employment and lengthy periods of unemployment. Their transitions to work often involve them being channelled into training schemes that do not always match the needs of the labour market and neglect individual aspirations and strengths; this results in de-motivation and disengagement. Importantly, however, research confirms that the linear equation 'more qualifications = more and better jobs' is simplistic and that the relationship between education and many economic dimensions is a far more complex one. Research demonstrates that reductionist popular beliefs that individual experiences of education (success or 'failure') have direct linear consequences for economic success assume that qualifications are the only legitimate outcomes of education and advocate greater individual investment and risk responsibility in education and training. By contrast, while outcomes continue to vary by gender, social class background and ethnic origin, research shows that poverty is cyclical – and, yes, a very real relationship between education and economics does exist, and that the origins of this cycle are in our social and economic relations, not in our schools.

Research shows that, in all systems, early educational experience has serious consequences for young people at later stages in life and that there is a need for policy intervention to reduce dropout. This will need to involve identifying those likely to drop out and providing them with incentives to remain in education. Research suggests that, given the diversity in education, training and labour market systems across Europe, the same policy interventions are unlikely to be equally effective in different contexts.

Research suggests that, contrary to existing conventional schemes, policies that involve the active participation and recognition of informal learning for young people in transition can have a major impact in enhancing motivation for active re-engagement in transitions to work. Research also suggests that active participation of young people should be a key principle in policies concerned with young people's transitions to work; that young people should be put at the centre of policies concerning their lives and be given negotiation power (López Blasco *et al.* 2003).

Research on new governance models for education and training suggests that the introduction of market mechanisms in education and training does not always correspond to a number of assumptions made by the advocates of decentralisation and marketisation of education. The effects that are reported include negative ones, in the sense that the introduction of market mechanisms could increase social and educational inequality and the exclusion of disadvantaged groups (Frade 2006).

Research demonstrates that external accountability mechanisms based on targets and performance can have damaging effects on disadvantaged schools and communities and can also distort educational processes (Power 2006).

Research on the use of information and communication technologies (ICT) in learning has shown that the use of ICTs is not a panacea for problems in education provision and their potential should not be overplayed. Research demonstrated that besides access to technology a number of other factors determine the success or failure of ICT-related educational innovation. Teacher training appears to be a critical factor. Research suggests that educational innovation involving the use of ICT should not be considered only as a matter of access to technology or only as a matter of implementation. The use of technology in schools and universities is found to be socially contextualised, interacting with the institutional and organisational cultures of schools and reflecting elements of the prevailing social relations in and around the context of use. Research demonstrates that educational institutions are social organisations that both influence the ways in which an innovation will be adopted and are influenced by that innovation. That the adoption of ICTs does not follow universal rules but is profoundly shaped by the context in which it is introduced.

Research leads to the conclusion that attempts to develop 'one size fits all' ICT-related innovation policies for adoption at national or regional level are unlikely to be successful. Rather, ICT policies need to be developed in a more bottom-up way, with the active involvement of a range of local social actors and sensitivity to the particular historical, institutional and cultural context in which the policy is to be implemented (Huws 2006).

Research on national, European and global education policies and policy rhetorics looks at the two main literatures dealing with learning (the literature on the learning society and lifelong learning and the literature on the learning or knowledge economy) and at the learning obsession and exhortations from politicians to 'learn, learn, learn':

> Learning is the new sex. Countries, firms and individuals are talking about it, wondering whether they are getting enough, enough of the right kind, with the right people, for long enough. And those who don't want learning ALL THE TIME, well they are just 'odd'.
>
> (Collins 2003: 4)

Research demonstrates that policies for learning, and their reflection of a 'learning society', are not merely policies for teaching and learning, or even for education and training, but form an integral part of wider social and economic policy. That the outcomes of learning are intimately connected to core economic *and* socio-cultural concerns and have social as well as economic consequences and opportunities attached to them.

Research shows that it is the latter – the economic implications – that dominate the European discourse over the 'learning society'. That while there are alternative conceptualisations of a 'learning or knowledge economy/society', it is the economic visions and rhetoric that have dominated the discourse on the 'learning society' and the relevant education policies in Europe:

> Although cultural enrichment does feature in EU and national policies, the overwhelming emphasis within policies at EU and national level is on the economic rather than socio-cultural gains of education.
>
> (Power 2006: 6)

Research in this area highlights the dangers from the uncritical acceptance of the currently dominant rhetoric surrounding the 'learning society' concept and demonstrates that there is an urgent need for a better balance between the economic and socio-cultural objectives, policies and practices of learning in Europe (Kuhn and Sultana 2005; Kuhn *et al.* 2005; Strieszka 2005; Collins 2003; Charles *et al.* 2003). It shows that rather than build artificial consensus, policy makers need to open up concepts such as the 'learning society' and 'widening participation' to critical debate so that they are not reduced to economic imperatives alone. Research suggests that policy makers need to work with academics and practitioners to debate the fundamental principles of education and to explore how the traditional strengths of European education systems can be reframed to meet contemporary economic *and* socio-cultural challenges (Power 2006).

A general lesson that we draw from EU-supported research on learning to date is that all too often we forget that in our attempts to 'innovate', to alter and 'reform' educational institutions, there are elements that should not be changed but need to be kept and defended. That:

> ... before we give a blanket condemnation to what schools do and turn to what we suppose is the alternative way,[4] we need a much clearer and more historically informed appraisal of what elements of the practices and policies of these institutions are already progressive and should be maintained.
>
> (Apple 1996: xvi)

Another lesson emerging from EU-supported research on learning is that various factors inside and outside education cause, or at least contribute to, processes of *social exclusion*. Research demonstrates that these factors are intertwined and appear to be mutually reinforcing, though in different ways and at different stages in life. While education has been seen by many national governments as a major tool for tackling social exclusion, European research demonstrates that the underlying factors involved are much broader and deeper than is often understood by policy makers and that any one area of social policy is unlikely, by itself, to be able to address the problem. That labour market or education or migration policy initiatives alone will have only limited success in removing barriers to inclusion unless they are articulated with policies that address wider social and economic inequalities. That policy makers need to consider the *combined* consequences of policies rather than see them as isolated strategies (Power 2006; Frade 2006).

This need for '"joined up" strategies for "joined up" problems' has been the driver behind the research topic on *Educational strategies for inclusion and social cohesion and their relation to other policies* which was available to the research community in FP6 to which I will now turn.

Educational research in FP6

In FP6 (2003–6), research in the social sciences and humanities was supported under Priority 7 'Citizens and Governance in a Knowledge Based Society'. The budget for social science research was increased to €225 million. Again, this represented a miniscule allocation of the total FP6 budget (in € million):

Priority 1. Life sciences, genomics and biotechnology for health	2.255
Priority 2. Information society technologies	3.625
Priority 3. Nanotechnologies and nanosciences	1.300
Priority 4. Aeronautics and space	1.075
Priority 5. Food quality and safety	685
Priority 6. Sustainable development, global change and ecosystems	2.120
Priority 7. Citizens and governance in a knowledge-based society	225
Priority 8. Supporting policies and anticipating scientific and tech. needs	1.300

The 1st call for proposals

Priority 7 was implemented through two different Calls for Proposals. The first Call had a budget that exceeded 100 MEURO and two different deadlines (April and December 2003). The research topics that this Call made available included the following education-related topics:

*Research should identify the **education challenges for the knowledge society** through improved understanding of the major challenges and opportunities faced by the education systems in Europe as it moves towards a knowledge-based society, and by identifying the policy options in response. The research should identify trends in the educational objectives, and the extent to which they adequately address the* *future in a knowledge society; effective pedagogical approaches at different levels of education; changes in education governance and their impact, including their overall effectiveness in improving learning. The school and vocational educational levels are of special interest.* Topic available for the deadline of 15/04/2003.

Research may identify and address key issues for improving the transmission of knowledge in **reinforcing the links between science and education** *and within the perspective of citizenship. This should lead, for example, to improved understanding of how different aspects of citizenship, including their affective and social dimensions, are promoted through studies in relation to environment, biology and health.* Topic available for the deadline of 15/04/ 2003.

Promoting the knowledge society through life-long learning. *Research capacities on various key aspects of lifelong learning should be integrated in order to compare the various discourses, improve conceptual clarity, better understand trends in lifelong learning policies and practices in Europe as well as their implications for the creation of a European knowledge society, for social cohesion, inequalities and quality of life. The themes to be integrated include: lifelong learning in the context of socio-economic change; objectives of lifelong learning; design of and access to lifelong learning strategies for all; articulation of lifelong learning policies with other key policy fields; issues of quality and relevance; recognition and validation of learning and qualification; effective learning methods. Attention is to be given to formal and informal aspects of learning, to perspectives from various relevant disciplines, and to the development of monitoring methods.* Topic available for the deadline of 10/12/2003.

In addition to these clearly education-related research topics, some references to education could also be found in other research topics in that Call. For example, in another research topic, education was linked once again to concerns about the intergenerational inheritance of inequalities and to other issues:

> There are close connections between the accumulation of socio-economic risks, current and past inequalities, quality of life, access to services, etc. Research is needed to better understand *the intergenerational inheritance of inequalities.* Work should identify ways to improve social mobility in Europe, the implications for relevant policies such as education systems and more generally public services, etc. Further changes in inequalities due to the emergence of the knowledge society should be considered, for example the consequences of the increasing value given in society to certain skills and knowledge.
>
> (European Commission 2002, pp. 7–8)

Fifty-nine new social science research projects started in 2004 as a result of the 1st Call for Proposals of Priority 7. These include the following projects that address directly issues of education:

- *Intercultural Active Citizenship Education* (INTERACT, started in March 2004 for 36 months, EU contribution: €550,000).
- *Biology, Health and Environmental Education for Better Citizenship* (BIOHEAD-CITIZEN, started in October 2004 for 36 months, EU contribution: €1 million).

- *European Universities for Entrepreneurship: their role in the Europe of knowledge* (EUEREK, started in September 2004 for 36 months, EU contribution: €1 million).
- *The Flexible Professional in the Knowledge Society: competencies required by higher education graduates and the new demands on higher education in Europe* (REFLEX, started in March 2004 for 36 months, EU contribution: €1,050,000).
- *Professional Knowledge in Education and Health: restructuring work and life between the state and the citizens in Europe* (PROFKNOW, started in September 2004 for 36 months, EU contribution: €1,350,000).
- *Empowerment of Mental Illness Service Users: lifelong learning, integration and action* (EMILIA, started in September 2005 for 54 months, EU contribution: €3,400,000).
- *Towards a Lifelong Learning Society in Europe: the contribution of the education system* (LLL 2010, started in September 2005 for 60 months, EU contribution: €3,200,000).

More information on these activities can be found at: http://www.cordis.lu/citizens/.

The second call for proposals of priority 7

The second Call of Priority 7 (December 2004–April 2005) was by far the biggest budget ever available for European research in the social sciences and humanities (€120 million). It was of interest and relevance to researchers from a wide range of disciplines in the social sciences and the humanities. It was explicitly open to and welcomed a wide range of approaches. The research topics available in the second Call included the following topic which is directly relevant to education.

Educational strategies for inclusion and social cohesion and their relation to other policies

Education and learning build the critical foundation for developing a knowledge based society and for combating social exclusion; links between education and other areas of policy are crucial to achieving both aims. *The objective is to assess the role of education and training, in interaction with other areas of social policy in addressing social inequalities, vulnerability, marginalisation, disengagement and as a means of fostering social cohesion.*

IP [Integrated Projects] and/or NoE [Networks of Excellence] may address: assessment of trends in education and learning, including lifelong learning, their interactions with other social policies and practices, and their implications for individuals and social groups; the role of education and training as a key factor in conceptualising social inequality and social cohesion and in building social capital; the impacts of specific and mixed interventions at different stages of the life-cycle; the impact of educational reform on social inequalities and exclusion and the possibilities and limits of formal education and training for individual, community and organisational learning; mapping of conditions to maximise the impact of educational measures in developing a knowledge based society; identification of strategies for related educational and social interventions that can prevent or reduce inequalities, combat exclusion, foster social integration and promote social justice and empowerment; ways of involving communities in learning to minimise disadvantage or the risk of disadvantage; the economic benefits of integrated strategies over the short, medium and longer term.

(European Commission 2004: 8)

This research topic set out to tackle the multiple fragmentations of the research community and combat the neat separation between research, policy and practice. It encouraged explicitly the cooperation between researchers working in various domains and levels of educational enquiry with researchers working on other areas of social policy and in other disciplines. In this sense, the topic was aimed at having an effect on the structure of the research community. Also, it was meant to create a platform for cross-disciplinary cooperation that would include significant opportunities for the training of a number of young researchers in this spirit.

This research topic aimed to generate research that could influence policy making in a number of policy areas. Research that could demonstrate – to policy makers also – the powerful interconnection of their respective fields of responsibility and the need for *combined* policies. In this sense, it was a research topic that aimed at demonstrating the possibilities but also the limits of what can be reasonably expected from education as a single policy area, to show that education cannot tackle all the issues alone.

It was a research topic able to accommodate researchers' concerns with a diverse range of issues related to policies, practices and methods. It was a topic permeated by the wish to explore the role of education within a broader social and economic context. Also a topic that was relatively focused while at the same time sufficiently open to interpretation in order to allow researchers to select their preferred approaches, perspectives and methodologies.

It was a research topic that invited the research community to explore the relationship of specific practices to wider social and cultural constructions and political and economic interests. It invited researchers to go beyond myopic optimistic accounts of school improvement and school effectiveness that almost always exaggerate the extent to which local agency can challenge structural inequalities.

It was a research topic that aimed to go beyond a simplistic notion of education research which makes a clear distinction between educational research and other kinds of research and suggests that policies and practices will be improved by a straightforward application of research findings.

It was a research topic that recognised explicitly the longer-term economic return from different kinds of interventions within education and training (as opposed to rather simplistic, narrowly focused and short-term returns) taking into account social cohesion and the implications for the wider welfare of citizens.

It was a topic that encouraged the wider social science research community to think of education research as social research and to engage seriously with education.

Challenges ahead

The novelty and creativity of EU-supported social science and educational research should not be taken for granted for the future, and guaranteed for ever. Rather, this sustainability is dependent on the actions and priorities of the various players involved. DG-Research of the European Commission is not acting in isolation, it is not the only (or the most powerful) player in the definition and implementation of social science research priorities. Other social, political and institutional players involved, include:

- *the European Parliament* and *the Council* (Member States); these institutions have the power to approve, disapprove or modify the Commission's proposals for a research Framework Programme and its contents through the so-called 'co-decision procedure';[7]
- *the social science research Programme Committee* (representatives of the Member States);
- *the research community* (through formal and informal consultation and through the results of projects);
- other services of the European Commission[8] which are formally consulted before the draft proposals of DG-Research for a social science research programme are submitted to the European Parliament and to the Council of research ministers.

Each of these players can influence the broad directions as well as the specific content of the social sciences and humanities research programme.

It can be fairly stated that consensus on European research priorities is the product of negotiation and struggle at various levels. Priorities are shaped by the concerns of the players involved. In this sense, the definition of European social science and humanities research priorities is one of the major sites in which different groups with distinct political, social, economic and cultural visions attempt to define what the socially legitimate means and ends of European societies are. The settlement of this struggle for consensus has implications for the overall direction of a social science and humanities research programme, for the specific research topics available to the research community, as well as for the degree of freedom allowed to the research community to interpret these research topics in creative, interesting and imaginative ways. The outcome of this struggle can have major implications within the global politics of knowledge, the commercialisation of research (Gieger 2004; Washburn 2005), the struggle for the heart and soul of universities and the struggle to protect powerful knowledge as an open and public dialogue (Seddon 2002: 161).

Also, within the Programme itself, the availability of sufficient and sufficiently competent human resources working for its management and implementation, their ability to contribute to policy making, their ability to aid the development of a progressive 'epistemic community' (Brine 2000) around it in a sustainable manner, the workload of staff and its impact on the quality of work, are all factors that affect the quality of the results, the Programme's impact on policy making, its image and credibility, and its constantly dynamic relationship with the research community (Kuhn and Remoe 2005: 300).

Another challenge is reflected in the alarming rift that currently exists between the rhetoric and the reality of support for learning-related research at a European level. While there is increasing recognition that every aspect of the European social, political and economic agenda is ultimately dependent on learning and thinking, the space given to learning-related research in FP5 and FP6 did not adequately reflect its post-Lisbon priority status and conceptualisation. Will more support then be given to learning-related research in the future? We do not know. At the time this book is going to the printers, important decisions are being made on Seventh Framework Programme (2007–13) probably the most ambitious of the framework programmes ever presented by the Commission. The Commission proposed to double the FP7 budget compared with FP6, rising to €72.7 billion for the period 2007–13, including €792 million for research in the social sciences and humanities. The European Commission's proposal for FP7 was submitted to the European Parliament and the Council (Member States) for approval in April 2005 (European Commission 2005[6]). On 21 September 2005, the European Commission adopted the so-called 'Specific Programmes' (the second stage of the process) that include the Programme for research in the social sciences and the humanities (full text available at: ftp://ftp.cordis.lu/pub/fp7/docs/fp7sp-cooperation_en.pdf, p. 62). In the third stage of the process, this Specific Programme will be 'translated' into a more detailed research agenda which will be the future work programme and the basis for future calls for proposals. Work on this began in autumn 2005 and includes consultations with the research community. Further information on the preparation of FP7 can be found at: http://www.cordis.lu/fp7/. It is expected that the new social science and humanities research programme in FP7 will continue to support research on learning; but how much and of what kind is not known at this stage. Issues of education are both present and strongly implied in several parts of the Specific Programme. In the next stage of the process (the preparation of a detailed research agenda, in spring–summer 2006), it is expected that these will become the basis for detailed research topics that will address issues of education explicitly.

Another challenge is related to the organisation of European social science and humanities research, the types of projects and the rationale behind them. As already mentioned in the early sections of this chapter, FP6 introduced and put a lot of emphasis on new and larger types of research projects and networks alongside the existing smaller ones. There is still concern as to whether these new, significantly larger types of projects (Integrated Projects and Networks of Excellence), and the way in which they are implemented represent a better way of organising European social science research. Since the first social science Integrated Projects and Networks of Excellence supported under FP6 started in spring 2004 with a five-year horizon, it is still too early for conclusions.

Conclusion

In the landscape of European social science research, disciplinary borders are still very strong and transnational cooperation is weak and difficult. The social sciences and humanities are relatively fragmented, their potential for addressing European-wide questions is limited and their capacity to contribute to Europe's future and to the citizens' quality of life is far from fully realised. Addressing the fragmentation and maximising the contributions of Europe's social sciences and humanities require a more coherent communicative approach involving all stakeholders to develop an inclusive strategy. This strategy must be a European strategy, including the actions of the Framework Programme as well as the actions of national governments and other stakeholders in Europe.

Within this wider research policy context, EU-supported collaborative research in the field of learning is an integral part of the process of developing and implementing a European strategy for the social sciences and humanities. It is seeking to reconcile the norms and cultures of basic and policy-relevant research. It provides an arena that affects what (and to some extent how) research can be undertaken, how it is perceived and the ways in which it is used – or ignored.

In terms of *content*, the research has been problem-oriented, policy-relevant and, where possible, multidisciplinary. Multiple perspectives have been encouraged on complex problems, in the belief that this is likely to produce a better understanding of the problems and policy responses. Much of the research is comparative in nature. The policy results are generally in terms of *orientations* for policy arising from the research, though there is a considerable range which at one end addresses specific policies at various spatial levels and even studies the implementation of policy; the policy process itself has also been addressed in a number of projects.

In terms of *process*, European social science research programmes have provided a new exciting arena for collaborative research. They have provided a transnational, transdisciplinary communicative space with a considerable European added value:

> European social science research programmes have proved to be an arena where new interpretations and new practices of research have been generated. The Commission has funded new areas of social and educational research and has requested that the policy relevant dimension be connected to practices of transnationality and interdisciplinarity. Consequently, conventional disciplinary hierarchies have come under pressure as well as conventional national barriers to research. Thus the interaction of policy relevance, trans-nationality and inter-disciplinarity has stimulated innovative social and educational research, in particular perhaps in terms of a closer interaction between the research community and the wider society.
>
> (Kuhn and Remoe 2005: 234)

EU-supported social science and learning-related research activities have already established a European research community with remarkable experiences. The answer to the question of whether there is 'an emerging European educational research space' is unreservedly positive. The question now is not whether there is (or not) an emerging European educational research space, but how to maintain the novelty and creativity generated in previous Framework Programmes.

In the light of the developments described in this chapter, the debate over the possible emergence of a 'European Educational Research Space' becomes somewhat problematic. On the positive side, this debate is useful in that it encourages researchers working in the wider field of learning to develop a more 'European' identity, a sense of belonging to a research community that crosses national boundaries; it also encourages some reflexive thinking about the role and character of this research community. On the negative side, however, this debate remains disappointingly myopic as it is largely mono-dimensional and self-referential, a self-examining debate *from, by, about, for* and *within* an 'educational research' community which is very diverse but for its greater part isolated from other social science research communities; it is the laborious (but largely introvert) soul-searching of a 'research community in crisis' (Flecha 1995, Badley 2003).

This inertia is also mirrored in the effort of several actors in the educational research field to nurture and defend their own tribes and territories which take the form of '[educational] research networks', '[educational] research associations', 'educational research conferences', or 'educational research journals' – all of them within, from and for the 'educational research' community (or smaller sub-communities) only.

Not surprisingly, some of the most refreshing contributions in the debate on the 'Europeanisation' of learning-related research currently come from individuals and research teams who do not perceive themselves as 'educational researchers' and/or from non-European researchers who are in the process of developing their understandings of Europe and European-ness from a certain distance.

The European Commission has so far operated as a broker that synthesises, accommodates and compiles the perspectives of a number of players, including – very importantly – those of the research communities. Without doubt, there is much space for improvement in what is a learning process for all of us involved in the design, negotiation and implementation of this rather new and exciting type of research (Teichler 2005). The research community plays and must continue to play a key role in this process.

Perhaps partly because of this complexity and uncertainty (but also because of the many difficulties and demands inherent in this new type of research and in its management), some social science and education researchers take a rather cynical view of European research. Some other researchers criticise (or avoid, or both criticise and avoid) European social science research not only because it is difficult and challenging, unpredictable and demanding; not only because it is linked to much administrative work, financial reporting and accountability; not only because it leads more often to the frustration of a rejected proposal than to the excitement of a funded project; not only because it has, by definition, a number of inherent difficulties that normally one may not encounter in other arenas; not because of the requirement for more policy relevance (which some researchers feel may domesticate or limit the ambitions of social science); not only because of the requirement for a clearly thought-out dissemination strategy of conclusions to policy makers; not only because narrow disciplinary business-as-usual advances one's career more easily. Rather, some social science and education researchers justify their retreat as a refusal to co-opt with the policies and practices of an institution (the European Commission or the EU as a whole) which they think is not doing enough for its citizens. They turn their back to an institution that they perceive as a technocratic bureaucracy, as a supra-national neo-liberal monster, as the enemy.

The activities of the European Commission are often criticised, in my view not always in a constructive way. A critical attitude is always necessary, albeit a fair and constructive one. We must demand more of the moral ideal, more social justice, more democracy, more transparency and more accomplishments, even as we articulate contradictions and dilemmas (e.g. Munchau 2005, Monbiot 2005, Parker 2005). However, I feel critical of the many educationists who indulge themselves with critique that they never have to explain or materialise to a wider socio-political and economic audience. To the negativists who favour the safe pseudo-radical blanket Euro-criticism, I say that we must be wiser and more strategic in our criticism of Europe, and that retreat to a reactionary *false certainty* (Badley 2003) of talking among ourselves within our particular comfort zone (even if we do that at 'our' annual conference) is no longer an option; that there can be no 'outside':

> The challenge is for researchers to recognise that they do not stand outside the reconfiguration of contemporary social spaces. There is no 'outside'. Rather, they

(we) are inside the processes and this is having an impact on both the character of research and the contribution of researchers.

(Seddon, 2002: 160)

In the business of building a better world and a better Europe within it, we are, as the Eagles sang in *Hotel California*, programmed only to receive, it is not possible to leave.

Appendix 1. Learning-related research topics in the first TSER call for proposals (1995)

In the *first Call for Proposals* (1995), the research topics available to the social science research community included the following education-related topics (grouped under three themes):

Theme 1. Effectiveness of policies and actions, European dimension and diversity

Objectives: To improve the understanding of the way education and training systems, in Europe, are responding and should respond to the new and emerging needs of European society and citizens: What kinds of skills are necessary to face the emerging type of knowledge, the new modes of organisation within enterprises, the multiplication of contacts between people with different cultural backgrounds, the development of new forms of communication?

To enhance understanding of the more specific European aspects of education and training in Europe, and the various components of the 'European dimension' in this field: What consequences will the variety of approaches and cultural differences as well as the existence of common values and needs in Europe have for education and training?

Research tasks
1. European policies in the field of education and training:

* Analysis and reformulation of educational goals in the light of anticipated developments in society at large (progress of technologies, evolution of the labour market, evolution of values in a multicultural society, development of new perspectives on knowledge) using notably case-study descriptions from various European countries.
* Comparative research on policies and restructuring efforts in various Member States aimed at a greater responsiveness of vocational education. Definition and effective utilisation of comparable success criteria.

2. Adaptation to change:

* The capacity for change and adaptation of educational systems. Building upon social sciences theories, clarifying the factors that determine the resistances of educational organisations to change as well as the means to improve the capacity for adaptation of the systems. Inventory and evaluation of the impact of

innovatory programmes. Identification and analysis of 'failures' and 'successes', also with respect to the possible influence of differences in national educational structures and cultures.

- Inventory and evaluation of opportunities for life-long learning. Points of attention are: facilities and services, media and tools (use of information technologies and telematics), public policies and private initiatives.
- Development of output indicators on capacities and qualifications obtained at the level of initial and continued vocational education as well as the university level. Inventory and evaluation of available assessment instruments within Member States. Comparative research at international level on key qualifications.

3. European unity and diversity:

- Research on common values in Member States' educational philosophies as well as specific articulation of these in a European perspective.
- The 'general education' issue. Comparative European research on the content of teaching and common core curricula in relation to general education, more particularly to languages, and social values.
- Education and cultural world of European young people: comparative research on the relations between education, values and cultural references.
- Research on the positive impact of European cultural diversity, the overall advantages of local differentiation of education and training.
- Cultural differences and integration of minorities (including gypsies): alternative schemes in the Member States, patterns of school integration and intercultural contacts.
- Education and training in Europe in the world: comparison of concepts, methods, values and policies in Europe, United States and Japan.

Theme 2. Methods, tools and technologies: quality and innovation in education and training

Objectives: To enhance understanding of the factors and mechanisms which contribute to an increase in the quality of education and training in Europe and to the improvement of the capacity of innovation of educational systems: What methods and criteria do we have to use for evaluation of quality; what role do the cognitive conditions and cultural factors play in using informatics and audiovisual tools for education and training; what are the attitudes of the teachers and the trainers to new technologies?

Research tasks
1. Educational effectiveness:

- Analysis of existing data on 'educational effectiveness' (in the broad sense) in the Member States. This research could offer a set of hypotheses of effectiveness-enhancing conditions that are generally applicable across Member States.

- Research on international transferability explanatory models of multi-level educational effectiveness. Study on the ways in which the social context, organisation and educational practices of schools determine the 'added value' of education.
- Assessment of European basic competences. The notion of basic competences can be applied to various educational and training contexts. Research on what happens to those pupils who do not master these basic competences and what remedial strategies are applied, if any.

2. Innovation in education and training:

- Designing and evaluating new kinds of learning environments taking into account available knowledge concerning cognitive, affective and socio-cultural factors that influence learning processes and school organisational conditions that are supportive to these learning processes. Focus on aspects that have not yet been frequently studied and are very relevant from a European perspective, such as history, language, civil and multi-cultural education and education on the environment.
- Scenarios of applications of new approaches to enhance the quality of education, focused on disadvantaged learners in primary education. Targeted studies on pupils in particular categories of special education.
- Science and technology teaching as components of general education. Approaches, concepts and methods in science teaching (including history and philosophy of science as a way of improving science understanding). Comparative research on the role of scientific education in the building of knowledge and general education.

3. Education, training and new technologies:

- The educational potential of the information society. Research to explore at the level of primary and secondary education to what extent mass media, home computers, and telematics can be seen as 'distractions' or 'aids' in education.
- Research on the cognitive aspects of the design and application of new technologies in education and training: cognitive processes and patterns of learning with the help of new knowledge technologies (multimedia, hypertexts, virtual reality). Research in cognitive science needed to produce new tools and devices allowing to increase flexibility of education and training in time and space.
- Research on cognitive aspects of the design of transparent and user-friendly interfaces and on the impact of application of new technologies for education and training. Scenarios for the combination of new technologies for education and training with conventional means and tools (face-to-face teaching; publishing, etc).
- Research on the impact of cultural aspects and on the effects of social factors in the design and utilisation of new technologies for open and distance learning and self-instruction technologies.

- Research on evaluation and methodologies for new education and training products (for example, hypertext).

Theme 3. Education, training and economic development

Objectives: To improve the understanding and mastering of education and training methods, patterns and means, allowing to cope with the problems related to unemployment, underqualification and economic and social needs in Europe and at European scale: What are the skills, qualifications and knowledge able to help to solve the problem of unemployment matching Europe's social and economic needs, those companies, public utilities, etc. with the current realities of the accelerating pace of discovery, the development of markets on the world scale, the demands for local services?

Research tasks

1. Evaluation of economic needs:

- Building scenarios concerning labour market demands and policy measures in targeted sectors of education and training. Each scenario should identify needs, policy measures and areas for further empirical research. Studying the concept of 'societal needs' with respect to education.
- Comparative research on methods, procedures and techniques to determine labour market requirements concerning vocational training as well as needs for training within companies.
- Comparative research on the effectiveness of labour-oriented training programmes for the long-term unemployed in Member States.
- The transition from school to work: comparative research on mechanisms and patterns of individual and group 'trajectories'.
- Scientific and technological literacy: research on social and cultural aspects of the teaching and mastering of technological knowledge.

2. Organisations and training:

- In-company training strategies and the learning organisation. Research on the way companies determine their training needs, together with new ways of organising in company training. Research on the concept of 'learning organisation' and the way it's applied.
- Conceptualisation and empirical investigation of core skills for certain branches of industry, and the potential for setting qualification in the mastery of core skills for enhancing (international) mobility.
- Comparative research on cooperation between universities and corporations aimed at the training of top specialists.

(Source: European Commission 1995)

Appendix 2. Learning-related research topics in the second TSER call for proposals (1996)

The second TSER Call for Proposals included some research topics that were directly relevant to education and training. These were again grouped under three themes: education and training policies, European dimension and diversity; quality and innovation in education and training; education, training and economic development:

Theme 1. Effectiveness of policies and actions, European dimension and diversity

Objectives: To improve the understanding of the way education and training systems, in Europe, are responding and should respond to the new and emerging needs of European society and citizens: What kinds of skills are necessary to face the emerging type of knowledge, the new modes of organisation within enterprises, the multiplication of contacts between people with different cultural backgrounds, the development of new forms of communication?

To enhance understanding of the more specific European aspects of education and training in Europe, and the various components of the 'European dimension' in this field: What consequences will the variety of approaches and cultural differences as well as the existence of common values and needs in Europe have for education and training?

Research tasks
1. European policies in the field of education and training:

* Analysis and reformulation of educational goals in the light of anticipated developments in society at large (progress of technologies, evolution of the labour market, evolution of values in a multicultural society, development of new perspectives on knowledge) using notably case-study descriptions from various European countries.
* Comparative research on policies and restructuring efforts in various Member States aimed at a greater responsiveness of vocational education. Definition and effective utilisation of comparable success criteria.

2. Adaptation to change:

* The capacity for change and adaptation of educational systems. Building upon social sciences theories, clarifying the factors that determine the resistances of educational organisations to change as well as the means to improve the capacity for adaptation of the systems. Inventory and evaluation of the impact of innovatory programmes. Identification and analysis of 'failures' and 'successes', also with respect to the possible influence of differences in national educational structures and cultures.
* Inventory and evaluation of opportunities for life-long learning. Points of attention are: facilities and services, media and tools (use of information technologies and telematics), public policies and private initiatives.

- Development of output indicators on capacities and qualifications obtained at the level of initial and continued vocational education as well as the university level. Inventory and evaluation of available assessment instruments within Member States. Comparative research at international level on key qualifications.

3. European unity and diversity:

- Research on common values in Member States' educational philosophies as well as specific articulation of these in a European perspective.
- The 'general education' issue. Comparative European research on the content of teaching and common core curricula in relation to general education, more particularly to languages, and social values.
- Education and cultural world of European young people: comparative research on the relations between education, values and cultural references.
- Research on the positive impact of European cultural diversity, the overall advantages of local differentiation of education and training.
- Cultural differences and integration of minorities (including gypsies): alternative schemes in the Member States, patterns of school integration and intercultural contacts.
- Education and training in Europe in the world: comparison of concepts, methods, values and policies in Europe, United States and Japan.

Theme 2. Methods, tools and technologies: quality and innovation in education and training

Objectives: To enhance understanding of the factors and mechanisms which contribute to an increase in the quality of education and training in Europe and to the improvement of the capacity of innovation of educational systems: What methods and criteria do we have to use for evaluation of quality; what role do the cognitive conditions and cultural factors play in using informatics and audiovisual tools for education and training; what are the attitudes of the teachers and the trainers to new technologies?

Research tasks
1. Educational effectiveness:

- Analysis of existing data on 'educational effectiveness' (in the broad sense) in the Member States. This research could offer a set of hypotheses of effectiveness-enhancing conditions that are generally applicable across Member States.
- Research on international transferability explanatory models of multi-level educational effectiveness. Study on the ways in which the social context, organisation and educational practices of schools determine the 'added value' of education.
- Assessment of European basic competences. The notion of basic competences can be applied to various educational and training contexts. Research on what

happens to those pupils who do not master these basic competences and what remedial strategies are applied, if any.

2. Innovation in education and training:

* Designing and evaluating new kinds of learning environments taking into account available knowledge concerning cognitive, affective and socio-cultural factors that influence learning processes and school organisational conditions that are supportive to these learning processes. Focus on aspects that have not yet been frequently studied and are very relevant from a European perspective, such as history, language, civil and multi-cultural education and education on the environment.
* Scenarios of applications of new approaches to enhance the quality of education, focused on disadvantaged learners in primary education. Targeted studies on pupils in particular categories of special education.
* Science and technology teaching as components of general education. Approaches, concepts and methods in science teaching (including history and philosophy of science as a way of improving science understanding). Comparative research on the role of scientific education in the building of knowledge and general education.

3. Education, training and new technologies:

* The educational potential of the information society. Research to explore at the level of primary and secondary education to what extent mass media, home computers and telematics can be seen as 'distractions' or 'aids' in education.
* Research on the cognitive aspects of the design and application of new technologies in education and training: cognitive processes and patterns of learning with the help of new knowledge technologies (multimedia, hypertexts, virtual reality). Research in cognitive science needed to produce new tools and devices allowing to increase flexibility of education and training in time and space.
* Research on cognitive aspects of the design of transparent and user-friendly interfaces and on the impact of application of new technologies for education and training. Scenarios for the combination of new technologies for education and training with conventional means and tools (face-to-face teaching; publishing, etc).
* Research on the impact of cultural aspects and on the effects of social factors in the design and utilisation of new technologies for open and distance learning and self-instruction technologies.
* Research on evaluation and methodologies for new education and training products (for example, hypertext).

Theme 3. Education, training and economic development

Objectives: To improve the understanding and mastering of education and training methods, patterns and means, allowing to cope with the problems related to unemployment, underqualification and economic and social needs in Europe and at European scale: What are the skills, qualifications and knowledge able to help to solve the problem of unemployment matching Europe's social and economic needs, those companies, public utilities, etc. with the current realities of the accelerating pace of discovery, the development of markets on the world scale, the demands for local services?

Research tasks
1. Evaluation of economic needs:

- Building scenarios concerning labour market demands and policy measures in targeted sectors of education and training. Each scenario should identify needs, policy measures and areas for further empirical research. Studying the concept of 'societal needs' with respect to education.
- Comparative research on methods, procedures and techniques to determine labour market requirements concerning vocational training as well as needs for training within companies.
- Comparative research on the effectiveness of labour-oriented training programmes for the long-term unemployed in Member States.
- The transition from school to work: comparative research on mechanisms and patterns of individual and group 'trajectories'.
- Scientific and technological literacy: research on social and cultural aspects of the teaching and mastering of technological knowledge.

2. Organisations and training:

- In-company training strategies and the learning organisation. Research on the way companies determine their training needs, together with new ways of organising in company training. Research on the concept of 'learning organisation' and the way it's applied.
- Conceptualisation and empirical investigation of core skills for certain branches of industry, and the potential for setting qualification in the mastery of core skills for enhancing (international) mobility.
- Comparative research on cooperation between universities and corporations aimed at the training of top specialists.

(Source: European Commission 1996)

Appendix 3. Learning-related research topics in the third TSER call for proposals (1997)

The third TSER Call for Proposals included the following research topics on education and training:

Objectives: In the short term: to provide a European base of information, knowledge and common references, covering more specifically the European aspects and the European dimension of education and training to researchers and policy makers. In the medium term, on the basis of the work on these European aspects, to build a community of research on education and training in Europe, linked to the developments in educational and cognitive sciences. In the long term, to strengthen the contribution of education and training to sustainable development, employment, and innovation in Europe.

Research tasks

- **Lifelong learning and educational goals:** Analysis and reformulation of educational goals in the light of anticipated developments in society at large (progress of technologies, evolution of the labour markets, development of new perspectives on knowledge) using notably case-study descriptions from various European countries. Of particular importance is the role of lifelong learning as a prerequisite for societies increasingly based on learning and knowledge; how social and working conditions could promote lifelong learning; and how this could be reflected in the formulation and implementation of educational goals. Key themes will be: identification of future educational needs and their implementation in policies; the relationship between the E&T sector and working life including strengthening apprenticeship training elements in schools and higher education systems; the role of general theoretical elements in vocational education and training; and new models for combining work and training over the life cycle.
- **Implications of societal developments for the E&T system:** E&T is facing a number of societal phenomena directly influencing the conditions of teaching and learning. It is widely acknowledged and often stated by educational experts and practitioners that developments in the society such as the changing family structures, the ageing of the population, social exclusion as well as the entertainment industry and deviant behaviour are also challenging the E&T systems. Empirical research assessing trends and interventions are needed on key issues: the influence of mass-media and the entertainment industry on the education process; violence and drug abuse in schools; new educational roles of schools in the context of changing family structures, including perceptions of teachers tasks, social integration models and relationships between educational and social policies at appropriate levels; new demands for education and training in the context of a growing elderly population; integration of disabled students, and consequences of multicultural societies for learning and teaching.
- **Educational implications of the European integration process:** Given the diversity of national systems, new efforts should be made in order to study the educational implications of the integration process. More specifically, attention should be given to comparative, empirical analysis of the strategies followed by national E&T systems to address the European dimension. Key thematic aspects of this should be: the impact of the European diversity on the practice of learning and teaching in Europe; the potential for common elements in curricula in the context of mobility and free movement of labour; and institutional and organisational adaptation in the E&T system in the context of European integration.
- **E&T, the labour market and economic growth:** In modern economies it is recognised that investment in human capital is a precondition for economic

growth. From the individual's perspective, the relationship between E&T, especially vocational education and training, and the potential for labour market participation, is of utmost importance. Attention should be paid to how flexible arrangements in working life could be used as institutionalised mechanisms for improved investments in E&T, as well as to developing a better understanding of training, competence and skill gaps and economic actors' capability to identify them. Other key themes will be: The effectiveness and flexibility of the E&T system vis-à-vis labour market demands with a critical view on the role of public policy aimed at enhancing human capital as a tool to avoid unemployment; vocational training needs in societies increasingly based on learning and knowledge; and the role of the social partners in the labour market in developing vocational training systems of high quality and relevance.

- **E&T's contribution to fostering innovation:** Research on innovation in the E&T system itself and the capabilities of E&T to foster or stimulate an innovation oriented culture in companies and society at large is of high relevance, as are lessons on how E&T systems, whether in collaboration with industry or other users, may develop schemes to support the excellence and high level competence required by innovative societies. A further theme where research is required, is on the identification and assessment of elements in the education process which are conducive to fostering an innovation culture. This includes new learning approaches directed towards the shift from teaching to learning (collaborative learning, problem-based learning, learning to learn etc). E&T will also have to respond to new challenges emerging from the information society. The E&T sector itself has to address the ICT-related issues. It needs to include learning demands stemming from the widespread use of ICT, as well as undergo transformations in order to make the best use of the new technologies and new educational material. The pedagogical and cognitive aspects of the innovative use of ICT in E&T programmes needs more specific investigation, in order, for example, to help improve the use of multimedia products and services, as well as bringing out the appropriate role for cognitive sciences and other approaches in this context. A key aspect of E&T innovation is the integration of new and emerging tools for learning and communication into existing or changing organisational structures, and research will be needed on pedagogical and organisational aspects of learning, with particular attention to the use of multimedia technology and telematic networks and to open and distance learning.

(Source: European Commission 1997)

Appendix 4. Learning-related research topics in the first call for proposals of the key action 'improving'

In the first Call for Proposals of the Key Action (March–June 1999), research on education and training focused on three main issues:

First, perspectives and methods (including in schools) for: developing tolerance and understanding between different cultures; supporting the sociability of learners; developing a more active involvement of learners as citizens; strengthening self-esteem. **Second**, preventing and addressing social inequality, marginalisation and exclusion in education and training; improving access to and successful participation in learning processes (partly by enhancing the attractiveness of learning). **Third**, the acquisition of new competencies enhancing employability, including identification of those required now and in the future, while bearing in mind the transition from education to work.

The research may address, critically, conceptual approaches, methods and policies, as well as barriers to innovation (cultural, economic, institutional, political, social etc.). Recommendations for policies and practices should be situated in their cultural and institutional contexts.

(Source: European Communities 1999b: 35, Task 5)

Appendix 5. Learning-related research topics in the second call for proposals of the key action 'improving'

In the second Call for Proposals of the Key Action (January–May 2000), the following research task on education was available to the research community:

Learning is recognised to be a crucial factor in relation to economic needs and employment prospects. It is also recognised that learning embraces the cultural values of the European society and touches on personal, civic and social dimensions. In view of the need to make decisions on long-term investments in human capital, we need to improve the understanding of the new forms of learning, taking into account the rich diversities in Europe.

The objective of this Task is to provide research support for the promotion of education and cultural resources. It is of particular importance to explore new ways of learning throughout life, to find ways of bridging learning to work experience as well as to prevent and combat social exclusion. At the core of the challenge are partnerships between schools, family, work and local communities and the need to improve related policies and actions.

Research challenges to be addressed include the following:

How can the 'school of tomorrow' be made more widely accessible? Specific research questions include: How to improve access to education for all in Europe, particularly for the youngest and children with fewer opportunities (e.g. immigrants) and how to support the growth of non-formal learning arrangements through family, work and/or local communities? Which learning strategies and policies may be put into place in order to prevent and combat social exclusion?

What may be the key features of teaching/learning at the 'school of tomorrow'? Specific research questions include: Which new sets of additional competencies, values and attitudes are necessary in the knowledge society of tomorrow: 'learning to learn', independent learning, 'learning to become citizen', social and communication skills, cultural and democratic values?

Part of the fundamental paradigm shift in education in Europe is related to the recognition that learning is a lifelong process. Specific research questions include: How do 'formal education and training systems' and the related policies and institutions respond and adapt to this process? Which new systems need to be developed to accompany lifelong learning? How to measure the impact and outcomes of these policies and programmes?

Facilitating transitions from education to working life, also from work to work; from inactivity to work, and from work to retirement are key to building lifelong learning policies. Which pathways and bridges between learning and work exist in Europe and how can they be developed? How do learning strategies and policies interact with the new trends in gender relations? How do collective organisations (companies, SMEs, trade unions, etc.) enhance employability and become learning organisations?

(Source: European Communities 1999a: 13)

Notes

1 Disclaimer: The views expressed in this chapter are purely those of the writer and may not in any circumstances be regarded as stating an official position of the European Commission.
2 This was reaffirmed by the Stockolm European Council of 23 and 24 March 2001, while the Spring 2005 European Council underlined that 'human capital is Europe's most important asset'.
3 COST is an intergovernmental European framework for international co-operation between nationally funded research activities, including activities in the social sciences. More information about COST can be found at: http://ue.eu.int/cost. 'Europe + 30' was a study of the feasibility of forecasting and assessment of science and technology. FAST (a programme on Forecasting and Assessment in Science and Technology) was a real social science research programme which shaped the ways in which social science research was going to be organised at Community level (see also Guzetti 1995).
4 For a discussion see Brine 2000.
5 A common feature in the rhetoric promoting the use of ICTs as a panacea in education.
6 See also the relevant Press Release at: http://europa.eu.int/rapid/pressReleasesAction.do? reference=MEMO/05/4&format=HTML&aged=0&language=EN&guiLanguage=en.
7 See Wallace *et al.* (2005) for more on the difficult but cxlosely interrelated layers of the decision-making mechanism of the European Union.
8 These can influence (through the 'inter-service consultation' process) the draft proposals for a research programme before these are submitted by DG-Research to the European Parliament and to the Council of research ministers. They can also influence the specific research topics available to the research community when a research programme is 'translated' into specific research tasks and topics.

References

Apple, M.W. (1996) *Cultural Politics and Education*, Buckingham: Open University Press.
Armstrong, Paul (2000) 'Include me out: critique and contradiction in thinking about social exclusion and lifelong learning', Paper presented at SCUTREA, 30th Annual Conference, 3–5 July , University of Nottingham.
Badley, G. (2003) 'The crisis in educational research: a pragmatic approach', *European Educational Research Journal*, 2(2): 296–308.
Becher, T. and Trowler, P. (2001) *Academic Tribes and Territories: Intellectual Enquiry and the Culture of Disciplines*, 2nd edn. Milton Keynes: Society for Research into Higher Education and Open University Press.
Benavot, A., Erbes-Seguin, S. and Gross, S. (2005) 'Interdisciplinarity in EU-funded social science projects', chapter 6 in Kuhn, M. and Remøe, S.O. (eds), pp. 115–75.
Bernstein, B. (1970) 'Education cannot compensate for society', *New Society*, 26 February: 344–7.

Biesta, G. and Burbules, N.C. (2003) *Pragmatism and Educational Research*, Lanham, MD: Rowman and Littlefield Publishers.

Brine, J. (1996) 'Over the ditch and through the brambles: negotiating the landscape of European funded educational research', Paper presented at the ECER conference, Seville, Spain, September 1996. A revised version of this paper was published as Brine, J. (1997) 'Over the ditch and through the thorns: accessing European funds for research and social justice', *British Educational Research Journal*, 23(4): 421–32.

Brine, J. (2000) 'TSER and the epistemic community of European social researchers', *Journal of European Social Policy*, 10(3): 267–82.

Charles, D., Conway, C. and Dawley, S. (2003) 'Urban knowledge economies'. Deliverable No. 4 of the research project *City-Regions as Intelligent Territories: Inclusion, Competitiveness and Learning* (CRITICAL), (project website: http://www.ncl.ac.uk/critical/).

Collins, G. (2003) 'Knowledge and learning societies', Deliverable No. 3 of the research project *City-Regions as Intelligent Territories: Inclusion, Competitiveness and Learning* (CRITICAL), p. 4 (project web-site: http://www.ncl.ac.uk/critical/).

European Commission (1995) DG-Research, *Targeted Socio-Economic Research* Programme, *Work Programme 1995*.

European Commission (1996) DG-Research, *Targeted Socio-Economic Research* Programme, *Work Programme 1996*.

European Commission (1997) DG-Research, *Targeted Socio-Economic Research* Programme, *Work Programme 1997*.

European Commission (2001) DG-Research, Work Programme of the Horizontal Programme 'Improving the Human Research Potential and the Socio-Economic Knowledge Base', Sixth Update, July.

European Commission (2002) DG-Research, Priority 7 'Citizens and Governance in a Knowledge Based Society'. *Work Programme 2002–2003*, Brussels, pp. 7–8.

European Commission (2004) DG-Research, Priority 7 'Citizens and Governance in a Knowledge Based Society'. *Work Programme 2004–2006*, Brussels.

European Commission (2005) *Proposals of the Commission for a Decision of the European Parliament and of the Council concerning the Seventh Framework Programme of the European Community for Research, Technological Development and Demonstration Activities (2007– 13)*. COM(2005) 119 final, Brussels, 6 April.

European Communities (1999a) *Guide for Proposers (Part 2 – Call Specific), Improving the Socio-Economic Knowledge Base*. December 1999 edn, ISBN 92-828-8711-1.

European Communities (1999b), Work Programme, *Improving the Human Research Potential and the Socio-Economic Knowledge Base (1998–2002)*. Office for Official Publications of the European Communities, Luxembourg, 1999, ISBN 92-828-6643-2.

Flecha, R. (1995) 'Out of the ghetto – a communicative perspective', *Adult Education and Development*, 45: 189–97.

Frade, C. (2006) *Policy Review of EU-supported Research Projects in the Field of Education, Training, Inequalities and Social Exclusion* (provisional title), European Commission DG-Research.

Geiger, R.L. (2004) *Knowledge and Money: Research Universities and the Paradox of the Marketplace*, Stanford, CA: Stanford University Press.

Greco, L., Landri, P., Tomassini, M. and Wickham, J. (2005) 'The Development of Policy Relevance in European Social Research', chapter 7 in Kuhn and Remøe (eds).

Green, A., (2002) 'Education, globalisation and the role of comparative research', Professorial lecture, University of London Institute of Education.

Guzetti, L. (1995) *A Brief History of European Union Research Policy*, Luxembourg: Office for Official Publications of the European Communities.

Hammersley, M. (2002) *Educational Research, Policy Making and Practice*, London: Paul Chapman.

Huws, U. (2006) *Policy Review of EU-supported Research Projects in the Field of Information Society* (provisional title), European Commission DG-Research.

Kuhn, M. and Remøe, S.O. (eds) (2005) *Building the European Research Area: Socio-economic Research in Practice*, New York: Peter Lang.

Kuhn, M. and Sultana, R. (eds) (2005) *Concepts of Knowledge and Learning: The Learning Society in Europe and Beyond*, New York: Peter Lang.

Kuhn, M. and Sultana, R. (eds) (2005) *'Homo Sapiens Europeus?'– Creating the European Learning Citizen*, New York: Peter Lang.

Kuhn, M. and Weidemann, D. (2005) 'Reinterpreting transnationality: European transnational socio-economic research in practice', chapter 4 in Kuhn and Remøe (eds).

Kuhn, M., Tomassini, M. and Simons, R.J. (eds) (2005) *Towards a Knowledge Based Economy? – The Forgotten Learner in European Educational Research*, New York: Peter Lang.

López Blasco, A., McNeish, W. and Walther, A. (2003) *Young People and Contradictions of Inclusion: Towards Integrated Transition Policies in Europe*, Bristol: The Policy Press.

Monbiot, G. (2005) 'Even scarier than Kilroy: a coup against social Europe has been foiled – for the time being', *The Guardian*, 8 March.

Montuori, A. (2005) 'How to make enemies and influence people: anatomy of the anti-pluralist, totalitarian mindset', *Futures* 37, 18–38.

Munchau, W. (2005) 'Barroso's misguided priorities', *Financial Times*, 6 February.

Nowotny, H. (2005) 'The researcher's perspective', contribution to the workshop on the role of the humanities and social sciences in the funding portfolio of the future European Research Council. Budapest, 11–12 February.

Ozga, J. (2000) *Policy Research in Educational Settings: Contested Terrain*, Buckingham: Open University Press.

Parker, G. (2005) 'Reform relaunch by EU likely to fall flat', *Financial Times*, 16 March.

Power, S. (2006) *Policy Review of EU-supported Research Projects in the Field of Education*, European Commission DG-Research.

Seddon, T. (2002) 'CODA: Europe, social space and the politics of knowledge', in Nóvoa, A. and Lawn, M. (eds) *Fabricating Europe: The Formation of an Education Space*, Dordrecht: Kluwer, pp. 157–61.

Sperber, D. (2003) 'Why rethink interdisciplinarity?'. Online. Available HTTP: http://www. interdisciplines.org/interdisciplinarity/papers/1/.

Strietska, O. (ed.) (2006) *The Clash of Transitions – Towards a Learning Society*, New York: Peter Lang.

Sultana, R. (2002) 'Quality education and training for tomorrow's Europe', in Nóvoa, A. and Lawn, M. (eds) *Fabricating Europe: The Formation of an Education Space*, Dordrecht: Kluwer, pp. 157–61.

Teichler, U. (2005) 'The European knowledge base on education: what can be expected from European research?', Contribution to the REDCOM Seminar, University of Kassel, 11–12 March.

Wallace, H., Wallace, W. and Pollack, M. (eds) (2005) *Policy-making in the European Union*, 5th edn, Oxford: Oxford University Press.

Washburn, J. (2005) *University Inc.: The Corporate Corruption of American Higher Education*, New York: Basic Books.

Weingart, P. and Stehr, N. (eds) (2000) *Practising Interdisciplinarity*, Toronto: University of Toronto Press.

Whitty, G. (2002) *Making Sense of Education Policy*, London: Paul Chapman.

4 International policy research

'Evidence' from CERI/OECD[1]

Tom Schuller

This chapter discusses, from the inside, issues involved in how OECD's Centre for Educational Research and Innovation (CERI) addresses the task of conducting international policy research. It begins with a brief descriptive account of CERI's work. I then consider three particular issues which relate to how research evidence is compiled. First, I consider why the rhetoric of lifelong learning is only weakly supported by systematic research. Secondly I suggest that an increasing focus on the outcomes of education raises questions about causality in a policy research context, for example what kinds of evidence are valued. Thirdly, I ask what might be meant by learning from international experience. I conclude that policy research conducted within the context of an international bureaucracy certainly differs from university-based research or consultancy contract work, but the differences may be less significant than the resemblances.

What forms of research inform educational policy, nationally and internationally? Who shapes the research, and what effects does it have? According to Rinne *et al.*, OECD 'has become established as a kind of "eminence grise" of the educational policy of industrialised countries', and 'has claimed for itself a central position in the collection, processing, classification, analysing, storing, supplying and marketing of education policy information – the extensive control of information on education' (2004: 456). The first observation is a clear judgement on the part of the authors, i.e. it is their own view of where OECD stands; the second is more ambiguous: does it mean that OECD has actually achieved this position of control, or merely that it claims it? In either case these are fairly extensive statements, which are both flattering and challenging to those of us who work within OECD's Directorate for Education.

Academic interest in OECD's role in educational policy analysis and formation is growing (see Papadopoulos 1994 for a historical account of OECD's education work up to a decade ago). A similar study to the Finnish one cited above is being carried out at the University of Bremen, located within a wider study of international governance (Mertens 2006 forthcoming). Both these projects cover OECD work on education at a very general level and over a long timespan. At the other extreme, a discussion of one specific one piece of work, the OECD review of Educational R&D in England, was published in the European Education Research Journal (Wolter *et al.* 2004), with the four roundtable participants expressing divergent views on the nature and quality of the review process. The review was criticised for adopting a linear model of the research–

practice relationship; for overriding the complexities of knowledge generation and for undermining the status of education as a discipline. But the commentators (though they did not share a common position) also referred to positive features of the review, such as the quality of the analysis and the attempt to provide a rational framework for discussing the effectiveness of research.

This chapter does not attempt either to justify or rebut these claims, or the broader ones cited in the first paragraph. It has a much more limited goal: to give a summary overview of the work of one part of OECD's education research capacity, the Centre for Educational Research and Innovation (CERI); and by drawing on some parts of that work to offer a perspective on current debates over how evidence is compiled and used in educational policy research. The first sections are largely descriptive and can be skipped by anyone familiar with CERI and OECD or uninterested in such an account, though they do give some insight into the mechanics of research programme formulation. The second part shifts gear into more of an epistemological and methodological discussion, but without high philosophical pretensions: it addresses the issue of evidence within a context of current policy concerns.

Education at OECD

The Directorate for Education was created as a separate directorate in 2002. Education was previously part of a joint directorate with Labour and Social Affairs, but education was considered sufficiently significant to warrant a discrete directorate (one of nine within OECD). The principal units within the Directorate are the Education and Training Policy division (ETP), which deals mainly with national and thematic reviews; the Indicators and Analysis division, including the famous Programme for International Student Assessment which is arguably OECD's highest profile activity; IMHE (Institutional Management in Higher Education); PEB (Programme on Educational Building), a programme building links with non-member countries such as China and Brazil; and CERI, the Centre for Educational Research and Innovation.

CERI was set up in 1968, with a mandate which is renewed every five years. It is what is known in OECD as a Part 2 operation. This means that Member countries are not obliged, when they join OECD, to take part in (and contribute financially to) its work, but may opt to join. In fact, all Member countries do participate in CERI, with countries such as Chile and Israel having observer status, but the Part 2 status allows a certain degree of latitude in comparison with Part 1 programmes (governed by the regular OECD Committees, including the Education Committee to which the Education and Training Policy Division reports). The CERI Governing Board is made up of nominees from the countries, the nominations being made mostly but not exclusively by ministries of education. Governing Board members may be policy makers, for instance from the ministry itself; or they may be researchers, for example from a university. The former category is larger, so that policy makers outnumber research representatives, but the Board's composition marks it out somewhat from Part 1 OECD Committees.

The Board meets twice yearly, and every two years agrees a programme of work for the next biennium. The most recent programme of work, for 2005–06, was approved at the May 2005 meeting of the Governing Board, which also approved the following as key themes cutting across the different CERI projects:

A. Lifelong learning, as an overarching theme
B1 Innovation and knowledge management
B2 Human and social capital
B3 Futures thinking
B4 Learning and teaching.

The substantive components of CERI's title – 'research' and 'innovation' – have meaning within the OECD context. That is, CERI is concerned with original knowledge accumulation of different kinds, and pursues lines of investigation which are not wholly predetermined; and it is oriented towards innovation in the sense of identifying and analysing new trends and issues in education. The research may be primary, in the sense of commissioning or executing work involve new data-gathering, or secondary and synthetic, bringing together results from existing research in Member countries. In both cases, however, one of CERI's key characteristics is the aim of developing new tools, frameworks and indicators for the gathering and analysis of data, both quantitative and qualitative. There is an agenda-setting as well as a reporting role, and this extends to the setting of research as well as policy agendas.

CERI operates with an extremely small core staff, as do all the units within the Directorate. At present we have about 18 professional and 10 support staff. Given the range of countries as well as issues to be covered this is very limited, especially when compared with some of the large education research units within universities or elsewhere in Member countries. CERI analysts themselves write reports, but also draw extensively on external consultants to provide thinkpieces, to contribute analyses of individual countries or to synthesise results from several countries.

The major tangible outputs are reports published by OECD. Dissemination also takes place through conferences and seminars, and through the posting of grey material, 'declassified' papers which are not formally published but are made available to the public. As everywhere, the Web is an increasingly important dissemination tool. We are now paying more strategic attention to the whole issue of CERI's public profile and the dissemination of its work.

Our principal audiences are, naturally, governments at national, regional and, to a lesser extent local levels. But they also include researchers, in education but also beyond, and practitioners such as school/university leaders or curriculum designers. 'Audience' may, however, give a misleading impression of one-way transmission. In the first place, successful policy research depends in some degree on some degree of user involvement in the selection, design and perhaps also execution of the research. But this is not straightforward, especially where the analysis challenges provider interests. Practitioner involvement can be extremely helpful, but for perfectly understandable reasons it may tend to close off certain options. Moreover the rhetoric of involvement can beg the question of who actually is the practitioner or user. Only in an unusually harmonious system will the views of teachers, researchers and policy makers converge. *Pace* the impression which the Finnish paper cited earlier may give, neither the Directorate for Education nor CERI within it is a free-ranging think tank with a self-determined educational agenda. The programme of work is set within parameters agreed by Member countries, and the outputs are monitored and scrutinised by their representatives. Of course the issues and to some extent the outcomes are shaped by a variety of political pressures, some of them emanating from the political stances of particular countries, some of them generated more generally from the interaction of different countries' positions and priorities, which are articulated to differing degrees of explicitness. To illustrate this, I turn now not to a specific example of a substantive educational project, but to the issue of how the nature of evidence itself is thought about. Although I do so in relation to CERI as an international educational research unit, these questions are common to researchers more generally, especially those engaged in policy-relevant research.

Evidence and policy research

No one seriously believes that policies are developed, implemented or evaluated by reference to research evidence alone, in some kind of aseptic rationalist bubble (see Levin 2004b). Occasionally one of those stages (development, implementation, evaluation) may be determined by evidence alone, but in general research evidence, where it figures at all, is just one part of the policy-making process (or rather several parts, since there can obviously be many different pieces of evidence, often conflicting). The extent to which evidence influences policy is subject to a whole number of factors, from political opportunism to pressure of public opinion to quality and capacity of both the producers and suppliers of research, but this is not the place to discuss the role of educational policy making in general. Instead, I deal with three aspects of the debate on how research evidence is compiled, understood and used. Much of the discussion results from work done as part of a small CERI project on 'Evidence-based Policy Research', which forms a strand within our activity on knowledge management.

Identifying and prioritising issues

In order for research to be carried out, and evidence compiled, a research agenda must be identified and, in some measure, legitimised. Agenda-shaping has always been a classic aspect of the exercise of power, whether it is done overtly or covertly (see e.g. Lukes 1963). The agenda not only concerns substance (what is to be researched) but also the techniques to be used, the expected outputs, the timescale on which they are to be delivered and the criteria for evaluation. All of these are of legitimate concern to bodies which fund or sponsor research, including governments, although different bodies will place different emphasis on the various aspects. Arguably, for example, a research council is more likely to give close scrutiny to research methodologies as well as to substance when reviewing the projects it funds, in order to ensure academic credibility, whilst a sponsoring government department will define the policy relevance more tightly.

This is a complex area, and I want here to focus only on two aspects, one substantive and one relating to evaluation. In the first part of the chapter I described, without further observation, how lifelong learning was proposed as the overarching framework within which CERI's research programme should be executed. This may appear as a rather bland affirmation of the unrejectable. After all, lifelong learning is hardly a new subject within OECD. Decades ago it was strongly promoted under the banner of 'recurrent education' (CERI/OECD 1973, 1975; see also Schuller and Megarry 1979 for a WYBE appearance). The 1996 Education Ministerial meeting adopted lifelong learning as an overall framework for OECD's work on education, and the 2001 Education Ministerial reaffirmed it. The Education Committee's programme of thematic reviews has addressed early childhood education and care, transition from initial education to working life and adult education, and substantial work has been done on strategies to increase incentives to invest in lifelong learning. Despite this, although most countries also support lifelong learning in their policy discourse and rhetoric, the extent to which actual policies are formulated and implemented within this frame of reference is very much open to question.

'Beyond Rhetoric', in fact, was the title of a recent major OECD publication on adult learning (OECD 2003), which posed serious questions on this front. Arguably, indeed, we do not even have the frameworks for understanding what progress if any is being made on lifelong learning (see e.g. Coffield 2000; Istance 2003; Istance *et al.* 2003). Thus the commitment to it as the overarching theme is potentially significant in itself. However, the key point here is the apparent vicious circle which exists in a policy research context – vicious in the sense that the interaction between existing institutional and sectoral structures, political visibility and data availability combine to make it difficult to establish lifelong learning as a central issue for policy and research. Schools, and to a lesser extent higher education, have an unmistakable policy home. To my knowledge, every country has a ministry of education dealing with primary and secondary education. Schooling is universal and compulsory. There are teachers to be recruited and buildings to be managed. Even in countries where education is highly decentralised, governments generally retain high profile responsibilities in respect of schooling. As noted, the same is not true to quite the same extent for higher education, where responsibility is often far more diffuse, and the governmental portfolio may be much more restricted and linked with one or more of a variety of other domains such as science or employment; but it remains the case that the institutional basis of the HE sector is easily identified in the public and political mind. Universities and colleges are easily recognisable, if not easily understood. Both schools and higher education are therefore relatively amenable not only to research as such but to research policy and funding, even though the research may not be good, effectively managed or properly disseminated (see Hargreaves 1999; Foray 2003; OECD 2004 on knowledge management in education).

Lifelong learning, by contrast, lacks an institutional base, a professional identity, an administrative location and a political profile. Moreover, although there is no shortage of general conceptual or philosophical views, some of high canonical status (e.g. Delors 1996), there is no agreed framework around which knowledge can be cumulatively constructed. This is one reason why the futures orientation of CERI work in this area carries such potential significance: by sketching out possible scenarios, and linking them to empirical trends and issues, we can aspire to generate such a framework. Several CERI projects make greater or lesser reference to lifelong learning: for example the work on learning sciences and education (see CERI/OECD 2001a) involves three networks of neuroscientific researchers, of which one, based in Japan, is focusing on the lifespan (the other two are on literacy and numeracy); and the work on Schooling for Tomorrow (CERI/OECD 2001b) includes scenarios which envisage the school at the heart of a lifelong learning community. But the task of redressing the balance in educational research so that initial formal education does not dominate to such an extent is a challenging one, as any analysis of the content profile of papers submitted to European or other educational research congresses, and to education research journals, will illustrate. As a mild test of commitment, it would be interesting to review national research agendas, or programmes funded by governments, to get an idea of how far these related in any meaningful way to a lifelong learning agenda.

The second issue is one of evaluation in relation to policy research. This is important in the light of the influence sometimes attributed to OECD's work (though the evidence on the extent and nature of that influence is usually somewhat impressionistic). How and by whom are quality and impact to be judged? For academic research the answer may be phrased primarily in terms of peer review and judgement, with no necessary dimension of application (but see e.g. Levin 2004a). For policy research, especially that funded directly by governments, this cannot be the response. But it is not immediately evident what the mechanisms are for judging impact, and this is something we at OECD wrestle with, both internally and as a matter of accountability. How is our work to be assessed and made publicly accountable in a meaningful and appropriate way? I pose this as a question, inviting constructive suggestions! All I would say here is that for CERI the impact should be judged in relation to the research community as well as the policy world.

There is one particularly important aspect of the research evaluation issue, and that is how any given piece of work resolves the tension between substantive significance on the one hand and degrees of certainty on the other. Put simply, is it better to produce a quasi-definitive answer to an issue of marginal importance, or a very patchy answer to an issue of central importance. Figure 4.1 presents a simple matrix to illustrate this. Research in the SE quadrant is what in management speak used to be called a 'dog' – no good to anyone. The NW corner is where we all want to be. But most research will be somewhere in a band stretching from SW to NE. The question, which applies to CERI but also to any reflective researcher – including, incidentally the purely theoretical one – is along what trajectory do we wish to progress: towards greater significance or greater precision?

The game is of course not always zero sum. But there is a further tension which follows from this first one. Do the difficulties of generalising across many countries, and of controlling for so many independent variables (even in non-quantitative work) mean offering conclusions which are almost always either heavily qualified or verging on the bland? I do not think so; but this is because the paradigm within which international policy research operates is specific to its circumstances. Hypotheses cannot usually be set up and tested in the same way as they can be in a more restricted social context, i.e. at national or local levels. Theoretical framing remains important, but contextualisation is inevitably coarser-grained. The claims made for 'results' are generally of a rather different order. The key feature of this, at least in relation to OECD, is that the conclusions of most projects are subject to debate and refinement as they emerge, as part of the

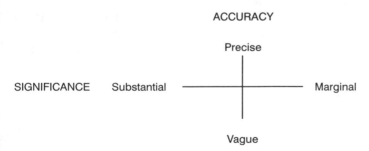

Figure 4.1 Significance and certainty in tension

process of international exchange and debate. That debate naturally sets certain limits which do not operate in the case of individual academic researchers, and these could be seen as imposing a restrictively consensual approach on our work. But it does not mean that challenging conclusions cannot be reached, and arguably the manufacture of consensus in OECD policy research is no stronger than in many other forms of research.

Explaining or describing? causality, confidence and capacity

The line between explanation and description is not clear-cut. Providing a clear and accurate description, whether it be of a national education system or a micro learning process, can itself go a long way to explaining how something works. It does this by sorting things into a meaningful pattern, which reveals causal or potentially causal relationships. This may involve developing new categories, typologies or conceptual frameworks which themselves embody a significant degree of analytical power. One person's description is another's explanation – and vice-versa: what one person considers to be an explanation is for someone else mere description. It is my own experience, most recently within a thriving interdisciplinary research team at the Research Centre for the Wider Benefits of Learning in London (www.learningbenefits.net), that what one person thinks is a 'result' – for example, an association between high levels of education and above average health – is for another just the starting point.

The development of new tools and frameworks is indeed a key function of CERI's work generally, which takes us beyond the gathering of regular statistics, fundamental though that is. But these conceptual innovations may be inspired as much by a perception of what is necessary to shape and inform the policy agenda (including the gathering of new statistics inspired by this conceptual work) as by an intention to use them to produce direct explanatory results. Our work rarely conforms to conventional models of theory-driven exploration or hypothesis-testing. But this does not mean that we can or should avoid the issue of assessing why some policies or practices appear to work better than others – or, if we want to eschew rankings or quality judgements, why different effects follow from different policies/practices.[2]

This raises two areas of concern to CERI but also to educational research more widely. The first is that the issues of causality and explanation are certain to become increasingly prominent as countries become more concerned with the outcomes of education and how to measure them. There is a distinct and highly significant trend within OECD countries to shift attention from inputs and processes to understanding what actually happens as a result of all these investments in education. The shift to outcomes can take many different forms, from the narrow, numerical and short term to the opposite of each of these. By this I mean that outcomes can be interpreted solely in terms of the proportions of students obtaining school or university diplomas immediately on completion of a given cycle. Or the evaluation process may directly address certain competences, independently of what proportion of students achieve a given level of qualification. PISA does this, and also aims to assess how far national systems succeed in laying down the foundations for lifelong learning (OECD 2004a). It thus points to a longer-term function for initial education, which should be assessed on its success in preparing people to continue to learn, as well as to be competent workers and citizens when they complete the initial cycle. But there is an even broader agenda when it comes to assessing outcomes. This involves evaluating the links between education and social domains such as health or civic engagement. Some work has been done on this at national level (see Schuller *et al.* 2004 for the UK; and Berhman and Stacey 1997 for the USA), and we shall be undertaking further work internationally as part of CERI's programme for 2005–06. The challenge of establishing causal relations when it comes to this broader agenda is very considerable (see Schuller *et al.* 2001).

The second issue, however, is what standards are set for establishing causality, or accepting analysis and explanation more generally. Educational research has been strongly criticised for its weakness in not even attempting to supply rigorous evidence on the effects of education (e.g. Angrist 2004). Some of the criticisms concern the low academic standing of educational research, and the low level of impact on policy or practice. What concerns us here, however, is what is understood to count as (rigorous) evidence, and that this is not a purely technical issue but one that reflects political and cultural practices. The understanding of what counts as evidence – whether or not this is geared to policy – varies from country to country, as well as within countries. There may be disagreement within and between academic disciplines, and between academic researchers and policy makers or practitioners. There are also varying degrees of tolerance, running from a strictly enforced 'one best way' philosophy to a laissez-faire relativism.

This can be illustrated by looking briefly at the case of randomised controlled trials (RCTs). The case for increasing the place of experimental design with random allocation is inspired by the failure of much educational research over the past decades to arrive at, or even aim at, conclusions which yield some causal explanation (Torgerson and Torgerson 2003). The approach is derived largely from medical, especially pharmaceutical, research, but has been used more widely in some non-educational social policy fields than in education (Oakley *et al.* 2003). In the USA, RCTs are seen in some quarters as the only form of rigorous research, setting a standard to which other studies should aspire but cannot attain (US Office of Education 2002; see also http://www.whatworks.ed.gov/). In other cultures, RCTs are treated with disdain, as wholly inappropriate to a field such as education. Why should this be so? I suggest that it is in part a function of American disillusion with educational effectiveness and the returns to public and private investment; in part a result of how educational policy is conceived of and developed – in the USA national education policy is far more a matter than elsewhere of funding specific interventions, which at least in principle offer themselves more to discrete evaluation and hence to RCTs;[3] and in part (and most interestingly) a reflection of what epistemic models are generally dominant within a particular culture, and why.

My own view is that experimental designs have a place in the range of educational research methodologies; that that place is larger than is currently accorded in most countries; and that although RCTs are very often inappropriate (as well as unfeasible) the concept has a certain heuristic value in prompting researchers to consider why such an approach is not appropriate and therefore to hone their alternative approaches more finely. However, the notion that randomised assignment should be the only, or even the main, accepted methodology is just bizarre. It cannot succeed: epistemologically, the privileging of a single mode of enquiry and definition of rigour is simply implausible; pragmatically any attempt to enforce this will not win the day within the research community; and politically the enthronement of randomisation will provoke reactions with wholly unpredictable consequences, invalidating any supposed rationality. The conclusion I draw is that the debate should certainly not be about which is the one best methodology; but somewhat about what the relative merits are of different methodologies and even more about how different methodologies complement each other; and how more mixed methods research could be conducted. Reflection on these issues within national, or for that matter disciplinary, research cultures could be extremely fruitful.[4]

This is far from a banal conclusion. It implies more than just the assumption – shared I imagine by most researchers – that more than one methodology has validity. It requires us to think how different kinds of evidence might interact, to reinforce each other or to allow refutation. This process is one which is best conceived of as iterative over time (rather than a kind of idealised synchronous collaboration). It challenges us to give substance to interdisciplinarity, at least to the extent of being able to understand and respond to the techniques and criteria of other disciplines and other approaches. (In my view iteration is probably more important than, and not exclusive of, interdisciplinarity; see Koizumi 1999 on the concept of transdisciplinarity as a way of capturing this.) It means paying more attention to cumulativity, the extent to which research builds on and refines other research – without supposing this to be a smooth, rational and consensual process.

All of this is a major challenge to capacity within the educational research community. Here there is an unambiguous message from the set of reviews of national educational R&D policies carried out by CERI in New Zealand, England, Mexico and most recently Denmark (see Wolter *et al.* 2004). In every case the review reported a significant shortage of capacity, most prominently in handling large-scale datasets and understanding statistical techniques. The weakness means not only that there is less good quality quantitative work than there should be; it also reduces the opportunity for interactive and 'intermethodological' work.

Learning from experience: whose and how?

'Learning from experience' often has a slightly negative connotation, as if the experience is usually painful. Most of us, except the saintly or the masochistic, tend to pass rather more quickly over our mistakes than our successes. This is one reason why knowledge does not accumulate as rapidly as it might: there is an in-built incentive to inhibit or abort the learning which can occur from mistakes – whether the mistakes be of policy or of research. Conversely, how might the lessons of success be more effectively shared? Or, more prosaically, how can we learn from the mix of good and less good which is the typical daily round?

In one sense, almost all of OECD's work is about learning from experience. It involves the gathering of data from a range of countries, which enables each Member country to do two things. First, it allows them to benchmark themselves against what is happening elsewhere. This does not necessarily take the form of league tables, but the most accessible forms are the comparative indicators on such items as educational expenditure per head at different sectoral levels, or the proportions of age-groups participating in education or attaining certain qualification levels. How this benchmarking information is actually used, and the status it is accorded as 'evidence', is an interesting question. The shift to a focus on outcomes gives this particular impetus. The prime example here is the case of Finland, which achieves top ranking in PISA but with middle-level inputs.

More significant from CERI's point of view is the second type of sharing, which provides the opportunities for countries to learn from successful and less successful practice elsewhere, ranging from national policy formulation to case studies of micro-level initiatives, without these data being put into any kind of rank order. OECD's national policy reviews are a prominent example of the former (see, e.g. the recent review of tertiary education in Ireland, OECD 2004c), whilst CERI's *What Works* series is a particularly strong example of the latter. The utility of the national reviews depends in part on the willingness of the country to confront issues and to be candid in the information it supplies. (It should be stressed that countries participate voluntarily in these reviews – OECD has no power to compel participation nor would it wish to.) Review teams conducting OECD country reviews on education make certain that they meet with a wide range of interest groups to ensure that they hear critical voices and do not receive just a government line. The more a review team can spend time addressing the issues as opposed to finding out about them, the fuller their analysis can be. On the other hand, it is precisely one goal of these exercises to identify issues of which the country itself might be only dimly aware. This points to a key feature of the work, already alluded to: the agenda-setting function. OECD analysis can help countries identify relevant policy items, whether these refer to early childhood education, to testing in secondary schools, to adult learning or to educational research and development. Recommendations will take the form of issues to address as well as of solutions to problems. Of course the review process is rarely straightforward or transparent. The invitation to OECD to conduct a review will often come because policy makers have an issue which they wish to see developed as a policy item, but would find it difficult to do so on their own initiative alone. Bringing in a review team can be a neat way of achieving this obliquely.

The *What Works* series, and other case-study-based work, offer the opportunity for policy makers and practitioners to learn directly from initiatives elsewhere. It is probably rare that direct wholesale imitation occurs, but the opening is there for them to adopt and adapt. However, there is a further component, potentially equally valuable, and this is the development and articulation of frameworks for the analysis of the cases. It is a question not so much of how far one can generalise from case studies (a standard topic for methodological debate) as of what concepts and tools emerge from the particular project which can serve as the basis for further and deeper analysis, within countries or beyond. Thus the current *What Works* project, on formative assessment, proposes a framework for thinking about the dynamic relationship between formative and summative assessment, at three different levels: classroom, school and system (CERI/OECD 2005). The framework, derived from the evidence of the case studies (19 in 8 different countries) as well as the literature, is itself very much a product to be tested, analytically and empirically. The significance of the work will therefore depend as much on the quality and applicability of the framework as on the results of the particular analysis.

One further point. It is legitimate to ask how cases of good practice or innovation are selected in the first place, and to pose the issue of circularity. Would we ever investigate a case and conclude that it was not in fact good practice? How do we handle the natural tendency of countries and project leaders to put as good a face as possible on the example they present for inclusion in a set of good practice cases? There is no easy answer to this.[5] In an ideal world one would have faith in the notion that there is as much to be learnt from failure as success, and explore cases on that basis. But that is more than a little ingenuous.

The policy learning process is heavily shaped by the quality of the relationships between the different stakeholders: the 'audiences' listed above (researchers, policy makers and practitioners), of course, but also students, parents and the wider public (this last also flags up the potentially critical role of the media in shaping the policy agenda). From a social capital perspective the nature of these relationships may be conceived of and analysed in terms of levels of openness, trust and communication. Where these are high, the links are more likely to bear fruit; but it is important to remember that this does not mean that all the stakeholders subscribe to the same objectives or values, but simply that they acknowledge the validity of the others' perspectives and are prepared to place some confidence in their judgements. Readers may wish to apply such an analysis to their own contexts.

Conclusion

Policy research conducted within the context of an international bureaucracy certainly differs from university-based research or consultancy contract work. But in what respects, and by how much? The implication of much of my argument above is that the differences may be less significant than the resemblances, at least in the areas covered above (and recognising of course that within each category of research there is considerable variation). The interesting issue is what these differences (whether they be of degree or of kind) might tell us about central issues such as the formation of research agendas, the validation of evidence and the utilisation of results.

The versatile physicist Richard Feynman once said:

> ... psychologically we must keep all the theories in our heads, and every theoretical physicist who is any good knows six or seven different theoretical representations for exactly the same physics. He knows that they are all equivalent, and that nobody is ever going to be able to decide which one is right at that level, but he keeps them all in his head, hoping that they will give him different ideas for guessing.
>
> (1995: 168, quoted in Mitchell 2003: 145)

Educational researchers are not physicists, and CERI/OECD work is not theoretical in the abstract sense. Other than that, this makes strikingly good sense to me. The qualification I would offer to Feynman's challenge, though, is that the most pressing need is for maintaining a diversity of models and tools over time rather than simultaneously, so that the cumulative impact is maximised. Whether that is more or less difficult than the Feynman challenge I do not know.

Notes

1 This chapter is written in a personal capacity and does not necessarily represent the views of OECD. A previous draft was presented to the European Congress of Educational Research in Crete, September 2004. My thanks to Barry McGaw and Janet Looney for helpful comment.

2 The issue of causality is well illustrated by OECD's most high profile educational activity, the Programme for International Student Assessment (PISA; see OECD 2004a, 2004c etc.; McGaw 2004 for an example of specific application to a single country). PISA is a huge exercise involving in its 2003 rounds nearly 300,000 15-year-old students in 62 different countries. Tests are administered across a number of domains, notably reading, maths and science, at different levels. PISA operates on a 3-yearly cycle. The results from 2000 and 2003 have had major political impact in many countries, largely because the design of the project enabled international rankings to be published. PISA's methodology has been quite

hotly debated (see e.g. Prais 2003 and the reply from Adams 2003), but that is not my concern here. The point here is that PISA produces results which can be related to factors such as socio-economic background and stratification within school systems, and shows relationships between average achievement levels and the patters of achievement distribution. But these relationships are highly complex. My colleague Andreas Schleicher, who is responsible for PISA, is always at pains to point out the limitations on PISA's power to provide strong causal explanations.

3   See the Education Department's description of itself, in relation to the fact that it handles only 10 per cent of the education budget: '[this] reflects the historical development of the Federal role in education as a kind of "emergency response system", a means of filling gaps in state and local support for education when critical national needs arise.' See http://www.ed.gov/about/overview/fed/role.html.

4   It is worth comparing the attempt to assert a single model of 'rigour' in social science/educational research, which bases itself primarily on a supposed model of rigour in natural sciences, with methodological debates in the natural science world. Mitchell (2003) provides a most illuminating discussion on this topic, with a cogent argument for non-relativistic pluralism in biological sciences. Understanding causality requires multiple approaches. For example, 'Redundancy of mechanism makes controlled experimental approaches problematic ... Knowing the causal laws that govern each process in isolation by experimentation will not automatically yield sufficient information for drawing an inference to their integrated contribution in situ' (2003: 155). Translated to education: we may be able to use experimental design to understand better the effectiveness (or otherwise) of some interventions, but this will almost never close the case on how that plays out within the wider educational context, still less within society more broadly.

5   The same point applies to the classic instances of management literature case studies, where the secret of commercial success is derived from a set of cases who do (or don't) stick to their knitting, take a long-term view, appoint charismatic leaders, etc. The medium-term survival rate of the cases which make up the management blockbusters would be an interesting index.

References

Adams, R.J. (2003) 'Response to "cautions on OECD's recent educational survey (PISA)"', *Oxford Review of Education*, 29(3), September, 377–89.

Angrist, J.D. (2004) 'American education research changes tack', *Oxford Review of Economic Policy*, 20(2): 198–212.

Berhman, J. and Stacey, N. (eds) (1997) *The Social Benefits of Education*, Ann Arbor, MI: University of Michigan Press.

CERI/OECD (1973) *Recurrent Education: A Strategy for Lifelong Learning*, Paris: OECD

CERI/OECD (1975) *Recurrent Education: Trends and Issues*, Paris: OECD.

CERI/OECD (2001a) *Understanding the Brain: Towards a New Learning Science*, Paris: OECD.

CERI/OECD (2001b) *What Schools for the Future?*, Paris: OECD.

CERI/OECD (2004) *Innovation in the Knowledge Economy: Implications for Education and Learning*, Paris: OECD.

CERI/OECD (2005) *Formative Assessment: Improving Learning in Secondary Classrooms*, Paris: OECD.

Coffield, F. (ed). (2000) *Differing Visions of a Learning Society: Research Findings Volume 2*, Bristol: The Policy Press.

Delors, J. (1996) *Learning: The Treasure Within*, Paris: UNESCO.

Feynman, R. (1995) *The Character of Physical Law*, Cambridge, MA: MIT Press.

Foray, D. and Hargreaves, D. (2003) 'The production of knowledge in different sectors: a model and some hypotheses', *London Review of Education*, 1(1): 7–19.

Hargreaves, D. (1999) 'The production, mediation and use of professional knowledge among teachers and doctors: a comparative analysis', in OECD, *Knowledge Management in Learning Society*, Paris, pp. 219–38.

Istance, D. (2003) 'Schooling and lifelong learning: insights from OECD analysis', *European Journal of Education*, 38(1): 85–98.

Istance, D., Schuetze, H.G. and Schuller, T. (2003) *International Perspectives on Lifelong Learning: From Recurrent Education to the Knowledge Society*, Buckingham: Society for Research into Higher Education and Open University Press.

Koizumi, H. (1999) 'A practical approach towards trans-disciplinary studies for the twenty-first century', *J. Seizon and Life Sci.* 9, No. B 1999.1: 19–20.

Levin, B. (2004a) 'Approaches to equity in policy for lifelong learning', Paper presented to the American Educational Research Association annual meeting, San Diego, May.

Levin, B. (2004b) 'Making research matter more', *Educational Evaluation and Policy Analysis*, 12(56) 1–20.

Lukes, S. (1963) *Power*, London: Macmillan.

McGaw, B. (2004) 'Australian mathematics learning in an international context', Paper presented at MERGA 27, the Conference of the Mathematics Education Research Group of Australasia, *Mathematics Education for the Third Millennium: Towards 2010*, Townsville, 27–30 June.

Mitchell, S.D. (2003) *Biological Complexity and Integrative Pluralism*, Cambridge: Cambridge University Press.

Oakley, A., Strange, V., Toroyan, T., Wiggins, M., Roberts, I. and Stephenson, J. (2003) 'Using random allocation to evaluate social interventions: three recent UK examples', *ANNALS of the American Academy of Political and Social Science* (AAPSS), 589, September: 170–89.

OECD (1996) *Lifelong Learning for All*, Paris: OECD.

OECD (2001) *Knowledge and Skills for Life. First Results from PISA 2000*, Paris: OECD.

OECD (2003) *Beyond Rhetoric: Adult Learning Policies and Practices*, Paris: OECD.

OECD (2004a) *Completing the Foundation for Lifelong Learning: An OECD Survey of Upper Secondary Schools*, Paris: OECD.

OECD (2004b) *Learning for Tomorrow's World: First Results from PISA 2003*, Paris: OECD.

OECD (2004c) *National Review of Education: Ireland*, Paris: OECD.

Papadopoulos, G.S. (1994) *Education 1960–1990: The OECD Perspective*, Paris: OECD.

Prais, S.J. (2003) 'Cautions on OECD's recent educational survey (PISA)', *Oxford Review of Education*, 29(2): 139–63.

Rinne, R., Kallo, J. and Hokka, S. (2004) 'Too eager to comply? OECD education policies and the Finnish response', *European Educational Research Journal*, 3(2): 454–84

Schuller, T. and Megarry, J. (1979) *Recurrent Education and Lifelong Learning. World Yearbook of Education*. London: Kogan Page.

Schuller, T., Brynner, J., Green, A., Hammond, C. and Preston J. (2001), *Modelling and Measuring the Wider Benefits of Learning: A Synthesis*, London: Institute of Education, University of London.

Schuller, T., Preston, J., Hammond, C., Brassett-Grundy, A. and Bynner, J. (2004) *The Benefits of Learning: The Impact of Education on Health, Family Life and Social Capital*, London: RoutledgeFalmer.

Torgerson, C.J. and Torgerson, D.J. (2003) 'The design and conduct of randomised controlled trials in education: lessons from health care', *Oxford Review of Education*, 29(1): 67–80.

Wolter, S., Keiner, E., Palomba, D. and Lindblad, S. (2004) 'OECD examiner's report on educational research and development in England', *European Educational Research Journal*, 3(2): 510–26.

5 A European perspective on international arenas for educational research

Sverker Lindblad

Introduction

This chapter focuses on international arenas for educational research: it explores how they are constituted and how international research communities work in relation to cultural and political influences and constraints.[1] I start with a discussion of the development of education research in different national contexts. I then turn to international rescarch associations and consider how they map the world of education research. Finally I consider how educational research is represented and located in the world through search engines such as the ISI Web of Science and ERIC.

My aim is to increase our understanding of international constraints on the making of educational research communities. A related ambition is to consider ways of dealing with such constraints in the formation of international research arenas in education. This chapter has a specific spatial location: I am writing as a Swedish, Scandinavian and European researcher questioning the current North-American dominance of international arenas of educational research.

Points of departure

Scientific work is often constructed on the basis of the stories told about different actors and their impact on the progress of science. This tendency has been criticised from within the sociology and history of science. Thus, Wittrock *et al.* write:

> The past decades have witnessed a widespread dissatisfaction with the traditional modes of historical reconstruction. It is now widely admitted that traditional textbook history suffers from anachronisms and whiggishness, displays all sorts of disciplinary biases and lacks truly historical scholarship as well as proper social sociological understanding.
>
> (Wittrock *et al.* 1998: 5)

There is a need to understand the development of scientific work, including that in the field of education, to describe and analyse this work in a social and historical context, i.e. to be scientific in the understanding of scientific work. Such a need fits well with the reflective turn in the social sciences and the demands to improve the scientific quality of social science (cf. Bourdieu and Wacquant 1992).

Educational research is considered here as a disciplinary field of study that is formed in different ways, depending on different preconditions as well as different actors' ambitions and strategies in a landscape of opportunities and constraints. One significant problem is that we as educational researchers are socialised in our fields of study and mostly take the landscape of that field for granted. International arenas for educational research are contexts where differences in the construction of research can be made visible through comparing different arenas and how researchers from different contexts orient themselves in these arenas. This text is a first attempt to do such comparative work, focusing on mapping of the arenas and the ways that they work.

In order to act within international arenas it is necessary to understand how such arenas are constructed. This in turn implies a consideration of the most influential ways of constructing educational research. We can ask such questions as: what categories and distinctions are used and how do they in turn contribute to the construction of the arena? There are important differences in different national contexts from evidence gathered from a series of symposia that we carried out in the European Educational Research Association (Lindblad and Mulder 1999, Hofstetter and Schneuwly 1999). According to Hofstetter and Schneuwly (2001: 8), educational research must be conceptualised as a disciplinary field, where different disciplines and different professional interests are at work:

> In our opinion, it seems interesting to make use of the concept *disciplinary field* to designate the sciences of education; we use this term mainly when we discuss its early developments and the uncertain, hazy, shifting boundaries of the sciences of education. We also use the concept to emphasize the referential plural of the sciences of education, which serves as an umbrella term for numerous fields that may, in turn, become established as disciplines. Finally, the concept is used to emphasize the close relationship of the sciences of education with practical reference fields and the professional knowledge that stem from them [italics in original].

Such a disciplinary field is transformed and moved because of two intrinsic tensions, or rather dilemmas, since there is no universal way to deal with them. These dilemmas are the implications for educational research of its relationship to the teaching profession as well as to other academic disciplines.

First, educational research has to deal with the tension that results from the need to be relevant to social and professional demands while at the same time it seeks acknowledgment in the academy which requires the maintenance of some distance from the object studied. This can be conceptualised as a *pragmatic* dilemma – between social relevance and scientific distance.

Secondly, educational research has to integrate approaches and findings based on other academic disciplines on the one hand, while at the same time emphasising the existence of a distinctive body of knowledge within education research. We have here an *academic* dilemma between academic subordination and academic isolation.

Based on these considerations I would argue that educational research as a disciplinary field is constituted by the way actors in this field deal with the pragmatic and academic dilemmas under the specific circumstances that are present in that field at a specific time.

Here I am concerned with scientific communicative events and contexts in international arenas for educational research. These include research associations, research congresses and scientific publications. I am focusing on broad categories and distinctions in these arenas and their work to construct the arenas, and drawing, in particular, on the work of Ian Hacking (Hacking, 1999). How do these arenas deal with these tensions and what are the implications of this for the construction of educational research? Are international arenas having an impact on the disciplinary field in its national contexts?

Different constructions of educational research

In Sweden education is a focus for research carried out in several disciplines. However, and this is a distinctive characteristic of Sweden and the other Nordic countries as well as Germany and Switzerland, there is a specific scientific discipline for educational studies, that is *Pedagogik*. In Sweden, Pedagogik was introduced in 1910. Around that time we also find similar patterns in those national contexts listed above. However, the construction of educational research is somewhat different. Education research in Sweden develops in three distinct periods (Lindberg 2000) that are related to transitions in education in Sweden. Such changes were not carried out in isolation from the rest of the world. Thus, after the Second World War the connections to US educational research became important as did connections to the OECD. Similar patterns are also found in other national contexts (Hofstetter and Schneuwly 2002).

Educational research and educational science(s) are somewhat problematic terms when used in different contexts. For instance Durkheim (1956) constructs education as a science in contrast to practical theories and in contrast to education as an art. Durkheim's point is that education as a science reflects on social facts concerning educational realities, while practical theories seek to move beyond current realities and seek improvements of current situations. Education as an art, according to Durkheim, is part and parcel of educational practice and is necessary for the making of education. This construction of education as a science is made by Durkheim in a specific French context that differs from that in Germany or Sweden.

Jürgen Schriewer compares the evolution of education sciences in Germany and two decades later in France. In Germany a coalition of university administrators organised themselves in order to prevent the questioning of the German education system by the political left, by the school teachers and the experimental psychologists

> In this situation, educational theory ... giving preference to historical interpretation of educational realities, and to the broad perspectives of reflection nourished by the philosophy of civilization – became in the eyes of the ministry an antidote to the attempts of 'modernist' psychologists to link positivistic research with political involvement, and experimental method with social and educational reform.
>
> (Schriewer 2002: 76)

This coalition counteracted an education science built on experimental psychology by means of the formation of an interpretative research paradigm for education research which also counteracted university studies for school teachers. A basis for education research was found in psychology and a specific discipline 'Pädagogik' was constructed with specific concepts and a canon of common references.

The historical development in France was quite different in this period, built on other coalitions of interests. Education as a science – as pronounced by Durkheim above – was dissolved. Instead, education was connected to foundation disciplines – e.g. philosophy of education or educational psychology. This in turn produced hierarchies between foundation disciplines, applications of disciplines in education, and knowledge in practice.

Comparing the German and the French cases from 1920–1970 we find that in Germany a relatively autonomous education science was constituted, while in France education sciences was not autonomous but subordinated to other disciplines. This in turn had implications for communication patterns – in the communication and reception of educational research according to Schriewer.

> In Germany, disciplinary communication in education … clearly centers around a compact kernel of almost unanimously acknowledged referenced authors. [...] In France by contrast, the most frequently cited authors do in no way represent the field of educational sciences proper.
>
> (Schriewer 2002: 86)

In Germany, disciplinary-oriented educational science constructed an independent communicative field, while French educational sciences became more fragmented, referring to different foundation disciplines. Since the 1970s the patterns of references seem to have converged to some extent, perhaps due to work in international arenas.

What objects are educational research referring to?

The different stories of education as a science in France and Germany suggest that it is important to capture the constitution of sciences based on different actors and their power, perceptions and strategies. This is a point that is well underlined in the US case by Lagemann (2000). Such stories are related to what is happening in education as a phenomenon: for example reforms, cultural contradictions, the financial situation and so on. But the stories also show the importance of capturing the impact of different concepts in the construction of educational research. There are parallel stories here – that is narratives in terms of scientific progress or the making of educational progress.

In this connection, the work of Fransson and Lundgren (2003) is useful. In the current Swedish debate on educational research they distinguish between an *object of study* (the phenomenon that is studied, such as early childhood education) and an *object of knowledge* (the conceptual framework or research approach that is used, for example Piagetian concepts of cognitive development). The object of study is the terrain to be mapped, while the object of knowledge is the mapping symbols and instruments.

In order to discuss educational research we are of necessity referring to these two objects: the object of study and the object of knowledge. One of them might be the figure and one of them the ground, but we need to combine the two to make meaningful statements. As researchers it is our task to develop the object of knowledge, the maps and the map making.

Research associations for educational research

In the study referred to in note 1, we used different search engines in order to capture the population of research associations. These included Ingenta and ERIC plus links at different sites. In total we identified 50 associations. We categorised them as 'umbrella organisations', 'knowledge object oriented organisations', and 'study object oriented organisations'. Selection of associations was based on the following criteria: (i) being international, (ii) having connections to the academy as well as the teaching professions, (iii) permitting a width in coverage. Information was collected by websites and conference catalogues and proceedings. In some cases this information was complemented by participant observations and interviews with researchers working in the organisations. A constraint is that subcategories dealing with education in disciplines such as psychology and linguistics are excluded from this mapping.[2]

From these associations we made a selection in each category as follows:

Umbrella associations:
AERA: American Educational Research Association
EARLI: European Association for Research on Learning and Instruction
EERA: European Educational Research Association
NFPF: Nordic Educational Research Association (a member of EERA)

These umbrella associations are built up by divisions, networks and special interest groups that refer to different objects of study and objects of knowledge. The overlap between these divisions or networks is considerable, as indicated by the existence of AERA division K: Teaching and teacher education, the EARLI special interest group on teaching and teacher education, and the EERA and NFPF networks on teacher education. To my knowledge there is little organised cooperation between AERA, EARLI and EERA divisions, networks and special interest groups (SIGs).

Associations oriented towards objects of knowledge:
CIES: Comparative and International Education Society
ISCHE: International Standing Conference on the History of Education

Both these associations are devoted to specific objects of knowledge – CIES towards historical and international comparisons of education and ISCHE with a focus on historical studies of education. ISCHE has history as a foundation discipline. The umbrella organisations also organise comparative education studies and studies in the history of education.

Associations oriented towards objects of study:
ISATT: International Study Association on Teacher Thinking
TNTEE: Thematic Network for Teacher Education in Europe
OMEP: World Organisation for Early Childhood Education
ESREA: European Society for Research on the Education of Adults

ISATT is an international study association dealing with teachers' professional competences and the education of teachers. TNTEE is a thematic network dealing with teacher education issues. OMEP is an international organisation with organised relations with, for example, UNESCO and is working in relation to early childhood education

Table 5.1 Disciplinary tensions and objects of educational research

Tensions	Objects of study	Objects of knowledge
Pragmatic dilemma	Social relevance vs Scientific distance	Not relevant
Academic dilemma	Not relevant	Subordination vs Isolation

and the conditions for children over the world. ESREA deals with adult education and is located in Europe.

What distinctions are at work in these organisations in terms of objects of study and object of knowledge? To a large extent categorisations are made in terms of object of study: researchers present the terrain in education that they are studying but not the research approaches or conceptual framework that is used to produced knowledge about this terrain. One example of this is when the object of study is based on educational levels.[3] Another is what category of education you are dealing with, for example[4] teacher education.[5] Different kinds of special education in relation to different needs offers another way of making distinctions.[6] Categorisations are also available through aspects of education systems such as administration and governance.[7] The influence and effects of information and communication technologies on education is another often recognised object of study in different research associations.[8] Of another kind are divisions and networks that deal with social contexts of education.[9]

Another approach that enables distinctions that is in widespread use is in relation to an object of knowledge. Here we find categorisations in relation to Foundation Disciplines, where the disciplines of history and philosophy appear frequently.[10] But we also find distinctions based on a certain independence from other disciplines, such as curriculum studies,[11] learning and instruction[12] and comparative studies in education.[13]

In sum, the distinction between objects of study and objects of knowledge identified categories at work in international research associations and their divisions, networks and SIGs. We could also identify two different objects of knowledge in the educational field, one subordinated to foundation disciplines and one autonomous object in the field of educational research. These categorisations are regarded as ways of dealing with the pragmatic as well as the academic dilemmas, where categories in terms of objects of study reflect a stress on social or professional relevance, while distinctions in terms of objects of knowledge reflect a tendency towards scientific distance.

In relation to the pragmatic tension the predominant tendency to make distinctions in terms of objects of study is regarded as a way of stressing the social relevance at the cost of scientific distance. Designations such as Inclusive Education, Instructional design, Quality assurance, School Effectiveness, Assessment and Evaluation, Moral and Democratic education, Social Justice and Intercultural Education, Information Centres and Libraries in educational research and Innovative Intercultural Learning Environments, are regarded as signs saying that this research is socially relevant. Conversely, research formulated in terms of objects of knowledge is a way of stressing scientific distance. Here we find tendencies to subordination when the categorisations are referring to foundation disciplines and towards isolation when the categorisations refer to autonomous objects of knowledge.

The different categories and distinctions are constructed by skilful actors manoeuvring in the disciplinary field of educational research. There is, however, a risk that the predominant way of solving the pragmatic dilemma results in a language of educational research that is not distinct from everyday language or from professional expertise. In the former case educational research is trivialised and in the latter we collapse the distinction between actors' and analysts' perspectives. My argument is not that we should correct the language in use but that we should reflect on what it does to us and to educational research. In addition, in considering international arenas of educational research it is important to recognise that the study objects are different in different societal contexts – e.g. education policy or interaction in teaching. Thus the same terminology refers to different objects of study. As a consequence, the seemingly universalistic language has little common ground.

Publications in educational research

The next step is to have a look at scientific publications as international arenas. By means of the search engines Ingenta, ERIC and ISI Web of Science we identified particular educational research journals.

Ingenta is a commercial enterprise that started in 1998 and which regards itself as a leading online search engine having access to 27,000 journals and 6,000 full text publications on line. There is a cooperation with 260 publishing companies and 14,000 libraries. Ingenta has more that 3 million users each month.

ERIC is short for Educational Resources Information Center. It was founded in 1966 in the USA and contains more that one million abstracts of education documents and articles in different kinds of journals. Here we find a large set of journals, more than 1,100, of different ambitions and orientations. Not all of these journals are included in this discussion.

ISI Web of Knowledge is a commercial company owned by Thompson ISIS and consists among other things of ISI Web of Science where more than 8,500 scientific journals are indexed. By means of these indexations there is an opportunity to study to what extent different journals and authors are cited and who is citing whom.

We identified 334 scientific journals relevant to the disciplinary field of education. Based on their titles,[14] we identified the following distinctions:

1. Almost 50 per cent referred to an object of study such as Adult Education or Computers and Education.
2. 20 per cent referred to professional practices such as Educational Psychology.
3. 10 per cent referred to foundation disciplines, e.g. *British Journal of Educational Psychology* or the *Journal of Philosophy of Education*.
4. 10 per cent referred to autonomous objects of knowledge such as Curriculum Inquiry or Learning and Instruction.
5. 10 per cent could not be classified.

Again, in the disciplinary field of educational research we find a predominant classification pattern in terms of objects of study.

The different research engines identified different journals: Ingenta identified 245 journals, ISI Web of Science 116 journals. Of these 42 – less than a half – were found in Ingenta as well.

Looking at the location of the identified scientific journals they are predominantly Anglo-Saxon. Looking at the ISI Web of Science and their social science journals and their national location 58 per cent were located in the USA and 23 per cent in Great Britain, while Germany and France *together* are the publication sites for 5 per cent of the journals. This is underlined by the fact that almost all journals represented in the search engines have English as their publication language. In sum, the journals represented are presenting globally and culturally biased arenas that are not internationally representative.

A more precise way to capture publication patterns in relation to local conditions is to consider in what ways researchers from a specific site are represented in different journals and search engines. Thus, we worked with Ingenta, ISI Web of Science, and ERIC in order to identify articles of Swedish origin. Swedish educational research is internationally recognised and considered to be of high quality according to reviews of research, e.g. Rosengren and Öhngren (1997). Given the more than 300 journals identified above, we found that in the period of 2000–02 almost 100 journals presented texts from Swedish researchers. The number of articles was more than 200, and the number of authors provided 302 cases. In Table 5.2 we show significant differences between the search engines. ERIC is the most efficient in finding Swedish researchers and ISI Web of Science is the least efficient for this purpose. In addition, there is not much overlap, as the results in Table 5.2 make clear.

Swedish educational researchers to a large extent publish in the refereed national research journal (*Pedagogisk Forskning i Sverige*) and the Nordic research association journal (*Nordisk Pedagogik*) neither of which is to be found in the ISI, ERIC or Ingenta. Thus, there is a considerable visibility problem here.

The dominant pattern was that Swedish publications in the current journals were mostly isolated events. Forty of the journals had during the current three years only one text of Swedish origin and almost 30 had two Swedish texts. Thus, in more than two-thirds of the journals Swedish publication was sporadic. Where do when find Swedish researchers? This is presented in Table 5.3.

The pattern is that within the limited numbers of journals that are located by the search engines used, only four are visible in the ISI journal citation reports. The highly ranked *Journal of Intellectual Disability* research is to a large extent a journal for researchers in the medical sector, e.g. psychiatry and neurology, which makes it a bit specific in this context.

In sum, the search engines and their ways of working are selective. They are located in the Anglo-Saxon part of the world, they do not very well represent other contexts, e.g.

Table 5.2 Search engines and their hits of Swedish educational research during 2000–02 (numbers and per cent)

Journal	Swedish Authors	Hits of journals by		
		Ingenta	*ISI*	*ERIC*
Total (*n* = 98)	302	29	27	63
Per cent		25	23	52
Only in relevant search engine (*n*)		11	11	43
Per cent within a specific search engine		37	41	68

Table 5.3 The most frequently used journals of Swedish researchers 2000–02 (numbers, names and citation index according to ISI Web of Science)

Number of articles with at least one Swedish author	Journal	Citation rank according to ISI journal citation reports 2002
3	Childhood	–
3	Journal of creative behavior	–
3	Learning and instruction	21
3	Current issues in language and society	–
3	Journal of adolescence	
4	Minerva	41
4	Instructional science	34
4	European journal of education	–
5	European journal of teacher education	–
5	International journal of inclusive education	–
6	Quality in higher education	–
6	Reading and writing	–
7	European journal of special needs education	–
23	Scandinavian journal of educational research	–
25	Journal of intellectual disability research	1*

* Rank based on Special Education Journal Impact

Swedish educational research, and in a word, they cannot be considered as culturally unbiased international educational research arenas. The universalistic claims and ambitions of search engines and international research journals found by means of these engines are contradicted in practice.

Concluding comments

In this text I have dealt with international arenas for educational research in two ways. I have reported on a study of research associations with international ambitions and the ways they construct themselves by means of categories and distinctions. And I have studied research engines and discussed their location and representation of research.

International arenas for educational research are vital for the building of research communities, at international as well as national and local levels. However, this is not an unproblematic enterprise. In considering international research associations we found a predominant way to identify different kinds of research in terms of objects of study, which means administrative ways of defining research relying on everyday language. This conceals the fact that such objects of study are different in different contexts. Thus, the internationalist ambition is based on a very shaky ground. Looking at educational research publications as international arenas I found that commonly used search engines are culturally biased to a large extent – where 'international' is equivalent to 'Anglo-Saxon'. In sum, researchers from Scandinavia, Continental Europe, Asia, Africa and Latin America are marginalised in these arenas. This does not only mean that the arenas are constructed in an unequal way. What is more important is that the cultural biases constrain our opportunities to understand education – to compare educational phenomena in different contexts and to capture the variation of educational processes in the making of individuals as well as societies.

As researchers interested in improvement of international arenas, we need to do at least two things. First, we need to identify the local bases for the international arenas (where do those who are acting in these arenas come from, where are they located in space, who is networking with whom?). Secondly, we need to work to make them international. We should not accept the universalistic claims of search engines such as ISI Web of Science and their claims to represent quality measurement in educational research.

Of special interest here are the ambitions in Europe to construct European Research Areas where resources are combined to improve research (see e.g. the European Commission) and the fact that European cooperation in such areas is developing rather rapidly (Dienel *et al.* 2002). As researchers we need to act to make such areas not only a site for 'Little Europe' but genuinely international. However, that does not mean that we should strive for a globalised homogenity in such arenas, suppressing local or regional variations in concepts of education and research. Instead, the basic idea should be acceptance of differences in the making of a 'robust' conception of educational research (cf. Nowotny 2003) in international research arenas – robust in the sense that it accepts complexities and ethical responsibilities for researchers as well as different contextualisations of education and research.

Notes

1 This text is based on a study on international arenas for educational research that I did together with Dag Kyndel and Lena Larson on behalf of the Committee of Education Research at the Swedish Research Council. It was presented at the 2004 AERA meeting at an International Relations Symposium. Miriam Ben-Peretz commented on my contribution to the symposium in a fruitful way.

2 Such internationally oriented associations are: International Association for Cross-Cultural Psychology, International Union of Psychological Sciences, Society for Cross-Cultural Research, American Psychology Association (which also has a division for school psychologists), International Association for Analytical Psychology, International Society for the Study of Individual Differences, International Sociological Association (which has a research committee on sociology of education), International Linguistic Organisation, International Mathematical Union, etc.

3 AERA: Post-secondary education, EERA: Vocational education and training, EERA: Research in Higher Education, EARLI: Higher Education, OMEP: World organisation for early childhood education, NFPF: Early childhood education, NFPF: Adult education, EERA: Open and distance learning.

4 AERA: Education of the professions, EERA: Continuing professional development in schools, EARLI: Learning and professional development.

5 TNTEE's activities in general, ISATTs activities in general, AERA: Teaching and teacher education, EARLI: Teaching and teacher education, EERA: Teaching and teacher education, NFPF: Research on teacher education.

6 EERA: Inclusive education, NFPF: Inclusive Education, EARLI: Special Educational Needs.

7 AERA: Administration, AERA: School evaluation and programme development, EARLI: Assessment and evaluation, EERA: Student assessment, EERA: Quality assurance and school effectiveness, NFPF: School leadership, NFPF: School development, AERA: Policy studies, EERA: Policy studies and politics of education.

8 EERA: ICT in education and training, EARLI: Learning and instruction with computers, NFPF: IT and education.

9 AERA: Social context of education, EERA: Communities and their schools, NFPF: Home–school cooperation, NFPF: Rural education, EERA: Partnerships in education.

10 AERA: History of education, EERA: History of education, ISCHE's activities in general, NFPF: History of education, AERA: Measurement and research methodology, NFPF: Philosophy of education, NFPF Sociology of education, EERA: Philosophy of education, EERA: Economics of education.
11 AERA: Curriculum studies, EERA: European curriculum research, NFPF: Curriculum research.
12 EARLI: Conceptual change, EARLI: Knowledge management, EARLI: Experience and understanding, EARLI: Writing, AERA: Learning and instruction, NFPF: Classroom research and ethnographic studies, EARLI: Social interaction in learning and instruction, EERA: Ethnography, EARLI: Individual differences in learning and instruction.
13 EERA: Comparative education network and CIES.
14 The categorisation was hierarchical in this way: if a journal was referring to a foundation discipline or an autonomous object of knowledge this was regarded as decisive compared to professional practices and objects of study. References to professional practices were decisive in relation to objects of study as such.

References

Bourdieu, P. and Wacquant, L. (1992) *An Invitation to Reflexive Sociology*, Chicago, IL: University of Chicago Press.
Dienel, H.-L., Hammarlund, K.-G. and Peterson, M. (2002) 'The historical context of the evolution of national research systems and international RTD collaboration', *Innovation: The European Journal of Social Science Research*, 15(4): 265–78.
Durkheim, E. (1956) *Education and Sociology*, New York: The Free Press.
European Commission DG XII (2001) 'Targeted socio-economic research', Project synopses 1994–8.
European Commission Research DG (2001) 'Improving the socio-economic knowledge base', Project synopses 1999–2001.
European Commission Research DG (2002) 'Key Action: improving the socio-economic knowledge base'. Synopses of key action projects funded as a result of 3rd Call for Proposals.
European Commission (2000) *The Sixth Framework Programme 2002–2006*, Brussels: EC.
European Commission (2000) *Towards a European Research Area*, Brussels: EC.
Fransson, K. and Lundgren, U.P. (2003) *Utbildningsvetenskap – ett begrepp och dess sammanhang*, Stockholm: Vetenskapsrådet.
Hacking, I. (1999) *The Social Construction of What?* Cambridge, MA: Harvard University Press.
Hofstetter, R. and Schneuwly, B. (1999) 'Sciences of education between disciplinary and professional fields. An analysis of tensions and pitfalls of the process of disciplinarisation', *European Educational Researcher*, 5(3): 19–25.
Hofstetter, R. and Schneuwly, B. (2001) 'The sciences of education in Switzerland: evolution and outlooks'. Centre of Science and Technology Studies. CEST 2001, No. 6.
Hofstetter, R. and Schneuwly, B. (2002) 'Institutionalisation of educational sciences and the dynamics of their development', *European Educational Research Journal*, 1(1): 3–26.
Lagemann, E.C. (2000) *An Elusive Science: The Troubling History of Educational Research*, Cambridge, MA: Harvard University Press.
Lindberg, L. (2002) 'Is "pedagogik" as an academic discipline in Sweden just a phenomenon for the twentieth century? The effects of recent education reform', *European Educational Research Journal*, 1(1): 65–82.
Lindblad, S. and Mulder, M. (eds) (1999) 'Changing conditions of educational research in Europe', *European Educational Researcher*, 5(3): 5–18.
Nowotny, H. (2003) 'Democratizing expertise and socially robust knowledge', *Science and Public Policy*, 30: 151–6.

Rosengren, K.-E. and Öhngren, B. (eds) (1997) *An Evaluation of Swedish Research in Education*. Stockholm: HSFR Brytpunkt.

Schriewer, J. (2002) 'Educational studies in Europe', in E. Sherman Swing, J. Schriewer, and F. Orivel (eds) *Problems and Prospects in European Education*, London: Praeger.

Wagner, P. and Wittrock, B. (1993) 'States, institutions and discourses: a comparative perspective on the structuration of the social sciences', in P. Wagner, B. Wittrock and R. Whitley (eds) *Discourses on Society. The Shaping of the Social Science Disciplines*, Dordrecht: Kluwer, pp. 331–58.

Wittrock, B., Heilbron, J. and Magnusson, L. (1998) 'The rise of the social sciences and the formation of modernity', in J. Heilbron, L. Magnusson and B. Wittrock (eds) *The Rise of the Social Sciences and the Formation of Modernity: Conceptual Change in Context 1750–1850*, Boston, MA: Kluwer.

Part II
Research steering in national contexts

6 Toward new government of education research

Refashioning researchers as entrepreneurial and ethical subjects

Kari Dehli and Alison Taylor

It has become commonplace to state that processes of globalisation are transforming economic, social and cultural relations within contemporary societies facilitated by neo-liberal government. The tightening relationship between knowledge, power and economy within neo-liberalism is signalled in terms such as 'the knowledge economy' and 'the information age'. Knowledge is viewed as a vital source and vehicle for economic prosperity, as integral to techniques, targets, sites and effects of power or, more profoundly, as implicated in regimes of discipline, regulation and government (Foucault 1991; Rose 1996a,1996b). It is not surprising then, that researchers in education and the human and social sciences more broadly, have encountered renewed interest in their/our work by governments, policy makers, corporations, media and all manner of so-called 'stake-holder' groups. Canadian policy reports over the past 15 years have constructed arguments for changes in the governance of research in terms of the demands of a new global economy, comparisons with other 'developed' countries, the need for innovation, and the challenges of migration, multiculturalism and social cohesion. There is also a growing scepticism about the worth and relevance of research and teaching, with complaints that scholarly labours produce little useful 'evidence' and dubious 'value for money'. Social science research, including education, is being called on to shift from so-called 'supply-driven' to 'demand-driven' priorities and questions (Levin 2003; SSHRC April 2002). The problem identified in some critiques is not merely that we have failed to disseminate and 'translate' knowledge that can be used to address educational and social problems, but rather that the questions we ask and the manner in which we ask are inappropriate or misdirected. In addition, problems with the organisation and conduct of 'the research enterprise' within universities have been identified.

Whether accurate or not, these sentiments come together to form a powerful frame for rethinking the purposes and organisation of social science and education research and its governance in Western societies. This occurs in at least two related ways. First, we are witnessing changes in how social science research is viewed. More explicit expectations are being fashioned for research with increased emphasis on its contributions to solving social, economic and cultural problems. Relevance, impact, evidence and effectiveness are key discursive concepts. Secondly, and simultaneously, there are changes in the governance of researchers and of the institutions in which they labour. Arguments for greater public accountability, transparency and value for money through target setting and performance indicators pepper the talk of policy makers, deans and university presidents. While working in shared registers, the resulting policy initiatives are uneven and have confusing effects: some invite individual scholars to exercise greater freedom and choice while others assert more detailed prescriptions for conduct and demands for meeting – and accounting for – transparent 'performance targets'.

In this chapter, we focus on two areas of neo-liberal governance that structure the field of possible action for researchers: first, the transformation of research granting councils to privilege entrepreneurialism and 'useful' knowledge; and second, the necessity for researchers to carefully manage the potential risks involved in research through adherence to ethical standards. While much of the chapter describes how new technologies of government work, we are also interested in the complicated 'subject effects' that they engender for university-based researchers (Burchell *et al.* 1991). Our perspectives are those of two critical education scholars working in different Canadian provinces, Alberta and Ontario. Although the governmental practices we discuss are federal, we do not claim to speak for Canada 'as a whole'. We write in a country where regional, cultural and linguistic differences mark the organisation of government and of research. We describe recent policy changes in general terms but do not presume to represent their effects for all researchers or across every education-related discipline, university or location.

Becoming entrepreneurial: transforming granting councils

> Public administration at the federal level in Canada has undergone huge changes over the past decade. As in many other countries in the developed world, there has been a marked shift away from the traditional bureaucratic emphasis on detailed control from the centre and preoccupation with process toward more autonomy and a focus on results. ... At the same time, however, the weakening of traditional controls can increase the risk of error, misjudgement or abuse. ... The downside risks of empowerment can be minimized if some key principles are applied to help guide action and set limits on the exercise of discretion in the new, decentralized environment of the public sector.
>
> (Auditor General, December 2000)

The above quote suggests that the changes now underway in the governance of research and researchers are not particular to these subjects and domains. Governing in a neo-liberal or advanced liberal way (Rose 1996a) may be seen as necessary to secure Canada's place in the global context, as fast-paced new 'knowledge economies' threaten to overtake the economic hegemony of 'the West' and 'the North'. Yet, such modes of government present their own peculiar problems. For example, the work of government involves 'empowering' local communities, organisations and individuals to be more responsive to new opportunities and contexts while instilling modes of management that are more flexible than those associated with the welfare state. But the risk is that such 'empowered' communities and individuals cannot be relied upon to pursue appropriate governmental ends. Thus, as the Auditor General's remarks suggest, what is required is not less government, but a different kind of government (for a good discussion of this point, see Cruikshank 1996 and 1999). The challenge is to envision new 'principles' and technologies of government that can 'help guide action and set limits'. In the quest to govern research more effectively, audit and ethics come together and researchers become both the target and vehicle of government (Rose 1999). Yet, as we will argue, these technologies and instruments are not always successful, nor do they necessarily generate consistent or desired effects.

The Social Sciences and Humanities Research Council (SSHRC), established in the late 1970s, is one of three major federal research-granting agencies which are a major source of funding for university-based research in Canada. In 2001–02, approximately 80 per cent of federal government expenditures on research and development in the higher education sector occurred in the natural sciences, engineering and health sciences while the remaining 20 per cent was spent in the social sciences and humanities. Operating at arm's length from the government, decisions about allocations are made through processes of peer-review, based mainly on the scholarly merit of proposals and the track record of researchers.

In 2004, SSHRC began a consultation process to talk about transforming the agency from a 'granting council' to a 'knowledge council' (SSHRC January 2004a). Three trends fuelled the perceived need for transformation in the way the Council operates:

• the perceived loss in status of social science research vis-à-vis research produced in the natural sciences;
• the emphasis on the 'knowledge economy' and the role of education in global competitiveness; and
• the rise of new public management and accountability practices.

The first trend was referenced in a speech given by the President of SSHRC:

The human sciences have not been able to produce, at the theoretical level, the equivalent to fluid mechanics or genetics, nor, at a practical level, anything quite like the jet engine or heart transplants. ... there is a sense that the human sciences ... have not lived up to their potential.[1] As a consequence, they have lost considerable status and prestige, not to mention their relative lack of research funding and the culture of poverty they now inhabit.

(Renaud, February 2004).

Here it is assumed that all disciplines can and should contribute to economic competitiveness, and that paying 'closer attention to the context of scientific inquiry' will eliminate the deficiencies in the human sciences (cf. Hamilton 2002: 48). The Minister of Industry, whose department oversees SSHRC, also expressed faith in the ability of SSHRC and the other agencies within his portfolio to improve Canada's business environment, create and commercialise knowledge, help build a skilled workforce, and strengthen communities (SSHRC 2004a). Researchers are encouraged to direct their efforts toward economic, social and cultural challenges and problems. The master frame of 'knowledge mobilisation' and 'technology transfer' reinforces this positioning of social and human science research, treating it as equivalent to the growth in commercialisation of knowledge in the natural sciences (Renaud 2004).

There is a palpable sense of impatience – governments are no longer willing to finance research and development without evidence of particular types of return on this investment. Encouragement alone is not generating the desired results. As the president of SSHRC notes, 'governments have switched from a rowing to a steering model' and are looking for ways to improve the 'evidence base for informing policy and creating new policy-research interfaces' (Renaud 2004: 8). Policy makers also recognise that SSHRC is able 'to influence how research is understood and carried out', even in areas such as education which is not under federal jurisdiction (SSHRC 2004a). Presuming, as it seems to do, that a new consensus has emerged regarding the purposes of human and social science research, the challenge is to devise the most effective means to assert these purposes.

Entrepreneurship, linked to audit and accountability, is seen as key. For example, the federal government in Canada has increased its emphasis on accountability through performance audits in all of its departments over time. As suggested in the opening quote from the Auditor General, new public management has several key features and implications for governance. One critical task is the development of technologies of control that inculcate new norms and values and allow 'action at a distance' (Rose 1996a; Miller and Rose 1990; Shore and Wright 2000). The specific principles outlined by the Auditor General for the public sector included the need to focus on prudent management of public funds by setting clear objectives and performance indicators, while providing appropriate incentives, and measuring results. A strong audit function to 'test the credibility of performance measurements' and 'systematic ongoing evaluation of programs' was seen as essential to good management.

A report called *Results for Canadians: A Management Framework for the Government of Canada* (Treasury Board Secretariat 2000) addressed several concerns outlined by the Auditor General and recommended the 'application of results-based management to all major activities, functions, services, and programs' of the government (p. 11). Costs must be linked to results to ensure value for taxpayers. Indeed, the Auditor General's recent annual report to Parliament expressed concern about the 'lack of progress' in subjecting government funded foundations and councils to transparent forms of 'performance audit'.[2]

Although consultations around transforming SSHRC to a 'knowledge council' occurred in 2004, changes in direction were evident before this. In particular, the council has been funding a 'growing proportion of tied, product-driven research' (Amit 2000: 219), and the SSHRC consultation paper refers to models of strategic programs 'designed to have impact outside of the walls of universities'. These include the Initiative on the New Economy (INE), Community-University Research Alliances (CURA) and Major Collaborative Research Initiatives (MCRI) (SSHRC 2004a: 9). In addition, the 2004 budget for the three federal granting agencies called for a tripling of their annual investments in programmes directly supporting the commercialisation of research (SSHRC 2004b: 27).

The INE, CURA and MCRI programmes share an emphasis on involving community, business and other 'partners' in the design and conduct of research. For example, specific objectives of the INE are to foster 'excellent' research using innovative and multi-disciplinary approaches; develop research partnerships involving the public, private and not-for-profit sectors; and enable research results to inform decision making in the public and private sectors. The government of Canada reportedly financed this programme because it believes that Canada's competitive position in the new economy depends on having a strong policy framework based on good research and evidence (SSHRC 2002). The programme's emphasis is not only to produce high quality research, but also to disseminate research to potential users:

SSHRC is directly accountable to the Ministers of Industry and Finance – partners in the initiative – for INE progress and impacts. SSHRC must provide annual INE reports which will detail how research results are being transferred to and applied by relevant stakeholders and users in the private sector, governments, the academic community and others.

(SSHRC 2002: 2)

The interest in bridging the contexts of research production and use is also a key theme in a document endorsed by SSHRC focusing on educational research (Levin 2003). This chapter recognises that there is not a direct line between research and subsequent policy and practice partly because complexities in the educational context make unambiguous recommendations difficult and because the policy-making process is itself complex. At the same time, Levin's analysis suggests that Canadian educational research tends to be 'modest, narrow, and often fragmented' (p. 16) and needs to be made more useful to users (governments, teachers, students, administrators, etc). His recommendations include building impact into the criteria for evaluating research grants; providing supports and resources to researchers to enhance research impact; supporting universities in building the same kind of effort in knowledge mobilisation in education as in science and engineering; strengthening the input of potential users in the development and review of research proposals; taking more steps to extract maximum value from existing research; and building networks of researchers as a way of developing large-scale programmes of research.

There are numerous effects of these initiatives, which come (not coincidentally) at a time when overall government funding for higher education is falling, and when university faculty must secure research grants in order to support graduate students and their academic units, as well as to attain tenure and build their scholarly reputations. New faculty members, in particular, are inducted into the practices of proposal writing, grants management and dissemination and may be invited to join large-scale research network programmes of more senior colleagues as junior partners. University faculty are invited to view and conduct themselves in entrepreneurial ways, to network and to look for opportunities. In the words of the SSHRC *Consultation Framework* document, times have changed from 'the academic world of the 1970s', when 'the role of a university professor working in the human sciences was to teach and write books' (SSHRC 2004a: 2). While we do not necessarily agree with this characterisation of the past, its description of the new reality of academic labour is familiar: 'to get grants, find money for graduate students, stimulate discussions with external audiences, participate in national research teams or to work with other disciplines' (SSHRC 2004a: 2).

At the same time, SSHRC has been developing an increasingly sophisticated results-based monitoring system. A report on SSHRC's performance explicitly outlines the various levels of control and specific steps for monitoring, measuring and reporting on the council's investments (SSHRC 2004c). The procedures retain peer review at the initial stage of proposal approval, as well as peer involvement in site visits to ensure that funded projects meet programme objectives. Universities are mandated, through a Memorandum of Understanding (MOU) with the three federal granting agencies, to manage agency funds according to clearly established and accepted guidelines and principles. SSHRC monitors how universities use these funds through regular on-site financial review and monitoring visits. Grant-holders are required to provide annual financial reports and a final report of research outcomes and SSHRC periodically conducts performance and evaluation studies on its programmes. In 2002/03, the Council put in place an evaluation strategy to better determine the results and impact of its funded research, and in order to establish, monitor and review its 'corporate' policy and programme priorities. It also developed a new Corporate Performance, Evaluation and Audit (CPEA) division. In 2004, this division planned to continue to promote the integration of a management culture that is explicitly based on results and risk assessment (SSHRC 2004b: 34). Other examples of the spread of an 'audit culture' can be seen in the development of a results-based management and accountability framework (RMAF) and a risk-based audit framework (RBAF) for evaluating SSHRC's Canada Research Chairs programme.

The development and expansion of regulatory structures related to evaluation and audit within SSHRC and the other two research councils have been replicated in universities across Canada that receive its funding as they render themselves 'auditable' (Power 1997). For example, financial monitoring reviews or audits of universities across Canada normally occur every five years. In the case of the University of Alberta, the Tri-Council's financial review in 2001 raised a number of concerns about grant administration. To maintain funding, the university responded by launching an initiative to change the way it manages research dollars and to more clearly define roles and responsibilities for different players within the organisation. In the fall of 2002, research functions were centralised into a Research Services Office and the university established a senior-level committee to act as bridge between central administration and faculties in the management of research administration. Around the same time, the Tri-Council signed an MOU with the university, which outlined basic requirements for maintaining eligibility to administer Agency funds. In 2003, Research Facilitators were hired to liaise between faculties and the Research Services Office. Their jobs involve assisting with the grant-writing process, monitoring applications and educating researchers about funding opportunities and the expectations of granting agencies. As Shore and Wright (2000: 62) comment, with regard to the audit culture in higher education in the UK, these new experts are charged with 'tutoring individuals in the art of self-improvement'.

As participants in and observers of these developments, we see that the need to set measurable goals around research outputs and to provide regular reporting on progress affects researchers' sense of worth (Ball 2000), while also narrowing the epistemological field on which research is based (Blackmore 2002, Hamilton 2002). Based on conversations with numerous colleagues it does seem that these developments affect the ability of researchers to engage in, and receive funding to conduct, critical and qualitative research where what counts as 'evidence' is not determined and defined in advance for the purposes of measurement, but rather is one of the questions that should be answered through investigation.[3]

En-coding ethics: managing the risks of research

Along with a growing sense of distrust in public institutions, researchers are subjected to more intense scrutiny and demands for accountability. The modernist presumption that science represents progress and knowledge and is innocent of politics and profit, can no longer be defended. Indeed, as we have argued, the work of researchers is to be more closely tied to 'innovation' and economic prosperity, while also addressing the social problems that arise in globalised economies. Moreover, science and research, including the social sciences themselves, 'are now recognized as a risk-producing endeavor' (Haggerty 2004: 392). Research ethics codes and protocols are one response to the heightened sense of risk in contemporary society. They also comprise instruments whereby university researchers and students can be recruited into their own self-government, thus allowing for devolved forms of management. We argue that ethics codes operate as rationalities and technologies for governing the conduct of researchers, relying on self-reflection and self-regulation of individual researchers.

In 1994 the three Canadian research-funding councils – the Medical Research Council of Canada, the Natural Sciences and Engineering Research Council of Canada and SSHRC – began a process to develop a shared set of policies and guidelines regarding research ethics. The intention was that the new policy, which became known as the *Tri-Council Policy Statement* or *TCPS*, would be applied to all institutions and individuals receiving funding from the councils. Prior to this, the research councils had disseminated guidelines for ethical conduct, but the specific criteria and procedures were left to universities and disciplines to work out. In addition, only research and researchers directly funded by the councils were subject to review. Practices within universities and disciplines varied, as did procedures used in different contexts and types of research.

The 1998 *Policy Statement* that resulted from the consultations is more encompassing, standardised and prescriptive than earlier recommended guidelines. In order to receive funds from any or all of the councils, institutions now have to demonstrate that *all* research conducted by its members (including students) complies 'with this policy regarding research involving human subjects'. Indeed, the opening page in the policy states that 'the Councils will consider funding (or continued funding) only to those individuals and institutions which certify compliance with this policy regarding research involving human subjects' (1998: i.1). Hence, all research conducted in or through Canadian universities, whether carried out by faculty and staff, or by students as part of course-work and dissertations, is subject to the new ethical review procedures. According to the policy, this wide reach allows the *TCPS* to promote a 'culture of ethics and responsible research' throughout higher education, a move that Haggerty (2004) more soberly has labeled 'ethics creep'.

Universities were given two years to demonstrate compliance with the *Tri-Council Policy*. This meant that ethical review committees were to be established, composed of faculty members from multiple disciplines, community representation, and in some cases, lawyers. While smaller universities operate with one committee, a large institution like the University of Toronto has several. The criteria that determine whether or not a review is required are detailed and framed within a bio-medical and psychological model of methodology and relation to 'human subjects'. Using the Tri-Council Policy as a template, each university's guidelines specify criteria for assessing research through a simplified or 'expedited' procedure versus a 'full review'.[4]

One justification for the new level of scrutiny of ethical conduct referred to growing 'public concerns' about 'the protection of human participants in research' (Interagency Advisory Panel on Research Ethics (PRE) April 2002, 1 of 6). Another rationale, presumably drawn from researchers themselves, asserts the 'cardinal principle of modern research ethics: respect for the human dignity of research participants'. By embracing these rationales as its foundation the policy therefore 'aspires to protect the multiple interests of the person – from bodily, to psychological, to cultural integrity' (PRE 2002:

1 of 6). A universal human essence – contained in the body, mind and culture – is thus asserted. Researchers must make two important promises to ensure that the 'human dignity' of research participants is protected: provide full information and opportunity to freely consent to participate; and ensure that privacy and confidentiality are protected. These promises are further specified and formalised. According to the *TCPS*, 'Evidence of free and informed consent by the subject or authorised third party should ordinarily be obtained in writing' unless it is 'culturally unacceptable' or there are 'good reasons for not recording consent in writing' (*TCPS* 1998: Article 2.1(b), A.4).

These framing statements assert a series of truth claims in which culturally specific notions of 'the subject' are naturalised and instrumentalised (Pels 1999 and 2000). Techniques of encoding and inscribing, through formal modes of writing and contractual agreements, are to secure ethical conduct by researchers. On the one hand, human subjects – or third parties acting as their representatives – are presumed able to consent to participate in research, and to sign a formal agreement to demonstrate their competence and willingness. At the same time, they require the monitoring of ethics committees to ensure they are not subjected to deception or coercion. Thus, 'human subjects' appear to possess conditional reason, positioned as vulnerable and subordinated to researchers who appear as powerful, capable of manipulation and in need of regulation. Moreover, 'human subject' participants in research are only exceptionally viewed as themselves capable of producing knowledge that would qualify as research, or to be included in the categories of users, stake-holders and partners that we discussed earlier.

The guarantee of privacy and confidentiality for participants suggests further that 'human subjects' in the research context are suppliers of data, anonymous members of 'populations', or individual 'cases' that can yield up 'evidence' for researchers' theories. This conditional view of 'subjects' (Hacking 1991) may have some rather troubling effects in the ways that ethics proposals are written up and reviewed and, quite possibly, for how they are conducted and understood. We would argue that the main target of these effects of power/knowledge is not the 'human subjects' of research, but researchers themselves.

When the draft of the Tri-Council Policy Statement was circulated for review in 1996, it elicited a barrage of criticism, much of it from researchers in social sciences and humanities (CAUT 1997; van den Hoonard 2001). Contested issues included the viability and appropriateness of generating one standard and procedure for all scholarly disciplines, the privileging of medical and psychological models of research, the difficulty of accommodating qualitative, critical, participatory or performance or arts-based research in the proposed review procedures, and the problem of monitoring compliance with the policy.[5] In 2004, a sub-committee of the Interagency Advisory Panel on Research Ethics reported that many criticisms and concerns remained, along with complaints about over-zealous review boards, unreasonable demands for revisions, slow reviews, no appeal procedures and a lack of transparency in relation to researchers. With regard to the last point, it is ironic that while ethical codes were intended to increase the accountability of Canadian researchers, ethics committee deliberations are not public, there is no provision for appeals, and committees are not obliged to justify demands for revisions in a submission (Haggerty 2004).

Above we suggested that the invitations for researchers to become more entrepreneurial and to seek out collaborative and ongoing relations with colleagues and partners imply a sense of research as a collective process and researchers as participants in extended social relationships. In the ethical review process, however, research is individualised and atomised. Moreover, research is viewed as an exceptional and potentially risky moment in potential participants' lives that warrants careful planning and external scrutiny. One illustration of paradoxical consequences of this 'discrepancy,' is that graduate students working on large-scale research programmes, encouraged and funded by SSHRC, must apply for separate ethics approval if they wish to make use of this research for their own dissertations.[6] Another concern is the legalistic nature of the code, and particularly the normalised expectation of written letters of consent, which can operate as a major deterrent to the recruitment of research participants.

While consideration is granted to cases where written consent is 'culturally inappropriate', such relations are seen as exceptional and must be justified. In other cases, applicants must go to extraordinary lengths to persuade ethics committees that it is not only inappropriate, but perhaps harmful, to insist that participants sign letters of consent before taking part in research. This may be the case in studies with undocumented migrants, for example, or with homeless youth who are seeking to maintain a connection to schooling. Relatedly, the procedures insist that third parties, parents or guardians, must give consent for children and youth, or others considered incapable of granting consent in their own behalf. While reasonable in many cases, to insist on such a requirement makes it difficult to conduct research with youth about activities considered risky or illicit. Is it inherently 'risky' for young people to talk to a researcher about sexuality? Does it increase or reduce risk to insist that parents give consent for 15-year-olds to take part in such research?

To reinforce the sense that research is inherently risky and potentially harmful, there is no category of 'no risk'. A category of 'minimal risk' allows for an 'expedited', less extensive and time-consuming review process. Minimal risk suggests that the proposed activity does not involve risks greater than what a person might expect in her everyday life, and the onus is on researchers to provide a rationale to demonstrate their study falls within this definition. Even so, all questions in the ethics protocol must be answered, and all relevant documents supplied – sample recruitment and information letters, consent letters, interview questions and observation schedules. A considerable number of studies in education are reviewed in the 'expedited' process, so much so that when monthly reports are assembled – as they must to satisfy audits for compliance – we have heard 'concerns' among review board members that 'too many' studies are being approved in this category. Such concerns suggest that members of review boards are also implicated in practices of self-government and audit.

A consultation conducted by the Social Sciences and Humanities Research Ethics Special Working Group in 2004 reported that ethics committees in some universities seem inclined to assume a worst case scenario, imposing restrictions that researchers find both unnecessary and even detrimental to their work. Some suggest that the teaching of research methods courses has been compromised because students are required to submit in-course research for review, a process that could consume an entire academic course. Another effect that Kari has observed is that students refrain from conducting complex, critical, innovative and multi-method research that would fall outside the model of what counts as normal research in the *Tri-Council Policy*. A few students in the masters programme declare they will 'stick to documents', to avoid the time-consuming process of ethical review. But it is not only critical researchers or those planning qualitative or interpretive studies that are frustrated. Paul Grayson (2004), a well-known Canadian scholar in social policy, has argued that survey research is in jeopardy in some universities where ethics committees insist on legalistic and cautionary wording on information letters, thus reducing the number of volunteer participants in a potential sample. Finally, Kevin Haggerty, who served on an Ethical Review Board at the University of Alberta, identifies a paradoxical effect of 'the formal ethics system ... that there is often a distinct but unquestioned rupture between following the rules and conducting ethical research' (2004: 410).

The administration of the Tri-Council Policy on ethics operates to normalise specific activities as 'research" to frame research as an inherently risky set of activities, and to codify particular relations and practices in response to these risks as ethical. At the same time, a range of epistemologies, research questions, relations and practices come to be viewed as marginal and exceptional, if not illegitimate or unethical. One of the potential long-term effects of the policy is the shaping of graduate student research and of future researchers, not only in terms of the research they feel is important, legitimate and recognised, but also in terms of what is possible. It seems the policy generates responses among students ranging from diligent rule-following and excellent form-filling, to frustration, anxiety and incomprehension – hardly the enhancement of an ethics culture. We do not doubt that important and productive conversations do occur between supervisors and students about respectful interactions with, and representations of, research participants. Yet, we would venture that such conversations took place long before these policies became mandatory. In addition, the standardised codes of conduct may reduce these interactions to matters of writing adequate answers to a prescribed set of questions. Ethics are confined to a moment and a protocol, reinforcing a fantasy that the ongoing, ambivalent and difficult relations of research can be anticipated and contained in advance. Power is fixed as a one-way relation that can be kept in check through adherence to prescriptive rules.

Conclusions

Ethical review procedures, along with the work of preparing grant proposals and submitting reports, are simultaneously practices of power and practices of inscription. They work because they draw us into apparently mundane and technical procedures of writing, reading instructions and responding, and filling in forms. They are also effective because they are repeated in a number of different contexts and relationships where we have to produce accounts of ourselves: activity reports, merit and performance reviews, departmental and programme reviews, reports on research 'outputs' reviews of teaching performance, submission of research proposals, drafts and revisions of ethical review protocols, reports on students supervised, and so on. Accounting for oneself or one's programme is no longer an event; it is integral to the ordering of everyday life in academia. Indeed, the ability to generate good accounts is becoming a key part of the performance and reward system of universities (Strathern 2000). New layers of expertise are emerging to 'train' academics in the practices of proposal development, budget preparation and management, ethical conduct, research dissemination and media relations.

One argument made by some observers is that we are witnessing a shift from governing through collective, systematic and social means to forms of government that are localised, specifically targeted and individualised, based on active participation and choice, rather than (overt) coercion and discipline (Rose 1999; Popkewitz 2000). Forms of audit and accounting, organised around continuous goal-setting, self-scrutiny and reporting on performance, feature centrally in emergent forms of government. The knowledges of human sciences are therefore subordinated to the calculative knowledges of accounting and audit (Miller and O'Leary 1987). Thus, programmes associated with new public management emphasise 'cost control, financial transparency, the autonomization of organizational sub-units, the decentralization of management authority, ... and the enhancement of accountability to customers for the quality of service via the creation of performance indicators' (Power 1997: 43). One of the new aspects of these forms of power is their emphasis on active participation, choice and responsibility. Stephen Ball (2000) has suggested with respect to the growing emphasis on accountability in schools, that they entail surveillance and self-monitoring that encourage 'internalized reflexivity', where issues tend to become matters of self-doubt and personal anxiety rather than public debate. Shore and Wright (2000) add that the audit technologies that are now working their way into higher education embody forms of rationality and morality designed to create self-managing individuals who render themselves auditable.

Ethical review codes and audit procedures are techniques of power that take individuals (researchers and participants) as the target and vehicle of government, ensuring that scholars will conduct themselves ethically as they venture into the terrain of partnerships to translate and disseminate research as products and outcomes to users. Our work and our worth are assessed in terms of the funds we are able to bring in, the contracts we are able to secure, the networks and partnerships in which we participate and the 'outcomes' of research. The assumption that reports to 'users' are the end product of research rather than the beginning of a process of discourse and debate could have troubling effects that narrow the scope and critical depth of inquiry (Atkinson 2000). Likewise, the attempt to 'package' education research for easy consumption by policy makers could stifle critical analysis, while moves to privilege partnerships could restrict the questions that are considered relevant and appropriate, producing monologues rather than dialogues (Robertson and Dale 2003). Willinsky (2001) similarly argues that attempts to frame education research in the USA around 'strategic priorities' are flawed because they focus too much on school improvement while missing opportunities to broaden the role of education research in relation to democracy and the capacity to participate in public deliberations.

In this chapter we have been particularly interested in forms of accountability, audit and ethics that structure the field of possible action for researchers, while at the same time encouraging particular kinds of subjectivities and relationships. Much like the teachers referred to by Ball (2000), Canadian university academics and graduate students are encouraged to think about themselves as individuals who are continuously improving their productivity, and live in an existence of perpetual calculation. At the same time, they are vested with responsibility for anticipating any possible harm their research might engender, and to manage the risks that are, according to Canadian ethical codes and procedures, inherent in all forms of research with 'human subjects'. Moves that engender entrepreneurialism among scholars and policies that regulate researchers' conduct through codes of ethics do not explicitly 'cause' people to behave in one way or another. Rather, these initiatives and policies shape a range of possible fields of action (Foucault 1982: 221).

Yet, when we examine the ways in which individuals are recruited into these practices, we see how we are variously invited, encouraged, cajoled, persuaded and/or compelled to reflect on our options and to make choices, for which we are then responsible. Thus, while entrepreneurial and ethical self-government is ascendant in Canadian universities, we have not entered a situation where coercion and discipline have become redundant. It seems that self-government alone cannot accomplish governmental aims, and coercive and disciplinary forms of power operate as well (Dean 2002; Valverde 1996). We therefore agree with Shore and Wright's argument that systems of audit in higher education rest upon 'a simultaneous imposition of external control from above and internalization of new norms so that individuals can continuously improve themselves' (Shore and Wright 2000: 61).

The developments we have discussed raise a number of issues. For example, while few researchers would disagree with the requirement for researchers to provide an account of their actions to funding sponsors, or with the need to be outward looking rather than insular, the effects on researchers and research of the expansion of audit functions within universities are troubling and potentially contradictory. While the audit functions embedded in ethical review codes require researchers to account for how they will protect confidences and manage anticipated risks, including potential conflicts between the interests of 'human subjects' and 'partners' of research, the audit functions requiring the demonstration of 'value for money' emphasise performance, dissemination and making public. Calculative knowledges are therefore asserted as a master frame in order to direct human sciences to analyse, and provide solutions to problems of the social in 'advanced liberal' conditions (Rose 1996a), as well as to govern human science research itself. In this sense, neo-liberal forms of government have complex subject-effects for research and the researched, as well for researchers.

Notes

1 The President of SSHRC's comments echo those made in England by Hargreaves when comparing the contribution of educational research to that of medical research (Atkinson 2000; Robertson and Dale 2003).

2 'Auditor urges more scrutiny of trust money', *The Globe and Mail*, Wednesday 16 February 2005, A7.

3 In a progress report required as part of a large SSHRC grant, one of the questions researchers were asked to respond to was: 'What are the main sources of evidence and rationale for their selection?' One researcher's response included the following comments: '[Our] qualitative account of learning involves neither measurement nor proof, but nevertheless counts as an authoritative research finding and a contribution to scholarly knowledge. Its validity and reliability are to be judged not by virtue of its basis in a representative sample, but rather in the non-positivist tradition, using criteria such as: the care and internal consistency of the study design; the suitability of the setting to the topic and the research questions; the knowledgeable and systematic use of recognised qualitative field methods; the analysis of findings in light of other relevant scholarship; and enough transparency that the study could be repeated by others in similar settings.' This represents an individual attempt to unsettle the assumptions made by evaluators but also indicates the need for researchers within communities of practice to play a greater role in the development of evaluation criteria. Like Ranson (2003), we would argue for a more democratic governance of accountability.

4 www.research.utoronto.ca/ethics_hshome/.

5 See Tri-Councils and AUCC Conference Report, 'Integrity in Research and Scholarship, a Collective Responsibility' September 1995; CAUT Responses to Tri-Council 1996 and 1997; SSHRC Standing Committee on Ethics and Integrity August 2001.

6 This observation was made by Kari in her work as a member of the Education Ethics Review Board at the University of Toronto.

References

Amit, V. (2000) 'The university as panopticon: moral claims and attacks on academic freedom', in M. Strathern (ed.) *Audit Cultures: Anthropological Studies in Accountability, Ethics, and the Academy*, London: Routledge, 215–35.

Atkinson, E. (2000) 'In defence of ideas, or why "what works" is not enough', *British Journal of Sociology of Education*, 21(3): 317–30.

Auditor General (December 2000) *Report of the Auditor General of Canada: Matters of Special Importance*. Online. Available HTTP: http://www.oag-bvg.gc.ca.

Ball, S.J. (2000) 'Performativities and fabrications in the education economy: towards the performative society'. *Australian Educational Researcher*, 17(3): 1–24.

Blackmore, J. (2002) 'Is it only "what works" that "counts" in new knowledge economies? Evidence-based practice, educational research and teacher education in Australia', *Social Policy and Society*, 1(3): 257–66.

Burchell, G., Gordon, C. and Miller, P. (eds) (1991) *The Foucault Effect: Studies in Governmentality*, London: Harvester Wheatsheaf.

Canadian Association of University Teachers (1997) 'CAUT responds to Tri-Council code', *CAUT Bulletin*, 44(8), 1–8 October. Online. Available HTTP: www.caut.ca/archive.

Cruikshank, B. (1996) 'Revolutions within: self-government and self-esteem', in A. Barry, T. Osborne and N. Rose (eds) *Foucault and Political Reason: Liberalism, Neo-liberalism and Rationalities of Government*, Chicago, IL: University of Chicago Press, 231–51.

Cruikshank, B. (1999) *The Will to Empower: Democratic Citizens and other Subjects*, Ithaca, NY: Cornell University Press.

Dean, M. (2002) 'Liberal government and authoritarianism', *Economy and Society*, 31(1): 37–61.

Foucault, M. (1991) 'Governmentality', in G. Burchell, C. Gordon and P. Miller (eds) *The Foucault Effect: Studies in Governmentality*, Chicago, IL: University of Chicago Press, 87–104.

Foucault, M. (1982) 'The subject and power', afterword in H.L. Dreyfus and P. Rabinow (eds) *Michel Foucault: Beyond Structuralism and Hermeneutics*, Chicago, IL: University of Chicago Press, 208–26.

Grayson, P. (2004, January) 'How ethics committees are killing survey research on Canadian students', *University Affairs*, 40.

Hacking, I. (1991) 'How should we do the history of statistics?', in G. Burchell, C. Gordon and P. Miller (eds) *The Foucault Effect: Studies in Governmentality*, Chicago, IL: University of Chicago Press, 181–95.

Haggerty, K.D. (2004) 'Ethics creep: governing social science research in the name of ethics', *Qualitative Sociology*, 24(4): 391–414.

Hamilton, D. (2002) ' "Noise, fallible and biased though it may be" (on the vagaries of educational research)', *British Journal of Educational Studies*, 50(1): 144–64.

Interagency Advisory Panel on Research Ethics (PRE) (2002) 'Process and principles for developing a Canadian governance system for the ethical conduct of reserach involving humans'. Online. Available HTTP: http://pre.ethics.gc.ca/english/publicationsandreports.

Levin B. (2003, August) 'Helping research in education to matter more: a brief discussion and proposals for action'. Paper prepared for Social Sciences and Humanities Research Council of Canada. Online. Available HTTP: http://www.sshrc.ca/web/whatsnew/initiatives/transformation/ben_levin.pdf.

Medical Research Council of Canada, Natural Sciences and Engineering Research Council of Canada, Social Sciences and Humanities Research Council of Canada (1998) *Tri-Council Policy Statement (TCPS): Ethical Conduct for Research Involving Humans*, Ottawa: The Councils.

Miller, P. and O'Leary, T. (1987) 'Accounting and the construction of the governable person', *Accounting, Organizations and Society*, 12(3): 235–65.

Miller, P. and Rose, N. (1990) 'Governing economic life', *Economy and Society*, 19(1): 1–31.

Pels, P. (2000) 'The trickster's dilemma: ethics and the technologies of the anthropological self', in M. Strathern (ed.) *Audit Cultures: Anthropological Studies in Accountability, Ethics, and the Academy*, London: Routledge, 135–72.

Pels, P. (1999) 'Professions of duplexity: a prehistory of ethical codes in anthropology', *Current Anthropology*, 40(2): 101–37.

Popkewitz, T. S. (2000) 'Globalization/regionalization, knowledge, and the educational practices: some notes on comparative strategies for educational research', in T.S. Popkewitz (ed.) *Educational Knowledge: Changing Relationships between the State, Civil Society, and the Educational Community*, Albany, NY: State University of New York Press, 3–27.

Power, M. (1997) *The Audit Society: Rituals of Verification*, Oxford: Oxford University Press.

Ranson, S. (2003) 'Public accountability in the age of neo-liberal governance', *Journal of Educational Policy*, 18(5): 459–80.

Renaud, M. (2004, February) 'Universities: change is mandatory; survival is optional; choose wisely', Fred A. Aldrich Lecture, Memorial University, Newfoundland. Online. Available HTTP: http://www.sshrc-crsh.gc.ca.

Robertson, S. and Dale, R. (2003) '"Designed" dialogues: the *real* politics of evidence-based practice and education policy research in England', in M. Ginsburg and J. Gorostiaga (eds) *Limitations and Possibilities of Dialogue among Researchers, Policy Makers and Practitioners*, New York: RoutledgeFalmer, 219–36.

Rose, N. (1996a) 'Governing "advanced" liberal democracies', in A. Barry, T. Osborne and N. Rose (eds) *Foucault and Political Reason: Liberalism, Neo-liberalism and Rationalities of Government*, Chicago, IL: University of Chicago Press, 37–64.

Rose, N. (1996b) 'The death of the social? Re-figuring the territory of government', *Economy and Society*, 25(3): 327–56.

Rose, N. (1999) *Powers of Freedom: Reframing Political Thought*, Cambridge: Cambridge University Press.

Shore, C. and Wright, S. (2000) 'Coercive accountability: the rise of audit culture in higher education', in M. Strathern (ed.) *Audit Cultures: Anthropological Studies in Accountability, Ethics, and the Academy*, London: Routledge, 57–89.

SSHRC (April 2002) *A Strategy for INE Knowledge Transfer*, prepared for INE Advisory Committee by SSHRC Knowledge Products and Mobilisation Division, Ottawa.

SSHRC (2004a) *From Granting Council to Knowledge Council: Renewing the Social Sciences and Humanities in Canada*, Consultation framework on SSHRC's transformation. Ottawa: Author.

SSHRC (2004b) *Social Sciences and Humanities Research Council of Canada: 2004–2005 Estimates, Report on Plans and Priorities*. Online. Available HTTP: http://www.sshrc-crsh.gc.ca.

SSHRC (2004c). *Departmental Performance Review: SSHRC Performance Report for Period Ending March 31, 2004*. Online. Available HTTP: http://www.sshrc-crsh.gc.ca.

Social Sciences and Humanities Research Ethics Special Working Committee (2004) *Giving Voice to the Spectrum: Report of the SSHWC to the Interagency Advisory Panel on Research Ethics*, Ottawa: Social Sciences and Humanities Research Ethics Special Working Committee.

Strathern, M. (ed) (2000) *Audit Cultures: Anthropological Studies in Accountability, Ethics and the Academy*, London: Routledge.

Treasury Board Secretariat (2000, March) *Results for Canadians: A Management Framework for the Government of Canada*, Online. Available HTTP: http://canada.gc.ca.

Valverde, M. (1996) '"Despotism" and ethical government', *Economy and Society*, 25(3): 357–72.

van den Hoonard, W. (2001) 'Is research-ethics review a moral panic?', *Canadian Review of Sociology and Anthropology*, 38: 19–36.

Willinsky, J. (2001) 'The strategic education research program and the public value of research', *Educational Researcher*, 30(1) January–February, 5–14.

7 The steering of educational policy research in neoliberal times

The case of Argentina

Jorge Gorostiaga, Mónica Pini,
Ana M. Donini and Mark B. Ginsburg[1]

Introduction

In this chapter, we analyse the changes that educational policy research has experienced during the last decade in Argentina. A central tenet of our argument is that research institutions and researchers – in education as well as in other fields – are increasingly influenced in their work by global research agendas and standards, which are often revealed in state policies and programmes as well as in the preferences and conditions set by major funding institutions (e.g. international foundations, multilateral agencies).

We argue that in Argentina educational policy research seems to be steered by a complex combination of forces that respond to globalisation trends, and that appear to be part of the neoliberal restructuring of the state and society. These forces, or influences, include adapting the educational system to the global economy; promoting the evaluation of academic institutions and scholars based on Anglo-American standards; increasing participation of local researchers and research institutions in global policy and research networks; and increasing influence of international agencies in the selection of research topics and methodologies. One of the main effects of these forces seems to be the adoption of a problem-solving approach to educational research that is expected to result in effective policy making.

The chapter begins by briefly describing the processes of state restructuring and of educational reform in Argentina during the last years. Then we turn to the analysis of the historical evolution of educational research, followed by the discussion of the scenario of the last decade. We locate educational policy research in the broader context of the steering of research in the national scientific system and in the field of education. At the same time, and in spite of several particularities, we locate historic and current Argentine processes in the wider landscape of Latin America.

Neoliberalism and state restructuring in Argentina

During the twentieth century Argentina achieved high levels of social equity and educational attainment.[2] It can be argued that the Argentine society lost its democratic and egalitarian character during the 1970s, when the military dictatorship of 1976–83 carried out, along with the systematic and extensive violation of human rights, a process of neoliberal economic restructuring that produced a weakening of state capacities for the implementation of public policies as well as an increase in social polarisation and poverty (Romero 2004). This process proved to be difficult to revert even after the return to democratic rule in December 1983, and the erratic economic policy of Raul Alfonsin's government ended up in hyperinflation. The two administrations of Carlos Menem (1989–99) implemented a deep neoliberal economic reform heavily influenced by the International Monetary Fund (IMF) and other multilateral lending organisations. The reform included the opening of the Argentine economy to international trade, the privatisation of state-owned companies, and the deregulation of economic activities.[3] In 1991, Argentina, Brazil, Paraguay and Uruguay formed the MERCOSUR (Southern Common Market), a very important step toward the integration of a regional trade block. More recently, Argentina has participated in negotiations about the establishment of the Free Trade Area of the Americas, an initiative promoted by the US government.

Argentina experienced high rates of economic growth during the early 1990s, but the decade ended with a situation of rising income inequality and high unemployment. Poverty dramatically increased after December 2001 with the devaluation of currency, which was followed by the declaration of default on external debt. At the beginning of 2003 the economic and social situation started to improve, but today poverty and unemployment still represent severe problems. During the first semester of 2004, 44 per cent of the population was living under the poverty line, and 17 per cent, below the subsistence line, according to official figures (INDEC home page).

Educational reform in Argentina

The process of state restructuring in Argentina has included the reform of education. At the end of the 1980s there was general consensus on the deep crisis of both basic and higher education sectors. The diagnoses focused on the problems of low quality and the lack of effective regulation of the education system (Krotsch 2001, Braslavsky and Tiramonti 1990). The first step in the restructuring of the education system was the decentralisation of secondary schools and teacher training institutes from the national to the provincial level, which was followed by the enactment of the Federal Law of Education (1993) and the Law of Higher Education (1995).

The reform was supposed to promote the improvement of quality, efficiency and equity. At the basic education level, changes included creating a new academic structure that extended compulsory education from 7 to 10 years; modernising provincial systems of educational administration; establishing a new mechanism of curriculum design; implementing compensatory programmes for the most disadvantaged social groups; developing student assessment, evaluation, and information systems; re-training teachers to upgrade their subject knowledge and teaching methods; and adopting a new model of school management.

The reform of higher education, in turn, involved establishing an accreditation system and evaluation mechanisms; encouraging institutional differentiation; and pushing institutions to search for new sources of funding other than the state (Donini and Donini 2003, Krotsch 2001, Mollis 2003). The changes introduced competition among individuals and among institutions, implying for universities a shift from public institutions to corporate enterprises regulated (or at least driven) by market principles (Araujo 2003) as well as a movement from a Latin American toward an Anglo-American model of higher education institutions (Krotsch 2001: 36).

The reform can be considered as an attempt to adapt the educational system to the demands posed – at least rhetorically – by international economic competition (see Ginsburg 1991). The implemented changes show a combination of the three kinds of responses that countries are adopting in the education and training sectors as a reaction to globalisation and changes in the world economy (Carnoy 1999). The first type, competitiveness-driven reforms, involves changes in at least the following four categories, all present in the Argentine case: decentralisation, standards development and implementation, improved management of educational resources, and improved teacher training. These changes were sometimes justified in terms of adapting the educational system to technological changes and the requirements of the global economy (e.g. Ministerio de Cultura y Educación 1996a, 1997a). On the other hand, the transfer of schools to provinces can be characterised as a finance-driven reform, while compensatory programs and some of the changes at higher education seem to reflect the rationale of equity-driven reforms.

The reform in Argentina reflects trends witnessed in other countries in Latin America and globally. As Fischman *et al.* (2003: 7) note:

> The educational debate in Latin America at the beginning of the twenty-first century appears to be dominated by polemics about standards, testing, school autonomy, decentralization, accountability of the public sector, privatization, and vouchers, indicating that the center of the debate is how to best accommodate educational institutions to the demands of the market.

The similarity of many aspects of current educational reforms throughout Latin America and the rest of the 'developing nations' is accompanied by a renewed interest in education as a key factor in economic and social development. This interest is reflected in the recommendations made by several governments and international agencies such as the United Nations, the Organization of American States, the World Bank and the International Monetary Fund (e.g. the 'World Conference on Education for All' held in Jomtiem, Thailand in 1990, and organised by UNICEF, UNESCO and the World Bank). A recurrent theme is the need to make basic levels of education widely available as a right and responsibility necessary for the development of human capital, as well as the need of higher levels of education for the workforce to adapt to rapid technological changes and to post-fordist organisation (see Kingsolver 1998).

During the last years the World Bank has assumed the leadership in educational international development, and has become the 'main expert' for education reform proposals in the developing world (Coraggio 1998). In Latin America, the World Bank and the Inter-American Development Bank (IDB) have adopted a key role in the restructuring of education (see Torres n/d). The influence of multilateral agencies in the educational field occurs through policy recommendations to governments – at international and regional meetings and more directly when involved in financing education reform — as well as more generally (and perhaps more powerfully) through their prominent role in shaping the supranational policy discourse (Lingard 2000).

In the case of Argentina, the World Bank and the IDB have participated in the design and financing of educational reform, supporting decentralisation, the modernisation of administrative systems in the provinces, the introduction of information technology in the schools, etc. The ideological and material support from the World Bank has been particularly important for the reform of higher education (Krotsch 2001).

Historical overview of educational research in Argentina with focus on educational policy research

In Latin America, educational research and theory have traditionally followed trends developed in Europe and the USA (see Tedesco 1987). Narodowski (1999) notes that, even though there are no detailed studies analysing the history of educational research in Latin America, it is possible to trace diverse experiences starting at the end of the nineteenth century and the beginning of the twentieth century. During the 1930s, for example, the development of school systems generated huge challenges to educational research in countries like Argentina, Brazil, Colombia and Mexico, but most studies were oriented to improving teaching methods (didactics) or to analysing the logic of learning processes (psychology).

A general diagnosis formulated at the end of the 1980s identified the poor coordination among government, productive, and scientific-technological sectors, and stated that in terms of educational research Latin American countries had not established 'lines of inquiry with clearly developed priorities' (Gutierrez 1990: 57). Another study (Tedesco 1987) highlighted the vulnerability of research capacities in the region due to political instability and budgetary limitations, as well as pointed out that research tended to:

1   ignore persistent regional educational difficulties;
2   highlight the role of dominant sectors in education; and
3   emphasise a passive or, at the most, resistant role for dominated groups.

Finally, it should be noted that Latin America seems to be no exception to the universal claim about the lack of impact of educational research on policy making and practice (Tedesco 1987; Tenti 2001; Lanza 1991).

Education research activities in Argentina, as scientific activities in general, have historically suffered from a lack of sufficient funding[4] as well from the limitation of relatively few full-time positions at universities (both at public and private institutions) (Palamidessi 2003). As tends to be the case in other countries' (see Ginsburg and Gorostiaga 2003) inadequate articulation between researchers, and public/private sector decision makers has been another characteristic of most academic fields, including education (Donini and Donini 2003). Actually, it is difficult to talk about a system of scientific research in Argentina; it is even more difficult to conceive of educational researchers and research institutions as forming an integrated system of research and academic activities, as following established guidelines, and being coordinated to even a moderate degree (Llomovate 1992; Palamidessi 2002).

Traditionally, most education research has been carried out in public universities, where *Universidad de Buenos Aires* (UBA) clearly stands out, but during the last decades independent research centres and some private universities have assumed a more significant role. One should bear in mind that universities in Argentina and other countries of Latin America have had in general a professional preparation orientation, with weak capacities in terms of the production of scientific knowledge and technological development (Donini and Donini 2003; see also Krotsch 2001).

The first academic degrees and research centres in education were established by UBA and *Universidad de La Plata* (also a public institution) during the first decades of the twentieth century (Suasnábar and Palamidessi 2004). At the end of the 1950s, a new impulse to the institutionalisation of educational research in Argentina took place in the context of a process of 'modernisation' and 'professionalisation' of state bureaucracy (in line with the global post-war trend toward the development of the planning capacities at the state), and the promotion of a scientific research system that included the creation of the *Consejo Nacional de Investigaciones Científicas y Técnicas* (CONICET, National Council for Scientific and Technological Research).[5] Along with other new academic degrees like Sociology, Psychology and Economics, *licenciaturas en Ciencias de la Educación* (bachelor degrees in Education Sciences) with a scientific orientation were established in different universities (Suasnábar and Palamidessi 2004). By contrast, after 1966, with the new military regime, universities entered a period of political persecution and censorship, and the policies to promote scientific research were abandoned.[6]

More specifically, the sub-field of educational policy in Argentina was built upon the fields of philosophy, pedagogy, history of education and law at the beginning of the twentieth century, receiving contributions from the sociology of education and the economics of education later on. During the 1950s and 1960s, the emphasis began to shift from school legislation studies, which had characterised the first decades of the century, towards the analyses of state activities in the area of public education. By the mid-1960s these lines of reflections were interrupted by the start of domination of human capital theories. These theories were oriented to efficacy and efficiency, and implied an optimistic perspective about the relationship between school achievement and economic development. By contrast, the development and spread of critical theories in education was one of the key phenomena of the 1970s. The school was seen by many scholars as an ideological apparatus of the state contributing to the reproduction of production and social relations within the capitalist society. The authoritarian reaction that followed in the late 1970s stopped the development of the field, and resulted in the dominance of religious educational agencies and ideas, as well as the elimination of education policy as a subject matter from all university syllabi. Many researchers emigrated from the country, while others left public universities for private institutions where they found more academic freedom. The democratic transition of the 1980s allowed recovering institutional spaces for alternative visions. Critical theoretical frameworks were revisited to include the analysis of authoritarian processes, and they inspired a lot of studies about school systems and reform in Argentina and in Latin America (Paviglianitti 1989).

During the period 1984–90, there was a strengthening of some education research centers, such as FLACSO (*Facultad Latinoamericana de Ciencias Sociales*),[7] and CENEP (*Centro de Estudios de Población*), which had been created outside universities during the previous two decades (Suasnábar and Palamidessi 2004). At the same time, there was a process of reconstruction of public universities, although limited by budgetary restrictions that affected the funding of research projects (Palamidessi 2003: 12). One of the results of these processes was the first studies and research programmes on higher education at universities and independent research centres (Krotsch 2001: 49). Another important development was an incipient recovery of technical capacities (statistics, research, planning) at the national government level.

A state-of-the-art study of research on the government and administration of education since the 1960s, released by the Argentinean Ministry of Education in 1988, noted scarce interest on these topics among educational researchers, and the lack of an organised body of knowledge and study in the area. Most of the studies were carried out by public institutions during democratic periods, and they focused on analysing educational services to optimise them, or on evaluating the effects of decentralisation of elementary schools. The research production from private centres was lower, but it included some valuable qualitative studies (Paviglianitti 1988). Additionally, Braslavsky and Tiramonti (1990:12) pointed out that during the 1980s educational debates had focused on the need for change. This focus on educational change resulted in renewed attention to educational policy research, an area they argue had been neglected or rejected during the 1970s by scholars adopting critical perspectives.

A study about the field of educational research published in 1992 revealed that educational policy was an under-represented topic, and that private institutions conducted more than a half of the educational policy studies (Llomovate 1992). This report also noted that little attention was being paid to financial and organisational topics, and that most of the studies referred to the whole school system rather than to particular levels or problems.

The restructuring of research in the 1990s and current trends

Educational reseach in Argentina has experienced important changes during the last years, in the context of restructuring of schooling, higher education and scientific research activities that reflect neoliberal globalisation trends. The funding from state agencies and international organisations has increasingly become linked to the promotion of problem-solving and positivistic approaches, of international evaluation criteria (based on models from the USA and other Anglo-American countries) and, in some cases, of topics that are central to the neoliberal reform agenda. At the same time, as new mechanisms of cooperation and competition among researchers and among institutions are introduced, research activities require new capacities (including the participation in international networks), while researchers are called upon to perform new roles as mediators between research and policy making. In what follows, we analyse what we consider to be the main elements framing the new scenario of educational research with a special focus on educational *policy* inquiry.

In 2003 the Argentinean Ministry of Education released a report describing the situation of research on education which was based on abstracts of studies submitted voluntarily by researchers to the Ministry beginning in 1966 (Serra and Landau 2003). The report documents sizeable increases in the number of research studies, the number of researchers[8] and the number of research institutions focusing on education. Moreover, in addition to educational researchers coming from traditional academic fields (e.g. psychology, educational sciences, sociology and history), the report documents an increasing number of specialists coming from fields like anthropology, linguistics, economics and policy analysis.[9]

The increase in the number of educational researchers and research studies is related to the expansion during the 1990s of institutions that are expected to do research, like graduate schools of education and teacher training institutes.[10] In addition, the changes implemented in the education system have created an important demand for information and research findings (Serra and Landau 2003, Palamidessi 2002), and have stimulated the debate on the nature and effects of educational policies (see Krotsch 2001 for the case of research on higher education). However, the growth seems to be mainly related to the implementation at public universities of the 'Incentives Program', which provides a small yearly grant to those public universities professors who participate in research activities (see discussion below).

As we described earlier, the national education reform of the 1990s implied a process of adaptation to the global economy. The reform included an organisational redesign of the national ministry of education, so that it could play its new role in a decentralised system in relation to schools operating as 'intelligent' organisations. One of the products of this redesign was the creation of the Secretary of Higher Education Policies, in charge of the close regulation of universities. The organisational redesign included the use of research products for decision making, but also the incorporation of a set of procedures. The Ministry introduced peer review practices, promoted critical readings, organised case-study seminars, developed data-bases, and encouraged participation in exchange networks, all in line with what was considered to be necessary for an effective management of the reform (Braslavsky 1999: 249). This move can be seen as constituting new techniques of regulation consonant with the neoliberal rationality of government (see Tikly 2003: 166–7).

These changes in the national Ministry were reinforced by the movement of a group of researchers from academia to policy-making positions. The Ministry's Office of Research and Development adopted a key role in the implementation of the reform during the 1990s, and educational researchers who were based at FLACSO, UBA and other public and private institutions were called on to occupy positions in different areas of the Ministry.[11] In addition, many researchers based in NGOs and universities were hired on part-time consultancy basis (Romero and Romero 2004: 94).[12] Apparently, these researchers were attracted to work with a government with a commitment and capacity to implement deep educational reform, in spite of the fact that the government's general neoconservative orientation and neoliberal economic policies contradicted the ideology of many of them.[13]

According to Braslavsky and Cosse (1997: 10), this incorporation of researchers into the state structures with 'significant levels of freedom and resources' involved a movement towards 'innovation and creativity', based on the use of empirical research and international comparison. However, according to Palamidessi (2002), the result was not a dialogue, but a kind of cooptation of scholars by the state, since researchers became involved after the definition and launching of the reform agenda.

The objectives of incorporating researchers in the reform initiatives, it was argued, were professionalising the Ministry, establishing 'state policies' (Braslavsky and Cosse 1997), and strengthening the state bureaucracy with specialised knowledge (Romero and Romero 2004).[14] At time, the incorporation of researcher can be seen as a response to a demand from multilateral agencies that funded educational reform, in that these agencies required or recommended the use of specific technical planning tools with which researchers are more likely to be competent than traditional bureaucrats (see Romero and Romero 2004: 115). Moreover, researchers could serve as effective links between government bureaucrats and the international agencies' officials.[15]

Meanwhile, the Ministry attempted to influence the research agenda in a more direct way, promoting what it considered to be a new kind of educational research, connected to policy needs, particularly with the reform agenda of the time, as well as encouraging researchers to adopt the role of mediators between research and policy making (Ministerio de Cultura y Educación 1996b, 1997b). The proclaimed objective was to solve the traditional disconnection between scientific knowledge and policy making (Serra and Landau 2003). In this regard, the Ministry started to organise meetings to discuss research findings, and to produce surveys of educational studies in order to identify gaps that needed to be filled.

At the same time, the government initiated discussions about establishing research plans and priority areas for the whole scientific and technological system. In this context, the government created in 1996 the *Agencia Nacional de Promocion Cientifica y Tecnologica* (ANPCyT, National Agency for the Promotion of Science and Technology), charged with awarding grants for technology innovations and scientific research (see Terneus Escudero *et al.* 2002). The ANPCyT has offered different types of grants, some involving private companies, and all requiring competitive proposals which are evaluated using similar criteria to those employed in the Incentives Program set up in public universities.

In 2003, the ANPCyT established a programme of research grants focused on important areas identified as under-researched. The first call included the areas of biotechnology, mathematics, urban violence and public security, information and communication technologies, and education. Within the area of education, the topics selected were: the educational system; education and work; the school and the cultural transformations; the school and citizenship education; and teacher training. (The second call (2004), however, did not include education as an area.) The programme promotes applied research with practical and/or policy-making implications. There are explicit demands for research that: has a social and economic impact; improves global competitiveness; contributes to 'the development of the Information Society'; and is performed in cooperation with state and civil society organisations and private corporations. In addition, the programme requires that at least four institutions participate in each research project, and that the research team of each institution demonstrates appropriate expertise by including at least three scholars with doctoral degrees or similar experience and a record of international publications (ANPCyT 2003). These requirements, together with the type of research that is promoted, imply an alignment with the standards of Anglo-American research institutions, and with the new functions that researchers are called to perform in the informational or knowledge society.

The 'Incentives Program' can be seen as another example of the way the work of researchers is being restructured along global standards. As mentioned above, this programme is administered by the national Ministry of Education and was created as part of the reform of higher education implemented during the 1990s. One of its main objectives is to improve research towards meeting international standards (Araujo 2003: 131). The programme establishes a small yearly grant for those university professors who participate in research activities. Professors are assigned a category that determines the amount of the grant, depending on an evaluation of their academic credentials, institutional experience (leadership positions at universities, research centres, government offices, etc.), teaching and research experience, human resource development (direction of theses and dissertations, supervision of teaching and research assistants, etc.), and performance (publications, knowledge transfer, etc.). The process of categorisation is coordinated by university rectors, and the evaluation is performed by researchers (Araujo 2003).

According to Araujo (2003: 86), the 'Incentives Program' represents a significant move by the state to define quality of research activities and of scholars, drawing upon evaluation models 'imported' from the USA and other developed countries. What is deemed 'good research practices' is based on the idealised images of the natural sciences and medicine (Araujo 2003: 88). The programme is designed to: increase the number of research projects (perhaps even at the expense of quality and originality); and encourage scholars to connect their research to teaching (Araujo 2003).[16]

International agencies have another important influence on the context and direction of educational policy research in Argentina and other Latin American countries. From the beginning of the 1990s there has been a concern about such influence and its impact on research agendas, as international agencies became major sources of funding (Lanza 1991).[17] The global agenda for educational policy and research is promoted in Argentina by multilateral agencies like the World Bank, IDB, the Organization of American States (OAS) and UNESCO, by major international philanthropic foundations (Ford, Kellog, Tinker, etc.), and Latin American regional organisations like PREAL. While the size of the research grants awarded by these organisations is usually not large, such external sources of funds can have a considerable impact in the context of very low level of national government funding for research.

During the last years, the Partnership for Education Revitalization in the Americas (PREAL) has become one of the main promoters of educational research in Latin America, with a focus on policy issues. PREAL is a network of private and public organisations jointly managed by the Inter-American Dialogue and *Corporación de Investigaciones para el Desarrollo* (CINDE, Chile), which aims at 'improving educational quality and equity' in the region. Launched in 1995 as a product of the Miami Summit of the Americas (Torres, n/d), PREAL generally espouses a positivist research orientation along with a neoliberal ideology.[18] Since 2002, PREAL has organised an annual competition for research funding open to all research institutions in Latin America; institutions based in Argentina have received six out of a total of 24 grants. In addition, PREAL provides funding for research projects that are commissioned through different institutions in Latin America (usually related to its programmes and working teams, which focus on evaluation and standards, school autonomy, professionalisation of teachers, etc.) and organises academic meetings on different topics (see PREAL home page).

Currently, educational policy research is carried out by five groups of institutions, although it should be noted that researchers usually have multiple affiliations, combining in many cases a part-time university position with a position at another kind of institution:

1   UBA and other public universities, where researchers usually espouse critical perspectives, with low impact on educational policy debates and policy making. Their funding mainly comes from research programmes at universities (funded by the state), and from national scientific institutions (e.g. CONICET).
2   Research centres that maintain high academic standards and do mainly policy-oriented research, contributing to educational debates at national and regional levels. These include centres associated with international organisations, like FLACSO, and UNESCO's International Institute for Educational Planning,[19] and other (more independent) centres like CENEP (*Centro de Estudios de Población*) and CEDES (*Centro de Estudios de Estado y Sociedad*).

3   Think tanks, most of them with a neoliberal orientation, and whose main concern is the influence of public policies at national, provincial and municipal levels.
4   A group of private universities, which usually employ a very small number of researchers and which focus their work on particular topics or education levels (e.g. *Universidad de Belgrano* and *Universidad de Palermo* both focus on higher education).
5   Research units of ministries of education (at the national level and in a few provinces), which employ a relatively small number of researchers and undertake a relatively small number of more policy-oriented research studies.

While higher education institutions have had problems to overcome their bureaucratic organisation and to perform new kinds of inquiry in addition to the traditional discipline-oriented research (Palamidessi 2002), think tanks and some independent research centres have been able to adapt to the new research scenario, responding to the demands of the 'market' and connecting their work to international networks. As a result, independent research centres and think tanks have gained more influence (and have been able to obtain more research funds), at the expense of public universities.[20] For example, in 2004, FLACSO, which, today, can be considered the main producer of educational policy-oriented research in Argentina in terms of quality and impact, received grants from the ANPCyT (4), PREAL (2), the national Ministry of Education, the European Union, and the Antorchas Foundation (local branch of an international foundation). Previously FLACSO had received funding for educational research projects from the IADB, Ford Foundation, Tinker and UNESCO (FLACSO home page).

From the end of the 1980s, think tanks have emerged in Argentina as significant actors in the discussion of public policies, and as places where researchers adopt the new roles of consultants and *knowledge brokers*, with funding from international agencies and local corporations (Thompson 1994, Suasnábar and Palamidessi 2004). In the case of education, the most influential think tanks include: *Fundación de Investigaciones Económicas Latinoamericana* (FIEL, founded in 1964 by the main national corporate associations, created an economics of education research programme in the early 1990s), *Fundación Grupo Sophia, Fundación Gobierno y Sociedad* and *Centro de Implementación de Políticas Públicas para la Equidad y el Crecimiento* (CIPPEC). Most of them are part of international networks or have important connections to foreign institutions, and are sponsored by multinational (Telecom, Telefónica, Siemens, McDonalds, Deutsche Bank Bank of Boston, etc.) and national companies (Techint, Bridas, Arcor, Roggio, etc.) (home pages of CIPPEC, *Fundación Grupo Sophia, Fundación Gobierno y Sociedad*, and FIEL).

The main and explicit goal of think tanks is to influence the design and implementation of public policies, generally espousing perspectives closely linked to neoliberal ideas and drawing on policies developed by central countries.[21] *Fundación Gobierno y Sociedad*, for example, was hired by a provincial government to design a policy inspired by the experience of charter schools in the USA.[22] We can find another example in a document of *Fundación Grupo Sophia*, which states that 'today, our society is part of the new knowledge and information society, of the globalised economy, where each nation stands out ... mainly because of its human capital' (Fundación Grupo Sophia 2004: 93, our translation). In addition, the document emphasises the need for higher levels of school autonomy, for providing material incentives to teachers and for granting more power to municipalities and more decision-making authority to school principals for the sake of efficiency. The Bush administration's 'No Child Left Behind' policy is cited as an exemplary programme (Fundación Grupo Sophia 2004: 49).

Conclusion

These changes in the national system of science and technology and in the functioning of higher education institutions have profound implications for scholars, particularly those in the humanities and education, resulting in new forms of power and prestige as well as new foci for their research activities (Araujo 2003: 153), notwithstanding the persistent poor material conditions in which research is produced.[23] Scholars are now pushed to obtain masters and doctoral degrees early on in their careers, to publish in peer-reviewed journals (prompting journals to adopt peer reviewed evaluation of manuscripts) and to orient research projects toward the topics and approaches preferred by funding agencies. The 'academic freedom' and the autonomy that researchers used to have in selecting topics appear to be replaced by what the 'market' (including the competition for governmental grants) demands. As Krotsch (2001: 40) points out, we have witnessed a movement from an autonomous and disciplinary way of doing research to a form that has to respond to the criteria of problem solving and applicability.

This phenomenon seems to be related to a change in the role of social scientists (Braslavsky and Cosse 1997, Brunner and Sunkel 1993), with more direct involvement in decision making, abandoning the classic separation between the activities of knowledge production and policy making (where knowledge produced by social scientists was supposed to be applied by policy makers) (see Ginsburg and Gorostiaga 2003).[24] In this regard, Castells (1994) points out that the informational society is characterised by work in networks, and exchanges through networks of organisations and institutions, which require people to constantly redefine their work roles. In this case, educational researchers in Argentina and other countries take on new roles as knowledge brokers and mediators, using their 'scientific' knowledge and 'academic' credibility to contribute to but also legitimate – for citizens of Argentina as well as representatives of multilateral agencies – national educational policies and practices.

Educational research in Argentina, however, continues to be carried out in a precarious institutional scenario, characterised by low levels of funding and production, lack of spaces for exchanges and articulation both among researchers and among institutions, and difficulties for establishing continuous research programmes (see Palamidessi 2002). Even when some of the changes we have discussed can be seen as having positive implications, like the strengthening of the local academic community in particular aspects (see e.g. Narodowski 1997), or like closer connections between research and policy making, or between local and international researchers and institutions, they may also entail the imposition – or self-imposition – of global topics and approaches as well as the fading of critical views and social transformation ideals. As Tikly points out in his analysis of the case of South Africa, 'One consequence of the utilitarian approach to research funding is the limiting of opportunities for funding research that is more critical of the underlying rationalities of government or is based on alternative epistemologies and knowledge systems' (2003: 168).

The institutions and individuals 'steering' educational policy research in Argentina are clearly diverse. As with the case of educational reform (see Ginsburg *et al.* 2005), one cannot validly explain the directions being taken only by reference to 'foreign' agents, in that Argentine governmental and non-governmental organisation actors can be seen to play important roles as well. Nevertheless, one has to question whether neoliberalism, positivism and the other ideologies informing their actions are indigenous to Argentina or part of a global discourse, and whether their capacity to influence the current direction of educational policy research in Argentina is at least partly a function of the coincidence of their perspectives and those promoted by international actors.

Notes

1 We would like to thank Myriam Feldfeber (Universidad de Buenos Aires, Argentina), Mariano Narodowski (Universidad Torcuato di Tella, Argentina) and Mariano Palamidessi (FLACSO Argentina) for their comments on a previous version of this chapter.
2 Notwithstanding the economic stagnation and the deterioration of social services that have prevailed during the last decades, the 2004 Human Development Report still places Argentina among high development countries (rank 34), and at the top of Latin American nations (UNDP 2004).
3 The policies of 'free' market economics, budget cuts and the reduction of the state structure were widely adopted in Latin America as a part of the 1990s neoliberal agenda (and even earlier in Chile and Argentina under military dictatorships) (Gamarra 1994). These policies were supposed to improve social services, to make public administration more efficient, and to fight the monopoly of the bureaucratic state.
4 In 1998, for example, Argentina spent US$1,530 on scientific and technological activities (while Brazil spent US$9,187), and invested 0.42 per cent of the GDP in R&D (while Japan invested 2.89 per cent, and the USA, 2.70 per cent) (Terneus Escudero *et al.* 2002). Funding problems are among the main obstacles for researchers, and emigration of the best 'brains' has been one of the historic phenomena characteristic of Argentine society (Ministerio de Educacion 2002).
5 The mission of CONICET is to promote, coordinate, and carry out research on pure and applied sciences. Since its creation, there has been a permanent tension between claims by the scientific community for public policies and funding for research, and claims for autonomy.
6 However, this military regime (the so called 'Revolución Argentina', 1966–73) promoted the development of education offices with planning and research functions, developments which were reversed by the military dictatorship of 1976–83 (see Paviglianitti 1988, Suasnábar and Palamidessi 2004).
7 FLACSO is an institution created by UNESCO with branches in several countries of Latin America.
8 A recent study suggests that in Argentina there are between 40 and 120 scholars (the number varies depending on the criteria used) devoted to doing educational research in a regular way and with a reasonable record of publications (Palamidessi 2003). While the number of researchers has increased in the last two decades, this is a still a very low number, even compared to some other Latin American countries. Within this small group of researchers, only a few of them focus their work on educational policy.
9 Similarly, Narodowski (1999) points to a variety of theoretical and methodological approaches to educational research that have been employed in Latin America during the last years, including post-structuralism, ethnography and constructivism.
10 This expansion was due to both the reform of basic education that involved a restructuring of teacher training, and to the changes in higher education, which have encouraged university professors to complete graduate studies. In addition, the new processes of institutional accreditation have also pushed universities to develop research programmes.
11 A prominent example is the current Minister of Education, a well-known scholar who was Director of FLACSO Argentina, and who has occupied different positions at the local and national government levels since the late 1980s.
12 In this respect, Narodowski (1997: 54) talks about the emergence in those years of the 'market educators' ('pedagogos de mercado'), who take advantage of the consultancy work

opportunities in the government and in other (local and international) organizations, and who are 'only concerned with responding to what comes into pedagogic fashion and with being competitive (reliable) in the market'.

13 According to Puiggros (1997: 48), the reform was the result of the confluence of almost all of the diverse groups that had historically been involved in the debates over education in Argentina, including groups with leftist, liberal and catholic ideological orientations (cited in Narodowski 1997). On the other hand, during the 1990s there was a general opposition to the national government from the academic community in national universities (Feldfeber 2000), as well as some strong criticisms of the participation of educational researchers in the national government (e.g. Cano 1997).

14 In addition, the 'professionalisation' of the administration had an important function of legitimating the government and the reform.

15 Many of the members of this group of researchers were part of global networks (particularly through participation in international conferences and research meetings) before becoming ministry officials and consultants, so they could be seen as part of the supranational educational community that helps to produce a more or less unified global discourse on educational policy issues (see Lingard 2000). At the same time, their positions in government allowed them to enter into new conversations with representatives of multilateral agencies, which reinforced their connections within the international network.

16 Some of the criticisms to the programme are that: (a) it functions as a mechanism for increasing the low salaries of (some, but not all) professors; (b) its evaluation criteria are controversial, giving high value to activities not directly related to research; (c) it 'inflates' participation in research projects, as many people are included on research projects and publications so they can receive the benefit; and (d) it bureaucratises research activities due to a permanent process of external evaluation (Araujo 2003, Donini and Donini 2003: 19).

17 Latin American NGOS, including research centers, receive the majority of their funding from foreign sources (Akkari and Perez 1998).

18 A core document of this organisation, 'Lagging Behind' (PREAL 2001), argues for increasing the decision-making power and the responsibility for results at the school level with performance goals and accountability mechanisms set at the central level. It also stresses the need for participation in international achievement tests that allow measuring up how Latin American students do in comparison to other countries and regions.

19 At the end of the 1990s the IIEP (UNESCO) established its first office outside of its headquarters in Paris. This office in Buenos Aires carries out educational policy research related to planning and management issues for Latin America, working especially with governments (Romero and Romero 2004: 127).

20 Albornoz (2004), however, points out that at the end of the 1990s public universities were making considerable progress in developing their scientific capacities, including learning how to obtain funds from different national agencies.

21 However, one should also note the emergence of think tanks which are opposed to neoliberalism (e.g. *Laboratorio de Politicas Publicas* and *Instituto de Investigaciones de CTERA*, the research institute sponsored by the main national confederation of teacher unions) and have some international links, but with less visibility and policy impact.

22 The programme has been carried out since 2001 in San Luis – a province characterised by an autocratic government and the lack of social participation, in spite of the strong opposition of the local teachers' union and other groups.

23 According to the final report of the National Commission for the Enhancement of Higher Education (Ministerio de Educacion 2002), the context of research activities was characterised by: recession, deteriorated institutional climate at universities, no business innovations, scarce links between institutional actors, dependence from foreign providers of knowledge, and weak public policies and funding for science, technology, innovation and higher education activities.

24 Braslavsky and Cosse (1997) argue that this move of educational researchers into policy-making positions has been characteristics of other Latin American countries as well (e.g. Brazil, Chile and Uruguay). Weiss (1994) makes a similar point with regard to the Mexican case. See also Tenti (2001).

132   *Jorge Gorostiaga, Mónica Pini, Ana M. Donini and Mark B. Ginsburg*

References

Akkari, A. and Perez, S. (1998) 'Educational research in Latin America: review and perspectives', *Education Policy Analysis Archives*, 6(7). Online. Available HTTP: http://epaa.asu.edu/epaa/v6n7.html (accessed 3 January 2005).

Albornoz, M. (2004) 'La investigación científica en las Universidades nacionales', in G. Delamata (ed.) *La universidad argentina en el cambio de siglo*, Buenos Aires: Jorge Baudino Ediciones/Universidad Nacional de General San Martín.

ANPCyT (Agencia Nacional de Promoción Científica y Tecnológica) (2003) 'Programa Areas de Vacancias: Bases Convocatoria PAV 2003', Buenos Aires: Ministerio de Educación, Ciencia y Tecnología, Secretaría de Ciencia, Tecnología e Innovación Productiva.

Araujo, S. (2003) *Universidad, Investigación e Incentivos: la Cara Oscura*, La Plata: Ediciones Al Margen.

Braslavsky, C. (1999) *Re-haciendo Escuelas: Hacia un Nuevo Paradigma en la Educación Latinoamericana*, Buenos Aires: Santillana.

Braslavsky, C. and Cosse, G. (1997) 'Las actuales reformas educativas en America Latina: cuatro actores, tres logicas y ocho tensiones', PREAL Document No. 5, Santiago de Chile: PREAL.

Braslavsky, C. and Tiramonti, G. (1990) *Conducción educativa y calidad de la enseñanza media*, Buenos Aires: Miño y Dávila Editores.

Bruner, J.J. and Sunkel, G. (1993) *Conocimiento, Sociedad y Política*, Santiago de Chile: FLACSO.

Cano, D.J. (1997) 'Conversos, técnicos y caníbales o acerca de las desventuras de la pedagogía en el laberinto del Estado Malhechor', in G. Frigerio, M. Poggi and M. Giannone (eds) *Políticas, Instituciones y Actores en Educación*, Buenos Aires: Novedades Educativas.

Carnoy, M. (1999) *Globalization and Educational Reform: What Planners Need to Know*, Paris: UNESCO, Institute for International Planning.

Castells, M. (1997) 'Flujos, redes e identidades: una teoría crítica de la sociedad informacional', in M. Castells *et al.* (eds) *Nuevas perspectives críticas en educación*, Buenos Aires: Paidós.

CIPPEC Home page. Online. Available HTTP: http//:www.cippec.org (accessed 8 January 2005).

Coraggio, J.L. (1998) 'Investigación educativa y decisión política: el caso del Banco Mundial en América Latina', *Perfiles Educativos*, XX(79–80): 43–57.

Donini, A.M. and Donini, A.O. (2003) 'La gestión universitaria en el siglo XXI: desafíos de la sociedad del conocimiento a las políticas académicas y científicas', Buenos Aires: Universidad de Belgrano, Documentos de Trabajo 107.

Feldfeber M. (2000) 'Una transformación sin consenso: apuntes sobre la política educativa de Menem', *Versiones* 11, Secretaría de Extensión Universitaria (UBA) y Ediciones Novedades Educativas, Buenos Aires.

Fischman, G., Ball, S. and Gvirtz, S. (2003) 'Toward a neoliberal education? Tension and change in Latin America', in S. Ball, G. Fischman and S. Gvirtz (eds) *Crisis and Hope: The Educational Hopscotch of Latin America*, New York and London: RoutledgeFalmer.

FLACSO, Home page. Online. Available HTTP: http://www.flacso.org.ar (accessed 16 February 2005).

Fundación Gobierno y Sociedad, Home page. Online. Available HTTP: http://www.fgys. org (accessed 17 February 2005).

Fundación Grupo Sophia, Home page. Online. Available HTTP: http://www.gruposophia.org.ar (accessed 17 February 2005).

Fundación Grupo Sophia (2004) *Puntos Fundamentales de la Agenda Educativa: Un Aporte a la Reforma*. Online. Available HTTP: http://www.gruposophia.org.ar/publicacion.htm (accessed 17 February 2005).

Gamarra, E. (1994) 'Market-oriented reforms and democratization in Latin America: challenges of the 1990s', in C.A.W. Smith and E. Gamarra (eds) *Latin America Political Economy in the*

Age of Neoliberal Reform: Theoretical and Comparative Perspectives for the 1990s, New Brunswick, NJ and London: Transaction: 1–15.

Ginsburg, M. (ed.) (1991) *Understanding Educational Reform in Global Context*, New York: Garland Publishing.

Ginsburg, M., Espinoza, O., Popa, S. and Terano, M. (2005) 'Globalization and higher education in Chile and Romania: the roles of the International Monetary Fund, World Bank, and World Trade Organization', in J. Zajda (ed.) *International Handbook on Globalization, Education and Policy Research: Global Pedagogies and Policies*, Secaurcus, NJ: Springer.

Ginsburg, M. and Gorostiaga, J. (eds) (2003) *Limitations and Possibilities of Dialogue among Researchers, Policy Makers, and Practitioners: International Perspectives on the Field of Education*, New York: RoutledgeFalmer.

Gutierrez, L.M. (1990) 'Educational research and decision-making in Latin America and the Caribbean', in M. Debeauvais (ed.) *National Educational Research Policies: A World Survey*. Paris: UNESCO.

INDEC, Statistics on poverty in Argentina. Online. Available HTTP: http://www.indec.gov.ar (accessed 3 March 2005).

Kingsolver, A. (1998) 'Introduction', in A. Kingsolver (ed.) *More than Class*, Albany, NY: SUNY Press.

Krotsch, P. (2001) *Educación Superior y Reformas Comparadas*, Bernal: Universidad Nacional de Quilmes.

Lanza, H. (1991) 'Posibilidades de producción de insumos de alto impacto con escasos recursos'. *Propuesta Educativa*, 3(5): 5–10.

Lingard, B. (2000) 'It is and it isn't: vernacular globalization, educational policy, and restructuring', in N. Burbules and C.A. Torres (eds) *Globalization and Education: Critical Perspectives*, New York: Routledge.

Llomovate, S. (1992) 'La investigación educativa en Argentina', *Propuesta Educativa*, 4(6): 92–102.

Ministerio de Cultura y Educación (1996a) 'Descentralización y autonomía', *Zona Educativa*. Buenos Aires: Ministerio de Cultura y Educación 6, 10–16.

Ministerio de Cultura y Educación (1996b) *Seminario de investigación para la transformación educativa*. Buenos Aires: Ministerio de Cultura y Educación.

Ministerio de Cultura y Educación (1997a, October) 'Argentine education in the society of knowledge', Presented at the 29th Session of the General Conference UNESCO, Paris.

Ministerio de Cultura y Educación (1997b). *I y II Seminarios de Investigación para la Transformación Educativa*, Buenos Aires: Ministerio de Cultura y Educación.

Ministerio de Educación (2002) *Informe Final de la Comisión Nacional para el Mejoramiento de la Educación Superior*. Online. Available HTTP: http//:www.ses.me. gov.ar/publicaciones (accessed 8 November 2004).

Mollis, M. (2003) 'Un breve diagnóstico de las universidades argentinas: identidades alteradas', in M. Mollis (ed.) *Las Universidades en América Latina ¿Reformadas o alteradas?*, Buenos Aires: CLACSO.

Narodowski, M. (1999) 'La investigación educativa en América Latina: Una respuesta a Akkari y Perez', *Education Policy Analysis Archives*, 7(2). Online. Available HTTP: http://epaa.asu.edu/epaa/v7n2.html (accessed 3 January 2005).

Narodowski, M. (1997) 'Del pedagogo de Estado al pedagogo de la diversidad', *Propuesta Educativa*, 17.

Palamidessi, M. (2002) 'La investigación educacional en la Argentina: una mirada al campo y algunas proposiciones para la discusión', discussion paper, Buenos Aires: FLACSO.

Palamidessi, M. (2003) *La Producción Académica sobre Educación en la Argentina*, Buenos Aires: FLACSO.

Paviglianitti, N. (1988) *Diagnóstico de la Administración Central de la Educación*, Buenos Aires: Ministerio de Educación y Justicia, Dirección Nacional de Información, Difusión, Estadística y Tecnología Educativa.

Paviglianitti, N. (1989) 'Política y educación: notas sobre la construcción de su campo de estudio', Lecture delivered at Universidad Nacional del Centro de la Provincia de Buenos Aires, Cátedra de Política Educacional de la Facultad de Ciencias Humanas, 6 October.

PREAL Home page. Online. Available HTTP: http://www.preal.cl (accessed 25 February 2005).

PREAL (2001) *Lagging Behind: A Report Card on Education in Latin America*. Online. Available HTTP: http://www.preal.org/infprogeduREG.php (accessed 12 March 2005).

Puiggrós, A. (1997) 'Espiritualismo, normalismo y educación', in A. Puiggrós (ed.) *Dictaduras y utopías en la historia reciente de la educación argentina 1955–1983*, Buenos Aires: Galerna.

Romero, L.A. (2004) 'Veinte años después: un balance', in M. Novaro and V. Palermo (eds) *La Historia reciente: Argentina en democracia*, Buenos Aires: Edhasa.

Romero, J. and Romero, P. (2004) *Los reformadores sin espíritu: ¿Quiénes hicieron la reforma educativa argentina en los 90?*, Rosario: Homo Sapiens Ediciones.

Serra, J.C. and Landau, M., with González, D. and Cappellacci, I. (2003) 'Relevamiento Nacional de Investigaciones Educativas. Aproximaciones a la investigación educativa en la Argentina (2000–2001)', Buenos Aires: Ministerio de Educación, Ciencia y Tecnología, DINIECE.

Suasnábar, C. and Palamidessi, M. (2004) 'Notas para una historia del campo de producción de conocimientos sobre educación en la Argentina'. Paper presented at the XIII Argentine Congress of the History of Education, Buenos Aires, 10–12 November 2004.

Tedesco, J.C. (1987) 'Paradigms of socioeducational research in Latin America'. *Comparative Education Review* 31(4).

Tenti, E. (2001) 'En casa de herrero cuchillo de palo: La producción y uso de conocimientos en el servicio educativo'. Paper presented at the IV Congress of Educational Research, COMIE, Manzanillo-México.

Terneus Escudero, A., Borda, M.E. and Marschoff, C.M. (2002) '¿Existe un sistema nacional de innovación en Argentina?', *Revista Iberoamericana de Ciencia, Tecnología, Sociedad e Innovación*, 4. Online. Available HTTP: http://www.campus-oei.org/revistactsi/numero4/borda.htm (accessed 21 February 2005).

Thompson, A. (1994) '"Think tanks" en la Argentina. Conocimiento, instituciones y política', Buenos Aires: CEDES. Online. Available HTTP: http://168.96.200.17/ar/libros/argentina/cedes/thom1.rtf (accessed 30 November 2004).

Tikly, L. (2003) 'Gobernmentality and the study of education policy in South Africa', *Journal of Education Policy*, 18(2): 161–74.

Torres, R. M. (n/d) '"Cooperación internacional' en educación en América Latina: ¿Parte de la solución o parte del problema?'. Online. Available HTTP: http://www.fronesis.org (accessed 9 November 2004).

UNDP (2004) *Human Development Report 2004*, New York: United Nations Development Program. Online. Available HTTP: http://hdr.undp.org/reports/global/2004 (accessed 21 February 2005).

Weiss, E. (1994) 'Situación y perspectiva de la investigación educativa', *Propuesta Educativa*, 5(10): 93–6.

8 The steering of educational research in post-Soviet Russia

Tradition and challenge

Irina Isaakyan

The context: globalisation and post-Soviet Russia

Globalisation and its effects on post-Soviet Russia set the context for this chapter. The characteristics of globalisation are well known: Morrow and Torres (2000) emphasise the following characteristics: post-Fordist production, new informational technologies and neo-liberal (privatisation) practices. Burbules and Torres (2000: 28), select 'the information society' and 'the global spread of post-modern culture' as key features. Globalisation encompasses 'the compression of the world and the intensification of consciousness of the world as a whole' (Robertson, 1992: 8), while Giddens (1990) highlights 'deterritorialisation' in his well-known comment that 'local happenings are shaped by events occurring many miles away and vice versa'.

Critical analysts of globalisation stress its contribution to the erosion of local customs and the spiritual, economic and political exploitation of impoverished communities and localities by affluent ones, along with the threat to the biosphere and the commodification of human culture in general (Kellner, 2002: 302). However, Kellner also acknowledges globalisation's beneficial effects in promoting cosmopolitanism and diversity. In this chapter, I look at the impact of these contradictory forces in a particular context, that of post-Soviet Russia, and consider the impact of rapid modernisation on a system and society that has had a particular relationship to knowledge production.

In Russia, the extremely rapid move towards global operations is fraught with unpredictable outcomes, including those in education. Azmanova (1992: 144) argues that the 'imitation of the West' is a long-established practice in Eastern Europe (EE). She suggests that the alterations on the East European periphery can be analysed as 'fundamental and economic innovations' and represent a transition from a 'closed' template of societal development, tailored to an authoritative regime with its military-based economy, to an 'open' economic pattern, which is egalitarian and market oriented (Azmanova, 1992: 144). For the EE communities this process is associated with liberation from totalitarianism. However, as she makes clear in her critical commentary on these developments, and as Graham's social constructionist approach to the shaping of social and intellectual life acknowledges (Graham, 1998),[1] there are undesirable consequences following from the rapid adoption of the Western path.

Azmanova (1992: 149) attributes Russian problems to the distorted version of marketisation in Russia, which contains alien 'standards of commodification and bureaucratization' (1992: 149). These alien standards and relations did not construct patterns of democratic participation. As a consequence, attempts to steer public resources through public participation were moribund. Late modernity in the EE region could almost be characterised as a distorted version of colonisation: a new society had been designed 'not organically, as a settlement [with a new, cosmopolitan, culture], but synthetically, as a building [with requirements imposed from the outside]' (Azmanova, 1992: 149). The principle of commodification implemented in the EE derives from the elite-serving nature of socialist organisation and distribution rather than mass consumption. Russia in transition, like other EE countries in the former socialist block, does not 'draw its new normativity from itself', but merely transplants Western legislative and administrative practices as a façade of democracy (op. cit. 150). The crux of the matter is the historically embedded nature of this experience for Russia. The top down application of the recent market-driven mode mirrors the building of Soviet communism 'from above' (Azmanova, 1992: 149). Castells describes the 'incoherent patchwork of people, nationalities and state institutions' as the chief consequence of the agonising annals of the USSR (1997: 36). The impact of the decline of the nation-state on the ideoscapes within the region is more than obvious.

Deficient in the cultural parameters of Western society, the EE ethos also lacks the nucleus of modernity, that is: 'the liberal individual or the liberal institutions of civic society' (Azmanova, 1992: 154). That is why the installation of egalitarian norms in Eastern Europe attempting to use configurations that are taken out of their original societal contexts produces an aberration from what is traditionally implied by democracy (Azmanova, 1992: 154). Appadurai would probably call it a departure from confirming the criteria of the 'ideoscape' (1996: 35).

Globalisation and higher education in Russia

Globalisation of the post-industrial economy is transforming the environment of higher education throughout the world, simultaneously compressing and expanding its ideoscapes, financescapes, ethnicscapes and so on.[2] Slaughter and Leslie (1997) argue that to facilitate change, convergent 'travelling' policies are designed in the Anglophone countries to promote organisational restructuring and other adjustments to academic capitalism. Governments reduce funding to universities, thus pressing the latter to alter their curricula, research and organisational development in a way that 'intersects' with the market (Deem and Johnson 2003). Slaughter and Leslie (1997) pinpoint a shift worldwide from 'basic' or 'curiosity-driven' research to 'targeted' or 'commercial' or 'strategic' research, which is strongly linked to the post-industrial corporate sector.

Russian higher education has been undergoing a significant transformation during the last 10 years from a centrally monitored to a market-focused system. Given major financial barriers and severe cuts in federal budgeting, Russia has modernised in line with dominant trends (UBuff 2002). The 1990s reforms embraced the following basic issues:

- diversification and humanisation[3] of higher education;
- decentralisation of management and promotion of university autonomy;
- creation of a non-state/private sector.

These initiatives have set the framework for an educational structure that seeks to meet international criteria of excellence. The Law on Education of 1992, followed by its 1996 Amendment, and the HEI Statute of 1993 became the landmark legislation for democratic governance and institutional autonomy in higher education (UBuff 2002). There are *new phenomena* in Russian higher education, which fit the worldwide mainstream of post-industrial change in academia. These innovations can be grouped as follows:

- *an educational boom*, with increased numbers of higher education institutions, where commercial universities comprise almost 40 per cent of provision;
- *commercialisation* or payment for higher education, with non-budget sources of financing as a major source for many universities;
- *a second tier of higher education*, which creates a multi-stage educational system rather than the traditional 'school-university' one (Smolentseva, 2003); and
- *international foundation grants for research and teaching* as a means of internationalisation of higher education.

According to Gorbunova and Zabaev (2002), Dailey and Cardozier (2002) and Smolentseva (2003), the global educational shift has offered Russia the following tangible benefits:

- *decentralization*, which is perceived by academics and universities as a means of achieving greater academic freedom and organisational autonomy;
- 'a reasonable level of *academic freedom*'. This comment is supported by Altbach's research (Altbach 2003);
- *more flexibility in thinking* or capability for redesigning curricula and instructional methods to accommodate urgent needs; and
- *a new attitude to research*, as part of the classic triad of teaching/training, research and community service, on the one hand, and research networking activities, on the other.

Following these changes, according to Dailey and Cardozier (2002), higher education in Russia is 'more readily adaptable to the marketplace' and more pliable and creative in dealing with innovation.

However, despite these positive assessments it is evident that the cultural transition to academic capitalism presents many challenges. The collapse of the Soviet Union and the loss of employment stability caused tangible 'cultural dislocations' (Altbach 2003: 389). The immediate implementation of widespread reform also contributed to social uncertainty and bewilderment that included the academic world (Dailey and Cardozier 2002). From the 1990s reforms onwards, Russian education has been in 'a continuous state of transition' (Smolentseva 2003), moving with difficulty towards 'a new civilisation based on the values of democracy and individual freedoms' (Gorbunova and Zabaev 2002). Investigating the Russian situation in 2003, Atlbach concludes that: '… there is no other world region where higher education is as much in turmoil' (389). The impact of a series of economic crises of 1993–94 and 1998 has been devastating. This had a particularly adverse effect on the hiring of academic staff and severely damaged the quality of higher education (Smolentseva 2003).

Russian science and scientists: yesterday vs. today

Academic research in the USSR: terms and conditions

Under the socialist regime, Soviet science had three basic characteristics:

1. it was entirely monopolised by the Communist Party;
2. it was generously sponsored by the state; and
3. it was located separately from teaching.

With very few exceptions, higher education institutions in the USSR concentrated on instruction with a tiny share in fundamental research (Markusova, Minin and Libkind 2001; Markusova, Minin and Libkind 2004). As Letokhov observes, Russia definitely suffers by comparison in this dimension with the West, where 'the best scientific research of Nobel Prize standard is mostly done at universities, while Russia's research is done only at the Academy of Sciences[4] (2004). Until the 1990s, Soviet knowledge emerged in a form of 'a simbiosis … of pure science, technology and engineering', with an emphasis on military and industrial needs.

As the exclusive source of sponsorship, the Soviet state was 'pumping money into funding science on a scale matched by a few if any other governments in history' (Graham 1998: 68). Consequently, the reputation of this 'big science'[5] was very high, especially in nuclear physics and astrophysics because of their military application (Markusova *et al.* 2004). All this was happening under 'the monopoly over intellectual life exerted by the Communist Party' (Graham 1998: 17). Researchers commenting on this period remind us of 'the unnecessary level of bureaucracy' (Zuyev 1998); of the limited access to militarised research institutions, with their 'secret mailboxes' (Zueyv 1998) and, indeed, 'secret cities' (Widdis 1995: 31); and of the imprisonment of scientists who did not conform to the rules of 'soviet science' (Graham 1998). Crude political control of soviet science had a devastating effect on its quality (Soyfer 2001: 724) and also produced an economy separated from the rest of the world and the intellectual ostracism of scientists (Ismail-Zadeh 2004).

Russian science in post-modernity

However, if the working conditions of Soviet scientists are assessed from an insider perspective, these did involve relatively high levels of payment and career stability, so that security existed but at the price of independence. Financial security may well outweigh many of the current advantages offered by globalising processes in the Academy. Severe reductions of state funding following the collapse of the Soviet system leaves scientists on very low salaries (Gerber and Yarsike-Ball 2002). There is a lack of experimental equipment, that is in most cases not compensated for by external grants (Bunchuk 2005; Zuyev 1998). In addition, there may be some psychological discomfort caused by the need to adjust to market competition (Ismail-Zadeh 2004). The scientific community remains quite conservative and nostalgic for the halcyon days of state support (Ismail-Zadeh 2004). According to Zuyev (1998), fundamental research in Russia today is funded at a level that is ten times below the level at which it was funded in the USSR, with a median salary constituting employment category number ten out of the eleven available in Russia. The costs of electricity reduce capacity to use equipment by half.

Gerber and Yarsike-Ball (2002: 4) suggest that a researcher's career in Russia is similar to that of a beggar: in these conditions there is no incentive for the most capable young scholars to enter research (Zuyev: 1998). Russia is losing its most able scientists to more lucrative domains outside academia or abroad (Ismail-Zadeh 2004, Letokhov 2004), at a rate of almost 30 per cent of the scientific personnel loss at the RAS institutes[6] (Zuyev 1998). According to data from 2002, 100,000 academics left Russia taking the equivalent of US$50 billion in value to the receiving countries (Ismail-Zadeh 2004) and consequently became successful in the West (Letokhov 2004). There is a great demand for 'new young blood' (Zuyev 1998) in the 'ageing' Russia academy (Gerber and Yarsike-Ball 2002). This suggests the needs for reformers in higher education to concentrate on the politics of science 'rejuvenation' (Gerber and Yarsike-Ball 2002) or 'repatriation' (Ismail-Zadeh 2004) by creating appropriate domestic conditions and rewards.

Funding Russian science today

Given these conditions and developments, some experts suggest that Russian science is in crisis or moribund. However, Gerber and Yarsike-Ball (2002) and Sher (2000) offer a more optimistic analysis that suggests that in this transitional period Russian knowledge is 'comatose' (Gerber and Yarsike-Ball 2002). They argue that, with time, the Russian environment will stabilise and a more accessible intercollegiate dialogue on a global level will emerge (Zuyev 1998), as will new forms of funding.

In the new system of multi-channel, competitive, funding (Markusova *et al.* 2001), there are several mechanisms, discussed by Bunchuk (2005), that appear as harbingers of a renaissance of knowledge (Bush 2004):

* domestic grants, distributed by the Russian Foundation for Basic Research (RFBR)[7] and other foundations;
* grants from foreign foundations;
* cooperation programmes; and
* the entrepreneurial activities of Russian scientists.

Ismail-Zadeh (2004) states that grants and donations from foreign foundations are a major source of funding Russian science. The West has responded to the crisis in Russian science 'to a surprising degree' (Sher 2000). In an effort to 'save Soviet science', France opened a $100 million fund (Sher 2000) and the USA allocated several billion dollars (Ismail-Zadeh 2004). Among the US participants in the rescue operation are such government organisations as ISTC, NATO, INTAS and CRDF as well as NGOs, including the George Soros and the MacArthur Foundations (Ismail-Zadeh 2004). Russia and western countries jointly run exchange programmes and twinning projects that include involvement by the UK Royal Society, the Swedish Royal Academy of Sciences and the strategic alliance of the European Union Framework Programme with INTAS.

Both foreign and domestic mechanisms for funding Russian science lay a particular stress on its repatriation. For example, RFBR issues prestigious fellowships for Doctors of Science (Ismail-Zadeh 2004). To sum up, Russian 'science is increasingly taking the shape of a commercial enterprise, and scholars ... become entrepreneurs in the market of ideas' (Bunchuk 2005). Sher (2000) concludes that learning 'how to survive in today's grant-driven environment', Russian intellectuals are shaping 'a much leaner, more cosmopolitan, less defence-oriented, more competitive community of scientists'.

Educational research as a critical issue in Russian science

Russian science is considered a vehicle for steering the Russian economy. Neumann (1957) would probably find this agenda unwelcome, since he argued that science should be primarily utilised for creating societal freedom and only then for advancing technology. In 1957 he warned against the reversing of this scheme: 'the transformation of the knowledge into technology' causes 'the technology of destruction' (205), when 'technological progress is determined completely by political utility' (207). As has been already observed by Loy (2003), this manner of knowledge utilisation derives from the Soviet regime.

Nevertheless, in a landmark decision the programme 'Integration of science and higher education of Russia 2002–2006', set out by the Ministry of Economic Development and Trade, the Ministry of Finance and the Ministry of Education of the Russian Federation in 2005, gives priority to the adaptation of Russian science to the market-style economy.[8] What is clear from this programme is that the new science is to be shaped with regard to regional problems and through the collaborative activities of higher education institutions, institutes of the Russian Academy of Sciences and scientific institutions of applied research (industrial branch institutions, known as NII). The Russian Academy of Sciences particularly emphasises 'the integration of the academic, university and industrial science of Russia' to facilitate 'the economic, social and spiritual development of society' (RAS 2000).

Educational research is aligned with this over-arching purpose and is viewed as a tool for the reform of education in the new Russia (ISRE n.d.). Educational research is part of the overall development programme for education, which is 'a complex socio-economic project' (ISRE n.d.). Conceptually, it is envisaged as a merger of new applied and fundamental research to serve as 'scientific support' for promoting the federal education development programme.[9] The scientific support is needed to create the legal and organisational base and developing a new economic base for the new system of education as well as for generating new education policy. It is crucial because 'the static school pedagogy [of the Soviet Union] must be replaced by new constructive theories and methodologies' (ISRE n.d.).

It will be evident from this chapter that Russian academics face two basic problems: the identification of sponsors and the development of market-like behaviours. Social sciences, in which educational research is an important element, also face the specific challenge of designing a *new epistemology*. The Social sciences have been especially injured by the Leninist version of Marxist ideology (Loy 2003), which penetrated into the scientific consciousness in the form of lysenkoism and supported the creation of dubious and rapid results. The most evident manifestations of lysenkoism in educational research are in management and special education, so that, for example, there is:

- the application of inappropriate instructional assessment techniques (such as TQM) in research on teaching and learning;
- the rejection and avoidance of approaches to understanding and classifying special education needs and categorising students accordingly so that, for example, large

numbers of dyslexic students are admitted without diagnosis or support. The problem
is exacerbated by the need to attract students in order to generate fee income;

• the incorrect understanding and application of the term 'disabled' which has made
this term synonymous with 'outcast' in Russia.

It is possible, given this history, that in pursuit of the ideas of democracy, equity and
inclusion, educational research in Russia may benefit from the adoption of some Western
thinking and practice. However, the emancipation from Marxist ties by copying the
West has its own dangers and will not revive educational thinking and research. Some
Western traditions cannot be transplanted into Russian education without necessary
modifications because the former have 'no exact parallel in Russian pedagogical theory'
(Michailova *et al.* 2002: 423). It is apparent that Western knowledge must be adapted
and only then transferred to the Russian context in order 'to create a new theory that will
be integrated into the Russian pedagogical tradition and accessible to Russian educators'
(Mikhailova *et al.* 2002: 424). A particular example is the efforts by Michailova and
colleagues to incorporate Action Research in teacher training into Russian pedagogical
science to build a new pedagogical tradition, without disregarding the existing one (2002).
According to the report by ISRE (n.d.), western approaches must be tested, transformed
and only then applied to the Russian context. New educational research in Russia may
be described as action research and model development and testing (in terms of basic
directions) and educational evaluation and policy research (in terms of methods), delivered
through partnerships and networking activities. The networking activities enhance
research in teaching practices through the international exchange of teachers and head-
teachers, for example, through the British Council (British Council Russia, n.d.).

Knowledge production and the social construction of Russian science

A key theme, throughout this chapter, has been the extent to which research practices
and dispositions, established during the Soviet era, continue to influence Russian science
as it faces the pressures of academic capitalism. Graham (1998) suggests applying social
constructivism, derived from the sociology of knowledge, supplemented with externalist
historical perspectives,[10] to understanding the Russian context and its effects. He argues
that the Russian case offers new parameters on the issue of the relationship between
society and knowledge production. Even those who advocate neo-liberal reform accept
that Russia has been always under pressure in relation to the links between politics and
knowledge. Graham agues that Soviet scientists were generously rewarded slaves of
totalitarian ideology, they became post-Soviet intellectuals who are financially abandoned
but mentally emancipated. Financial deprivation gradually develops into entrepreneurship
in the search for new funds, which in turn produces a form of vassalage to the developing
Russian academic market.

Politicisation of Russian science is tied to funding: who pays the scientists, how
generously, how regularly and who sets the conditions of payment. In these terms, the
Soviet researcher can be described as married to the state (Ashwin 2000, Mamonova
1984) and the post-Soviet researcher is married to the market. During the period of state
marriage there were deep contradictions, for example, five Nobel Prizes in the 1930s
and 1940s (Graham 1998) on the one hand, and lysenkoism on the other. That influence

may be felt today in the opportunistic drive to achieve fast results for commercial purposes, especially aggravated by imitation of the West.

Married to the market, modern scientists have to adopt market-style competition with its rigid norms of conduct, which mean 'learning how to live in a competitive world at every level, from junior research fellow up to every academician' (Gerber and Yarsike-Ball 2002). They suggest that 'scientists are no longer free to work on what interests them: rather they are compelled to engage in work that attracts grants' (Gerber and Yarsike-Ball op. cit.). Commercialisation 'destroys the ethos of the Russian science' (Bunchuk 2005).

The pressure of commerce and enterprise has much in common with the Soviet system of 'planning for research' (Graham, 1964, 146) or planning for knowledge. Both are oriented towards the professionalisation of knowledge production and knowledge enterprise: political or ideological knowledge enterprise in the first case and commercial knowledge in the second (Loy 2003). Graham (1998: xii) asks: 'How robust is science under stress? What is more important to science, freedom or money?' Russian knowledge has survived under difficult conditions, and he concludes that such conditions produce an orientation to monetary rather than intellectual values. For example, the leading motive for academic emigration is money, and improvement of material working conditions is the most desired policy. Graham (1998: 98) argues that 'the best science will be done when both freedom and money are present'.

Recent discussions of changes from mode 1 to mode 2 knowledge (Delanty 2001; Jacob and Hellstrom 2001), highlight the significance of the control of knowledge production in Russia. When knowledge and ideology collide, who creates the approved form of knowledge? The answer to that question may still be politicians and lysenkoists: as Seitz argues, 'Legislators and bureaucrats shape the decisions that determine which paths scientific research should take' (Seitz 1995) or, as Graham puts it (1964: 146), 'plan for science'. Their message is carried forward by lysenkoists. As the Lysenko paradigm illustrates (Graham 1998; Loy 2003; Soyfer 2001), when politics seeks to control knowledge, the abnormal tends to become the norm (Kuhn 1970). The Communist Party monopoly of knowledge under the metaphorical name of 'Lysenkoism' sets many challenges for the future of research in Russia and requires a re-examination of the historical record (Graham 1998; Kuhn 1970; Neumann 1976). What does survival mean for intellectuals under such a paradigm? What bargains or compromises are necessary and how can researchers preserve their intellectual status and avoid 'intellectual degradation' (Neumann 1976)? To what extent does the new situation and the discipline of the market create conditions that sustain conformist science or that threaten the future of the new and fragile autonomous research cultures?

In the past, intellectual survival in Russia has been associated with geographical mobility (Neumann 1976). In Russian academic culture, science or research and what may be termed *parvenuation* are closely linked. The terms 'parvenu' (endless traveller or knowledge searcher) and 'pariah' (outcast) were used by Baumann in 1998 in discussing the sociology of knowledge (24), though the latter term had been coined much earlier by Max Weber as applicable to a broader sociological context (Giddens 1997). These terms capture the Russian phenomenon of the alienation of research from and by ideology and the search by Russian scientists for ways of preserving their intellectual culture and identities and avoiding the degradation of knowledge.

Russia traditionally has its own approach to the notion of territory, associated with a lack of boundaries and overabundance of space, and defined as 'a symbolic landscape' (Willis 1995: 38).[11] Russian intellectuals were traditionally understood as sojourners, travellers or truth seekers. The idea of scientific pilgrimage is important in understanding the professional attitudes and identities of Russian academics. To gain one's own intellectual place and privacy, to be able to breathe scientifically with ease, was, and perhaps is, paramount for Russian researchers who, for political or other reasons, become outcasts in their domestic culture. As Baumann (1998) suggests, globalisation makes categories such as pariah redundant, because it 'deterritorialises' (Giddens 1990), and 'compresses' the world (Robertson 1992: 8). For some researchers, this process of becoming an 'endless traveller' or 'truth seeker' is simply achieved within the framework of their own culture. Others become migrants. Academic migration means the geographical or metaphorical transmission or dislocation of the intellectual in search of another country, or geo-region, or scientific domain. In any case, it could be argued that a true researcher must 'migrate' in order to avoid stagnation and become a parvenu. Parvenuation enables researchers to identify a circle of supporters and to create their own research culture, or 'academic tribe' and research paradigm, shared within this community (Becher and Trowler 2001: 23). Parvenuation is especially meaningful for those who aim at scientific revolutions (Kuhn 1970.) Talented Russian researchers might be categorised as: *Intelligentsia* (traditional, pre-Soviet and early-Soviet, intelligentsia); *Dissidents* or *dissenting intelligentsia*; and participants in the *brain drain*, comprising *global labour* or *globalists* (itinerant scholars (Neumann 1976) and emigrants). As indicated above, the current migration of Russian researchers seems to be economically rather than intellectually driven, and, while mobility may increase, 'parvenuation' may be disappearing as a phenomenon of Russian intellectual life. This, perhaps, is another feature of globalisation's effects on intellectual and academic culture in Russia.

Conclusion

Two basic points emerge from the discussion above. First, Russian science is, and has been, greatly impaired and suffers from severe intellectual and financial difficulties, some of them historically rooted, some related to the rapid modernisation and marketisation of the system. Both the Soviet regime and the changes following its breakdown are contributory factors to the current difficulties. Some writers believe that Russian knowledge is being resurrected and revitalised in the present modernisation process. Others see its condition as 'comatose' (Gerber and Yarsike-Ball 2002), with unpredictable outcomes. What is undeniable is the dependence of the functioning of science and the development of scientific careers on a risky and unstable external environment. Secondly, the case of Russia is a distinctive one, and throws into particularly sharp relief some of the trends in academic migration, commercialisation and economic pressures that feature in the reshaping of the academy globally. Within that general situation there is particular and specific pressure on educational research, which is harnessed to the modernisation project, and which is charged with considerable responsibilities while simultaneously seeking to develop, in a balanced way, making appropriate use of some Western research practices while seeking to maintain some indigenous characteristics.

Notes

1 According to the social construction thesis, the state of intellectual life and knowledge development depends on the external environment and on the societal processes. See Graham (1998) for more detail.
2 See Appadurai (1996: 33–7).
3 Humanisation of education is meant to convey a shift to accommodating individual instructional needs.
4 The Russian Academy of Sciences (RAS) was founded as the country's fundamental research hub. For more detail, refer to the website of the RAS: http://www.ras.ru. Specific information about the Academy's history can be found at http://www.pran.ru/eng/history/.
5 The term 'big science' is used by Kojevnikov (2002: 421).
6 RAS or the Russian Academy of Sciences has a network of academic institutions, where the major part of the country's fundamental research is conducted. These institutions recruit the most talented scientists and offer post-graduate (PhD and Doctor of Science) programmes of study.
7 RFBR is 'a government organization whose primary goal is to support the most promising research initiatives in all fields of fundamental science on a competitive basis. Nearly 70 per cent of its budget is to support research groups and individual scientists' (Markusova *et al.* 2001: 541). For more detail, refer to the RFBR website: http://www.rfbr.ru/.
8 More information on this programme can be found on the website: http://www.informika.ru/text/goscom/ntp/pol.html.
9 The fundamental research in Russia is conducted in the academic institutions of the Russian Academy of Sciences, higher education institutions and in some industrial branch institutes (NIIs).
10 Graham (1998) refers to the analysis provided by sociologists (the social construction hypothesis) and *the externalist school of historians*. Externalists consider scientific phenomena in historical perspective as *shaped by external conditions* or external environment, for example, Neumann (1957, 1976).
11 This perception of territory conveys a keener sense of geographical domain in the light of the 'shifting borders of the real [Russian] landscape', affiliated with the USSR political map dissection (Widdis 1995: 33), and assists in comprehending the place of parvenuation in Russian culture.

References

Altbach, P. (2001) 'Academic freedom: international realities and challenges', *Higher Education* 41: 205–19.
Altbach, P. (2003) 'Introduction to higher education theme issue on the academic profession in Central and Eastern Europe', *Higher Education*, 45: 389–90.
Appadurai, A. (1996). *Modernity at Large*, Minneapolis, MN: University of Minnesota Press.
Ashwin, S (2000) *Gender, State and Society in Soviet and Post-Soviet Russia*, London and New York: Routledge.
Azmanova, A. (1992) 'Dictatorships of freedom', *Praxis International*, 12(2): 144–57.
Bauman, Z. (1990) 'Modernity and ambivalence', in M. Featherstone (ed.) *Global Culture: Nationalism, Globalization and Modernity*, London: Sage Publications.
Bauman, Z. (1998) *Globalizatoin: The Human Consequences*, Cambridge: Cambridge University Press.
Becher, T. and Trowler, P. (2001) *Academic Tribes and Territories*, 2nd edn, Buckingham: Society for Research into Higher Education and Open University Press.
British Council Russia (n.d.) 'Partnerships in education', Retrieved 22 June 2005 from: http://www.britishcouncil.org/ru/russia-partnership-education.htm.
Brooks, N. (1998) 'Alexander Butlerov and the professionalization of science in Russia', *Russian Review*, 57(1): 10–24.

Bunchuk, M. (2005). 'The impact of the new funding mechanisms on Russian natural sciences', Abstract. Retrieved 26 May 2005 from: http://www.geocities.com/CollegePark/Lab/5590/absimp.htm.

Bush, J. (2004, August 9). 'A renaissance for Russian science'. *Business Week On-line.* Retrieved 26 May 2005 from: http://www.businessweek.com/magazine/content/04_32/b3895103_mz018.htm.

Burbules, N. and Torres, C. (2000) 'Globalization and education: an introduction', in N. Burbules and C. Torres (eds) *Globalization and Education: Critical Perspective*, New York: Routledge, 1–26.

Castells, M. (1997) *The Information Age: Economy, Society and Culture. Volume 2. The Power of Identity*, Oxford: Blackwell Publishers.

CRDF Immediate Release (2005, May 12) 'MacArthur Foundation $10 million grant helps CRDF strengthen research capacity of Russian universities', CDRF News and Press Releases. Retrieved 7 June 2005 from: http://www.crdf.org/News/051205macarthur.htm.

Dailey, M. and Cardozier, V. (2002) 'Higher education in Russia', Retrieved 17 October 2004 from: http://studentorgs.utexas.edu/heaspa/library/rus.htm.

Deem, R. and Johnson, R. (2003) 'Risking the university? Learning to be a manager academic in UK universities', *Sociological Research Online*, 8(3).

Delanty, J. (2001) *Challenging Knowledge: The University in the Knowledge Society*, Buckingham: SRHE and Open University Press.

Gerber, P. and Yarsike-Ball, D. (2002) 'From crisis to transition: the state of Russian science based on focus groups with nuclear physicists', *PONARS Policy Memo 220*, Washington, DC: PONARS Policy Conference.

Giddens, A. (1990) *The Consequences of Modernity*, Cambridge: Polity Press.

Giddens, A. (1997) *Sociology*, 3rd edn, Cambridge: Polity Press.

Gorbunova, E. and Zabaev, I. (2002) 'The role of universities in the transformation of societies: an international research project', Retrieved 17 October 2004 from: http://www.open.ac.uk/cheri/Trmsesprgress.htm.

Graham, L. (1964) 'Bukharin and the planning of science', *Russian Review*, 23(2): 135–48.

Graham, L. (1998) *What Have we Learned about Science and Technology from the Russian Experience?*, Stanford, CA: Stanford University Press.

Ismail-Zadeh, A. (2004) 'Russian science in transition', *EuroScience News*, 26: 9–11.

ISRE (n.d.) 'ISRE virtual newsletter: the reform of education in new Russia'. Retrieved 20 June 2005 from: http://www.indiana.edu/~isre?NEWSLETTER/vol16no2/OECD_CH5.htm.

Jacob, M. and Hellstrom, T. (2001) *The Future of Knowledge Production in the Academy*, Buckingham: SRHE and Open University Press.

Kellner, D. (2002) 'Globalization and new social movements: lessons for critical theory and pedagogy', in N. Burbules and C. Torres (eds) *Globalization and Education: Critical Perspective*, New York: Routledge, 299–322.

Kojevnikov, A. (2002) 'The Great War, the Russian Civil War, and the invention of big science', *Science in Context*, 15(2): 239–75, Cambridge: Cambridge University Press.

Kuhn, T. (1970) *The Structure of Scientific Revolutions*, 2nd edn, Princeton, NJ: Princeton University Press.

Letokhov, V. (2004, October 18) 'Science reforms hopelessly lagging behind', *Pravda*, Retrieved 26 May 2005 from: http://english.pravda.ru/science/19/94/377/14459_Science.html.

Loy, J. (2003) 'Trofim Denisovich Lysenko', Retrieved 25 May 2005 from: www.jimloy.com/biograph/lysenko.htm.

Mamonova, T. (1984) *Women and Russia*, Oxford: Basil Blackwell.

Markusova, V., Minin, V, Libkind, A. and Arapov, M. (2001) 'Russian grant-holders' opinion on competitive funding: results of a survey', *Scientometrics*, 51(3): 541–51.

Markusova, V., Minin, V., Libkind, A., Jansz, M., Zitt, M. and Bassecoulard-Zitt, E. (2004) 'Research in non-metropolitan universities as a new stage of science development in Russia', *Scientometrics*, 60(3): 365–83.

Michailova, N., Yusfin, S. and Polyakov, S. (2002) 'Using action research in current conditions of Russian teacher education', *Educational Action Research*, 10(3): 423–48.

Morrow, R. and Torres, C. (2000) 'The state, globalization, and educational policy', in N. Burbules and C. Torres (eds) *Globalization and Education: Critical Perspective*, New York: Routledge. 27–57.

Neumann, F. (1957). *The Democratic and the Authoritarian State: Essays in Political and Legal History*, Glencoe, IL: Free Press.

Neumann, F. (1976) 'The intelligentsia in exile', in P. Connerton (ed.) *Critical Sociology*, London: Penguin Books, 423–41.

Robertson, R.(1992) *Globalization: Social Theory and Global Culture*, Thousand Oaks, CA: Sage Publications.

Russian Academy of Sciences (2000) 'The primary objectives of the Russian Academy of Sciences', Retrieved 22 June 2005 from: http://www.intertec.co.at/itc2/partners/RAS/Default.htm.

Seitz, F. (1995) 'The present danger to science and society', *COSMOS: Science and Society*. Retrieved 19 April 2005 from: http://www.cosmos-club.org/journals/1995/seitz.html.

Sher, G. (2000) 'Why should we care about Russian science?' *Science*, 289, 389.

Smolentseva, S. (2003) 'Challenges to the Russian academic profession', *Higher Education*, 41: 390–423.

Slaughter, S. and Leslie, L. (1997) *Academic Capitalism*, Baltimore, MD: Johns Hopkins University Press.

Soyfer, V. (2001, August) 'The consequences of political dictatorship for Russia science', *Nature* 2: 723–9.

UBuff – SUNY/University at Buffalo, The State University of New York (2002) 'The Russian federation: The International Comparative higher Education Finance and Accessibility Project'. Retrieved 17 October 2004 from: http://www.gse.buffalo.edu/org/inthigheredfinance/region_europe_Russia.html.

Widdis, E. (1995) 'Russia as space', in S. Franklin and E. Widdis (eds) *National Identity in Russian Culture: An Introduction*, Cambridge: Cambridge University Press, 30–50.

Zuyev, K. (1998, June 11) 'Russian science in peril', *Moscow Times*. Retrieved 26 May 2005 from: http://www.prometeus.nsc.ru/science/scidig/june.ssi#1.

9 The politics of educational research in contemporary postcolonial Malaysia

Discourses of globalisation, nationalism and education

Cynthia Joseph

Introduction

The contradictions and tensions between Malaysia's prevailing institutionalisation of educational research and its engagement with the knowledge-based economy and the need to grow are examined in this chapter. The Malaysian political and cultural context of educational research offers interesting insights about the clash of globalised, national agendas of educational research and postcoloniality.

The first section of this chapter provides a brief discussion of the important concepts used to unpack the politics of educational research in contemporary Malaysia. A critical understanding of policy with interconnections to the Foucauldian notion of discourse and power (Foucault 1980, 1982) and feminist theorisations of the notion of difference (Brah 1996; Mohanty 1994; Weedon 1999) is adopted. The second section of this chapter unpacks these concepts within the context of contemporary postcolonial Malaysia and extends the debate to the politics of education and educational research. This discussion is also considered in the interplay between the global, national and institutional levels. The next section draws on my own experiences as a Malaysian-Indian academic and researcher in Malaysia and now as a Malaysian-Indian academic located within Australian academe. The concluding section focuses on the contradictions and tensions between Malaysian and Western-Eurocentric orientations to research at the levels of practice, organisation and institutionalisation.

Theoretical framework: the interplay of discourse, power and difference in the politics of policy

A critical approach to the politics of policy is used as an overarching conceptual framework to unpack the interplay between educational research and policy in contemporary postcolonial Malaysia. The notion of policy as conceptualised within such a framework is understood not only as a document or a product but as a continuous, complex and political process (Ball 1990; Colebatch 2002; Taylor *et al.* 1997). Ball (1990) argues that 'policy cannot be divorced from interests, from conflict, from domination or from justice' (p. 3). Whose values are validated in policy and whose are not are linked to the power play between the dominant groups and other groups in society (Ball 1990; Gale 2003; Taylor *et al.* 1997). Notions of discourse, power and difference are important to such critical understandings of the politics of policy. These concepts enable researchers to contextualise and historicise the notion of policy. The complexities of the interplay of the various social dimensions such as race, ethnicity, class and gender are also considered in unpacking the politics of policy within this conceptual framework.

A Foucauldian analysis of power uses the notion of discourse to examine practices through which power is exercised (Sarup 1993; Weedon 1999). Foucault wants to shift the attention from questions such as 'who has the power?' to the processes by which subjects and objects are constituted as effects of power (Sarup 1993). Foucault argues that relations of power cannot themselves be established, consolidated not implemented without the production, accumulation, circulation and functioning of a discourse.

While individuals are the vehicles of power, power relations have come more and more under state control (Foucault 1982). Power relations have been elaborated, rationalised and centralised under the auspices of state institutions. This does not discount discourses that are sustained through the power relations within a specific site that might operate either in harmony or in opposition with the wider societal power relations. The intertwining of power and knowledge is important in examining the interplay between policy and educational research. Foucault (1977: 27) states that 'the production of knowledge is always bound up with historically specific regimes of power and, therefore, every society produces its own truths which have a normalizing and regulatory function'.

Foucault posits that power is a dynamic of control, compliance and lack of control between discourses and the subjects constituted by discourses, who are their agents (Weedon 1999). Discourse is a historically, socially and institutionally specific structure of statements, terms, categories and beliefs (Foucault 1980). Discourses represent political interests and are constantly vying for status and power (Weedon 1999). Discourses authorise what can be said and what cannot be said. There are discourses that constrain the production of knowledge, dissent and difference and those discourses that enable new knowledges and difference (Foucault 1980, 1982; Weedon 1999).

The notion of difference is also intertwined with the politics of power in examining the intertwining of policy and educational research. Difference here is not just attributed to diversity but to differences that are embedded within webs of power as argued by Mohanty (1994). Whose values, interests and knowledge are validated and silenced in research practices is located within hierarchies of power that are linked to the interplay of social dimensions such as ethnicity, class and gender.

Research in Malaysia: then and now

Research practices do not exist in isolation within the culture of academe. The political, economic and educational agendas of a nation shape the politics of research at the national, institutional and individual levels. Globalisation, new regionalism, supranational political forms, information technology and diasporic public (Appadurai 1996; Lingard 2001) also impinge on the interplay between policy and educational research.

The unique character of multiethnic contemporary postcolonial Malaysian society provides a non-Eurocentric context in understanding the link between the global, national, meso and micro in doing educational research. The politics of ethnic identification are deeply embedded within institutional, societal and personal practices in multiethnic Malaysia. I use the term 'politics of ethnic identification' to refer to the multiple and shifting power dynamics related to the social, economic and educational privileges and positionings associated with the official ethnic labellings. The official public and political discourse on identity in Malaysian society categorises each Malaysian as either *Bumiputera*, Chinese, Indian or Others. These communal divisions in multiethnic Malaysia with these major ethnic groups have resulted in contestation as well as encouraged consultation and compromise (Lee 2000).

The *Bumiputeras* are Malays and other indigenous people who constitute 67.3 per cent of the society (Malaysia 2001). This group has indigenous status that guarantees them attendant privileges. The Malays, the largest ethnic group, comprise 80 per cent of the *Bumiputera* category and exercise political dominance and monopolise the public and government sector. All Malays are Muslim and speak Malay. The standard form of Malay is the official and national language of Malaysia.

The Chinese and the Indians constitute 24.5 per cent and 7.2 per cent of the Malaysian population respectively (Malaysia 2001). The Chinese ethnic collective, a significant minority, monopolise the private or corporate business sector having had the historical experience of capital accumulations (Phang 2000). The Indians lag behind economically, educationally and socially in comparison to the Malays and Chinese (Santhiram 1999). These are the three major ethnic groups but there are also minor groups who trace their ancestries through intermarriage and cultural diffusion from inter-ethnic interactions centuries ago. Another group is the *Orang Asli*, who are the aboriginal people of Peninsular Malaysia.

The notion of ethnicity as played out within the Malaysian context is socially constructed and discursively produced and always involves a political dimension (Brah 1996, Mac an Ghail 1999, Yuval-Davis 1997). Past and present political events also contribute to heterogeneity between and within the ethnic groups in contemporary Malaysia. There is the historical context of colonial rule premised on division that brought about the social and economic imbalance of the ethnic groups (Andaya and Andaya 2001). Independence in 1957 brought with it nationalistic feelings and intense identifications. The ethnic bargaining during Independence and the 1969 ethnic riots led to implementation of various state policies to address the economic, social and educational imbalance amongst the ethnic groups brought about by British colonisation. These policies generally ensure that the affirmative action policy for the *Bumiputera* remain untouched. Islam also plays an important role in the in the dynamics of Malaysian society. Ong (1999) describes Islam in contemporary Malaysia as a patchwork of the most liberal as well as radical strands of Islam. There is also the emergence of a Malaysian middle class due to the period of economic boom in the late 1980s and early 1990s. This new middle class on the one hand wanted national security and are consumption-oriented, yet they also demanded greater democratic space and were critical of issues concerning democracy, political transparency, good governance, abuses of power and corruption. Malaysians in contemporary postcolonial Malaysia constantly negotiate competing and contradictory ideological discourses of colonialism, globalisation, nationalism, capitalism, Islam, populism and ethnic politics.

State policies and structures are structured along ethnic lines as well as classed and gendered. Most of the top government leaders and department heads are Malay-Muslims. Affirmative action policies for the *Bumiputera* still guide the practices of the government sector in Malaysia. There is a discourse of 'Malayness' or '*Bumiputera-ness*' within the public and government sectors. The leaders and top management echelon of most multinational companies within the corporate sectors tend to be Chinese. There is a discourse of 'Chineseness' within the corporate sectors. However, this does not discount exceptions to this general patterning. There are discourses that are sustained through the power relations within specific sites or context that might operate either in harmony or in opposition with the wider societal power relations. Furthermore, there is the interplay between the state and the corporate sectors.

These negotiations, contradictions and tensions in the sociocultural and sociopolitical scenario of contemporary Malaysia are played out within the politics of educational research in contemporary Malaysia in different ways. The next section of this chapter will examine these contradictions in discussing Malaysia's recent engagement with the global agenda of the knowledge-based economy, Malaysian educational strategies and plans that relate to educational research and the culture of Malaysian academe.

The politics of educational research in contempory Malaysia

Global influences

The Malaysian government in wanting to be globally competitive and part of the global hierarchy, where there is a privileging of Western/Eurocentric and malecentric ways of education, research and knowledge production, engaged with the notion of a knowledge-based economy. This notion of a knowledge-based economy is the dominant discourse of transnational agencies and OECD countries with Eurocentric ideologies. Knowledge, creativity and innovation are considered the driving forces for the economic success of a nation. The Malaysian government launched the Knowledge-based Economy Masterplan in 2002. The discourse of a knowledge-based economy, as adopted by Malaysia advocates for an economy in which knowledge, creativity and innovation plays an important role in generating and sustaining growth (Malaysia 2002). One of the recommendations in this Masterplan is the improvement of the quality of research, researcher and academicians.

Dominant discourses operating within the OECD educational policies and practices in the present globalising times are focused around 'an ascendant neo-liberal paradigm of policy in which education has been largely (though not solely) framed as human capital investment and development. Such a paradigm serves to legitimate a set of educational values feeding off and feeding into the broader culture of rampant individualism and consumerism unleashed by the ideological victory of capitalism over communism' (Burbules and Torres 2000: 175). The notion of education as advocated by the OECD now operates within the global economic framework (Henry *et al.* 2001). The importance of a highly skilled and flexible workforce within the global knowledge economy is important to national success. A culture of performativity where performance indicators are used to assess the success of an education system are emphasised within such a model. Burbules and Torres (2000) argue that the interplay between discourses of globalisation and neoliberalism are played out within the implementation and ideology of bilaterial, multilaterial and international organisations through an educational agenda with particular policies for evaluation, financing, assessment, standards, teacher training, curriculum, instruction and testing.

Malaysia aims to achieve the OECD benchmarks of economic, social and educational success through the development of various policies and programmes so as to be positioned within the global hierarchy of knowledge and power. The discourse of knowledge-based economy as advocated for by Malaysian government focuses on developing an individual's creative, innovative and analytical as well as learning abilities and skills. Information Communication Technology and moral values are important as well. The knowledge-worker is represented as one who 'should have a strong formal education, have learned how to learn, have a habit of continuing to learn throughout his or her lifetime, be an expert or learn throughout his or her lifetime, be an expert or specialist and be able to work in a team' (Amat 2001: 107).

In Malaysia's aspirations to be part of this transnational and neo-liberal ideology of a knowledge-based economy, Malaysians would need to be located within an educational environment that encourages and develops the intellectual and social potential of researchers and workforce that are highly skilled, globally competitive, ICT-savvy, analytical, creative and place importance on cultural mores adhered to by the Malaysian society and ethnic collectives. Educational research would have to be cutting-edge, highly creative and innovative and at the same time taking into account the global and national needs of the nation and her peoples. The knowledges generated from such educational research will emphasise the ways in which the intellectual, social and cultural potentials of Malaysians can be fully realised in order to move the nation forward in present globalising and transitional times.

However, there are tensions and contradictions between the nation's global aspirations and the discourse of education and educational research as advocated in the practices of the various Malaysian educational institutions. A number of Malaysianists have written on the discrepancy between stated objectives of educational policies and the planned strategies that are outlined for the achievement of these objectives (Lee 2004; Loo 2000). Education and educational research in Malaysia is highly politicised and ethnicised. This is further exacerbated by the institutionalisation of ethnic politics as manifested through the politics of ethnic identification. The Malaysian government does take into account the educational needs of the ethnic groups, but always ensures that the dominance of the *Bumiputera*-Malay ethnic collective is never threatened within the state's machinery and politics. Such practices create ethnic, economic and educational divisions and inequalities between and within the different ethnic groups in Malaysia. The hierarchies that result from these practices are disadvantageous to the nation's aspirations and goals of developing a productive and creative workforce where all citizens are able to contribute significantly to the knowledge-based economy.

Educational practices that promote social and educational inequalities result in an unequal distribution of social and economic benefits that do not contribute to the prosperity and progress of the nation. Connell (1993) states: 'Education systems are busy institutions. They are vibrantly involved in the production of social hierarchies. Further, education is centrally involved in the creation of social identities for groups who are stake-holders in the system' (p. 27).

Every child, youth and adult in Malaysia has to have access to educational opportunities that will enable them to develop their maximum potential for the notion of the knowledge-based economy to be successfully implemented in contemporary multiethnic Malaysia. This is the challenge for Malaysia.

Competing discourses of globalisation, nationalism and the politics of ethnic identification shape the agendas and practices of educational research in Malaysia. The next section examines the policies and strategies guiding education and educational research in Malaysia.

National influences: policies guiding educational research

There are no specific education policies that relate to educational research in Malaysia. However, there are major strategies and plans that are considered as policy. The discourses that are represented in these strategies and plans guide the educational agenda and practices which in turn drive the agenda of educational research. As argued by Luke (2003), policy should be understood as 'something which is historically produced through discourse generative zones, their everyday exchanges of capital and face-to-face dynamics' (p. 97).

Strategies and plans for education and educational research developed in the 1970s, 1980s and early 1990s aimed at transforming Malaysia from a commodity-export country to an industrialised and developed country. Such measures also focused on developing a national Malaysian system of education and moving away from the influence of the British colonial system. In recent years, Malaysia has also had to engage with the global agenda of education and research, and at the same time maintaining a Malaysian culture in its state's machineries in the midst of the ethnic politics.

The current official and public discourses on education are the Education Development Plan (2001–10) and the Eighth Malaysia Plan (2001–5). In addition to these, there is the Vision 2020 plan to ensure that Malaysia becomes a crucial player in the global scene in being globally competitive in areas of economic and educational activities by the year 2020. The official discourse on Vision 2020 promotes this plan as an instrument for promoting national unity, social equality and economic development (Lee 2000). Education is seen as a major vehicle for achieving the objectives of Vision 2020.

The Malaysian Ministry of Education developed the Education Development Plan for Malaysia (2001–10) or the Blueprint as the official and public discourse on education development in present globalising times. The Blueprint focuses on the development and strengthening of preschool, primary, secondary and tertiary education levels through the development of support programmes, funding, management and integration of information and communication technology. This Blueprint 'takes into account the goals and aspirations of the National Vision Policy to build a resilient nation, encourage the creation of a just society, maintain sustainable economic growth, develop global competitiveness, build a knowledge-based economy, strengthen human resource development, and maintain sustainable environment development' (Malaysian Ministry of Education 2001: 2). This plan outlines specific strategic action plans aimed at producing a research and development culture of international standards within higher education institutions. These action plans include providing appropriate infrastructure, incentives, research grants and facilities for a dynamic research culture; increasing the number of researchers and research centres; and facilitating the growth of a research culture in both the public and private education sectors. Collaborative efforts between public and private higher education institutions; and industry and international organisations are also emphasised in this plan.

The Eighth Malaysia Plan outlines strategies and programmes to ensure the nation's growth strategy from being input-driven towards one that is knowledge-driven with an emphasis given to improving management and organisational techniques, upgrading research and development and science and technology as well as strengthening innovative capacity (Malaysia 2001). In relation to research and development, there is a drive to restructure existing research and development institutions to undertake more market-oriented activities, promote technology applications in industry as well as expand and strengthen science and technology manpower.

These public and official discourses clearly indicate an education and research agenda that will enable Malaysia to be competitive in the global arena. Notions of social justice, economic growth and global competitiveness are represented in these discourses. However, as discussed earlier, the Malaysian education system and research agenda that are portrayed as unbiased systems are full of tensions and contradictions. These contradictions are examined in relation to the interplay between the national, institutional practices and professional of researchers as played out within the Malaysian academe.

Institutional practices: the culture of Malaysian academe

The 2003 OECD data indicates that, in comparison to international standards, Malaysia is under-performing in research and development in education and higher education, even though Malaysia has a high public expenditure on education and tertiary education. The Research and Development funding overall is at 0.5 per cent of GDP which is well below levels in the OECD countries. This figure is also much too low for Malaysia to be internationally competitive in research. Malaysian academics have a research publications output that is much lower than countries like Australia, Ireland and Singapore (Taskforce on Higher Education and Society 2000).

The public Malaysian universities and the Malaysian Ministry of Education are the major institutions in Malaysia that conduct educational research (Keeves *et al.* 2003). Educational research in Malaysia is conducted by university lecturers and ministry officials who have academic training. The main foci of this research has been on curriculum, language education, teacher education and on the educational development of the system (Keeves *et al.* 2003). The Ministry of Science, Technology and Environment through its Intensified Research Priority Areas Funding Program is also a major player in the funding for educational research in Malaysia. The major priorities in Malaysian research are in the field of study of Applied Sciences and Technologies (MASTIC 2000) with more than half the funded research in ICTs and Engineering. There is now a move from research focusing on construction-related applications and ICTs to research in the life sciences, medical technologies and biotechnologies in keeping with the global trends. The spending on social sciences, which includes the field of education was 3.8 per cent of the total. There is a privileging of research in the applied sciences and technology field over the social sciences in the allocation of national expenditure.

In 2002, there were in existence 11 public universities, 5 university colleges, 6 polytechnics and 27 teacher-training colleges (Lee 2004). The Malaysian state is the main provider to public higher education in allocating financial resources to institutions of higher learning, research and capital expenditures (Lee 2004). In the late 1990s with the massification of higher education and the Asian economic crises the Malaysian government encouraged the private sector to play an active role in the provision of higher education (Lee 2004). The number of private educational institutions has increased from 156 institutions in 1992 to 707 in 2002 (Lee 2004). Most of these private educational institutions are profit-oriented enterprises and do not have a strong research agenda. This liberalisation of government policies towards private higher education is also due to the lack of places in the public institutions of higher learning to meet the increasing demands as well as the ethnic quota system. The ethnic quota system in public universities determines access and success along ethnic lines.

The private educational institutions in Malaysia offer transnational educational programmes through institutional arrangements with foreign universities from Australia, the UK, the USA and Canada. These institutions offer their educational programmes to students on Malaysian soil. Some overseas universities like Monash University, Curtin University and Nottingham University have also set up branch campuses in Malaysia. The institutional arrangements can take the form of twining programmes, credit-transfer, external degrees, distance learning and joint programmes (Lee 2004).

The Malaysian government also corporatised some of the public universities in line with the global trend of changing universities into enterprises and to develop corporate culture and practices that enable them to compete in the marketplace (Lee 2004). However, there is a lack of institutional autonomy within Malaysian public universities and other public educational institutions as the Malaysian government exerts its authority over the administrative, academic and financial operations of these higher education institutions. Furthermore, the Malaysian government provides most of the funding for public universities.

The governance of all Malaysian public universities and colleges comes under the Universities and University Colleges Act (UCCA) of 1971 (Lee 2004). Under this Act, the Malaysian government has total control over student enrolment, staff appointment, educational programmes and financing. The Ministry of Education determines the appointment of Vice-Chancellors and Deputy Vice-Chancellors and these appointments are political in nature.

The 1975 amendment of UCCA forbids students or academics from being affiliated to any political party or trade union or to be involved in any political activities. Legislation is also used by the Malaysian government to ban academics and students from participation in shaping public discourses and national debates (Lee 2004). The UCCA was further amended in 1995 but these restrictions were not removed. These amendments were related to the governing structure within universities, namely the reduction in the size of the university senate and council which has led to the further erosion of the academics' power in the governance of the university. Teaching staff in the private educational institutions have even less power in the governance and management of their institutions. These institutions are governed by a board of governors or directors, who are representatives from the stakeholders of these institutions.

There are also various measures put into place at the national level to curb dissent and these practices filter down to the various educational institutions. There exist articles of legislation that are used to curb civil liberties: the Internal Security Act (ISA), Official Secrets Act (OSA), Printing and Presses Act (PPA) and the Sedition Act (SA). An important tool in implementing Malay economic and cultural policies is the Sedition Act. This Act prohibits public or even parliamentary questioning on constitutional matters that are regarded as 'sensitive issues'. These issues include the sovereignty of the Malay rulers as they symbolically represent the Malays' exclusive historical link with the country. Others are the Malays' special privilege, status of Malay as the official and national language, the status of Islam as the official religion and the citizenship rights of non-Malays. The government may also prohibit any other controversial issue if it is perceived to directly or indirectly challenge political stability.

This discourse of fear and control as manifested through the various articles of legislation and Acts limits academic freedom in Malaysia. A critical research approach to examining issues to do with the ethnic politics and other politically sensitive topics is not encouraged in Malaysian academic research. Lee (2004) argues that there have been cases of censorship of research findings which are considered to be politically sensitive by the powers that be.

The politics of ethnic identification at the national level is also translated into academic, research and management practices within these institutions. There is a dominant discourse of Malay-*Bumiputera* bureaucracy within Malaysian public universities as most of the university staff are *Bumiputera* Malay-Muslims. There are spaces for the non-Malays within these institutions but again this is political and strategic to ensure the dominancy and power of the *Bumiputera*-Malay ethnic collective.

The majority of academics in the public sector are *Bumiputeras* while most of the teaching staff in the private sector are non-*Bumiputeras*, generally the Chinese. Furthermore, the majority of students enrolled in the private sector are non-*Bumiputeras*, generally the Chinese and the majority of students in the public universities are *Bumiputeras*. The educational institutions within the private sector are located within a hierarchy with the financially successful and top colleges having a majority of Chinese students and top management and teaching staff members. The ethnic divide is also linked to class as the interplay between these social dimensions determines access and success to educational opportunities within both the public and private educational sectors.

The ethnic politics at the national level has impacted on the opportunities for career advancement for non-*Bumiputera* academics in public universities. There are hardly any non-*Bumiputeras* who hold positions higher than the deanship. The few non-*Bumiputera* deans and deputy deans are tokenistic in nature. The promotion exercise to associate professor or professor is also embedded within the politics of ethnic identification in Malaysia. The promotion exercise is also not very transparent or democratic (Lee 2004). The ethnic politics in Malaysian public universities and general lack of meritocracy have caused much frustration and grievances among the non-*Bumiputera* academics and this has resulted in a brain drain with a number of these academics migrating to overseas countries like Singapore, Hong Kong and Australia.

The politics of academe in Malaysia is complex. The public universities, where most of the educational research is conducted, are highly bureaucratic and hierarchical in its administrative culture and this in turn impacts on the academic culture. This academic bureaucratic culture has also degraded academia in Malaysia. Lee (2004) argues that:

> The development of such a culture has also tightened the government's grip on the universities because many of the academic bureaucrats would turn to the government and political leadership for recognition and rewards which have nothing to do with academic achievements.
>
> (Lee 2004: 109)

Lee further adds that:

> Academics are no longer promoted based on academic performance but based on non-academic criteria such as 'favouritism, political patronage, administrative experience and other kinds of cronyism' (Pernyataan 1985).

This form of politics has resulted in many of the academics who are promoted to leadership positions lacking in intellectual rigour and academic leadership.

Language also plays an important issue in the knowledge production through research activities in Malaysian universities. Generally, the medium of instruction in most of the programmes in public universities tend to be the Malay language. There is an increasing decline in the standard of English of Malaysian academics and university students (Lee 2004). There are academics and students who are unable to engage critically with the international body of literature in their particular field which are in the English language.

Other factors like the lack of recognition given to research and international publications also contribute to the lack of motivation to do research. Lee (2004) argues that the majority of Malaysian academics believe that research and publications make little difference to their promotion. Lee (2004) quotes Osman (1999) in stating that 'what matters are their political stance and connections'. Such an academic environment also results in the lack of networking between Malaysian academics and the international intellectual community.

The absence of post-doctoral fellowships and research is also a significant gap in the research system in Malaysia. There is a low proportion of PhDs completed by Malaysians who are trained inside Malaysia. There is also low level of incentives for research collaboration between universities.

There is research that is commissioned by various government agencies, statutory bodies and private companies. This form of research may focus on the client's social or national needs. This form of research tends not to be critical in nature.

The interplay of various contradictory discourses as represented through the strategic action plans, legislative documents and practices contribute to weakness of research capacity and of research activity among academics and researchers. This culture of educational research is also prevalent within other Ministry agencies and departments that conduct educational research. This is turn impacts on the educational research agenda for Malaysia

Such a discourse of academia within the Malaysian public universities with the politics of ethnic identification and the '*Bumiputera*-isation' of academe and the entrepreneurship of the private higher education institutions have led to the lack of intellectual rigour in educational research in Malaysia. The research environment in general does not encourage cutting-edge research which can contribute to the global competitiveness of the nation and the social, economic and educational development of the nation and her ethnic collectives along the lines of democracy and social justice. This is the general representation of the state of educational research in Malaysia. However, I do not wish to discount that there are spaces and discourses operating within these dominant discourses that enable a small number of educational researchers in Malaysia to engage critically with notions of intellectual rigour, social justice and democracy in their professional and academic practices.

Contradictions in research practice

These conflicts, challenges and negotiations in doing educational research in Malaysia are examined through the micro-politics of experiences of a Malaysian-Indian academic. I draw on my experiences as an educator and researcher within the Malaysian schooling and university sectors in unpacking the politics of doing educational research in Malaysia.

Two major research projects are discussed in relation to this. The first, doing my doctorate as a Malaysian doctoral researcher in an Australian university. The second, my experiences and involvement in a research consultancy project funded by the United Nations Development Programme (UNDP) and the Prime Minister's Department of Malaysia that examined the Malaysian schooling and the other education sectors against OECD indicators and the benchmark countries of Ireland, Korea and Australia. Both research contexts were of different scales, had different funding sources and had different impacts.

I am now located within an Australian university, teaching and researching in the areas of Critical Social Theory and International Education. I had taught and did research for 3½ years in a Malaysian university before going to Australia to pursue my doctorate in 1999. In my doctorate research (Joseph 2003), I investigated differences and similarities in personal and collective identities in ways of being Malay, Chinese and Indian schoolgirls within the context of schooling as an institutional practice. I used the notion of resistance as an analytical tool, emphasising its sociopolitical significance and multidimensionality, to understand the complex link between ways of being Malay, Chinese and Indian schoolgirls, schooling and the wider Malaysian society. The doctoral research was very much linked to my own personal journey and life experiences as a Malaysian-Indian female – as a school and university student and university lecturer located within the interplay of discourses of the politics of ethnic identification, education and other competing and contradictory discourses.

I had always wanted to examine the link between gender and ethnicity in ways of being and knowing in Malaysia as this was very much part of my experiences. I was told when I was doing my Masters at a Faculty of Education in a Malaysian university that this topic was politically sensitive. I compromised my research passions with the research agenda at the faculty and adopted a positivistic research framework for my Masters thesis titled 'The relationship between self-concept, value system and academic achievement among Form Four Malay students in a residential Junior Science College'.

Access to academic journals as a postgraduate student and later on as a university lecturer still provided me with the curiosity to read in the area of gender studies and critical sociology. That notion of globalisation where there are flows of ideology and ideas through engagement with media and text materials, colleagues who had been trained overseas within Western academic institutions, and international visiting scholars provided me with ideoscapes (Appadurai 1996) of doing doctoral research within a transnational context. I was told when I spoke to academics in the faculty of education at Malaysian universities about my proposed doctoral topic, that issues to do with gender, ethnicity and feminist research approaches were not important in educational research in Malaysia.

Furthermore, the academic culture within the faculties of education in Malaysian universities with markers of discourses of fear, control and the politics of ethnic identification did not provide me with the academic freedom, environment or the conceptual tools to embark on a critical sociological approach using a postcolonial feminist theorisation of identity and difference to unpack the politics of ethnicised-gendered identifications of Malaysian teenage schoolgirls. As argued earlier, generally, there is a lack of educational research in Malaysia that engages with notions of difference, power, resistance and oppression within a critical social theory framework. However, I do not wish to discount that such politics of research do not exist in educational institutions in other countries. Educational research is political and is influenced by the political and economic agenda of nations.

The irony of this is that I could do this doctoral project within an Australian university that generally adopted a Western tradition of academic ideology. For my doctoral research, I drew mainly on feminists of colour, post-colonial feminists and feminists of identity and difference for notions of identity and difference, ethnicity, gender, agency, power, oppression and patriarchy. Experience as a source of knowledge is also important within such a framework. I also looked to theorists such as Foucault for notions of discourse and power and critical educational theorists such as Giroux for notions of resistance. Equally important is the conceptualisations of the Malaysian ethnoscape in relation to the social, political and educational dimensions and I drew on the works of Malaysians social theorists for this. I attempted as best as I could within this eclectic theoretical framework to construct as Sheth and Handa (1993) and other feminists of colour have argued for 'a feminist, anti-capitalist, anti-imperialist, anti-colonialist standpoint'. This allows for the experiences as well as the social, political and historical contexts of the research participants, research site and researcher to be used in theorising. This also avoids adopting a Eurocentric perspective in trying to understand the complexity of ways of being within different societal contexts. Moreover, it emphasises the role of the researcher in knowledge production and power dynamics of the research project.

The dynamics of globalisation shaped my doctoral research and allowed for that exchange and flow between the Malaysian experiences and Australian context in constructing this thesis which I would argue is a tapestry of theoretical concepts – be these postcolonial or Malaysian, or Australian or Western and that makes it unique in being a Malaysian feminist thesis. I had the academic freedom to research gender and ethnicity using a critical postcolonial feminist approach, a topic and approach considered politically sensitive within Malaysian educational research.

I do not wish to privilege the Australian academe over Malaysian academe as the basis for comparison is complex when historicity, politics and culture are considered. What is important here is that the research framework and practices adopted in my doctoral studies resulted in the production of knowledge that are, as in Mohanty's (1991) terms, based on specific locations and struggles of people of colour and postcolonial peoples and on the day-to-day strategies of survival utilised by such peoples. The findings of the doctoral study provided a critical understanding of the ways in which inter and intra ethnic differences impacted on the schooling experiences and outcomes of young Malaysian women. The study also provided results in relation to the Malaysian schooling system which stratifies on the basis of testing in relation to ethnicity and gender. This doctoral research that considers the interplay between the national, institutional and micro levels are not considered in most Malaysian educational research. Such critical research can contribute significantly to the development of the Malaysian education system as the interplay between national, institutional and experiences of the personal are considered. Theoretical and analytical understandings of the intersectionalities of the macropolitics of education and the micropolitics of experiences are essential in developing models of best practices for education. There has to be an unpacking of grounding of the politics and policies within the experiences of students and educators in order for the Malaysian educational system to move forward.

With the next project I embarked on upon the completion of my doctoral studies, I was negotiating a different political and research agenda. I was involved in a consultancy project funded by the United Nations Development Programme (UNDP) and the Malaysian Government that developed a Human Resource Development Masterplan in line with the notion and global discourse of knowledge-based economy. I examined the schooling sector in Malaysia in relation to the notion of knowledge-based economy against OECD education indicators and the benchmark countries of Ireland, Korea and Australia. These countries were chosen as benchmarks as these nations are major contenders in the global education sector having been hailed into the discourses of educational success and knowledge-based economy. This consultancy project involved fieldwork in interviewing Malaysian students, teachers and education officers. The framework and consultancy reports were done within a culture of positivism (Giroux 1997).

As with the general framework of most consultancy projects, this model essentialised and homogenised notions of education, students, teachers, curriculum and other aspects of schooling and silenced the complexities in the interplay between the various social dimensions such as gender, class and ethnicity. Social, economic and political specificities were not considered. This model enabled comparisons to be made between the various dimensions of schooling models and systems within different cultural and political contexts. An integrated model of best practices from each of the benchmark countries and OECD was developed.

There is a sense of neo-colonialism in that power is exercised through and within social, cultural, political and educational global hierarchies that privilege models of education and schooling as developed by transnational agencies and countries with Eurocentric ideologies. There is a privileging in difference. I refer to the notion of difference as posited by Mohanty (1994) that is linked to power and hierarchy. Difference is not seen as benign variation (diversity) that bypasses power as well as history to suggest a harmonious, empty pluralism but rather is seen as conflict, struggle and the threat of disruption embedded within webs of power. Having said that, it is not such a simplistic explanation as nation-states do have agency and control over the educational reforms and educational research within the state while having to engage with global education and schooling trends located within hierarchies of power.

There are the paradoxes and tensions between discourses of colonialism, nationalism, capitalism, globalisation, Islam and ethnicity. In the consultancy research project, Malaysia did negotiate with these differences but within a homogenised model that once again silenced complexities in the interplay between social dimensions. So while Malaysia did negotiate with the essentialised model of education system through the notion of a knowledge-based economy that was based on OECD education indicators and that of the benchmark countries, there was also the politics of nationalism that determined the educational reforms that were considered for future implementation within the various educational institutions. This politics of nationalism is intertwined with the politics of ethnic identification. Furthermore, the consultancy project was coordinated and managed by the Malaysian government where there is a dominant discourse of 'Malayness' or '*Bumiputera-ness*'. There are processes of contestation and negotiations within the interplay between discourses of the state, transnational agencies and the global educational, social and educational hierarchies that determined the agenda for this research consultancy project.

In referring to Brah *et al.* (2002), the political and sociological macro-analysis of the politics of globalisation as played out in this project is one way of understanding the complex processes of globalisation and educational research. Such a model results in immediate analysis with the 'hegemonic global power' as transnational agencies at its centre, through the OECD education indicators. International agencies such as the OECD have been important in proselytising a micro-economic version of human capital theory, new managerialism and spreading a new rationalisation through the development of global educational performance indicators (Henry *et al.* 2001; Lingard 2001).

Malaysia positioned herself and was positioned by these markers of transnational educational success through the various OECD reports along a hierarchy. As argued earlier, this hierarchy is based on markers located within Western-Eurocentric ideologies of education and knowledge-based economy and discourses of neo-liberalism.

In Malaysia's attempts in moving up this hierarchy and being globally competitive, she would have to ensure that the education system maximises the creative and analytical potential of each student and citizen to the fullest. To do so, issues to do with social, economic and educational inequalities between and within the ethnic groups would have to be addressed. However, the politics of ethnic identification as manifested through the politics of nationalism in Malaysia also impacted significantly on the conduct and outcome of this consultancy research project. The silences in this project resulted from the lack of engagement with the politics of difference as manifested through the interplay between ethnicity, gender and class. The values and voices heard in this consultancy project was linked to the politics of essentialism as manifested through the politics of ethnic identification and nationalism. The discussion so far has indicated the ways in which the tensions and contradictions of Western-Eurocentric ideologies of education and development and Malaysian nationalism are played out in the public discourses of education and research and the culture of academe in Malaysia.

Negotiating the research enterprise: the dilemmas and challenges for future research in Malaysia

Generally, there is the prevalence of a 'culture of positivism' (Giroux 1997) in the politics of educational research in Malaysia. Educational research is generally conceptualised within a positivistic framework where construction of knowledge becomes countable, measurable and impersonal. There is a culture of homogenisation and essentialism in doing educational research in Malaysia that fails to critically interrogate the social and political dimensions of gender, ethnicity and class and the notion of difference in the various educational contexts. There is a lack of engagement with critical social theory and critical approaches to research among Malaysian education researchers. Again, I do not wish to discount that there are pockets of spaces for Malaysian educational researchers to be critical researchers.

Education is seen as an important political mechanism for the state to maintain its dominant ideology, in the case of Malaysia, the politics of ethnic identification. This in turn impacts on the agenda for educational research in Malaysia. Adopting a critical approach to educational research in addressing issues to do with inequality, power, oppression and social injustice might destablise to some extent the status quo of the politics of ethnic identification currently in operation within the Malaysian context.

While it is understandable that there is a need for some legislation and policies to maintain peace and harmony in a multiethnic and multi-religious country, these practices should not impede on research and knowledge production for the betterment of the Malaysian peoples and society. Malaysia still has to address issues to do with ethnic politics, social injustice and democracy within its own specific historical and sociocultural context, in general, and in particular in education through educational research. This is so Malaysia can be globally competitive in the production of knowledge. As Henry *et al.* (2001, 174) states: 'the nation-state still is and ought to be, the prime site of education policy production, serving important national purposes of social justice ... including economic prosperity for all citizens ... and social cohesion'.

A recent research project titled 'Ethnic interaction among students in secondary schools in Malaysia' (Jamil *et al.* 2004) funded by the Intensified Research Priority Areas Grants has conclusions such as 'our research has shown that students have learned to tolerate other ethnic groups ... Although there were cross ethnic conflicts, but the situation is not so serious' (p. xii). This research project failed to adopt a critical approach to the issue in interrogating issues to do with power, social injustice and oppression. Such an approach will assist in dealing with the social, economic and educational inequalities within the education system. This in turn will assist the teachers, educators, policy makers and the government in making the education environment a more conducive one that will enable each Malaysian child/student to fully achieve her or his potential. Malaysia needs to deal with these matters should the nation want to be competitive globally. Unless the citizens are educated in an environment where issues to do with fairness, equality and democracy are addressed and debated, there will continue to be that politics of identification that impinges on the social, economic and educational productivity of the nation. I am not advocating an egalitarian society where all is fair and equal as such a society does not exist given that power always operates at every level of society and in every interaction. What is advocated for in the Malaysian context is to engage with notions of social justice, equality and democracy in the midst of the politics of power.

A critical approach to Malaysian educational research that considers the interplay of the global, national and the micro-contexts will create a significant space for Malaysia in the global order of knowledge production. This would entail a Malaysian approach that draws on the uniqueness and complexities of its multi-ethnic context to provide critical theorisations of the various dimensions of education within the interplay of nationalism and globalisation. These different and new forms of educational research in Malaysia can provide valuable knowledge about the facets of education in a multiethnic and multi-religious context. It is not a simple matter of adopting transnational or Western-Eurocentric or Malaysian ideologies of research. The discourses and representations of education, development and research of transnational agencies, Western ideologies, non-Western ideologies and that of Malaysia inform each other and respond to the cultural, social and political milieus these are located within.

Malaysia, in the midst of negotiating discourses of colonialism, globalisation, neoliberalism, nationalism and the politics of ethnic identification, has to reconceptualise the intertwining between policy and educational research and address notions of equity, fairness and democracy in the educational research agenda in order to take this contemporary multiethnic nation forward in the global arena. There has to be some move away from Malaysian educational research being constructed as an organised, political, state-financed and state-directed academic activity to an academic and societal intellectual activity that is driven by the global and nationalistic agendas and the needs of the different social, ethnic and cultural groups in Malaysia. Malaysian educational research has to engage with the notion of difference at the global, national, institutional and personal levels that will be beneficial to her at the macro, meso and micro levels to move forward in her educational research agenda.

References

Amat, Taap Manshor (2001) 'Challenges and potentials in human resource development in a knowledge-based economy: A Malaysian perspective', in D. Abdulai (ed.) *Malaysia and the K-Economy*, Malaysia: Pelanduk Publications.

Andaya, B. and Andaya, L. (2001) *A History of Malaysia*, 2nd edn, Basingstoke: Palgrave.

Appadurai, A. (1996) *Modernity at Large: Cultural Dimensions of Globalisation*, Minneapolis, MN: University of Minnesota Press.

Ball, S. (1990) *Politics and Policy Making in Education: Explorations in Policy Sociology*, London: Routledge.

Brah, A. (1996) *Cartographies of Diaspora: Contesting Identities*, London: Routledge.

Brah, A. (2002) 'Global mobilities, local predicaments: globalisation and the critical imagination', *Feminist Review*, 70: 30–45.

Burbules, N. and Torres, C. (2000) *Globalisation and Education: Critical Perspectives*, New York: Routledge.

Connell, R.W. (1993) *Schools and Social Justice*, Toronto: Our schools/our selves Education Foundation.

Colebatch, H. (2002) *Policy*, Buckingham: Open University Press.

Gale, T. (2003) 'Realising policy: the who and how of policy production', *Discourse*, 24(1): 51–66.

Giroux, H. (1983) *Theory and Resistance in Education: A Pedagogy for the Oppositions*, South Hadley, MA: Bergin and Garvey.

Giroux, H. (1997) *Pedagogy and the Politics of Hope: Theory, Culture and Schooling*, Boulder, CO: Westview Press.

Foucault, M. (1997) *Discipline and Punish*, New York: Vintage.

Foucault, M. (1980) 'Two lectures', in C. Gordon (ed.) *Power and Knowledge: Selected Interviews and other Writings by Michel Foucault 1972–1977*, Brighton: The Harvester Press, 78–108.

Foucault, M. (1982) 'The subject and power', in H. Dreyfus and P. Rabinow (eds) *Michel Foucault: Beyond Structuralism and Hermeneutics*, Chicago, IL: University of Chicago Press, 26–47.

Henry, M., Lingard, B., Rizvi, F. and Taylor, S. (2001) *The OECD, Globalisation and Education Policy*, Oxford: Pergamon.

Jamil, H., Lee, M., Santhiram, R., Ismail, H., Razak, N., Nair, S., Yusog, N. and Lee, L. (2004) *Ethnic Interaction among Students in Secondary Schools in Malaysia*, Malaysia: Universiti Sains Malaysia.

Joseph, C. (2003) 'Theorisations of identity and difference: ways of being Malay, Chinese and Indian schoolgirls in a Malaysian secondary school'. Unpublished Ph.D thesis. Australia: Monash University.

Keeves, J.P., Watanabe, R. and McGuckian, P. (2003) 'Educational research in the Asia-Pacific region', in J.P. Keeves and R. Watanabe (eds) *International Handbook of Educational Research in the Asia-Pacific Region*, Dordrecht: Kluwer Academic Publishers.

Lee, M. (2000) 'The politics of educational change in Malaysia: national context and global influences', in T. Townsend and Y.C. Cheng (eds) *Educational Change and Development in the Asia-Pacific Region: Challenges for the Future*, Lisse: Swets & Zeitlinger.

Lee, M. (2004) *Restructuring Higher Education in Malaysia*, Malaysia: Science University of Malaysia.

Lingard, B. (2001) 'Some lessons for educational researchers: repositioning research in education and education in research'. *Australian Educational Researcher*, 28(3): 1–46.

Loo, Seng Piew (2000) 'The Malaysian educational system: societal trends and issues for the twenty-first century', in H.J. Steyn and C.C. Wolhunter (eds) *Education Systems of Emerging Countries: Challenges of the 21st Century*, Noordburg: Keurkopie Uitgevers.

Luke, A. (2003) 'After the marketplace: evidence, social science and educational research', *Australian Educational Researcher*, 30(2): 87–107.

Mac an Ghail, M. (1999) *Contemporary Racisms and Ethnicities: Social and Cultural Transformations*, Buckingham: Open University Press.
Malaysia (2001) *Eighth Malaysia Plan (2001–2005)*, Kuala Lumpur: Economic Planning Unit, Prime Minister's Department.
Malaysia (2002) *Knowledge-Based Economy: Master Plan*, Malaysia: Institute of Strategic and International Studies.
MASTIC (Malaysian Science and Technology Information Center) (2000) *Malaysian Research and Development Classification System*, Kuala Lumpur: Ministry of Science, Technology and Innovation.
Ministry of Education (2001) *Education Development Plan (2001–2010)*, Kuala Lumpur: Ministry of Education.
Mohanty, C.T. (1991) 'Introduction: cartographies of struggle – third world women and the politics of feminism', in C.T. Mohanty, A. Russo and L. Torres (eds) *Third World Women and the Politics of Feminism*, Bloomington, IN: Indiana University Press.
Mohanty, C.T. (1994) 'On race and voice: challenges for liberal education in the 1990s', in H. Giroux and P. McLaren (eds) *Between Borders: Pedagogy and the Politics of Cultural Studies*, New York: Routledge.
OECD (2003) *Education at a Glance: OECD Indicators 2003*, Paris: OECD.
Ong, A. (1999) 'Muslim feminism: citizenship in the shelter of corporatist Islam', *Citizenship Studies*, 3(3): 355–71.
Osman, S. (1991) 'Politik akademia kini dan menjelang tahun 2000', Dalam Wan Muda, W.M. dan Mh. Jadi, H. (Penyunting), *Akademia* (ms. 34–43), Pulau Pinang: PKAPUSM, Universiti Sains Malaysia.
Phang, H.E. (2000) 'The economic role of the Chinese in Malaysia', in K.H. Lee and C.B. Tan (eds) *The Chinese in Malaysia*, Kuala Lumpur/Oxford: Oxford University Press.
Santhiram, R. (1999) *Education of Minorities: The Case of Indians in Malaysia*, Kuala Lumpur: Child Information, Learning and Development Centre.
Sarup, M. (1993) *An Introductory Guide to Poststructuralism and Postmodernism*, Athens, GA: University of Georgia Press.
Sheth, Anita, and Handa, Amita (1993) 'A jewel in the frown: striking accord between India/n feminists', in H. Bannerji (ed.) *Returning the Gaze: Essays on Racism, Feminism and Politics*, Toronto: Sister Vision Press.
Taskforce on Higher Education and Society (2000) *Higher Education in Developing Countries: Perils and Promise*, Washington, DC: The International Bank for Reconstruction and Development/The World Bank.
Taylor, S., Rizvi, F., Lingard, B. and Henry, M. (1997) *Educational Policy and the Politics of Change*, London: Routledge.
Weedon, C. (1999) *Feminism, Theory and the Politics of Difference*, Oxford: Blackwell Publishers.
Yuval-Davis, N. (1997) *Gender and Nation*, London: Sage.

10 Research as consultancy in the African university

A challenge to excellence

Kenneth King

With the substantial erosions in income and living conditions, faculty have tended to concentrate on the struggle to keep body and soul together – by any and all means available. The quest for alternative income through moonlighting, contract research and consultancies has become desperate … The result is a decline in the dedication to scholarship and teaching. In many, though not all cases, faculty have little time for lectures and tutorials, and those who do, tend to be demoralised by the bloated classes, inadequate teaching facilities and the generally poor educational environment. There is not much research and hardly any fieldwork, and dissemination of research results through publication has taken a back seat, as has supervision of graduate work. In general, the life of the mind, which has for decades defined and sustained academic communities everywhere in the world, is an endangered category on many an African university campus.

(Sawyerr 2004: 25)

Renewing the African university and developing centres of excellence in science and technology were core concerns of the Report of the Commission for Africa (2005) and specific proposals for this revitalisation went to the meeting of G8 leaders in Scotland in July 2005. Amongst the issues mentioned was a claim that due to lack of funding and other pressures, the research capacity of African tertiary education had declined (Commission for Africa 2005: 137). This very topical crisis has longer historical roots, and it will be argued here that a crucial element in the undermining of the African university's mission to create knowledge over the long term has been the switch from disciplinary research to short-term consultancy. Indeed, this is exactly the point made by Sawyerr, the Secretary General of the Association of African Universities (AAU), in the quotation above.

It is important, however, to be clear from the outset about the relations between research and consultancy. In many universities, including those with the highest reputation in the OECD countries, research and consultancy co-exist, and do so in an entirely interdependent fashion. Moreover, the relationship between them also differs by discipline, with it being more common for consultancy to be undertaken in academic areas which have a strong link with professional and commercial bodies outside the university, including law, management, economics, engineering, pharmacy, etc. But, in conceptual terms, it is also worth acknowledging, following Gibbons *et al.* (1994), that research, whether fundamental or more applied, is not the prerogative or monopoly of the university. Increasingly, and again there are important differences by discipline and by country, research is to be found outside the universities, in think tanks, medical and industrial research centres, directly supported by the private corporate sector.[1]

The particular challenge of the consultancy research mode in the African setting is very different from the consultancy arm of the mainstream Western universities. In Africa, it is not a short-term alternative to the pursuit of long-term disciplinary research; rather it has, for many scholars, become a necessary accompaniment to the pursuit of an academic career. It is important to stress, however, that consultancy is not itself being identified as the direct cause of the weakening of research capacity and research production. It is rather a symptom of the malaise which derives from the reduction of the real value of university salaries over the last 20 and more years.

This itself is by no means restricted to the university sector, but has affected the entire civil service, including very large numbers of primary and secondary school teachers. Its economic causes are complex, but they include the dramatic worsening of the terms of trade for Africa's primary products, the reduction of foreign direct investment in Africa, and the widespread problems with governance and conflict that affected so many African countries in the lost decades of the 1970s, 1980s and early 1090s. Whatever the causes, the perception by very large numbers of civil servants – and by university lecturers – that their salaries no longer constituted a living wage has resulted in a very widespread search for second – or even third sources of income. In the case of university teachers this has frequently meant the pursuit of consultancy income.

In this particular account, the analysis will be drawn principally from Anglophone African universities, and more particularly from East Africa. It should be acknowledged, however, that although the phenomenon of short-term consultancy has been noted there for over 20 years, there has been little detailed quantitative analysis of the extent of consultancy in the university environment. One reason that this has not happened is that the bulk of consultancy activity, like much other engagement in seeking second incomes, is not mentioned to the tax authorities.

The role of external influence and demand

External donor agencies have played a critical role in the emergence of the consultancy culture. In addition to the more general forces mentioned above which have undermined the value of salaries, there have been some external factors which have accentuated the problems of the university sector. From as early as the 1970s, bilateral and multilateral agencies, many of which had played a key part in the initial establishment and support of the new universities in Africa, began to withdraw that support. The reasons were complex but they included a belief within the donor community that universities were high cost and were predominantly patronised by the elite. As agencies shifted their funding priorities in support of what they termed basic needs, and pro-poor development, they found it easy to assume that the universities had little direct or even indirect connection with poverty reduction. This tendency became much more widespread after the World Conference on Education for All took place in Thailand in 1990. It suggested that basic education should be the first priority for nations and for the development assistance community. It was a trend that was reinforced by the International Development Targets of the OECD in 1996, and by the Millennium Development Goals (MDGs) announced by the United Nations in 2000. Primary schooling was the only sub-sector of education explicitly singled out for support (King 2004).

There can be little doubt that tertiary education in sub-Saharan Africa suffered from the withdrawal of donor agency support. It is important to point out that this was never a complete withdrawal; several key foundations, such as Ford and Rockefeller, continued their support of research, as did bilateral research agencies from Canada and Sweden. But the result of dramatically reduced national sources of income for universities, and particularly local sources of support for research, meant that increasingly university staff turned to external development agencies to secure additional income. There is therefore something of a paradox here; donor agencies had withdrawn their earlier general support for the university sector, but they continued to be hugely influential in being one of the only sources of financial support for analytical work in tertiary education.

It is, however, with the character of this analytical work that we are concerned here. In most cases, the requirement of the donor agencies, whether bilateral, multilateral or non-governmental organisations (NGOs), was for immediate policy-oriented tasks such as feasibility studies, evaluations and appraisals. The philosophical orientation of this kind of analysis is developmental and problem solving. The focus is frequently on whether particular projects or programmes have been effectively delivered or implemented, and hence there is a preoccupation with assessing inputs and outputs, and then analysing the challenges, the constraints and the 'lessons learned'. In this kind of evaluation, there is normally little room for historical reflection, let alone for critical analysis. The emphasis is on rapid elucidation of practical issues. Typically, the task involves a minimum of fieldwork, but it has to be completed by a specific date, and to be presented in a particular style.

Even though there is little external support for the university sector, there is a plethora of development assistance agencies operating in Africa, and in most countries, including in East Africa, there is a prodigious range of both small and large projects and programmes which need to be evaluated and appraised for reasons of accountability (King 2001). Occasionally, such work can be reflective, critical and even provocative, but in general it requires a measured problem-solving approach to all the subjects and topics being evaluated or appraised. David Court, a long-term analyst of the university sector in East Africa, has commented on the implications of this particular modality for the wider goals of the university research community:

> In a context like the Kenyan one, however, there are dangers in a situation where research is perceived and justified exclusively in terms of its problem-solving capability. One is the risk of diminished credibility arising from the fact that it cannot provide the 'developmental answers' that may be expected. A second is the risk of extinguishing other types of research, e.g. basic and theoretical work, on which the ultimate strength of the educational profession depends.
>
> (Court 1983: 182)

A consequence of the widespread opportunities for evaluative, analytical work is that the contract research mode has become dominant in East Africa, but particularly in those disciplines which are potentially most applied. There are several implications of this dominance both for the research profession and for the wider institutional embedding of research within the academy. First, because the primary audience for consultancy is the donor agency, there is little or no obligation to disseminate the findings more widely to peers in the scholarly community. Indeed, there is often a specific condition from the sponsor prohibiting wider circulation. Thus, these products of evaluation and appraisal cannot be assessed as academic publications or used for career advancement. Secondly, because of the monetary value attached to consultancy, and the very short time frames involved, it has been commonplace for enterprising academics to set up consultancy firms, or to be associated with existing companies. The attractions of additional finance, often accessible in hard currency, are understandable in the wider climate of national under-funding of the university sector. But, thirdly, the result of this availability of substantial revenue from contract research is that lecturers and professors find little to attract them to the regular mission of the university, such as the building up of the next generation of scholars through masters and doctoral supervision. Equally, when compared to the need to secure supplementary income on a regular monthly basis, there is little to commend an open-ended, long-term research project which might take two or three years to complete, and, at best, might translate into one or two articles, or, over a longer period still, an academic text.

Consultancy in the wider research environment

It was argued earlier that the consultancy mode was not the cause of the deterioration of the university research environment, but more a response to it. In a situation where library budgets have been unable to keep up with the costs of foreign journals or books, and where it is very far from commonplace for academics to have routine access to the internet in their own offices, consultancy has provided an opportunity for individual academics to buy computers and secure the key texts (many of them derived from the agencies) that are required to carry out their contracts. But if the contract research mode was a response to an already deteriorating academic environment, there can be little doubt that the intensification of the consultancy mode has itself made the situation worse. It has underlined the fact that regular, time-consuming tasks like research supervision do not generate additional income. And it has discouraged academics from the long-term and uncertain process of trying to place articles in prestige journals or to complete academic monographs. There is simply no money involved in these pursuits, unless a major research grant is obtained. Indeed, the absence of the most up-to-date international journals and relevant texts, and the hugely problematic challenge of access to the internet have, in combination, made the pursuit of conventional academic objectives very unattractive. In addition, there are few accessible publishing outlets locally available, and great difficulty in ensuring that if a book is published, it is widely disseminated and marketed.

Consultancy is not, however, restricted to the pursuit of analytical work for the agencies, or for national governments. Academics often find themselves supplementing their regular salaries by teaching, on a contract basis, in a nearby private college or university. Through the consultancy mode, the private university sector can get regular access to the skills and expertise of what are meant to be full-time academics in the public sector. It is admitted by staff that they can double their ordinary salary through contract teaching, but it means that timetables in their own universities get changed to allow substantial teaching duties elsewhere. In some public East African universities, moreover, this private teaching option has been incorporated into the mainstream of the university, in the form of parallel degree streams in the afternoon and evening, which bring fee-paying students in very large numbers on to the campus. In this situation, many academics get their regular pay cheque, and a second cheque for their contract teaching in the parallel courses. Such has been the popularity of this approach that there are now famous universities like Makerere in Uganda where the number of fee-paying students greatly exceeds those with bursaries from the state (Musisi and Muwanga 2003). But here, it should be noted that this contract teaching in the private streams of the public university has major implications for equity. There is a real sense in which it constitutes the privatisation of the public university.

'Public–private partnerships' of the sort illustrated in Makerere at least have the advantage of containing the additional contract work of the academic staff within their mother university. In the case of much other consultancy work, academics prefer for the moneys not to be channelled through their own university. Partly, this is to ensure that the fees reach them directly, and often without any tax having been removed. But there is also substantial anecdotal evidence that routing the consultancy through the university finance office can mean major delays, and bureaucratic hurdles in accessing the moneys. Again, therefore, there is a two-way relationship between the dominance of consultancy and the weakness of institutional capacity within the university. Arguably, academics have avoided their universities because of the lack of financial transparency within the institution. But the less the academics bring their research and consultancy within the university, the weaker that financial capability may become.

Conclusions about research, consultancy and revitalisation

We mentioned at the outset that an agenda item for the renewal of African universities and for the development of centres of excellence went to the meeting of the G8 leaders in early July 2005. One of the elements in the background proposal for renewal was a scheme whereby African academics could be encouraged to remain in their universities by the introduction of a salary incentive scheme that would, in essence, come close to doubling their salaries (ACU, AAU, SAUVCA, 2005). The suggested mechanism would select 100 of the 'best academics' in all the AAU universities across the continent. The financial resources for this would be derived from the agreements by the G8 and other countries to double aid to Africa (King 2005).

This particular scheme may or may not be put into place. But our analysis of the operation of consultancy and contract research in the university environment would indicate that many of the more enterprising academics, in particular disciplines, are already doubling their small salaries by a variety of local solutions. The process of individuals pursuing these financial requirements has over time fundamentally altered the character of the research and analytical work being undertaken in many African universities. Reversing this process and prioritising longer-term research of a more fundamental and critical character will need much more than a salary incentive scheme. It will require a dramatic improvement in the libraries, journal provision and internet access. It will also demand greater financial transparency in the running of the university, and a whole series of new incentives to reward the training and supervision of the next generation of scholars.

There is evidence, however, that more fundamental research, as well as highly relevant, poverty-oriented analysis, can be drawn back into the universities of East Africa, through schemes of long-term cooperation with universities in Europe, North America and Japan. But the impact of more than 20 years of the culture of consultancy and contract research will remain powerful for some time to come. The tradition of individual academics working on a whole series of short-term assignments on quite different topics, none of which may relate to the original doctoral focus or preferred subject area of the particular scholar, may well prove difficult to shift. But it would be timely, since radical reform and renewal of the African university are on the world's agenda, to carry out much more detailed analysis of the long-term effects of the contract research and consultancy mode in a variety of different university contexts, in East, West and Southern Africa.

Notes

1 It is worth noting that, as Chapter 8 points out, in the Russian tradition, which continues to influence countries of Eastern and Central Europe, and Central Asia, even after the collapse of the Soviet Union, research was located outside the universities in the Academies of Science, while teaching principally remained with universities.

References

AAU, ACU, SAUVCA (2005) *Renewing the African University. Nine Points of the Draft Programme*, London: Association of Commonwealth Universities.

Commission for Africa (2005) *Our Common Interest. The Report of the Commission for Africa*, London: Commission for Africa.

Court, D. (1983) 'Kenya: educational research environment in Kenya', in S. Shaeffer and J. Nkinyangi (eds) *Educational Research Environments in the Developing World*, Ottawa: International Development Research Centre.

Gibbons, M., Limoges, C., Nowotny, H., Schwartzman, S., Scott, P. and Trow, M. (1994) *The New Production of Knowledge: Science and Research in Contemporary Societies*, London: Sage.

King, K. (2001) 'Knowledge agencies: making the globalisation of development knowledge work for the North and South', in W. Gmelin, K. King, and S. McGrath (eds) *Development Knowledge, National Research and International Cooperation*, Edinburgh: Centre of African Studies, University of Edinburgh.

King, K. (2004) 'Development knowledge and the global policy agenda: Whose knowledge? Whose policy?', Paper to conference of the United Nations Institute for Research on Social Development (UNRISD) in Geneva, 19–21 April 2004 on 'Social Knowledge and International Policy Making: Exploring the Linkages'. To be published as 'Knowledge management and the global agenda for education', in P. Utting (ed.) *Reclaiming Development Agendas: Knowledge, Power and International Policy Making*, Geneva: UNRISD (forthcoming).

King, K. (2005) 'The Commission for Africa: A changing landscape for higher education and capacity development in Africa?', Paper to Conference on 'A Changing Landscape – making support to higher education and research in developing countries more effective', 23–25 May. The Hague: NUFFIC. Published in *The Aging Landscape: Making Support to Higher Education and Research More Effective*, The Hague: NUFFIC.

Musisi, N.B. and Muwanga, N.K. (2003) *Makerere University in Transition 1993–2000*, Oxford: James Currey.

Sawyerr, A. (2004) *Challenges Facing African Universities: Selected Issues*, Accra: Association of African Universities.

11 Redesigning what counts as evidence in educational policy

The Singapore model

Allan Luke and David Hogan

Two decades of policy critique show us that the making of state policy and the reshaping of pedagogy is both ideologically located and intellectually untidy. Yet in the context of a dominant transnational model of neoliberal educational governance the use of critical educational research in policy making is largely unexplored. We define educational policy making as the prescriptive regulation of flows of human resources, discourse and capital across educational systems towards normative social, economic and cultural ends (Luke 2005). This chapter proposes a version of evidence-based educational policy formation, one not narrowly determined by standardised achievement test scores but rather one that is based on triangulated quantitative and qualitative research. We describe work underway in Singapore as a possible model, discussing the potential of nested, multilevel longitudinal research design in reconceptualising and tracking the differential construction and distribution of educational capital.

Having spent two decades expanding the methodologies and epistemologies, discourses and practices of educational research, it is appropriate that the task of defending educational research should fall back upon this generation of critical researchers. For current debates over what counts as evidence in state policy formation are indeed debates over what counts as educational research and what should count as curriculum and pedagogy. This is only in part a matter of finding the proper and right educational 'science'. It necessarily entails contention over the normative goals, purposes and outcomes of education in new economic and social conditions. Our aim here is to reassess available epistemological and methodological toolkits for looking at current policy issues. We then turn to make the case for a different approach to evidence in policy formation, one that is multidisciplinary, critical and interpretive.

Critical research and neoliberal policy

A major achievement of work of the last two decades was an expansion of what counts as educational research beyond the longstanding boundaries of the Thorndike behaviourist tradition. That American legacy, coupled with the industrial design and expansion of the educational system, translated into a large-scale focus on pre/post-test experimental design, with standardised achievement test performance as the index of efficacy. The models owe as much to industrial assembly-line 'time on task' studies of early Taylorism and agricultural crop yield studies as they might to medical/epidemiological science

(Callahan 1962). As subsequent histories showed, the early twentieth-century push towards 'fairness' through test-driven streaming and placement systems by Terman, Thorndike and colleagues had as substantive roots in eugenics and social Darwinism as it might have relied upon Behaviourist or developmental models of mental measurement (Gould 1991).

In the 1960s and 1970s, neomarxian critiques began to document reproductive effects of the model, its claims to scientific means and meritocratic ends notwithstanding. These critiques came from several sources – in the reanalysis of achievement and test score data (e.g. Bowles and Gintis 1977); histories of schooling and urbanisation (e.g. Hogan 1986); and curriculum studies based on ideology critique (Apple 1978). The historical and political grounds were set for scepticism towards quantitative research models as positivist and reductionist. Beginning first from the cognitive and linguistic turns in social science, and later drawing from French discourse theory, poststructuralist feminism, postcolonial and cultural theory, the critical turn in educational research moved towards a broad repertoire of theoretically driven qualitative and case-based, narrative and discourse analytic work. Prototypical ethnographic and sociological work showed the mechanisms of cultural and class reproduction at work. At the same time, there was a general shift to language and discourse processes as constitutive of learning, development and cultural practice (Cazden *et al.* 1972). The theoretical and epistemological grounds for the rise of sociohistorical psychology, discourse analysis of social interaction, and studies of the construction of identity and subjectivity were established. These, not coincidentally, are key to current and recent work in understanding how cultural, socioeconomic, gender and sexual 'difference' and 'diversity' work in educational contexts – and they have been taken as a 'natural' fit to issues of equity and social justice (Luke 2003).

Over the past two decades, there has been a rebalancing of quantitative psychometric research with a focus on qualitative and text-based work in methods courses and theses, including discourse analyses of students' and teachers' narratives, critical analyses of curriculum documents and policy texts, and face-to-face classroom interaction. These changes, of course, have occurred in the context of shifts in political ideology in the West, including a progressive opening of educational systems to women, indigenous peoples and minorities. But while the educational research community moved towards diversity of theory, method and scholarship, the political economy of education underwent major restructuring.

There are, of course, contending accounts of the rise of neoliberal educational policy in the North/West. But the result has been dominant discourses of markets and corporatism, economic rationalism and accountability. These have formed the grounds for 'evidence-based' educational policy in the USA and UK and, later, Australia, New Zealand and Canada, with roots in two historical contexts. The first is the domination of international policy by the premises and practices of a highly decentralised US system, where state-based regulation, school-based management, district autonomy and separate taxation bases, state curriculum and local ideologies are allowed to play themselves out against broad regulatory backdrops. The second was the beginning of a retreat by the postindustrial state from the postwar social contract of expanding social services with an explicit policy focus on minority and lower socioeconomic groups. The emphasis on educational performance and neoliberal management later was exported through Asia and emergent economies via non-government organisations and international aid projects, and World Bank structural adjustment policies (Tan 1998; Mok and Chan 2000).

In new educational economies and cultures, the key policy issue is not the shift to cultures of performativity, but what will count as performance, efficacy, outcome, consequence and, indeed, learning, knowledge and capital. Curriculum debates typically become public, legislative and professional contests over taxonomies of standards, outcomes, skills and competences. But the latest iteration of neoliberal ideology turns on a version of the 'scientific', both as source of legitimation and as a means for supplanting critical work in educational faculties internationally. This was epitomised in ranking Bush advisor Reid Lyon's call to 'burn down the faculties of education'. The centrepiece is the US Federal *No Child Left Behind* legislation, based on the findings of the National Reading Panel (National Institute of Health and Child Development 2000). It is among the first legislative acts to name and set targets for minority groups, with test score goals set by local schools and districts for minority achievement. While the stated intent of this bipartisan educational bill is to force a major refocus on early reading, early intervention and the achievement of the bottom quartile of students, the legislation has two interesting ideological effects.

The first is its version of 'scientific evidence'. The National Reading Panel only admitted 'proof' based on studies of reading programmes that met criteria of classical experimental design and randomised field trials. In Lyon and others' rhetoric, the 'gold standard' is randomised drug trials (US Department of Education 2002), the same models that have most recently brought us VIOXX. This meant that the qualitative observational, ethnographic and discourse analytic work by educational researchers was dispatched from the policy field as speculative, soft and biased. This included quantitative and qualitative classroom observation. So its first major effect was to politically cleave educational research into an artificial divide between the Thorndike tradition and 'everybody else', indexing a crude division between quantitative and qualitative, deductive and inductive, positivist and interpretive, scientific versus speculative – a move, it is worth mentioning, that no responsible medical organisation from the World Health Organisation to the Center for Disease Control would make in trying to track and engage with the complexity of an epidemiological problem. The consequence for education is that local qualitative proof via local or smaller scale teacher-based curriculum implementation, action research and school-based teacher development work is ruled out of court as a grounds for local, regional or state-based policies, including those governing curriculum adoption and implementation.

The second major effect was to tie failure of proof of efficacy to mechanisms of public accountability, including web-accessible, published league tables for parent consumers, and to the withdrawal of support for state schools and redirection of funds to private schools, charter schools, voucher systems and so forth. Collateral effects, students' social and non-cognitive outcomes, tend to be downplayed on the radar screens of accountability. The ostensibly 'scientific' measurement of school success, the test score, is the cornerstone of a neoconservative policy regime of marketisation and commodification, deregulation and privatisation.

But how 'scientific' is such a move? And does this translate, even in its own stated terms, into effective or powerful education and social policy committed to interventions that will alter patterns of the achievement of marginal groups of students or that will address the demands of new economies and cultures, knowledges and discourses? The response of the educational research community to this situation is important. A first wave of responses has been to argue that quantitative paradigms by definition present a narrow version of educational practice and attainment, elements of which can only be explained through qualitative research. A further option is to mount a strong critique of neoliberal educational ideology, the privatisation and marketisation agenda. But a prior question is whether any and all evidence-based educational policy is inherently reductionist, and whether its ways of rationalising and legitimating educational practice are necessarily part of a regime of 'countability' that serves a conservative attack on state education and social equity.

Elsewhere, we have argued that policy formation in many educational jurisdictions, even when committed to goals of educational equity and social justice, is often made according to arbitrary blends of precedent, political pressure and established ideology – independent of any systematic research or data, however defined (Luke 2005). The issue is not whether or not educational culture and governance will shift towards an ethic of performativity, but rather what will count as evidence, data and, indeed, teaching and learning under these educational economies. This is not to treat neoliberal standards and performativity as a *fait accompli*. Rather, it is to begin from the assumption that the matter of social policy formation is indeed a matter of 'translating facts into norms' (Habermas 1998), and that our job is to both expand and make problematic what will count as facts and to expand as broadly and critically as possible the available theoretical resources for the translation of these into normative educational goals.

Normative goals of equality of access and improved achievement can be qualitatively and quantitatively evaluated, but an exclusive reliance on the 'experimental design' approach is a blunt and crude approach to policy. To make the case, we argue here that the educational research community needs to recover and join two principal traditions of research that enabled the critical analysis of social reproduction in the early 1970s: quantitative sociology and the ethnography of communications.

Alternative models

Debates about what constitutes research evidence have varied by national context. In the UK, policies have led to the development of multilevel statistical procedures that assess, at the school level, the value added by schools to student learning (as measured by key national performance indicators, including national examination results), taking into account prior achievement levels and family background characteristics. In Australia, the debate also has moved towards the development of comparative value added measures, pushed by a federal government that has progressively expanded funding for non-state schooling and state governments working for curriculum reform. But interschool and cross-systems comparisons in Australia have been checked by lack of consistent and comparable data sets within and across states and the technical limits of existing test instruments.

The most comprehensive approach to evidence is the New Zealand Ministry of Education's *Iterative Best Evidence Synthesis Programme*. Its author, Adrienne Alton-Lee (2004) defines this as a 'collaborative knowledge-building strategy to draw upon and synthesise … valuable but inaccessible and fragmented research literature in education' on both English and Maori-medium settings in New Zealand. It weighs quantitative and qualitative research data on a case-by-case data, depending upon the policy questions at issue. The result is both a 'fitness for purpose approach', focused on contextual validity and relevance – on 'what works, under what conditions, why and how' (Alton-Lee 2004: 1). What is distinctive about the New Zealand approach is its willingness to consider all forms of research evidence regardless of methodological paradigms and ideological rectitude, and its concern in finding contextually effective, appropriate and locally powerful examples of 'what works'. Its focus is on capturing and examining the impact of local contextual variables (e.g. population, school, community, linguistic and cultural variables). Indeed, 'what authentically works' in educational interventions may be locally effective with particular populations, in particular settings, to particular educational ends. This stands against the base assumption of the US model: that there are instructional treatments that can be shown to have generalisable and universal efficacy across and in spite of contexts, that this efficacy at the production of educational outcomes can be assessed solely through standardised achievement test results, and that the matter of 'reform' of systems requires the mandating, standardisation and implementation of these approaches.

Our position concurs with the New Zealand approach and is based upon prior work that we have done in systemic reform of curriculum and pedagogy in Queensland (Lingard *et al.* 2002) following prototypes by Newmann and Associates (1995) in US school reform studies. We agree that rigorous, scientific research is required for policy formation:

• That there are material, cognitive and social conditions, discourse interactions and linguistic processes that can be studied, tracked and examined empirically, through rigorous observation and careful theorisation.

Many dominant approaches to evidence in the USA and UK fail to capture these variable processes and practices adequately. This is principally because they adopt, inter alia, a 'black box' approach, controlling inputs, with a reductionist quantification of educational outcomes. There is little emphasis on the close study of pedagogy, classroom face-to-face teaching, where the work of teaching and learning occurs. This precludes a finer grained set of analyses and interventions that can address the host of cultural and institutional variables that might influence performance and, indeed, make elements of them valid and replicable in local sites. Finally, there is no attempt to systematically study the full range of cultural and linguistic, social and economic 'outcomes', including quality of life, psychological health, values and other 'non-cognitive' educationally related outcomes.

In contrast to the New Zealand model, the US model assumes that contextual variables can be controlled in the search for generalisable pedagogic approaches. In fact, the National Reading Panel's (National Institute of Child Health and Human Development, 2000) first report did not consider studies of minority students and second language speakers that did not meet its randomised field trial criteria. In so doing, it wrote off almost all studies of the largest target groups of students with potential reading and early achievement difficulties. These studies were ruled out of the scientific database that was used for making curriculum and funding policy for these same target groups.

Hence, we share with Alton-Lee (2004), the core assumption:

• That these can be optimally studied through a rigorous multidisciplinary social science – and not a narrow, selective psychometrics – that examines sociodemographic data, data on the contexts of schools and teachers, studies of face-to-face pedagogy, and a broad array of educational outcomes.

Yet the practical problem is this. Policy makers typically draw from available studies and existing research. In many countries, there has been a decline in overall government and non-government funding of educational research over the past decade, in part spurred by the ideological divisions identified here. But what if we could build from scratch a large-scale research design that followed the principles we have outlined here? In what follows, we propose a design that blends quantitative and qualitative, cross-sectional and longitudinal studies, with a comprehensive socio-demographic and linguistic database on student population, a central focus on descriptive and observational accounts of classroom pedagogy, and a multidimensional definition of educational outcomes and pathways.

The Singapore core research project

In 1965 Singapore gained independence from Malaya, a former British colony. By 2005 it has become a post-colonial nation-state, economic power and global city. It is a strong centralised state, a centrally regulated market economy, featuring a competent and corruption-free public administration dominated by a single political party since independence (Tan, Gopinathan and Kam 1998). The resultant policy environment is frequently characterised as a 'pragmatic' blend of direct social and economic intervention with evidence-driven medium and long-term planning.

The twin normative goals of the educational system have rested for some 30 years on a meritocratic system of human capital formation (in a context where the country has virtually no resources other than its people, institutions and built infrastructure) and a curricular focus on the maintenance of a cohesive multiracial and multilingual society. The system is well funded, with streaming in year 6 and high stakes examinations in years 5, 10 and 12. The track record of this system is strong. Basic literacy rates jumped from 68.9 per cent to 94.2 per cent between 1970 and 2004, and the percentage of university graduates in the population increased from 1.9 per cent in 1970 to 12.1 per cent in 2004. Additionally, Singapore has over a 95 per cent retention rate through to the end of year 10. Singaporean students consistently do exceptionally well in comparative international assessments in maths and science, ranking first or second in all TIMMS categories since the late 1990s.

In the late 1990s, the Ministry of Education introduced *Thinking Schools, Learning Nation* – a suite of policy initiatives aimed at engaging with new technologies, better curriculum integration and relevance, and a broad embrace of critical and higher order thinking. As in other postindustrial countries, the general premise is that new conditions demand worker citizens equipped with different skills, knowledges and dispositions than industrial models of schooling afforded. Service-based, diversified and decentralised, information and discourse-based economies are said to require more than the basic skills, functional rule compliance and reproductive capacity of manual laborers, primary and secondary industry workers, and the hierarchical management of the 'old' industrial economies. In these discourses around education and globalisation, then, the general push is for worker/citizens who are able to independently weigh risks and develop strategies for the creation and realisation of capital, and for worker/citizens who have the motivational dispositions to cope with rapid change, potential volatility and changing demands of these same, globalised markets.

In a speech on 2 April 2005, the Minister of Education, Thaman Shamugaratmun, called for a 'spirit of innovation' and the 'skills and attitudes required to succeed in an innovation-based world'. In his inaugural 2004 National Day Address, Prime Minister Lee Sing Loong argued that:

'... above all, we should work to *avoid a convergence of ideas*, even as we foster an abiding loyalty to Singapore and an interest in seeing Singapore succeed. ... [W]e have to *start young*, encourage our children to question as they learn, and to experiment with new ways of doing things – not just follow the rest of the class. We have to allow a spread of ideas and learning habits ... [original emphasis].'

By 2002 the Ministry of Education and the National Institute of Education announced the establishment of the largest funded educational research centre, setting aside S$48 million to establish the Centre for Research in Pedagogy and Practice (CRPP). The purpose of the Centre was to develop a comprehensive research programme that would provide the evidence for evaluating reforms to date and enable the Ministry to plan medium and long-term policy interventions (Luke, Freebody, Lau and Gopinathan 2005). By April 2004 it had grown into the largest educational and social science research centre in East Asia, with 100 research staff and over 80 school-based research projects of varying size and emphasis.

The Ministry and National Institute defined the Centre's foundational role as the study of pedagogy. The foundational assumption is that research and development required for educational policy in these conditions needed to focus on the core business of teachers' and students' work in classrooms, treating reform of school management, assessment and curriculum, marketisation and deregulation as adjunct issues. Accordingly, the Centre has established the *Core Research Program*, a comprehensive four-year longitudinal study of Singapore schooling. The Core Program addresses six interrelated key research questions:

1.   What institutional rules and discourses shape educational practice in Singapore?
2.   What are the principal patterns of student achievement and attainment in Singapore?
3.   How is pedagogy practised in Singapore?
4.   Why do Singaporean teachers teach the way they do?
5.   What are the principal academic, economic, cultural, social, civic and psychological outcomes of schooling?
6.   What are the distinctive life plans, choices and pathways that young Singaporeans set for themselves?

To address these questions, the *Core Research Program* is divided into six discrete panels, each linked and nested to enable triangulation of quantitative and qualitative data, and HLM analyses of the relationships.

The Core Program begins from an analytic map of the broad variable pathways from diverse linguistic/cultural communities and socioeconomic backgrounds to and through schooling. This will generate a picture of the social, demographic and cultural factors that impact upon school performance and outcomes and assess whether and to what

Table 11.1 Core panel design (2004–05)

Panels	Sample	Key focus
Panel 1: student background/achievement	Entire school population from 1993–2002+ (500,000 students pa)	Modelling impact of SES, race and MT on student achievement in high stakes assessment in primary, secondary and post-secondary levels
Panel 2: teacher and student survey	Sample (*n* = 19,000) primary and secondary students in random stratified sample of schools. Sample linked to Panels 3, 4 and 5 and linked to Panel 1. Sample of teachers (*n* = 4000) in same Primary and Secondary schools across all subjects.	Students: modelling impact of classroom pedagogy on student achievement in Maths and English controlling for student characteristics. Teachers: mapping pedagogical capacities and teaching practices. Also school climate and leadership.
Panel 3: classroom observation and coding	2004/5: sample of 950+ lessons in Maths, English, Science, Social Studies, Chinese, Malay and Tamil in 36 schools using the Singapore Coding Scheme.	Structure and distribution of classroom pedagogical practices with respect to knowledge, teaching and assessment.
Panel 4: discourse analysis of classroom interaction	Audio-taping and selected video of lessons drawn from Panel 3 above.	Structure of classroom talk, patterns of social interaction, language patterns and knowledge construction.
Panel 5: analysis of student work	Same sample as Panels 3 and 4 above.	Teacher assessment tasks and student work artefacts evaluated by expert teachers.
Panel 6: longitudinal survey of student experiences, choices, pathways	Sample of students (*n* = 27,500) 130 schools and post-secondary institutions.	Longitudinal measures of life experiences, patterns of social participation and attainment and life goals, choices and pathways.

extent these patterns fit the meritocratic ideals of the system (see Panel 1). At the same time, the design focuses on the practices of pedagogy: on both the everyday patterns of classroom talk and work, and on how system policies, school structure and leadership, teacher training, belief and attitude, curriculum, assessment influence and motivate teachers' work (see Panels 2, 3 and 4). The design also expands the definition of educational outcomes, including conventional indicators of achievement (year level retention, marks and grades, test and examination performance), but also analysing student artefact production (see Panel 5), and surveying social outcomes, choice and agency, acquired capital, psychological, vocational and lifestyle choices of students (see Panel 6).

The aim of the Core design, then, is to provide a comprehensive overview of variable levels of schooling. In so doing, it is an attempt to capture the complexity of a system in a way that the experimental design approach to 'evidence' cannot. The resultant design is:

- Multi-method: the different panels enable the blending and triangulation of quantitative (survey, observational) and qualitative (observational, discourse analytic, interview) data.
- Multi-level/ hierarchical: samples of students, classrooms and school are nested across panels, and linked to a comprehensive population database on achievement and sociodemographic background.
- Cross-sectional and longitudinal: cross-sectional samples and multi-year repeated measures are combined.
- Representative and generalisable: schools, teachers and students are selected from random stratified samples.
- Multiple outcome: cognitive and social outcomes are assessed through conventional test and exam scores, teacher evaluation of student artefacts, and longitudinal surveys.

The Core Program, then, sets out to build a comprehensive, multidisciplinary evidence base for medium and long-term policy formation. In what follows, we take up a range of the conceptual and methodological challenges it raises. We then summarise some of its key findings and policy impacts to date.

Conceptual and methodological issues

Educational policy that attempts to 'steer from a difference' without a multilayered empirical data base on teachers' and students' work, everyday lives and interaction in classrooms is inherently limited. It is limited in terms of its capacity to represent teachers' and students' work and classroom lives, and thereby to shift, mobilise or transform teaching/learning relations; and it is limited in terms of its actual analysis of strengths and weaknesses of teaching and teachers.

The Core Program focuses on classroom pedagogical practice – on how school knowledge is classified and framed, taught and assessed in large representative samples of Singaporean schools. Classroom units and phases are coded using a systematic coding system (Luke *et al.* 2003), which draws categories from sociocultural psychology, discourse analysis and curriculum theory. This model brings together behavioural and interactional observational protocols with curriculum theory and discourse analytic categories. All individual lessons are audio-taped for subsequent transcription and linguistic corpus analysis. This enables secondary qualitative analysis (sociolinguistic, systemic functional, ethnomethodological) to explore and detail which patterns of classroom talk can be systematically linked to efficacy claims in particular disciplinary fields, and with particular student populations. The corpus of transcripts, further, is large enough to enable more generalisable claims about subject, level and stream variability of discourse, interaction and knowledge representation. We have to date used transcripts and audio-tapes to illustrate to senior ministry policy makers and administrators the 'state of the art' in the field, providing cases of, for instance, Chinese, Tamil and Malay language pedagogy.

Process/product, teacher effects, qualitative case studies and teacher effectiveness studies focus on pedagogical practices and their impact on students. At the same time, many of these are small, quasi-experimental or non-experimental design studies that do not attempt to measure, map and model pedagogical practices or their effects on student outcomes systematically. Unlike traditional school effects or educational value added studies, the aim here is to blend quantitative classroom coding, teacher accounts and discourse analysis to yield detailed, thick description of classroom practices and model how they mediate the impact of student background characteristics and prior achievement on student outcomes. In this way, then, the Core Program is empirically focused on precisely what is missing from the US policy approach – the complex, multileveled and multi-mediating 'black box' of everyday student/teacher pedagogical interaction around knowledge, artefacts and text.

The design, further, overcomes one of the central methodological issues in discourse analysis and classroom ethnography, where sampling numbers tend to be small, with high levels of local contextual validity but limited generalisability across the system. The hierarchical design goes beyond the conventional multilevel models that locates students in particular classes and classes to particular schools and communities. Rather, the Core Program is designed in such a way that the sample of students, classrooms and schools that are the focus of work in Panels 3, 4 and 5 are nested within the sample frame for Panel 2 (the cross-sectional study of teacher and student effects). In turn, the large sample drawn for Panel 2 is nested within the population of all students in Singaporean schools that is the basis of our analysis of the impact of social background on student high stakes assessment performance in grades 4, 6, 10 and 12 in Panel 1.

The nested sample design permits us to link and triangulate data sets across panels. This adds to the depth and comprehensiveness of measures of pedagogical practice, classroom processes and student outcomes. For example, it allows linkage of the teacher and student self-reported measures of pedagogical practice and the assessments of student achievement that are the focus of Panel 2 to the detailed observations of pedagogical practice in Panel 3, the corpus of classroom talk and interactions in Panel 4, the collection of student artefacts and assignment tasks in Panel 5, and the family background and student achievement data of Panel 1. The result is a range of input, process/practice and outcome measures for modelling purposes, and a descriptive and analytical picture of classroom life. In sum, the findings of both quantitative classroom observation, teacher and student accounts of these interactions, and qualitative discourse analyses of the same events can be triangulated. Because the classrooms, teachers and students are parts of random stratified samples, qualitatively detailed patterns of classroom interaction can lead to meaningful generalisations about typical and ubiquitous patterns of discourse and exchange.

Furthermore, the repeated measure longitudinal design of some of the panels permits far more exact or precise modelling of student outcomes by modelling changes in student outcomes at the individual level over time (Singer and Willett 2003). Indeed, for understanding the causal structuring of student outcomes, longitudinal growth modelling provides a superior design approach over randomised controlled field trials. Randomised controlled field experiments depend upon the hypothetical construction of socially artificial classroom and school settings (in effect, socially *inauthentic* experimental settings), since the social composition of classrooms and schools in the real world are far from randomly constituted or socially heterogeneous in composition. Pedagogical practices and educational outcomes are routinely shaped in interaction with social and demographic factors, including the highly stratified credentialing projects and practices of communities and families. It is for this very reason – the violation of the multivariate assumption of independence of observations – that statisticians have developed multilevel models in organisational research over the past 15 or so years in order to take into account the nested nature of observations in either cross-sectional or longitudinal studies.

In longitudinal studies, for example, Raudenbush and Bryk (2002, 5) note, 'studies of student growth involve a doubly nested structure of repeated observations within individuals, who are in turn nested organizational settings'. Ignoring the clustered or nested nature of observations results, among other perfidious statistical outcomes, in serious mis-estimates of standard errors and unreliable causal models (Singer and Willett 2003).

At a policy level, our view is that research findings generated in artificial randomised controlled experimental settings are unlikely to have significant purchase in the real world of classrooms and schools, no matter how big the effect sizes, and are therefore likely to be of relatively limited value.

Longitudinal designs, on the other hand, do not ignore powerful institutional rules or violate important validity assumptions. Instead, they take advantage of natural variance and historical change within and across human populations, cultural and institutional settings to develop models of the impact of pedagogical practices on student outcomes over time controlling for family background and individual characteristics, including cultural and linguistic diversity. Indeed, longitudinal studies can reveal the institutional rules and the embeddedness of schools in particular social, cultural, political and institutional contexts and their impact on classroom processes and student outcomes. It is exactly this kind of realistic and naturalistic evidentiary database that policy making requires.

Unlike conventional randomised field trial designs, multilevel designs allow accurate modelling of variance in student achievement at the student, class and school level (cf. Newmann and Associates 1995). This enables policy makers to gauge whether interventions need to be targeted at the classroom level within schools, at differences between schools that students attend, or at the individual and family background characteristics of the students attending schools. If most of the variance is located at the student level ('Level 1') in rather than at the classroom or school level, policy makers would be well advised to focus on initiatives that address student, family and community capital formation and mobilisation. If much of the variance is located at the school ('Level 3') rather than at the individual or classroom level, then policy would need to focus on aggregate composition effects, and the mobilisation of school organisational capacity. But if most of the variance is located at the classroom level ('Level 2') within schools, then policy attention clearly needs to focus on face-to-face social interactional and affiliated organisational practices (tracking within subjects, streaming across subjects, the allocation of teachers to streams and classes, pedagogical practices) within schools at the classroom level. And where sources of variance cross levels (as they generally will), then precisely targeted mixed policy initiatives – however difficult these may be for educational bureaucracies and systems – are necessary.

Where the strength of cross-sectional and longitudinal designs is augmented by multiple and triangulated measurements of pedagogical practice, classroom processes and student outcomes, the theoretical and policy benefits can be even more substantial. Rowan *et al.* (2002), for example, not only argue that longitudinal school and teacher effect studies produce vastly superior and realistic estimates of the impact of family background and classroom practices on student outcomes, but that multiple measures of pedagogical practice – for example the use of teacher logs as well as survey data – provide substantially improved measures of pedagogical practice. Again, Alton-Lee (2004: 11) observes:

> ... longitudinal micro-genetic studies carried out in classrooms (not laboratories) that intensively trace learner experiences and changes over time ... optimise validity through multiple observational approaches (e.g. broadcast microphones, multiple videos and observers) and in depth assessment of learner outcomes. Within micro-genetic method, prediction can offer a foundation for theoretical development and explanatory power about cause, and interrelated influences, even when those influences are not directly observable such as processes in the mind.

We have already discussed the use of observational coding data, survey (teacher, student) data and qualitative (transcript, interview) data to measure pedagogical practice in Panels 2, 3 and 4. But we are also committed as a design principle to developing multiple (as well as longitudinal) measures of *multiple* student outcomes. Thus, on the one hand, we are endeavouring to analyse or develop multiple measures of cognitive performance or academic achievement: academic performance in national high stakes assessments in grades 4, 6, 10 and 12, standardised and scaled achievement in Maths and English in grades 5 and 9, and artefact production in grades 5 and 9. On the other hand, the Core Program develops measures that capture key non-cognitive outcomes of schooling, and to do so in a methodologically rigorous way. For example, Panel 2 develops a range of measures of non-cognitive skill, including measures of motivation, engagement, learning orientation, meta-cognition, self-regulation and academic self-efficacy. Panel 6 also includes a comprehensive array of measures of agentive, economic, social and civic capital that promote participation and attainment in a broad range of institutional practices – in schools, in labour markets and work places, in communities, in friendship groups and in civil society.

The rationale for developing multiple measures of student academic performance is obvious: it enhances validity. But the same rationale also applies to the measurement of multiple outcomes. Almost all school systems are committed to a broad range of educational outcomes in addition to academic achievement. As noted earlier, there is a shared rhetoric across OECD and other countries around the new educational outcomes required by 'knowledge economies' and the new work order, including non-cognitive competences in values and cultural disposition, communication and social relations, and so forth. Although specifications and emphases vary, school systems generally want students to develop particular arrays of intellectual habits, to become good community members and citizens, to develop moral character, to become productive workers, to grow into psychologically balanced and healthy individuals who are able to derive substantial existential meaning out of their lives. Yet, despite the broad commitment to these goals, school systems and researchers have done precious little to establish what 'value adding' they contribute to these outcomes. This is arguably one of the most glaring gaps between strategic policy making on the one hand, and programmatic policy making and educational research on the other. Indeed, we have only the most rudimentary understanding of the impact of schooling on the development of these broader goals and 'non-cognitive skills' or the complex relationships (and possible zero-sum exchanges) between cognitive and social skill development. This leaves policy makers more or less in the dark about the broader impact of schooling on the development of individual capital, capacities and commitments (Rothstein 2004: 95).

A critical realist approach to evidence

What is entailed in making educational policy committed to a fair and equitable distribution of educational capital in an age 'after neomarxism', 'after deconstruction', 'after poststructuralism', following on from three decades of increasingly sophisticated theory wars within critical educational studies, and indeed, after naïve appeals to psychological experimentalism? Whatever methodological form it takes, critical educational research continually needs to be re-enlisted and re-invented to address the tenacious material and social problems faced by schools and teachers, communities and cultures.

In Singapore, we have begun this process. To date, work on the impacts of socioeconomic background, race and linguistic difference on achievement (Liau *et al.* 2005), on pedagogical patterns in the teaching of Chinese, Tamil and Malay (Liu *et al.* 2004; Shegar 2005; Abu-Bakar 2005) and on pedagogical capacity to generate skills and knowledges for the new economy (Luke *et al.* 2005) has been tabled. This in turn has been influential in the development of new policy and curriculum interventions – the impact of which the Core Program will continue to track.

We have here argued for a 'critical realist' approach to educational research and policy making. Such an approach enlists the full range of educational research tools to generate as broad an empirical picture of educational practices, patterns and institutional outcomes as possible. But even then, having established a comprehensive picture of an educational system at work, the serious work of theorising and modelling only begins: for policy analysis and construction is theoretical, interpretive and discursive work. It requires historical narratives and scenario planning, explanations about how things came to be, and about how alternative scenarios might be constructed (Luke 2003). The myth underlying the current approach to scientific evidence is that there is something akin to a hypodermic effect between a particular educational 'treatment', however construed, its articulation in policy or curriculum discourse, its implementation and application in the complex fields of an educational system, and consequential student results.

Life, work and policy would be much easier if indeed any of us lived in such a simple and pristine educational universe. If there is a single lesson from the school improvement reform literature of the past two decades, it is that educational policy making and implementation entails a complex set of embeddings and mediations through and across the nested organisational cultures of educational systems. Where this is the case, nothing less than the multidisciplinary, multilevel and longitudinal approach that we have presented here will do.

Acknowledgements

The authors acknowledge our colleagues in the Core Research Project: Lau Shun, Albert Liau, Kim Koh, Trivina Kang, Anneliese Kramer-Dahl, Courtney Cazden, Ridzuan bin Abdul Rahim, Dennis Kwek and Savandra Gopinathan. We thank Peter Freebody and James Ladwig for design work and the ongoing support of the Singapore Ministry of Education, schools and teachers in this work. Regular updates and technical reports are available at: http://crpp/nie/edu/sg.

References

Abu-Bakar, M. (2005) 'The teaching of Malay in Singapore classrooms', Technical Report. Singapore: Centre for Research in Pedagogy and Practice.

Alton-Lee, A. (2004) *Iterative Best Evidence Synthesis Programme*, Wellington: Ministry of Education (www.minedu.govt.nz/goto/bestevidencesynthesis).

Apple, M.W. (1978) *Ideology and Curriculum,* London: Routledge.

Bowles, S. and Gintis, H. (1977) *Schooling in Capitalist America*, New York: Basic Books.

Callahan, R.B. (1962) *Education and the Cult of Efficiency*, Chicago, IL: University of Chicago Press.

Cazden, C.B., Johns, V. and Hymes, D. (eds) (1972) *Functions of Language in the Classroom*, New York: Teachers College Press.

Gould, S. (1981) *The Mismeasure of Man*, New York: Norton.

Habermas, J. (1998) *Between Facts and Norms*, Boston, MA: MIT Press.

Liau, A.K., Tan, T.K. and Aye, K.M. (2005) 'The multilevel effects of SES and race on student achievement in Singapore', manuscript under review, *London Review of Education*.

Liu, Y.B., Kotov, R. and Rahim, R. (2004) 'The teaching of Chinese in Singapore classrooms: a preliminary analysis', Technical Report. Singapore: Centre for Research in Pedagogy and Practice.

Lingard, R., Ladwig, J., Mills, M., Hayes, D., Bahr, M., Chant, D., Gore, J., Christie, P. and Luke, A. (2002) *Queensland School Longitudinal Restructuring Study*, Brisbane: Education Queensland.

Luke, A. (1997) 'The material effects of the word: apologies, stolen children and public speech', *Discourse*, 23(3): 151–80.

Luke, A. (2003) 'After the marketplace: evidence, social science and educational research', *Australian Educational Researcher*, 9(3): 43–78.

Luke, A. (2005) 'Evidence-based state literacy policy: a critical alternative', in N. Bascia, A. Cumming, A. Datnow, K. Leithwood and D. Livingstone (eds) *International Handbook of Educational Policy*, Dordrecht: Springer, 661–75.

Luke, A., Cazden, C., Lin, A., and Freebody, P. (2005) 'A coding scheme for the analysis of Singapore classrooms', Technical paper. Singapore: Centre for Research in Pedagogy and Practice.

Luke, A., Freebody, P., Lau, S. and Gopinathan, S. (2005) 'Towards research-based innovation and reform: Singapore schooling in transition'. *Asia Pacific Journal of Education*, 25(1): 5–28.

Luke, A., Rahim, R., Koh, K.H., Lau, S., Ismail, M. and Hogan, D. (2005) 'Innovation and enterprise in classroom practice: a discussion of enabling and disenabling pedagogical factors in P5 and S3 classrooms, Technical Report. Singapore: Centre for Research in Pedagogy and Practice.

Mok, J.K.H. and Chan, D.K.K. (2002) *Globalisation and Education: The Quest for Quality Education in Hong Kong*, Hong Kong: Hong Kong University Press.

National Institute of Child Health and Human Development (2000) *Report of the National Reading Panel.* (NIH Publication No. 900-4769), Washington, DC: US Government Printing Office.

Newmann, F. and Associates (1995) *Authentic Achievement: Restructuring Schools for Intellectual Quality*, San Francisco, CA: Jossey-Bass.

Rowan, B., Correnti, R. and Miller, R. (2002) 'What large-scale survey research tells us about teacher effects on student achievement: insights from the prospects study of elementary schools. *Teachers College Record*, 8: 104.

Rothstein, R. (2004) *Class and Schools: Using Social, Economic and Educational Reform to Close the Black-White Achievement Gap*, New York: Teachers College Press.

Raudenbaush, R. and Bryk, A. (2002) *Hierarchical Linear Models: Applications and Data Analysis Methods*, 2nd edn, Thousand Oaks, CA: Sage.

Shegar, C. (2005) 'The teaching of Tamil in Singapore classrooms', Technical Report. Singapore: Centre for Research in Pedagogy and Practice.

Singer, J. and Willett, J. (2003) *Applied Longitudinal Analysis: Modelling Change and Event Occurrence*, New York: Oxford University Press.

Tan, J. (1998) 'The marketisation of education in Singapore: policies and implications', *Review of Education*, 44(1): 43–63.

Tan, J., Gopinathan, S. and Kam, H.W. (eds) (1998) *Education in Singapore*, Singapore: Prentice Hall.

US Department of Education (2002) 'Report on scientifically based research supported by US Department of Education', Press Release. Office of Public Affairs, November 18.

12 Performativity, measurement and research

A critique of performance-based research funding in New Zealand

Peter Roberts

Introduction

Over the past two decades, tertiary education in New Zealand has undergone some significant changes. One recent development with far-reaching implications for educational research is the introduction of a Performance-Based Research Fund (PBRF). Initiated by a Labour-led government but foreshadowed by the White Paper on tertiary education policy released under the previous National administration, the PBRF system is ostensibly designed to recognise and reward (through increased funding) those institutions performing at the highest levels in their research activities. The PBRF was introduced in 2003 following a careful review of similar schemes in the UK, Hong Kong and other countries. The results of the first round, released in 2004, attracted considerable attention in educational communities and the popular media. A second (partial) round is scheduled for 2006.

This chapter provides an overview and critique of performance-based research funding in New Zealand. The first section sets the PBRF in its broader policy context, details some of the main features of the scheme, and discusses the results of the 2003 exercise. The second part of the chapter provides a critical evaluation of the PBRF. A number of positive points are noted. These include the comprehensiveness of the deliberations that led to the development of the scheme, the relatively high degree of openness in the policy development process, and the expressed commitment to enhancing the quality of research in tertiary education institutions in New Zealand. At the same time, some important concerns are raised. These include the emphasis on measurement and the logic of performativity, the narrowing of our sense of what counts as worthwhile inquiry, the problematic nature of the appeal to 'quality' and the development of a competitive research culture. It is argued that the PBRF, while seeking to address problems created by the market-driven approach to tertiary education in the 1990s, ultimately reinforces and extends some of the key neoliberal ideas and practices that underpinned the process of marketisation.

Neoliberalism, 'third way' politics and research

When New Zealand's Labour-Alliance coalition government was elected in 1999, there was a sense of considerable relief among many educational commentators. After nine years of National Party rule, many students and academics were ready for an alternative to the relentless process of marketisation in education and other areas of social policy. Through the 1990s, New Zealanders were encouraged to view education as a commodity: something to be sold, traded and consumed. There was a heavy emphasis on choice and competition. In the tertiary education sector, institutions were expected to operate like businesses, with a chief executive officer, a 'Board of Directors' style of governance, performance indicators, and a strong entrepreneurial thrust. Image creation and aggressive marketing became the order of the day. The marketisation agenda found expression in a number of policy documents on tertiary education, culminating in the Green and White Papers of 1997 and 1998 respectively (Ministry of Education 1997, 1998).

The newly elected Labour-Alliance government wasted no time in setting up a major review of tertiary education. In early 2000, the Tertiary Education Advisory Commission (TEAC) was established, and by the end of 2001 four reports had been completed: *Shaping a Shared Vision* (TEAC 2000), *Shaping the System* (TEAC 2001a), *Shaping the Strategy* (TEAC 2001b), and *Shaping the Funding Framework* (TEAC 2001c). Senior Labour ministers were keen to distinguish themselves from both their National Party counterparts in the 1990s and the neoliberal policies promoted by Roger Douglas, Richard Prebble and other key figures in the fourth Labour government (1984–90). Following the release of the TEAC reports, the government has developed a *Tertiary Education Strategy* (Ministry of Education 2002) setting out priorities for the sector over the next five years. A permanent Tertiary Education Commission (TEC) has been formed to oversee the administration of tertiary education in New Zealand. There have also been policy initiatives in a number of related areas, including industry training (Ministry of Education 2001a), export education (Ministry of Education 2001b), Pacific education (Ministry of Education 2001c), and adult literacy (Ministry of Education 2001d).

Influenced by the 'Third Way' politics of Tony Blair in the UK, the New Zealand government has in recent years pushed for the development of a 'knowledge society and economy'. This ideal figures prominently in the *Tertiary Education Strategy* (Ministry of Education 2002) and it was also important in the TEAC reports (see especially, TEAC 2000). From the beginning of the process of post-1999 reform, there has been an explicit attempt to reduce the emphasis on choice, enhance cooperation, recognise diversity, preserve New Zealand's cultural heritage and foster innovation. There is, however, a significant degree of continuity between the policies of the current government and those introduced in the preceding 15 years. In some respects, the commodification of knowledge, research and education has been taken several steps *further* by Labour than it was by National. While there is now noticeably less talk about 'choice' in education policy, many other defining features of the market model promoted by National remain in place. There have been no substantial changes in structures of governance within tertiary education institutions, competitive marketing of courses and programmes continues, and the emphasis on 'accountability' and 'performance' remains in place. Indeed, the logic of performativity is arguably becoming more deeply entrenched, as the development of the Performance-Based Research Fund shows.

New Zealand's Performance-Based Research Fund has been developed by the current Labour-led government, but the conditions for its emergence were already in place more than a decade earlier. The Hawke Report (Department of Education 1988), released during the second term of the fourth Labour government, advocated a separation of teaching from research. The National government extended this idea in the latter half of the 1990s, tying the proposal more directly to a neoliberal education agenda. In the

White Paper of 1998 (Ministry of Education 1998) it was proposed that from 2000 a new system of research funding would be introduced. Traditionally, government research funding for universities in New Zealand had been tied to student numbers. Tuition subsidies have varied across different programmes, with higher-cost areas such as medicine receiving a greater share of the funding relative to the number of students enrolled. The White Paper suggested a system through which contestability in research funding would be progressively increased. Initially, 20 per cent of the government's contribution would be placed into a contestable pool, while the remaining 80 per cent would continue to be allocated through tuition subsidies based on numbers of effective full-time students (EFTS). The contestable component would increase by 20 per cent each year, with a review in 2001, until the ratio had been reversed (leaving 80 per cent contestable and 20 per cent based on student numbers).

While some of the key proposals in National's White Paper (e.g. further changes in systems of governance) have been abandoned, the notion of introducing greater contestability in research funding is one of several mooted changes to have found continuing support. The White Paper was thin on detail in establishing the criteria and processes through which the funds in the contestable pool would be allocated. The TEAC Commissioners, by contrast, were very thorough in their work on such questions. *Shaping the Funding Framework* (TEAC 2001c), the final and largest of the four TEAC reports, addressed funding issues at length. The report provided the foundation on which all subsequent policy developments in research funding have been built. The commissioners based their recommendations on a careful review of similar schemes elsewhere in the world. They also considered some of the distinctive features of the New Zealand context that had a bearing on research and tertiary education in New Zealand. Their intention was to find a funding scheme that would recognise and reward those institutions performing at the highest levels in their research activities.

In *Shaping the Funding Framework* the Commissioners discussed two major approaches to performance-based research funding: a performance indicator system (used in Australia and Israel) and a peer review model (used in Britain and Hong Kong). The performance indicator approach involves three main quantitative measures: the volume of 'research output' (based largely on the number of publications, with different weightings for different types of publication), the amount of external funding gained, and postgraduate degree completions. The peer review model considers not just quantitative measures but also the quality of research, measured against national and international standards of excellence. Judgements about research quality are made by peers – in the case of Britain's Research Assessment Exercise (RAE), by expert disciplinary panels – and the unit of assessment becomes not the institution but the disciplinary-based department (p. 92). The Commissioners saw advantages and disadvantages in both systems, and concluded that neither would be ideal for the New Zealand tertiary education environment. They advocated a 'mixed model' incorporating elements of both approaches. Institutional performance would be measured on the basis of three criteria: a quality rating of academic staff; the level of external research income; and the number of postgraduate research degree completions. The Commission proposed that the first of these criteria should count for 50 per cent of the allocation, with the other two weighted at 25 per cent each. The assessment of academic staff would be repeated in three years and be conducted on a five-yearly basis thereafter. Assessment for the other two categories would be carried out on a yearly basis (pp. 96–7). The

Commission recommended that the PBRF account for approximately one-third of the total estimated expenditure on research by New Zealand's universities.

Further work on this issue was continued, from July 2002, by the Performance-Based Research Fund Working Group. Set up to provide detailed advice for the Transition Tertiary Education Commission and the Ministry of Education on the design and implementation of the PBRF, the Working Group reported in December 2002 (PBRF Working Group 2002). The Working Group recommendations were similar to those of the Tertiary Education Advisory Commission. The Working Group maintained that the absence of performance-based incentives placed New Zealand at a disadvantage relative to other nations. With an increasingly globalised market for high-quality researchers, it was argued, this country must find ways to remain internationally competitive and to attract talented academic staff (p. 6). The primary focus of the PBRF would be to 'reward and encourage excellence' (p. 7). This would be vital, it was claimed, if the country was to achieve its growth and innovation goals. Excellence, the Working Party suggested, pertains not just to the production of respected books, articles and other forms of research 'output' but to the creation, application and dissemination of leading-edge knowledge and the support of others (including postgraduate students) in these pursuits. The Working Group recommended a funding model with the three elements identified in the fourth TEAC report, but with slightly altered weightings: 60 per cent to be based on ratings of academic researchers (the 'Quality Evaluation' part of the process), 25 per cent to be based on research degree completions, and 15 per cent to be based on the external research income gained by participating tertiary education organisations (p. 10).

The first 'Quality Evaluation' of individual academics was completed in 2003. A total of 22 Tertiary Education Organisations (TEOs) participated in this process. In addition, one TEO submitted a return for the research degree completions component of the PBRF assessment while another submitted a return for external research income. There were thus 24 TEOs involved in at least one of the three PBRF components (TEC 2004: 4). Academics in participating institutions and organisations were required to prepare individual 'evidence portfolios' (EPs) in which their research 'outputs' for the period 1 January 1997 to 31 December 2002 were listed. There were three sections in each EP: one devoted to the quality and quantity of research outputs (on which 70 per cent of the individual rating would be based), another detailing evidence of 'peer esteem' (15 per cent), and a third setting out contributions to a research environment (15 per cent). Within the first section, academics were required to nominate what they considered to be their four best research outputs. In addition, they were to list up to 50 other outputs. A spreadsheet was supplied for the purposes of developing the portfolio. Suggested descriptors for each type of output were provided, a column was supplied (in the first section) for indicating whether an output had been 'quality assured', and small spaces (with preset word limits) were set aside for comments and explanations of any 'special circumstances'. The submitted portfolios from each participating institution were evaluated by external panels in the relevant disciplinary areas. Each academic was assigned a grade: 'A' ('research of a world-class standard'), 'B' ('very good quality research'), 'C' ('good quality research') or 'R' ('did not meet the requirements for a "C"') (TEC 2004: 6). These grades were made available to the rated individuals. The aggregated ratings of individual academics, when combined with measures of postgraduate completions and external research funding, would determine the total PBRF allocation for each participating institution.

The results of the 2003 round showed major differences between the participating TEOs, with the seven traditional universities (the University of Auckland, the University of Canterbury, Victoria University of Wellington, the University of Otago, the University of Waikato, Lincoln University and Massey University) achieving markedly higher quality scores than the other institutions. The country's newest university, Auckland University of Technology (formerly Auckland Institute of Technology), was ranked around the middle of the results table. The TEC report on the 2003 exercise notes that '[r]elatively few researchers outside the university sector secured an "A" or "B" Quality Category, and some TEOs have very few researchers rated "C" or above' (TEC 2004: 11). The best results, generally speaking, were achieved by 'long-established disciplines with strong research cultures, such as philosophy, chemistry and psychology' (p. 9). Newer areas of study such as design, sport and exercise science, and television and multimedia studies fared less well. Subject areas within the biological and physical sciences, social sciences and humanities tended to achieve higher scores than those within business and the creative and performing arts (p. 9). According to the TEC report, a 'substantial number' (5.7 per cent) of staff in TEOs are undertaking research of a world-class standard and there are 'significant numbers of high-calibre researchers in a good range of the 41 subject areas'. Nearly 40 per cent were rated 'R'. The report stresses, however, that 'there is a large proportion of new and emerging researchers, many of high-calibre and potential' among these 'R' ratings (p. 8). Of the participating TEOs, 15 lodged returns for external research income. A total of approximately $195 million in external funding was recorded, all but about $1 million of which was generated by the eight universities (p. 4). Thirteen TEOs listed research degree completions, of which approximately two-thirds were for Masters programmes and one-third for doctorates (p. 4). The results of this round and subsequent PBRF assessments will count for a successively greater proportion of the total government funding for research in TEOs over the next few years, with the enrolment-based 'top ups' being phased out completely by 2007 (p. 12).

A critique

The process of developing the PBRF scheme has been thorough and, by comparison with research funding proposals in the 1990s, well grounded in research and appropriate academic expertise. The fourth TEAC report sets the question of research funding in a wider international context and provides a reasoned account of strengths and weaknesses in the New Zealand system. The merits of different overseas performance-based research funding schemes are considered carefully, potential problems are noted, and the recommendations flow logically from the preceding analysis. While it was already accepted that some form of performance-based research funding was likely to be implemented by the time the PBRF Working Group was formed, the Working Group's report is generally lucid and systematic in laying out what form the scheme would take. The Working Group's report, like the fourth TEAC report, draws attention to potential problems and responds to these. Throughout the PBRF development process, there has been a consistent expressed commitment – on the part of the Tertiary Education Advisory Commissioners, the PBRF Working Group, and the government – to the goal of improving the quality of research in New Zealand. There has also been a relatively high degree of openness in the policy development process. This has been evident, for example, in the manner in which key documents have been made available for public scrutiny through the internet. By all appearances, the move to a performance-based approach has been motivated, to a considerable extent, by a desire to improve the fairness, transparency and effectiveness of the system through which government funding for research is allocated.

Intellectual activity, measurement and 'outputs'

Despite these significant strengths of the policy process, the overall effect has been a narrowing of what counts as worthwhile intellectual activity. It is not that the definition of 'research' has been unnecessarily restrictive (both the fourth TEAC report and the Working Party report provide clear, well developed definitions); rather, it is the deeper logic behind the process and the practical consequences for intellectual life that are of concern. Performance-based research funding, in New Zealand as in Hong Kong, Australia and the UK, reinforces the view that only *measurable* forms of intellectual activity are worthwhile for research funding purposes. The PBRF process, far from disrupting the language of neoliberalism, has played a significant role in cementing it more firmly in bureaucratic and institutional consciousness. Harley (2002: 188) reports that in the British context, 'there is a growing body of evidence to show that academics on the ground feel themselves increasingly constrained to produce and disseminate that knowledge which has immediate value in terms of RAE rankings ... rather than intrinsic value and potential worth'. The same pattern is likely to be established in New Zealand, with academics changing their scholarly priorities *and themselves* to meet the demands of the PBRF system. All forms of research activity must now be translatable into the language of 'outputs' if they are to count under the PBRF scheme. The key policy actors in the PBRF process have been at pains to stress that a variety of forms of academic work can count as 'outputs'. Those completing portfolios were informed that it was not merely academic books and articles in refereed journals that could be included but also musical performances, poems, works of art, dramatic performances and so on. This expansive view of acceptable 'outputs' has allowed a wide range of subject areas to be included in the PBRF exercise. It has, however, also encouraged many who wished to participate (or who were required to do so by their institution) to think about their work in a new light. The idea of academic life being a vocation will come to seem quaint and irrelevant, and the notion that research should be driven by a deep form of *inner* commitment (e.g. to the process of investigation, to truth, to seeking knowledge for its own sake, to dialogue with others pursuing similar questions, or to the interplay of ideas) will quickly become overwhelmed by extrinsically defined demands to *perform* – to produce higher scoring units of measurable output for assessment at periodic intervals by external panels.

The most obvious indication of the importance of measurable indices in the PBRF scheme is the calculation of total externally generated research income. This counts for 15 per cent of the funding a TEO receives through the PBRF process. The problems with indexing government funding against externally generated research funding are numerous, but perhaps the most obvious – and important – is that some domains of study are far more likely to receive this sort of funding than others. Possibilities for external, non-government funding are comparatively plentiful in areas such as medicine, engineering, business and the applied sciences, but they are scarce in areas such as classical studies, romance languages, art history and many other fields within the arts and humanities. Universities without traditionally strong revenue generating faculties and departments will thus be at a significant disadvantage. It is not clear, in a system devoted to 'performance', why the external research income criterion should be applied across the board at all. *If* the logic is that performance must be measured, then performance in relation to the generation of external research income should arguably apply only to those areas where funding is readily available and researchers might reasonably expect to compete against each other for it. A similarly problematic form of measurement instituted in the PBRF scheme is the number of Masters and doctoral completions. This counts 25 per cent towards the total PBRF funding for a TEO. Here the problems are of a rather different order. Having a measure of this kind encourages institutions, against the rhetoric of 'quality, quality, quality' surrounding the PBRF process, to 'pump out' as many graduates and postgraduates as possible, risking a *decline* in quality.

Problematising 'quality'

The promoters of the PBRF scheme have emphasised the importance of quality over quantity in assessing individual researchers' evidence portfolios. This, it has been asserted, is one of the features that distinguishes the New Zealand PBRF from similar schemes in some other countries (e.g. Australia). The concept of quality is, however, not without its problems. 'Quality', both in New Zealand and elsewhere, has become a vacuous term: one with no fixed content of its own but with an almost infinite potential to be manipulated and reshaped according to the purpose at hand. Vidovich and Porter (1999: 568) argue that the 'complex and contested' nature of quality has, in Australia, allowed the concept to serve the interests of the government in 'increasing higher education's accountability to external stakeholders which have traditionally been held at "arm's length" from universities'. Bernard, in discussing the impact of the British RAE on the field of history, maintains that identifying the 'best' historians is problematic because:

> ... in history there are no objective or repeatable and verifiable tests of exceptional quality of work comparable to those in the physical sciences, not least because it is not a race to discover new knowledge. That makes judgements of quality ... inescapably subjective and provisional.
>
> (Bernard 2000: 103)

There is no agreement among New Zealand researchers about the meaning of 'quality' in exercises such as the PBRF, at least not in some subject areas; yet when the results appear we are encouraged to act *as if* such agreement existed. The grounds for distinguishing higher quality 'outputs' from those of lesser quality are always contestable. Even where agreement can be reached on certain distinctions between, say, different journals, academics may *choose*, with good reasons, to work against their own PBRF interests in the publication of their research. They may, for example, seek to publish an article in a freely available electronic journal rather than a subscriber only print-based journal (even where they suspect a PBRF panel will rank the latter higher than the former) on ethical grounds, believing that the results of research should be open to as many people as possible. They may place commitment to their profession higher than publication in refereed journals, and seek first and foremost to disseminate the results of their work directly to their colleagues. An academic may feel he or she can make a more worthwhile contribution by helping a struggling student to finish a Masters thesis rather than seeking out likely scholarship winners for the extra 'output' points they are likely to earn on an evidence portfolio. A researcher may wish to publish a book in New Zealand rather than attempting to secure a prestigious overseas publisher who may have no particular commitment to New Zealand book buyers or who may set a price that will place the book out of reach for New Zealand students. Performance-based systems of research funding assume a certain kind of self-interest that is not always evident in the decisions academics make about how to prioritise their time and intellectual energies.

While there has, on the face of it, been an attempt to move away from purely quantifiable indices of performance, the logic of performativity underlying the PBRF has tended to push the process closer towards such measures. There has been considerable rhetoric in recent years about the importance of research 'impact'. This has been pushed by both policy makers and institutional leaders. Within universities, for example, creating 'impact' with one's work as a researcher is a significant factor in determining promotion at higher levels on the academic scale. Similar thinking has prevailed elsewhere in the world, leading to the development of a 'star' culture among researchers. The PBRF process has continued this trend, with a move – at least in some areas of study – to create rankings of journals according to their supposed 'impact factor'. This follows a trend already established in Britain with the circulation within university departments of '[u]nofficial and not so unofficial lists of journals ... believed to count most' in the RAE (Harley 2002: 188). With weightings assigned to publications according to the 'impact factor' of the journal, an apparently qualitative measure can quickly become a quantitative one. But even if numbers are not assigned to journals (or, say, to book publishers according to their alleged prestige and international significance), and other measures of 'impact' are taken into account, the logic remains intact. The idea is for researchers to stand out from the crowd, gain as much attention as possible, and thus increase their value in the educational marketplace.

Competition, accountability and the 'consumer'

At the heart of neoliberal economic and social policy is the ontological construct *homo economicus*: the rational, competitive, self-interested individual consumer (Peters and Marshall 1996). The PBRF reinforces the importance of the 'consumer', the value of competition, and the significance of self-interest in contemporary tertiary education. In setting up a system of rankings for departments and institutions the PBRF encourages a 'league table' mentality. Universities have been quick to exploit their results, where they can be construed favourably, in seeking to entice students. Where the results have been less than encouraging, new advertising angles (e.g. linking an institution with 'real world' learning) have been developed in an effort to retain and expand the existing student base. Overall, the level of competition between institutions has increased, and 'branding' has become even more important than it was in earlier years. Massey University, for example, increased its spending on marketing to $3.16 million in 2004, an increase of more than 47 per cent from the previous year. In the same period, Auckland University of Technology increased its marketing expenditure by 56 per cent to $1.6 million. Such increases have not been confined to universities. Spending at Te Wananga o Aotearoa, for example, was up by 97 per cent in 2004. Manukau Institute of Technology and the Open Polytechnic of New Zealand also devoted comparatively large sums to marketing in this period ($2.5 million and $3.1 million respectively). The total spent on marketing across all public tertiary education institutions amounted to $26.5 million, an increase of $3 million from 2003 and $13 million from 1999 when the Labour-Alliance coalition government was elected (Association of University Staff 2005a: 2). Students are now, as much as ever, regarded as self-interested consumers who must be 'won over' by institutions through intense competition with each other. The PBRF has played a crucial role in the aggressive advertising campaigns that have formed part of this competitive ethos.

The PBRF also signals the arrival of new forms of competition among academics. Armed with their PBRF scores, academics can now regard themselves as 'research entrepreneurs' (cf. Ozga 1998). Given what is at stake in the PBRF process, institutions will become increasingly keen to recruit proven higher scorers. One or two academics with high scores will not be sufficient for most departments, however, and moves will be made to form strategic groupings of such individuals. Low scoring departments with little hope of building a critical mass of PBRF 'stars' will find themselves under increasing pressure and may, over time, be closed down altogether. Some will adapt by changing their focus and seeking out new forms of external funding (e.g. through closer relationships with industry: see Willmott 2003). The individual academic thus becomes both a 'seller' and a 'buyer' in the new system. Top PBRF scorers will be able to market themselves as highly saleable commodities, while institutions, in turn, will seek to develop and sell more attractive working packages to recruit such 'stars'. The enticements might include higher salaries, lighter or no teaching loads, more internal research funding, better computing or secretarial support, more impressive collections of scholarly materials, stronger groupings of other high achieving researchers, larger numbers of promising research students and so on. Strong incentives are in place, then, for not only students but academics to continue the legacy bequeathed by 15 years of neoliberal reform in seeing themselves as self-interested consumers in a highly competitive tertiary education environment. In the longer term, the results of the PBRF could mirror those of the British RAE, which one commentator (Elton 2000: 281) has described as inherently 'competitive, adversarial and punitive'.

Underpinning the PBRF process is the assumption that tertiary education institutions ought to be held accountable for public money invested in research. Few would argue against the principle that those funded by the government, and hence by taxpayers, have a responsibility to ensure that the money is well spent. 'Accountability' and 'responsibility' are, however, rather different concepts. The former is one of the cornerstones of neoliberal discourse and its roots in New Zealand education policy date back to the second half of the 1980s. At that time, the New Zealand Treasury (1987) argued that education had suffered from a form of 'provider capture'. For Treasury officials, the solution was to reduce the excessive power teachers exercised over educational decisions and to make them more 'accountable' for their performance in the classroom. The notion of accountability gained a strong foothold in the tertiary education sector in the 1990s, with a heavy policy emphasis on competition and student choice. It was believed that when students were given stronger incentives to 'shop around' for courses and programmes, tertiary education institutions would respond by performing at a higher level to retain and enhance their enrolments (and hence their funding). Accountability is essentially a *punitive* concept: it assumes that those being funded cannot quite be trusted, or can be trusted in only a limited way (see Gibbs 2001), and must be monitored and audited at regular intervals. It wrests power away from those to whom the demand for accountability applies and places it squarely in the hands of 'consumers' of the services provided by those being judged. 'Consumers' can be students, parents, employers, the government or taxpayers. Discourses of accountability depict educational decisions and actions as *transactions*, with similar characteristics to transactions in the economic sphere. The relationship between 'providers' (institutions, organisations and individual teachers or academics) and 'consumers' becomes a *contractual* one. Accountability, as Delanty (2003: 75) points out, is 'in effect about increased accounting'. Responsibility, on the other hand, places the teacher or academic at the centre and implies professional, pedagogical and personal obligations to others. Taking responsibility seriously demands new words that have no place in the discourse of accountability: words such as commitment, sincerity, respect, and authenticity (cf. Nixon 2004: 249–51).

Putting the PBRF in perspective

The old system of research funding in New Zealand tertiary education was certainly not without its flaws, some of which have been highlighted, very effectively, by the TEAC commissioners and supporters of the PBRF scheme. Allocating money for research to tertiary education institutions on the basis of student enrolments can mean that some who are not actively engaged in research, or not producing a sufficient quantity of work (whatever that might be), or delivering 'outputs' of the required quality (however that might be defined), receive funding they do not deserve. Indeed, as the TEC report on the 2003 PBRF round points out, questions can be raised about 'the extent to which all degree providers are meeting their current statutory obligations; under section 254(3)(a) of the Education Act 1989, degrees must be "taught mainly by people engaged in research"' (TEC 2004: 13). Such questions, however, have been raised long before the PBRF exercise and the release of the TEC's evaluation. The genesis of the problem lies in the proliferation of new tertiary education 'providers', new programmes and new qualifications under the banners of 'choice' and 'competition' in the 1990s. This was a consequence of a vigorous and sustained programme of marketisation in tertiary education under the National government, the main features of which have been discussed at length by critical education policy analysts for more than a decade (see e.g. Peters *et al.* 1993; Fitzsimons 1995; Gordon 1995; Peters 1994, 1997; Roberts 1999; Roberts and Peters 1999; Peters and Roberts 1999; Olssen 2001; Codd 2001). Policy makers within government, the Ministry of Education and the New Zealand Qualifications Authority, among other bodies, were determined to break down distinctions between the 'academic' and the 'vocational', and between universities and other tertiary education institutions. Degrees are now offered by multiple institutions and the number of private tertiary education establishments has grown dramatically. The ideology of neoliberalism demands 'quality' in the provision of degrees and other qualifications in only a strictly limited way. In a marketised system of tertiary education, it is assumed that if 'consumers' *want* higher quality programmes, they will pay for them and the institutions will respond. Such an approach assumes, and this is one of its most telling flaws, that all who 'consume' tertiary education are adequately prepared to make good decisions about what counts as 'quality'. There is, however, no *necessary* connection between higher quality tertiary education and increases in student enrolments. In practice, the massive growth in 'providers' and qualifications – including degrees – has made it difficult to even *address* the question of quality, let alone assess it. After a series of controversies over courses in computing, diving, English for speakers of other languages, and other areas, the New Zealand government has finally announced that it will be undertaking a review of private tertiary education and training (TEC 2005). This has been welcomed by the Association of University Staff (AUS), who note that '[d]espite the significant differences in quality and accountability, private training establishments and universities are funded at almost the same levels'. For example, in the arts and social sciences, non-degree programmes in private training establishments are funded at a rate of $5,331 per equivalent full-time student, while degree programmes in universities receive $6,049 per equivalent full-time student. The AUS claims that the review will 'lead to less money being wasted on tertiary courses which are of low quality and value which should never have received public funding' (AUS 2005b: 1).

In this context, the PBRF occupies an ambivalent position in tertiary education policy. On the one hand, the PBRF process has produced results that the Tertiary Education Commission and supporters of the scheme believe will be helpful in allocating more research funding for those who deserve it. For the most part, the beneficiaries here will be the traditional universities. To this extent, the PBRF exercise could play an important role in redressing the apparent inequities thrown up by the enrolment-based funding schemes of the past. Yet, in the middle of all of the information and activity associated with the PBRF process, it is easy to lose sight of the bigger picture. A focus on the *total funding* from government for universities and research, relative to the overall budget for tertiary education and government spending in other areas, helps put the PBRF scheme into perspective. Government funding for universities has fallen significantly over the past quarter of a century. Between 1980 and 2002 the decline, in inflation adjusted terms, was 34.76 per cent, with a particularly marked drop (23 per cent) in the period from 1991 to 2002. Teaching ratios (total EFTS per full-time academic staff member) increased from 12.5 to 18.3 between 1980 and 2002. In 1991 73 per cent of total operating revenue was covered by government grants; by 2002 this had fallen to 42 per cent (Scott and Scott 2004). With the introduction of a student loans scheme in the 1990s, student debt has spiralled and now amounts to over $6 billion. This places a considerable burden on students, their families and, in cases where the debts are not repaid, taxpayers. Spending on private training establishments has increased dramatically over the past decade and now runs to hundreds of millions of dollars each year. Far larger sums are now devoted to advertising, marketing and consultants' fees in tertiary education institutions (including universities) than was the case in the past. Other areas of government spending (e.g. defence: see Campbell 2005) make the total sums devoted to research appear miserly by comparison. New Zealand's research spending relative to other First World nations also makes for sobering reading, comparing unfavourably with Australia, Britain, Canada and the USA, among other countries. The effects of comparatively low levels of government spending on research are exacerbated by other factors. There is, for example, no well-developed culture in New Zealand of wealthy individuals and groups donating large sums for the creation of substantial endowment funds. (Endowments for universities such as Harvard and Princeton in the USA are these days counted in the *billions* of dollars.) This further reduces the total resource base for undertaking research and makes it more difficult to retain academic staff. Set in this broader context, the gains (in purely financial terms) made by individuals, departments and institutions who commit to improving PBRF scores seem ridiculously small.

Concluding comments

The PBRF, as one element in the government's vision of a knowledge society and economy, provides tacit reinforcement for the view that the 'Third Way' is the *only* way for New Zealand. The 'Third Way', as has been argued at greater length elsewhere (e.g. Roberts 2005), is, in many respects, still a *neoliberal* way. The New Zealand government remains committed to international economic competitiveness as a fundamental goal; globalisation is viewed in a largely favourable light; so-called 'free trade' is encouraged; the logic of performativity continues to prevail in government departments and public institutions; the commodification of education continues (e.g. with the growth of 'export education' as a major industry); and human beings are still regarded, for the most part, as self-interested, utility maximising consumers. While the government has made important moves in recent years towards greater cooperation and collaboration in the tertiary education sector, the PBRF reinvigorates an ethos of competition and aggressive marketing. There is nothing in the PBRF that actively encourages either those being measured or those viewing the results to 'see the world otherwise': to imagine social ideals *other* than those driven by the imperatives of international economic competitiveness.

The PBRF Working Group believed that performance-based research funding could, in conjunction with other policy developments in the tertiary education sector, make a 'major contribution to the development of "our knowledge society" and "a prosperous and confident nation"' (PBRF Working Group 2002: 4). But it is 'our' knowledge society only in so far as we accept that prosperity and confidence ought to be the key goals for New Zealand as a nation. This is *one* ideal of a 'knowledge society' only. With the election of the Labour-Alliance government in 1999, there has been a shift in the policy discourse from the 'knowledge economy' to the 'knowledge society and economy'. Yet the emphasis remains the same: it is the *economic* dimension of the ideal that dominates. Other conceptions of ideal knowledge-based societies are hardly ever mentioned, let alone explored in detail or implemented in policy. Seddon (2004: 184) notes that in contemporary Australia 'the capacity to imagine universal public goods and the democratic ideal, and the necessity of ethical judgement (of truth rather than lies) is faltering'. A key challenge for educationists and others, she argues, is to 'refuse the blinkering that has accompanied the ascent of an economic paradigm for understanding life'. Bullen *et al.* (2004), similarly, contend that the techno-economic orientation of knowledge economy policy in Australia has impeded the growth and development of creative arts and humanities. They propose an alternative approach to the knowledge economy based on the notion of reflexive modernisation. Investigating ideals other than those governed by the rules of neoliberal global capitalism could, in the New Zealand context, provide a very interesting research agenda and contribute to a broadening of the government's current 'shared vision' for the country and its citizens.

The concern in this chapter has not been with the efficiency of the PBRF as a funding mechanism but with the underlying philosophical assumptions and the 'hidden' (or unspoken) consequences of such a system. The Tertiary Education Commission's 'quality evaluation' of the 2003 PBRF round (TEC 2004) contains exhaustive analyses of the assessment process, the performance scores for different subject groupings and the funding allocations based on these results. Evaluations from individual panels (subject groupings) are also available. The reports are, in many respects, systematic, thorough and informative. Missing from them, however, is a robust, explicit account of what this all means for our conception of 'research' and *of ourselves* as researchers. The reports remain silent on fundamental ontological, epistemological, ethical and political questions. What view of knowledge, knowing and knowers is implied by the PBRF system? Whose interests are served by the scheme? How should we conceive of a well-lived academic life in the light of the PBRF exercise? To what extent and in what ways might the PBRF help (or impede) universities in meeting their statutory obligation to serve as the 'critic and conscience of society'? What view of the human being underpins the PBRF process? What global and national influences have shaped, and will continue to shape, the PBRF scheme? What will be gained – and lost – if institutions place greater pressure on their staff to produce more and more 'quality assured' research 'outputs'? How does the PBRF contribute to the creation of a 'good society' in New Zealand? These questions have been almost completely ignored. The PBRF process has produced a flood of information, and it is easy to become lost in the numbers and tables and acronyms. Underlying all of the information is tacit agreement that the process is ultimately worthwhile and that any problems with it can and should be addressed by further tinkering with the system. The analysis in this chapter suggests that such changes will not address some of the deeper problems with performance-based research funding and that a more fundamental rethinking of the nature, purpose and value of research in tertiary education will be necessary.

References

Association of University Staff (2005a) 'Tertiary update', 3 March 2005. Online. Available HTTP: http://www.aus.ac.nz (accessed 3 March 2005).

Association of University Staff (2005b) 'Review should mean less waste in tertiary education courses', media release. Online. Available HTTP: http://www.aus.ac.nz (accessed 1 March 2005).

Bernard, G.W. (2000) 'History and research assessment exercises', *Oxford Review of Education*, 26(1): 95–106.

Bullen, E., Robb, S. and Kenway, J. (2004) '"Creative destruction": knowledge economy policy and the future of the arts and humanities in the academy', *Journal of Education Policy*, 19(1): 3–21.

Campbell, G. (2005) 'Poor little rich military', *New Zealand Listener*, 29 January–4 February: 19.

Codd, J. (2001) 'The third way for tertiary education policy: TEAC and beyond', *New Zealand Annual Review of Education*, 10: 31–57.

Delanty, G. (2003) 'Ideologies of the knowledge society and the cultural contradictions of higher education', *Policy Futures in Education*, 1(1): 71–82.

Department of Education (1988) *Report of the Working Group on Post-Compulsory Education and Training* (Hawke Report), Wellington: Department of Education.

Elton, L. (2000) 'The UK research assessment exercise: unintended consequences', *Higher Education Quarterly*, 54(3): 274–83.

Fitzsimons, P. (1995) 'The management of tertiary educational institutions in New Zealand', *Journal of Education Policy*, 10(2): 173–87.

Gibbs, P. (2001) 'Higher education as a market: a problem or solution?', *Studies in Higher Education*, 26(1): 85–94.

Gordon, L. (1995) 'Human capital theory and the death of democracy: tertiary education policy in New Zealand', in M. Olssen and K. Morris Matthews (eds) *Education, Democracy and*

Reform, Auckland: New Zealand Association for Research in Education and Research Unit for Maori Education (University of Auckland).

Harley, S. (2002) 'The impact of research selectivity on academic work and identity in UK universities', *Studies in Higher Education*, 27(2): 187–205.

Ministry of Education (1997) *A Future Tertiary Education Policy for New Zealand: Tertiary Education Review* (Green Paper), Wellington: Ministry of Education.

Ministry of Education (1998) *Tertiary Education in New Zealand: Policy Directions for the Twenty-first Century* (White Paper), Wellington: Ministry of Education.

Ministry of Education (2001a) *Skills For a Knowledge Economy: A Review of Industry Training in New Zealand*, Wellington: Ministry of Education (Office of the Associate Minister of Education – Tertiary Education).

Ministry of Education (2001b) *Export Education: Towards a Development Strategy for New Zealand*, Wellington: Ministry of Education.

Ministry of Education (2001c) *Pasifika Education Plan*, Wellington: Ministry of Education.

Ministry of Education (2001d) *More Than Words: The New Zealand Adult Literacy Strategy*, Wellington: Ministry of Education.

Ministry of Education (2002) *Tertiary Education Strategy, 2002/07*, Wellington: Ministry of Education (Office of the Associate Minister of Education – Tertiary Education).

Nixon, J. (2004) 'Education for the good society: the integrity of academic practice', *London Review of Education*, 2(3): 245–52.

Olssen, M. (2001) 'The neo-liberal appropriation of tertiary education policy in New Zealand: accountability, research and academic freedom', 'State-of-the-Art' Monograph No. 8, Palmerston North: New Zealand Association for Research in Education.

Ozga, J. (1998) 'The entrepreneurial researcher: re-formations of identity in the research marketplace', *International Studies in Sociology of Education*, 8(2): 143–53.

Performance-Based Research Fund Working Group (2002) *Investing in Excellence: The Report of the Performance-Based Research Fund Working Group*, Wellington: Ministry of Education and Transition Tertiary Education Commission.

Peters, M. (ed.) (1994) 'The corporatisation of New Zealand universities', Special issue of *Access: Critical Perspectives on Cultural and Policy Studies in Education*, 13(1).

Peters, M. (1997) 'Neo-liberalism, privatisation and the university in New Zealand: the democratic alternative', in K. Morris Matthews and M. Olssen (eds) *Education Policy in New Zealand: The 1990s and Beyond*, Palmerston North: Dunmore Press.

Peters, M. and Marshall, J. (1996) *Individualism and Community: Education and Social Policy in the Postmodern Condition*, London: Falmer.

Peters, M., Marshall, J. and Parr, B. (1993) 'The marketisation of tertiary education in New Zealand', *Australian Universities' Review*, 36(2): 34–9.

Peters, M. and Roberts, P. (1999) *University Futures and the Politics of Reform in New Zealand*, Palmerston North: Dunmore Press.

Roberts, P. (1999) 'The future of the university: reflections from New Zealand', *International Review of Education*, 45(1): 65–85.

Roberts, P. (2005) 'Tertiary education, knowledge and neoliberalism', in J. Codd and K. Sullivan (eds) *Education Policy Directions in Aotearoa New Zealand*, Palmerston North: Thomson/ Dunmore Press.

Roberts, P. and Peters, M. (1999) 'A critique of the tertiary education White Paper', *New Zealand Annual Review of Education*, 8: 1–22.

Scott, W.G. and Scott, H.M. (2004) 'University income and student numbers between 1980 and 2002', report of a study commissioned by the New Zealand Vice-Chancellors' Committee and the Association of University Staff. Online. Available HTTP: http://www.aus.ac.nz (accessed 3 March 2005).

Seddon, T. (2004) 'Remaking civic formation: towards a learning citizen?', *London Review of Education*, 2(3): 171–86.

Tertiary Education Advisory Commission (2000, July) *Shaping a Shared Vision*, Wellington: TEAC.

Tertiary Education Advisory Commission (2001a, February) *Shaping the System*, Wellington: TEAC.

Tertiary Education Advisory Commission (2001b, July) *Shaping the Strategy*, Wellington: TEAC.

Tertiary Education Advisory Commission (2001c, November) *Shaping the Funding Framework*, Wellington: TEAC.

Tertiary Education Commission (2004) 'Evaluating research excellence: the 2003 assessment', overview and key findings. Online. Available: http://www.tec.govt.nz (accessed 3 March 2005).

Tertiary Education Commission (2005) 'TEC announces reviews of education and training provision', media release, 28 February 2005. Online. Available: http://www.tec.govt.nz (accessed 3 March 2005).

Treasury (1987) *Government Management: Brief to the Incoming Government, Vol II: Education Issues*, Wellington: Government Printer.

Vidovich, L. and Porter, P. (1999) 'Quality policy in Australian higher education of the 1990s: university perspectives', *Journal of Education Policy*, 14(6): 567–86.

Willmott, H. (2003) 'Commercialising higher education in the UK: the state, industry and peer review', *Studies in Higher Education*, 28(2): 129 41.

13 Global trends towards education and science

Tension and resistance

Barbara Schneider, Zack Kertcher and Shira Offer

Introduction

Globalisation, some have argued, has led to a worldwide convergence of models and attitudes toward education and science (Boli and Thomas 1997, Guillen 2001, Sassen 1996). Whereas some envision globalisation as structural, others perceive it as a symbolic discourse (Fiss and Hirsch 2005). Whether globalisation is understood as the adaptation of physical or organisational structures, such as computers on desks in classrooms in rural areas of Africa, or as the language used by the media and others to provide meaning and make sense of information such as 'the re-engineering of education based on scientific evidence', the concept of globalisation has become increasingly complex and ontologically dominant in academic and public spheres. In a growing number of developing and developed countries, educational systems have adopted goals emphasising rationality and scientific modes of inquiry, and instituted programmes aimed at enhancing students' skills in preparation for an increasing competitive global labour market (Carnoy 2000). This has resulted, according to some neoinstitutional scholars, in systems of mass education around the world that have become increasingly similar in their educational ideologies, administrative structure and instructional practices (Meyer *et al.* 1992).

This process of convergence, however, has not occurred without tension. Contrary to the paradigmatic schema articulated by the neoinstitutionalist perspective, the penetration and institutionalisation of ideas and practices associated with world culture have been subject to opposition by social groups whose belief systems have been challenged by these global trends (Hirst and Thompson 1996; Wade 1996). One example pertaining to education can be seen with the increasing public discourse and international emergence and adoption of scientific principles for the conduct of educational research and the resistance to this approach expressed by critical theorists (*Educational Researcher* November 2002, *Teachers College Record* January 2005, *Qualitative Inquiry* February 2004). With respect to science, public and religious leaders, oftentimes representing ultra-conservative religious groups, are leading challenges to theories of evolution and expressing support for creationism (Bhattacharjee 2005). Although resistance to US trends towards a more formalised scientific approach to educational research has been documented in the literature, relatively few empirical studies have been conducted about such resistance internationally. In this chapter, we investigate forms of resistance to converging trends in education and science by: (1) discussing global trends to further the 'science' of educational research; and (2) examining divergence in attitudes towards education and science using social science survey data obtained from a generalisable sample of adults in the USA, Sweden, the Netherlands, France, Chile, Russia and the Philippines.

Global convergence and mass education

Neoinstitutionalism is emerging as one of the most prevalent theoretical frameworks for the study of globalisation and has been receiving considerable attention among scholars in the field of education. According to the neoinstitutionalist framework, globalisation is regarded as a worldwide intensified process, commonly referred to as isomorphism, which has led to a standardisation of beliefs, models and policies. Professional associations, scientific communities, and international organisations, such as the World Bank and the United Nations Educational, Scientific and Cultural Organization, constitute the major engines that are driving this process (Meyer 2002). Facilitated by their institutional actors, the diffusion of beliefs, models and policies has occurred both horizontally and vertically. Horizontally, it has led to the standardisation of various types of institutions across countries, so that institutions such as professional societies, whether in the USA, France or Chile, are organised to perform similar functions (Mcyer *et al.* 1997; Meyer 2002). Vertically, these beliefs, models, and policies have penetrated 'all of the domains of rationalized social life–business, politics, education, medicine, science, even the family and religion' (Meyer *et al.* 1997: 145). Together the formation of these institutions and the beliefs, models and policies that incorporate and sustain them have spread around the world, converging into what Meyer *et al.* (1997) have termed 'world culture'.

The observed worldwide growth of mass education, as evidenced by the increasing number of children enrolled in elementary, secondary and postsecondary schools since the 1980s, rising costs and governmental expenditures on education, and the infusion of science concepts and scientific principles throughout the educational curriculum and research and development systems are emblematic of world culture diffusion (Meyer *et al.* 1992; Meyer *et al.* 1997). Although an expansion of state-run education systems does not necessarily imply uniformity, mass education systems have converged on several fundamental objectives, one of which is to deepen the knowledge base and enhance the skills of students in preparation for an increasingly high-skilled technological job market. Extending the knowledge and skills of future workers is seen as crucial for ensuring that nation states gain a favorable position in the highly competitive global economy (Meyer *et al.* 1997; Astiz *et al.* 2002).

One of the more immediate consequences of this world cultural focus on producing highly skilled workers has been an international interest in assessing the academic performance of elementary and high school children in science, mathematics and reading (Carnoy 2000). Although interest in comparisons of student achievement across nation states has existed for nearly 50 years, the results of international academic assessments took on new meaning in the 1990s, particularly when student performance in mathematics and science in the USA and other industrialised states trailed less economically capitalised and developing countries (Schmidt *et al.* 2001; Schmidt *et al.* 1997). Evolving from the International Association for the Evaluation of Educational Achievement (IEA), the major data source for comparative quantitative studies of school organisation, curriculum and achievement, The Third International Mathematics and Science Study (TIMSS) was created.[1] This study, conducted in the mid-1990s and involving 40 countries, had a complex design that included not only standard survey and achievement tests of mathematics and science performance, but also videos of classrooms and ethnographic studies in selected countries (Baker and LeTendre 2000). TIMSS was unique in that it was funded by several national governments, including the USA and Canada, and was fielded through the coordinated efforts of participating nation-state governments. TIMSS was a global highly technological comparative quantitative study and its findings have had significant implications for the USA as well as other countries.

Results from the TIMSS showed that a country's wealth was not strongly related to achievement gains in mathematics and science (Schmidt *et al.* 2001). And in the instance of Japan, an economic competitor of the USA, students scored significantly higher. Not only was the performance of US students significantly below students in other countries, there were significant gaps in academic performance within the USA among students of different racial and ethnic groups. Some of these findings have been confirmed with the National Assessment of Educational Progress (NAEP), a national study conducted in the USA that measures trends in student achievement. Results show little progress in students' performance between the 1970s and early 1990s, and the gaps in academic performance among students of different racial and ethnic groups appear to have persisted or widened over time (National Center for Education Statistics 1998; Lee 2002). The US government policy response to the poor performance of US students has been a series of national reform efforts to: institute standards of performance and accountability measures that monitor school compliance; promote alternative forms of school organisation; and restructure curricular content and instruction in subjects such as mathematics and reading (NCLB 2001).

The prominent position of science in the curriculum is one manifestation of the increasing penetration of scientific and rational principles to mass education. This process can be observed in research and development activities where there has been a general increase in the use of scientific principles to evaluate educational interventions designed to improve educational outcomes (Schneider, in preparation). One of the most striking examples of this at the global level is the creation of the Campbell Collaboration, an international not-for-profit organisation currently funded by various foundations and government agencies and designed to prepare and maintain systematic reviews of studies of the effects of polices and practices in education and the social and behavioural sciences.[2] Formally established in 2000 with members from four countries, the organisation strives to produce better information for the public on what works based on high quality evidence. To further this aim the collaboration prepares, maintains and disseminates systematic reviews of studies of interventions that involve randomised and nonrandomised trials. Diffusion of information is facilitated through products of the collaboration that include summaries and electronic brochures of reviews and reports of trials for policy makers, practitioners, researchers and the public.

The Campbell Collaboration grew from the Cochrane Collaboration, which is an international not-for-profit organisation of over 10,000 people working in over 90 countries to ensure that up-to-date information about the effects of healthcare interventions is available world wide.[3] The Cochrane Collaboration and the Campbell Collaboration have as their goal to inform not only policy makers but consumers about the effects of systematic scientific studies so that people can make better decisions; in the instance of the Cochrane Collaboration, about health care, in the instance of the Campbell Collaboration, about education, criminal justice, social policy and social welfare. The Campbell Collaboration describes the Cochrane Collaboration as a sibling organisation and notes that the two are establishing joint methods groups.

In both the Campbell and Cochrane Collaborations, the intent is to promote evidence-based studies that use randomised field trials. The randomised field trial is a research design that places individuals, or schools or other units of study, into an experimental group which receives an intervention or a control group which does not, on the basis of a random process, such as the toss of a coin. The idea behind random assignment is that, on average, the two groups that result from the selection process will differ only in terms of the intervention. The US Department of Education has established as one of its chief goals to transform education into an evidence-based field; in congressional law, scientifically based research is defined as studies that use experimental or quasi-experimental designs in which individuals, entities, programmes or activities are assigned to different conditions and with appropriate controls to evaluate the effects of the condition of interest, with a preference for random-assignment experiments, or other designs to the extent that those designs contain within-condition or across-condition controls. The seriousness of the US government's determination to make educational research more scientifically based was recently underscored in the 25 January 2005 *Federal Register*, where it was noted that random assignment and quasi-experimental designs are considered to be the most rigorous methods to address the question of project effectiveness (p. 3586), and research using these designs are established as a priority for all US Department of Education programmes, not only those in the Institute for Education Sciences, the major research arm of the US Department of Education.

The press for randomised field trials has been aided in part by the What Works Clearinghouse, a federally funded website that reviews results of randomised trials that have a demonstrated beneficial causal relationship to student outcomes, such as improving early reading comprehension and reducing high school dropout rates. Guided by a technical advisory panel, the What Works Clearinghouse has established quality standards to review available research, using criteria similar to the Campbell and Cochrane Collaborations, which place a high priority on randomised field trails (What Works Clearinghouse 2003).[4] Acknowledging that randomised field trials are not feasible in certain situations or for some research questions, they also advocate the use of quasi-experiments, that is, comparative studies that isolate the effect of an intervention through means other than randomisation.

Despite the somewhat mixed response of the educational research community to these new funding guidelines, a number of websites and foundations have also supported the new direction being taken by the government, and current solicitations in federal and private not-for-profit foundations are recommending the use of random assignment (William T. Grant Foundation).[5] Some researchers have raised objections to the emphasis on this type of design, arguing that the model of causation that underlies it is too simplistic to capture the complexity of teaching and learning in diverse educational settings (Towne *et al.* 2004). On the other hand, there are a group of researchers who advocate for and are involved in a series of randomised trials in education (Cook and Payne 2002; Mosteller and Boruch 2002; Slavin 2004).

The movement in the USA towards more scientifically based research can now also be seen in several other countries. This is in part due to the international focus of the

Cochrane and Campbell Collaborations, which in addition to randomised clinical trials have recommended a series of measures to make research more transparent through better reporting standards, structured abstracts of studies and comprehensive registry of studies. This trend towards a more systematic reporting of studies is not only being recommended for quantitative work; in England, for example, there is a major governmental initiative underway to establish guidelines for all educational research studies including those that use observations and interviews (Towne and Hilton 2004).

The pressure to transform educational research into a more scientific enterprise is in part a response to the field, which has been characterised as fragmented and inconclusive (Lagemann 2000). The push for a more scientific foundation for educational research is rational given the goal of improving student performance, although some critical theorists have argued that merely 'scientising' the field may not lead to the desired outcome (Popkewitz 2004; *Teachers College Record* 2005). Despite the controversy in the USA regarding this approach, the overriding orientation has been a major change in favour of evidence-based research, a change that is also affecting other countries. Educational research is being 'scientised' and even those studies that take a qualitative approach are being asked to follow similar guidelines in the conduct of research, the sharing of data and the reporting of results (Ragin *et al.* 2004).

Accompanying the increased attention to academic performance has been the inclusion of topics that deal with ethnic diversity and multicultural education in the elementary and high school curriculum (Ueda 1995). Since the 1970s, such topics have become a central focus in the USA and other industrialised nations in contrast to more traditional curricular areas that address national identity and culture, such as geography and national history. This shift in emphasis from building a common education for national citizenship towards one that recognises and builds a stronger sense of ethnic and cultural identity has been criticised as potentially undermining democratic beliefs and encouraging stereotypical perspectives and exclusionary practices. From a global perspective, this focus on racial and ethnic distinctiveness is not entirely inconsistent with the scientific approach, which has championed the merits of individual discovery. Overall, these isomorphic trends both in increasing achievement and focusing on ethnic and cultural diversity appear to be shifting educational systems all over the world to adopt a more scientific, rational and individualistic perspective toward education (Meyer *et al.* 1997: 131).

Convergence and resistance

The worldwide process of convergence towards scientific research, particularly in education, and the focus on rationality and individualism has in turn led to a decline in practices that stress religion and community, a movement predicted by early sociologists such as Durkheim (1900) and more recently by Coleman (1992). This movement towards science might alienate social groups whose core beliefs and practices differ from those promoted by world culture institutions. The neoinstitutionalist framework posits that these groups will eventually adopt world culture ideas so that, for example, religious fundamentalists will 'reformulate their religious doctrine in accordance with typical modern conceptions of rational-moral discipline' (Meyer *et al.* 1997: 161). The neoinstitutionalist approach thus assumes that the process of isomorphism is likely to occur without disturbance.

This assumption, however, may be unfounded. Under certain circumstances, social groups, whose belief systems have been challenged by the diffusion of ideas and practices associated with world culture, have been able to effectively resist their institutionalisation. In other words, we can expect to find particular social forces in various countries that counter isomorphic tendencies and consequently lead to the reiteration of existing beliefs that are at odds with world culture.

The expansion of religious fundamentalism has been regarded by many as a manifestation of this phenomenon (Barber 1996; Beyer 1994). That is, fundamentalism, and, more generally, the revival of religion around the world, is viewed as an active response to the diffusion of world culture institutions and a way of reinforcing existing beliefs that diverge from world culture. As some scholars have suggested, fundamentalism should be viewed 'as a series of related responses to the globalization process per se' (Miszal and Shupe 1992: 7, see also Riesebrodt 2000). The growing prominence of fundamentalist movements has also been perceived as a reaction against modernity and a threat to the individualistic and secular values that constitute the core of liberal Western societies.

Consequently, it might be expected that the ideologies and practices of the mass education system will be of major concern for fundamentalists. Some indication as to the attitude of fundamentalists toward public education can be found in Sikkink's study (1999), which demonstrated that Christian fundamentalists in the USA are more likely to distrust and feel alienated from the public education system. As in other countries, public education in the USA is widespread, and in some cases the only possibility for primary and secondary education. Therefore, it is not surprising that those who hold fundamentalist beliefs, and, due to lack of more suitable alternatives, take part in the public educational system, have generally lower achievement scores and complete fewer years of formal education than their peers (Darnell and Sherkat 1997; Lehrer 1999). Given the strong relationship between family educational expectations and educational attainment (Coleman and Hoffer 1987), it may be that very religious families, particularly those who are fundamentalists, do not perceive educational performance as important or desirable for future career success and do not support their children's educational endeavours while in public schools. Such norms and values are likely to be transferred to their children, who adopt similar positions and perform accordingly.

When the option is available, many fundamentalists choose to opt out of the mass schooling system to study in their own schools, not other private religious schools.[6] These types of educational institutions have grown considerably in past decades all over the world. A striking example is the USA, where since the mid-1980s enrolment in these fundamentalist schools has surpassed enrolment in Catholic schools (Sikkink 2001: 38). A similar expansion has been noted in other economically developed Christian countries, such as in the Netherlands and the UK (Walford 2001), and in Muslim developing countries, such as Pakistan (Singer 2001; Zia 2003).

It has been suggested that parents enrol their children in these schools to protect them from the influence of world culture.[7] Consequently, these schools are governed by a very different logic than public schools. They stress the word of God as written in the scripture; emphasise parent and teacher authority; reinforce 'traditional' gender roles; and promote the family–church–school trinity (Peshkin 1986; Rose 1988; Sikkink 1999; Singer 2001; Zia 2003).

The logic of fundamentalist education is manifested in the curriculum where time devoted to subjects such as science and social studies comprise only a small fraction of the time devoted to core curricular subjects. These subjects are taught in a very different way than in public schools. The atmosphere in fundamentalist schools fosters a negative attitude toward science, both in the textbooks used, and in class, and the word of God (as written in the scripture) is preferred over science (Rose 1988). In fact, the teaching of science is utilised as means to teach the word of God and to better understand God's creation (Peshkin 1986; Rose 1988; Menenedez 1993). A quote from a biology textbook, which is widely used in US Christian fundamentalist schools, captures this attitude (Menenedez 1993: 118): 'The people who have prepared this book have tried consistently to put the Word of God first and science second … If the conclusions contradict the Word of God, the conclusions are wrong no matter how many scientific facts may appear to back them.'

Consequently, it could be expected that fundamentalism, as an expression of the conflict aspect of trends in global convergence, would be associated with negative attitudes towards science and education. This source of tension, moreover, may be manifested globally, that is, negative attitudes towards science and education will be found among fundamentalists in countries that differ in their religious and cultural background and level of economic development. Given this assumption, we began investigating different datasets in order to determine whether such tension and resistance towards education and science would be associated with strong religious identity and practice and whether this pattern would occur in both industrialised and developing nation states. After examining several data sets, the International Social Survey Program (ISSP) seemed especially well suited to explore these issues.[8]

Since 1985 the ISSP, an international consortium of research organisations representing 40 different countries, has collected survey data on a wide range of social science research topics. For purposes of this analysis we rely on the 1998 Religion II module which is an extension of the previous 1991 module that included a series of questions regarding religious practices and beliefs. The ISSP dataset is constructed so that it is possible to link individual religious practices and beliefs with attitudes towards science and education.

From 1998 through 2000 the ISSP was administered to a random sample of 39,000 adults in 31 countries, mostly in Europe. This analysis uses data from the USA, Sweden, Netherlands, France, Chile, Russia and the Philippines because these countries are experiencing an increased growth in the proportion of adults who identify themselves as having a strong sense of religiosity (e.g. see Iannaccone 1994 for the USA; Stoffels 2001 for the Netherlands). Another consideration in selecting particular nation states was the inclusion of a range of countries that differed in terms of their GNP and level of industrialisation.[9]

An international comparison of attitudes towards education and science

The ISSP surveys adults about their perceptions of the educational system, attitudes towards science, and confidence in political systems, using items similar to the General Social Survey (GSS), a national survey that examines US adults' trust and confidence in social systems.[10] Items included in the ISSP are determined by the governing committee, which assesses whether the items are viewed as meaningful by and relevant to all participating countries and can be expressed in equivalent languages. Questions are drafted in British English and back translated. With respect to education, the survey, much like standard items used in Gallup and Roper Polls, queries individuals about how much confidence they have in the schools and the educational system, using a five-point Likert scale. Attitudes towards science are derived from questions that ask about the relative 'good' of science and its relationship to faith. These items are also asked using Likert scales, and specifically inquire as to whether the individual agrees or disagrees with the statements, 'Modern science does more harm than good'; and 'We trust too much in science and not enough in religious faith'.[11]

Measuring religiosity

There are no standard conventions as to how to measure religiosity (Hill and Hood 1999). Recently researchers have attempted to conceptualise religiosity by distinguishing among personal faith, participation in organised religious activities and identification with a particular religious community (Ellison *et al.* 1989). Looking more specifically at conservative forms of religious practice and faith, with respect to fundamentalism there is little agreement about the scope and definition of the term. For instance, some scholars suggest broader inclusion criteria (Marty and Appleby 1993), while others prefer a stricter perspective (Woodberry and Smith 1998). Recently, fundamentalism has taken on a pejorative meaning in some countries, and is seen by some as an unreliable term to use in surveys, even if people have to self identify. With the exception of the USA, the ISSP 1998 module does not have a category that enables respondents to identify themselves as fundamentalists.[12]

Despite the limitation of identification with a particular religious community, the ISSP has a series of items that previous research has shown to be valid and reliable measures of fundamentalism (Kellstedt and Smidt 1991; Marty and Appleby 1993: 3). First, fundamentalists were found to identify themselves as being more religious, and to attend religious services more frequently. Secondly, fundamentalists read the Bible, or the scripture, literally, and consider it the highest source of authority. And finally, although the various religious denominations associated with fundamentalism are likely to have different moral attitudes corresponding to the varied social contexts in which they operate, having a strict attitude towards gender roles, in which men are breadwinners and the women's place is in the home, has been suggested as a fairly reliable measure of more conservative religious beliefs across cultures. Clearly, none of these measures on its own is sufficient for capturing fundamentalism. We therefore aggregated four survey items to construct a 'fundamentalist' measure. This measure included the following items: self-identification as being religious; frequency of church attendance; feelings about the Bible; and gender attitudes with respect to family, that is, 'Family life suffers when the woman has a full-time job'.

There is a conceptual difference between having a positive attitude towards religion and fundamentalism. For instance, while in general fundamentalists are more likely to have a strongly positive attitude towards religion, not all those who have a strong positive opinion on this matter can be considered fundamentalists. We therefore used two items that would assist in capturing this important distinction. The first was an item measuring attitude towards organised religion that asked respondents, 'How much confidence do you have in churches and religious organizations?' The second item measured connections between religious orientation and politics and asked respondents the degree to which they agreed with the statement: 'Religious leaders should not try to influence how people vote in elections.' [13]

Much of the literature on fundamentalism deals with the so-called process of being 'born again', in which a person experiences a spiritual or a religious revelation and as a result adheres to the word of God. Not all those experiencing a turning point in their life could be characterised as fundamentalists, and not all fundamentalists have had a born again experience (Woodberry and Smith 1998). Nonetheless, this concept was important for our study for two main reasons – its alleged relationship with fundamentalism, and its dynamic property, indicating a *process* of attitudinal change during a person's life course. We stress the dynamic quality of this concept as we suspect that those who regard themselves as 'born again' would be more likely to be involved in religious practice, see themselves as religious and have a negative attitude towards education and science.[14]

By allocating and controlling school resources, and more generally by determining educational policy, nation states are the engine that shape and steer the education system. In most cases, states also influence the curricula (e.g. increasing the focus on science), albeit with varying degrees of control (Stevenson and Baker 1991). A success or a failure of the education system, for example in terms of overall academic achievement on standardised tests, is interpreted as a success or failure of the state. Thus, we expected to find a positive relationship between confidence in the state and education and science. To measure confidence in the state we constructed a measure that included two questionnaire items: 'How much confidence do you have in the government?' and 'How much confidence do you have in the courts and the legal system?'

Fundamentalism in most countries is usually associated with low income and lower levels of education (cf. Coreno 2002). Thus, our aim was to determine whether there was a pattern of association between social groups with different socioeconomic status and these characteristics. Our categories for income range from very low (approximately $27,000) to very high (over $75,000). With respect to education, measuring education across countries only in terms of years might be misleading because there are substantial differences in mandatory education requirements across countries or number of years required to obtain a university degree, for example. Therefore a measure was created that included the following categories: less than high school, completed high school, some college and university degree.

Evidence of convergence

As shown in Table 13.1, level of confidence in education is relatively similar across countries, with respondents indicating considerable to high degrees of confidence in their education and school systems. The highest levels of confidence in the education system are reported in the Philippines and Russia, while the lowest levels of confidence in education are reported in France and Sweden. In contrast, results for attitude towards science indicate a somewhat different pattern, as the difference across countries is more substantial. The most positive attitudes towards science are reported in Sweden, France and Russia. Respondents in the USA, on average, report considerably lower levels of confidence in science than most other countries, including those that are less wealthy and industrialised.

Table 13.1 Descriptive statistics for attitudes towards education, science and religion

	US Mean	Sweden Mean	Netherlands Mean	France Mean	Chile Mean	Russia Mean	Phillipines Mean
Confidence in Education[a]	3.1673	2.9885	3.3939	3.0045	3.3894	3.5568	3.9614
Confidence in Science[a]	3.5805	5.4630	5.0582	5.3623	3.5812	5.1833	3.8794
Confidence in State[a]	4.5546	4.7189	5.0226	4.0674	3.5994	3.3634	5.8096
Confidence in Church[a]	3.3131	2.6009	2.7373	2.3672	3.5512	3.0417	3.9267
Religion in Politics[a]	2.1855	2.0661	1.9367	1.5696	2.2108	1.8622	2.2569
Turning Point[b]	0.4614	0.1214	0.2344	0.2456	0.4025	0.1999	0.2342
Fundamentalism[c]	11.2718	7.4405	8.8190	7.9804	11.8904	9.0485	13.8717

Source: www.ISSP.org.

Notes
Differences across countries were not significant (not shown) with the exception of education and fundamentalism in the USA being significantly different (p < .01) from all other countries

a   Scales range from 1–5, 1 being 'complete confidence' and 5 being 'no confidence at all'.
b   Turning point is a dummy variable based on the question, 'Has there ever been a turning point in your life when you made a new and personal commitment to religion', 1 being "Yes" and 0 being 'No'.
c   Scale ranges from 1–20, 1 being 'extremely religious' and 20 being 'extremely non-religious'.

Table 13.1 further indicates that the countries in the sample vary considerably in their levels of religiosity. The mean of the fundamentalist variable, for example, is highest in the Philippines, followed by Chile and the USA. In the USA and Chile almost half the respondents report that they have experienced a change in their level of commitment to religion, a number nearly twice that of other countries in the sample. Such a high percentage of the respondents who have experienced a turning point in their life connotes a general shift towards religion in these countries. This percentage is very low in Sweden, where 12 per cent of the respondents reported experiencing a turning point.

This pattern is stable for the other two predictors that capture religiosity: confidence in church, and attitude towards religion in politics. Americans, Chileans and Philippians have a much higher degree of confidence in the church in comparison to Swedes, Dutch, French and Russians. Similarly, Americans, Chileans and Philippians prefer stronger involvement of religion in politics in contrast to the other countries in the sample. Thus, based on the religious dimension, two groups emerge from the sample: the more religious countries – USA, Chile and the Philippines – and the group consisting of the less religious countries.

Results from Table 13.1 suggest that global trends towards support for education and science are somewhat uneven, with countries most supportive of education not necessarily being the least religious; in fact Philippians are the most religious and have the most confidence in education. However, the situation for science is slightly different, with Swedes being the most positive in their attitudes towards science but the least religious, which would seem consistent. At the general level there is some pattern of globalism; the next step was to determine if there were also patterns of resistance. One conjecture could be that because ultra-conservative religious groups, some Christian, some Muslim, are different across nation states they would exhibit different attitudes towards education and science. To explore this question we engaged in a series of analyses, taking into account individual characteristics such as gender, age, level of educational attainment, income, confidence in government and attitudes towards organised religion, to determine if there was an association between fundamentalists' attitudes towards education and science by country.

Turning to Table 13.2, we find that the fundamentalist scale exhibits a consistent pattern of negative coefficients, especially for science. In all six countries, individuals who are more religiously devout are more likely to report negative attitudes towards science. While the association between religiosity and science is negative in all of these countries, there is a positive relationship between religiosity and confidence in the government. Because state institutions run mass school systems, it is not surprising to find that there is a highly significant positive relationship in all countries between confidence in state institutions and confidence in the educational system. This pattern seems to suggest an inherent tension between science and religiosity that is mediated in part by confidence in government.

The association between fundamentalism and confidence in education is less stable across countries in comparison to attitudes towards science. Only in the USA and France do more religiously devout individuals lack confidence in the education system. However, in all the other countries, while the numbers are not statistically significant, the association between fundamentalism and confidence in education is in the expected direction, with the exception of the Philippines. These results corroborate evidence found in other studies about the negative attitude of US fundamentalists towards public schools (Sikkink 1999).

Table 13.2 Regression results for confidence in education and attitude towards science by country

	US E β	US S β	Sweden E β	Sweden S β	Netherlands E β	Netherlands S β	France E β	France S β	Chile E β	Chile S β	Russia E β	Russia S β	Philippines E β	Philippines S β
Gender	−	− **	+	− ***	+	− ***	−	− ***	+	+	−	−	+	+
Age	−	−	+	− **	+	− **	+	+	+	−	+	−	−	−
Less than H.S.	+	− **	+	− ***	+	+	−	−	+	− *	+	−	−	− *
Some college	+	+ ***	+	+	−	−	−	+ **	+	+	−	−	+	−
University	+ **	+ ***	+	+ ***	−	+ *	+	+ ***	−	+	−	+ *	+	−
Very low income	+ ***	− ***	−	−	−	− ***	+	+ **	+	−	+	−	+	+ **
Low income	+	−	−	−	−	− **	+	+	+	−	+	+	+	+
High income	+ *	−	−	−	−	− **	+ **	+	− **	−	+	+	+	+
Very high income	−	−	−	+ *	+	+ **	+	+	+	+	−	+	+	+
Confidence in state	+ ***	+ ***	+ ***	+ ***	+ ***	+ ***	+ ***	+ ***	+ ***	+ ***	+ ***	+ ***	+ ***	+ ***
Confidence in church	+ ***	+ **	+ **	−	+ **	−	+ ***	+	+ ***	−	+ ***	−	+ ***	+ ***
Religion in politics	− **	+ *	−	−	+ *	−	− *	+	−	+ *	− *	− ***	− *	+ *
Turning point	−	−	+	−	−	−	−	−	−	+ ***	+ *	−	+	+
Fundamentalist	− ***	−	−	− ***	− ***	−	− ***	− ***	−	− ***	− ***	−	+ ***	− **

Source: www.ISSP.org

Notes

Standardized coefficients are not reported due to the disparate scales of the different measures of the model.

*p < 0.10, **p < 0.05, ***p < 0.01 (two-tailed test)

E = Education

S = Science

Except for the Netherlands, no significant differences were observed between those who experienced a turning point and those who did not, with respect to confidence in the education system. Since this variable captures changes in religious commitment during one's life course, one possibility is that turning to religion does not substantively alter pre-established attitudes towards the school system. However, in nearly all countries, experiencing a turning point is negatively associated with attitudes towards science, an association that is particularly strong in the Netherlands. It may be that experiencing a turning point is more related to a world view that focuses on problems with technology and labour economics.

Finally, it is worth highlighting a few relationships found between confidence in education and science and other predictors, particularly socioeconomic status. First, as could be expected, those who have completed higher education are more likely to have a positive attitude towards science than those who have only completed high school. Secondly, having a high income is not necessarily associated with a more positive attitude towards science, although in five countries the pattern is positive but not significant.

Conclusion

Two trends are observed in this chapter. The first relates to the global movement towards the use of evidence-based scientific studies to inform the implementation of policy. This trend is not without controversy or challenge. The situation in education is not unlike scientific intellectual movements in other disciplines where substantive specialties evolve, rarely sharing and more often competing with other specialties for 'intellectual attention space' (Collins 1998). A recent article by Frickel and Gross (2005) compares the development of a scientific intellectual movement with certain aspects of other social movements, and specific elements of their general theory are particularly relevant here. An intellectual movement has to articulate a coherent programme for change; one could argue that the movement towards scientifically based educational research could be thought of in these terms. A movement requires some type of collective, coordinated action, and one might see the establishment of the Campbell Collaboration and the What Works Clearinghouse as examples of this. Frickel and Gross argue that such a programme will be embraced by some and rejected by others, and that all who subscribe to the change will necessarily agree on what constitutes its knowledge base. They argue that intellectual movements are bound to be contentious, as they conflict with normative expectations, and are inherently political because they call for a transfer of power. The US federal legislation advocating a specific scientific approach to educational research certainly suggests a transfer of power. And finally such movements are influenced by the broader cultural and political environment. In this instance, we argue that the movement towards science and technology is now converging into a world culture.

In our second example, we more intensively examined resistance to this world culture through religious practices and beliefs. Much as scientific principles in the education movement fit the Frickel and Gross (2005) general theory of scientific intellectual movements, the pattern of resistance among religious fundamentalists also suggests a common global movement of divergence. Although the countries examined in this chapter greatly differ in their level of economic development, as well as cultural and religious background, fundamentalists report very similar attitudes towards science and education. This finding indicates that resistance to world culture might itself be a global phenomenon.

That is, although we find that fundamentalists' negative attitudes towards science and education are manifested independently in different countries, this type of reaction might constitute a different form of convergence, one which is motivated by opposition to world culture (Marty and Appleby 1992). This finding further suggests that the approach treating fundamentalism as a reaction against Western conceptions of modernism, despite critiques of reinforcing a culturally biased view of fundamentalist movements, can still make an important contribution to our understanding of the shared moral base of fundamentalist groups in different contexts.

From these two examples it would appear that the concept of scientifically based evidence is not a unique US phenomenon but is part of a converging normative emphasis on using evidence to support treatments in medicine and policies in health and criminal justice. Resistance to this approach and resistance to science among religious groups suggest that an inherent aspect of globalism is the tension between convergence and divergence. However, the resistance to world culture is itself a global phenomenon and may serve to strengthen globalism.

Notes

1 Beginning in the 1960s, IEA designed a series of studies on curriculum and achievement that were fielded by academics in different countries throughout the world (see Baker and LeTendre 2000; Heyneman and Loxley 1983; Comber and Keeves 1973).
2 For more information on the Campbell Collaboration see http://www.campbell collaboration.org.
3 For more information on the Cochrane Collaboration see http://www.cochrane.org/docs/ descriphtm.
4 For more information on the What Works Clearinghouse, see http://www.w-w-c.org/july 2003.html.
5 For more information, see http://www.wtgrantfoundation.org.
6 Fundamentalist schools are associated with different religious movements, have varied organisational structures and maintain a relatively wide range of educational practices (see Rose 1988 and Sikkink 2001 for the differences between Pentecostals, Charismatic and fundamentalist schools). However, the conceptual approaches that orient this chapter call for a focus on the similarities rather than the differences among these schools. As we argue above, these similarities justify the use of this umbrella term.
7 The methods for protection vary by religious movements. Those who identify themselves as Christian fundamentalists tend to be more separatist, whereas Pentecostals are more likely not to disconnect from the rest of the population. But they would pray for saving their children and would put great effort into maintaining for their children a symbolic universe that virtually shields them from world culture (cf. Rose 1988). Furthermore, not only fundamentalists send their children to fundamentalist schools. The curriculum and the educational environment, that is, the discipline and moral values, are probably more important for some non-fundamentalist parents than religion. On the other hand, from the educator's perspective their primary goal is religious education (Peshkin 1986: 280–1; Rose 1988: 32).
8 More information on ISSP and the on the Religion II dataset can be found at: http:// www.issp.org.
9 The Gross Domestic Product (GDP) for these countries is based on information reported by the United Nations Statistics Division (2005).
10 For more information on the GSS and its relationship to the ISSP, see http://www.norc. uchicago.edu/projects/gensoc1.asp.

11 These items were aggregated to create a single score. In the instance of the USA only one of the two science questions was asked, and the score for these individuals represents only one item.
12 The US fundamentalists can identify themselves as such. In fact, for the US population, it has been suggested that self-identification as a fundamentalist be included as a reliable measure (Kellstedt and Smidt 1991).
13 Since we analyse an international dataset, respondent's affiliation with a specific party, or respondent's identification with left-right ideology, is country specific and does not adequately serve our analysis.
14 This measure was created from the item 'Has there ever been a turning point in your life when you made a new and personal commitment to religion?' (1=experienced a turning point).

References

Astiz, F.M., Wiseman, A.W. and Baker, D.P. (2002) 'Slouching toward decentralization: consequences of globalization for curricular control in national education systems', *Comparative Education Review*, 46(1): 66–88.
Baker, D.P. and LeTendre, G.K. (2000) 'Comparative sociology of classroom processes, school organization, and achievement', in M.T. Hallinan (ed.) *Handbook of the Sociology of Education*, New York: Kluwer Academic/Plenum Publishers, 345–64.
Barber, B.R. (1996) *Jihad vs. McWorld: How Globalism and Tribalism are Reshaping the World*, New York: Ballantine Books.
Beyer, P.F. (1994) *Religion and Globalization*, Thousand Oaks, CA: Sage Publications.
Bhattacharjee, Y. (2005, April 29) 'Kansas gears up for another battle over teaching evolution', *Science*, 308(5722): 627.
Boli, J. and Thomas, G.M. (1997) 'World culture in the world polity', *American Sociological Review*, 62(2): 171–90.
Carnoy, M. (2000) *Sustaining Flexibility: Work, Family, and Community in the Information Age*, Cambridge, MA: Harvard University Press.
Coleman, J.S. (1992) 'The rational reconstruction of society', *American Sociological Review*, 58(1): 1–15.
Coleman, J.S. and Hoffer, T. (1987) *Public and Private Schools: The Impact of Communities*, New York: Basic Books.
Collins, R. (1998) *The Sociology of Philosophies: A Global Theory of Intellectual Change*, Cambridge, MA: Harvard University Press.
Comber, L. and Keeves, J. (1973) *Science Education in Nineteen Ccountries*, New York: Halsted.
Cook, T.D. and Payne, M.R. (2002) 'Objecting to the objections to using random assignment in educational research', in. F. Mosteller and R.F. Boruch (eds), *Evidence Matters: Randomized Trials in Education Research*, Washington, DC: Brookings Institution.
Coreno, T. (2002) 'Fundamentalism as a class culture', *Sociology of Religion*, 63(3): 335–60.
Darnell, A. and Sherkat, D.E. (1997) 'The impact of Protestant fundamentalism on educational attainment', *American Sociological Review*, 62(April): 306–15.
Durkheim, E. (1900) *Professional Ethics and Civic Morals*, London: Routledge.
Educational Researcher (2002, November) Theme issue on Scientific Research and Education [Special issue], 31(8).
Ellison, C.G., Gay, D.A. and Glass, T.A. (1989) 'Does religious commitment contribute to individual life satisfaction?', *Social Forces*, 68: 100–23.
Fiss, P.C. and Hirsch, P.M. (2005) 'The discourse of globalization: framing and sensemaking of an emerging concept', *American Sociological Review*, 70: 29–52.
Frickel, S. and Gross, N. (2005) 'A general theory of scientific/intellectual movements', *American Sociological Review*, 70: 204–32.

Guillen, M. (2001) 'Is globalization civilizing, destructive or feeble? A critique of five key debates in the social science literature', *Annual Review of Sociology*, 27: 235–60.

Heyneman, S. and Loxley, W. (1983) 'The effect of primary-school quality on academic achievement across twenty-nine high- and low-income countries', *American Journal of Sociology*, 88(2): 1162–94.

Hill, P.C. and Hood, R.W. Jr. (1999) *Measures of Religiosity*, Birmingham, AL: Religious Education Press.

Hirst, P. and Thompson, G. (1996) *Globalization in Question: The International Economy and the Possibilities of Governance*, Cambridge: Polity Press.

Iannaccone, L. (1994) 'Why strict churches are strong', *American Journal of Sociology*, 99(5): 1180–211.

Kellstedt, L. and Smidt, C. (1991) 'Measuring fundamentalism: an analysis of different operational strategies', *Journal of Scientific Study of Religion*, 30(3): 259–78.

Lagemann, E.C. (2000) *An Elusive Science: The Troubling History of Education Research*, Chicago, IL: University of Chicago Press.

Lee, J. (2002) 'Racial and ethnic achievement gap trends: reversing the progress towards equity', *Educational Researcher*, January/February: 1–12.

Lehrer, E.L. (1999) 'Religion as a determinant of educational attainment: an economic perspective', *Social Science Research*, 28: 358–79.

Marty, M.E. and Appleby, R.S. (1992) *The Glory and the Power*, Boston, MA: Beacon.

Marty, M.E. and Appleby, R.S. (1993) *Fundamentalism and the State: Remaking Polities, Economies, and Militance*, vol. 3, Chicago, IL: University of Chicago Press.

Menenedez, A.J. (1993) *Visions of Reality: What Fundamentalist Schools Teach,* Buffalo, NY: Prometheus.

Meyer, J.W. (2002) 'Globalization, national culture, and the future of the world polity', *Hong Kong Journal of Sociology*, 3: 1–18.

Meyer, J.W., Boli, J., Thomas, G.M. and Ramirez, F.O. (1997) 'World society and the nation-state', *American Journal of Sociology*, 103(1): 144–81.

Meyer, J.W., Ramirez, F.O. and Soysal, Y.N. (1992) 'World expansion of mass education, 1870–1980', *Sociology of Education*, 65(2): 115–49.

Miszal, B. and Shupe, A. (eds) (1992) *Religion and Politics in Comparative Perspective: Revival of Religious Fundamentalism in East and West*, Westport, CT: Praeger.

Mosteller, F. and Boruch, R.F. (eds) (2002) *Evidence Matters: Randomized Trials in Education Research*, Washington, DC: Brookings Institution Press.

National Center for Education Statistics (1998) *The Condition of Education, 1998*, Washington, DC: Institute of Education Science, US Department of Education.

No Child Left Behind Act of 2001(2002) Pub. L. No. 107-110, 115 stat. 1425.

Peshkin, A. (1986) *God's Choice: The Total World of a Fundamentalist Christian School*, Chicago, IL: University of Chicago Press.

Popkewitz, T.S. (2004) 'Is the National Research Council Committee's report on Scientific Research in Education scientific? On trusting the manifesto', *Qualitative Inquiry*, 10(1): 62–78.

Qualitative Inquiry (2004, February) Theme issue on Scientific Research in Education, 10(1).

Ragin, C., Nagel, J. and White, P. (2004) *Workshop on Scientific Foundations of Qualitative Research*, Washington, DC: National Science Foundation.

Riesebrodt, M. (2000) 'Fundamentalism and the resurgence of religion', *Numen*, 47: 265–87.

Rose, S.D. (1988) *Keeping Them out of the Hands of Satan: Evangelical Schooling in America*, New York: Routledge.

Sassen, S. (1996) *Losing Control? Sovereignty in an Age of Globalization. The 1995 Columbia University Leonard Hastings Schoff Memorial Lectures*, New York: Columbia University Press.

Schmidt, W.H., McKnight, C.C. and Raiszen, S. (1997) *A Splintered Vision*, Dordrecht: Kluwer.

Schmidt, W.H., McKnight, C.C., Houang, R., Wang, H.A., Wiley, D., Cogan, L. and Wolfe, R. (2001) *Why Schools Matter: A Cross National Comparison of Curriculum and Learning*, San Francisco, CA: Jossey-Bass Publishers.

Schneider, B. (ed.) (in preparation) *Scale-up in Practice*.

Sikkink, D. (1999) 'The social sources of alienation from public schools', *Social Forces*, 78(1), 51–86.

Sikkink, D. (2001) 'Speaking in many tongues: the common stereotypes of Christian schools mask their healthy diversity', *Education Next*, 1: 37–44.

Singer, P.W. (2001) *Pakistan's Madrassahs: Ensuring a System of Education not Jihad* (Analysis paper #14), Washington, DC: Brookings Institute.

Slavin, R.E. (2004) 'Education research can and must address "What Works" questions', *Educational Researcher*, 33(1): 27–8.

Stevenson, D.L. and Baker, D.P. (1991) 'State control of the curriculum and classroom instruction', *Sociology of Education*, 64(1): 1–10.

Stoffels, H. (2001) 'Survival strategies of conservative Protestants in Dutch society', in L. van Vucht Tijssen, J. Berting and F. Lechner (eds) *The Search for Fundamentals: The Process of Modernization and the Quest for Meaning*, Dordrecht, The Netherlands: Kluwer.

Teachers College Record (2005, January) Theme issue on Scientific Research in Education, 107(1).

Towne, L. and Hilton, M. (2004) 'Implementing randomized field trials in education', Report of a workshop. Washington, DC: National Academic Press.

Towne, L., Wise, L.L. and Winters, T.M. (2005) *Advancing Scientific Research in Education*, Washington, DC: National Academic Press.

Ueda, R. (1995) 'Ethnic diversity and national identity in public school texts', in D. Ravitch and M.A. Vinovkis (eds) *Learning From the Past*, Baltimore, MD: Johns Hopkins University Press, 265–80.

United Nations Statistics Division (2005) *Social Indicators*. Online. Available at: http://www.unstats.un.org/unsd/demographic/products/socind/inc-eco.htm. Last accessed: 17 March 2005.

Wade, M.J. (1996) 'Globalization and its limits: reports of the death of the national economy are greatly exaggerated', in S. Berger and R. Dore (eds) *National Diversity and Global Capitalism*, Ithaca, NY: Cornell University Press.

Walford, G. (2001) 'Evangelical Christian schools in England and the Netherlands', *Oxford Review of Education*, 27(4): 529–41.

Woodberry, R.D. and Smith, C.S. (1998) 'Fundamentalism et al.: conservative Protestants in America', *Annual Review of Sociology*, 24: 25–56.

Zia, R. (2003). 'Religion and education in Pakistan: an overview', *Prospects*, 33(2): 165–77.

14 Neoliberalism liberally applied

Educational policy borrowing in Central Asia

Gita Steiner-Khamsi, Iveta Silova and Eric M. Johnson

Introduction

The study of educational policy borrowing occupies a prominent place in comparative education research. From early comparative studies when 'gentlemen traveled extensively and wrote about differences between nations' (Kelly 1992: 14), to recent comparative research on globalisation, the fascination with reforms that have been transplanted from one cultural context to another has remained constant. To some extent, educational borrowing implies isolating education from its political, economic and cultural contexts. Therefore, numerous warnings have been articulated about policy borrowing, whether wholesale, selective or eclectic. This chapter deals with a policy that went global and with a considerable delay landed in Central Asia. The programme under scrutiny is neo-liberalism, particularly the policy of outcomes-based education (OBE) and its emphasis on data-driven, evidence-based accountability in the education systems in the three countries under review – Kazakhstan, Kyrgyzstan and Mongolia.

Research on policy borrowing and lending

We purposefully avoid using the term 'travelling policies' for its lack of agency. It tends to direct us towards obsolete research questions, many of which have already been answered in the diffusion of innovation studies of the 1950s and 1960s (Rogers 1992). Typically, their pre-occupation lay with the 'adoption rate', the 'degree of adoption' and 'receptiveness' towards innovations of reforms. The question of which policies travel internationally, which do not, and why, were beyond their scope of research interest. In the past decade, however, diffusion of innovation research experienced a re-incarnation of a superior kind with social network analysts and Small World researchers revitalising earlier concepts, and filling them with a notion of agency. One such useful concept, on which we will draw later in this section, is the notion of 'late adopters'. Unless research on travelling policies directs its attention to the individuals, networks and institutions that make policies travel, or as we would say, are engaged in the business of policy lending, there is little to be gained from introducing the new term, 'travelling policies'.

We prefer to stay with the more commonly used terminology of educational transfer, in particular with the conceptual twins 'policy borrowing' and 'policy lending', for an additional reason. Only in the past decade or so have comparative researchers started to tackle a series of understudied areas such as the reasons for policy attraction (Phillips

2004), the politics of borrowing and lending (Steiner-Khamsi 2004a), or the processes of local adaptation and re-contextualisation of borrowed reforms (Anderson-Levitt 2003). Illuminating these dark corners of an old research terrain of comparative education yields new insights. The authors of this chapter, for example, interpret borrowing as a policy strategy that is used to resolve protracted domestic policy conflict (Steiner-Khamsi 2004b), and view borrowing as a result of a re-orientation in a transnational educational space (Silova 2005). This new terrain not fully explored, it appears premature to dismiss an entire body of literature on policy borrowing and lending and replace it with a term that is more elusive.

Arguably, comparative research on policy borrowing and lending has undergone several major discursive shifts. An initial shift was the move from normative to analytical studies; the first being concerned with what *could* and *should* be borrowed and the latter interested in understanding *why* and *how* references were made to experiences from elsewhere. Jürgen Schriewer (1990) needs to be credited for criticising normative and meliorist approaches to the study of policy borrowing. At a time when many scholars were still pondering which lessons could be drawn from reforms in other countries, and ideally be imported, he turned the very act of lesson drawing into an object of study. Why are references made to experiences from elsewhere, or in what local policy context is emulation likely to occur? Why have the most common types of references, that is, references to own experiences (tradition), values or scientific rationality (Luhmann and Schorr 1979) been suspended giving way to external references? Embedded in the theoretical framework of system theory (Luhmann 1990), Schriewer proposed to study local contexts in order to understand the 'socio-logic' (Schriewer and Martinez 2004: 33) of externalisation. According to this theory, references to other educational systems are used as a leverage to carry out reforms that otherwise would be contested. Schriewer *et al.* (2004) also find it indicative of the 'socio-logic' of a system that only specific educational systems are used as external sources of authority. Which systems are used as 'reference societies'[1] (Schriewer and Martinez 2004: 42) and which are not, tells us something about the interrelations of actors within various world-systems. Pursuing an analytical rather than a normative approach to the study of educational borrowing, we reach the conclusion that is quite the contrary of what borrowing advocates might have us believe: borrowing does not occur because the reforms from elsewhere are better, but because the very act of borrowing has a salutary effect on domestic policy conflict.

In line with Schriewer's conceptual framework, we applied the concept of externalisation to comparative policy studies and found that it is precisely at moments of heightened policy contestation that references to other systems are made. Thus, borrowing, discursive or actual, has a certification effect on domestic policy talk (Steiner-Khamsi 2004b). Against this backdrop of system theory, three common phenomenon that at first appear to be nonsensical, make perfect sense:

1   very often the language of the reform is borrowed, but not the actual reform (Steiner-Khamsi 2005);
2   borrowing occurs even when there is no apparent need, that is, even when similar reforms already exist in the local context (Steiner-Khamsi and Quist 2000); and
3   if the actual reform is borrowed, it is always selectively borrowed and sometimes locally re-contextualised to the extent that there is little similarity left between the copy and the original.

Global borrowing and lending: rationales, impacts and trajectories

This shift from normative to analytical studies in policy borrowing research, however, has only triggered a revolution among certain comparative education researchers. While the orphans of normative borrowing studies continue to compete over which 'best practices' to disseminate around the globe, the analytically oriented borrowing researchers have turned their attention to the interplay between borrowing and globalisation. They notice that policy makers increasingly generate reform pressure by making references to globalisation. Panic-stricken, no educational system wants to be 'left behind'. Whether globalisation in education is real or imagined, it is uncontested that the 'semantics of globalisation' (Schriewer 2000: 330) is increasingly tied to accelerate educational reform.

Given the epidemiological model of global reforms, timing matters a great deal (see Luschei 2004). In social network analysis, we distinguish between three phases of reform epidemic, including the slow growth, explosive and burnout phases of reform dissemination (Watts 2003: 172). In this chapter, we propose to examine adoption of global reforms at their burnout stage. In particular, we propose to study the 'late adopters' of a reform that had already reached its peak of global dissemination and in some cases faced a decline in its popularity. By the time global reforms land in 'late adopter' countries, they are at the same time everybody's and nobody's reforms. They are generally de-territorialised or global reforms characterised by a 'referential web' (Vavrus 2004) rather than by clear references to one or two educational systems that served as exemplars for emulation. The very fact that we examine the adoption of a global reform movement during its burnout phase means that we investigate not only different local responses to a global reform, but also the global reform movement itself. By implication, the investigation of the late adopters becomes the study of global reforms.

In light of globalisation studies in education, this chapter addresses three unresolved issues in global policy borrowing and lending research pertaining to the rationales, impacts and trajectories of global policy borrowing. First, scholars examining the rationale for borrowing have relied on studies of transnational borrowing and have averted attention from other types of borrowing, notably *cross-sectoral* and *intra-sectoral* borrowing. Given the amount written on the impact of neo-liberal thought in current school reforms, there is no need to reiterate the evidence that the education sector is soaked in language and concepts borrowed from the economic sector (e.g. supply/demand, accountability, cost-effectiveness, etc.; see Henig 1994). We also learn from Tyack and Cuban (1995) that the penetration of the education sector with principles typically applied to markets and the economic sector has been a recurring theme, emerging cyclically every couple of years. Nevertheless, the phenomenon of cross-sectoral borrowing is striking from a sociology-of-knowledge perspective because it entails an interaction between two sectors that, by virtue of being different subsystems or sectors of society, manifest different epistemes and regulatory mechanisms. Nevertheless, cross-sectoral transfer is well documented in the general educational research literature (albeit not in the comparative education research), especially the transfer of principles of market regulation from the economic sector to the education sector and the transfer of TQM (total quality management) principles from the health to the education sector. However, relevant for our analyses is the transfer of principles of accountability from the finance sector, in particular from public and administration reform, to the education sector. In contrast to these different variations of cross-sectoral or horizontal borrowing, intra-sectoral or vertical transfer processes have been little investigated. Eric Johnson will discuss in this chapter a case (Kyrgyzstan) where the rationale for standardised testing and assessment reform was first applied in higher education and then passed down to general education.

Second, the question of how existing practices are impacted by policy import is often brushed off with a general comment on hybridisation. The case studies in Anderson-Levitt's edited volume (2003), as remarkable as they are, exclusively focus on how a global reform such as, for example, OBE takes on different meanings in various contexts. The destiny of existing policies in light of such global forces is not explicitly addressed. Arguably, it is no small feat to examine how one and the same reform is re-interpreted differently as this tells us something about culture and in particular about the culture of reform in the various policy contexts. However, hybridisation resulting from the encounter between imported and already existing policies is but one of several conceivable outcomes. Other conceivable outcomes are a replacement of previous policies, and at the other extreme, a reinforcement of what had already been in place. Again, hybridisation has been amply documented (e.g. Anderson-Levitt 2003), and replacement as an outcome of borrowing has also been well studied in societies that have undergone revolutionary changes (e.g. Spreen 2004). Both strands of research view policy borrowing, or more broadly speaking, globalisation, as a form of external intervention that inevitably triggers change. Even if we qualify this assumption by adding that, for a variety of political and economic reasons, so-called external interventions are frequently internally induced when politicians and policy makers utilise the semantics of globalisation to generate reform pressure, we are still left with those cases where policy import exclusively served to reinforce existing policies. Other than Silova's study on bilingual education policies in post-Soviet Latvia (Silova 2005a), there is little in the way of empirical evidence to suggest that policy borrowing is sometimes used to legitimise and reinforce existing practices. In this chapter, Gita Steiner-Khamsi supports Silova's earlier findings (Silova 2005a), and presents an additional case (Mongolia) where the introduction of OBE merely reinforced an elaborate monitoring system that had been in place for the past 30 years.

Third, the difficulty with mapping trajectories of transplanted reforms has been highlighted by several scholars in globalisation studies and has rendered the spatial connotation of borrowing and lending research highly problematic. Is OBE, for example, *originally* a New Zealand, Australian, Canadian or US reform? The answer varies, depending on the time period one is referring to and on the expert asked. In the end, how valid is the genealogical approach to the study of reform epidemics that, as in the case of OBE, spread like wildfire around the globe? Today, OBE is as much a Chilean, South African and European reform as it is a New Zealand or Australian reform. Late adopters of a reform do not necessarily resort to the original(s), but rather orient themselves towards early adopters of the reform from their own world-system, educational space, or reference horizon. In contrast to nineteenth-century borrowing research when scholars were content with tracing transplanted policies across the Atlantic (between North America and Europe), many scholars nowadays suggest giving up the idea of actually mapping the itinerary of a travelling policy. Frances Vavrus (2004) has coined the term 'referential web' to acknowledge multiple references for policy borrowing and invites us to abandon mapping exercises in borrowing and lending research. There is a special type of reference that has caught our attention in recent years (Steiner-Khamsi 2003). Politicians and policy makers increasingly make deterritorialised references to an imagined international community. They generate reform pressure domestically by invoking fears of 'falling behind' and urge their constituents to comply with 'international standards' in education. In this chapter, Iveta Silova discusses a case (Kazakhstan) where the trajectories of OBE are ubiquitous and different OBE models were simultaneously used as exemplars for emulation.

The centrality of Central Asia

> May this help convert Central Asia from the sort of dark hole in the middle that it was, to a real black hole whose gravitational attraction can soon engulf the outside and outsiders.
>
> (Frank 1992: 52)

Andre Gunder Frank (1992: 52) ends his book *The Centrality of Central Asia* with this powerful statement demanding that Central Asia be given a place in world-systems theory. There were periods in history in which the three countries of our case studies viewed themselves as part of the same world such as, for example, in the thirteenth century under the Mongol Empire and in the twentieth century as Soviet Central Asian Republics (Kazakhstan, Kyrgyzstan) or as socialist 'fraternalist countries' (Mongolia, Kazakhstan, Kyrgyzstan), respectively. These are but two periods in history during which the three case studies inhabited the same geo-political space. We focus in this chapter exclusively on the latter space and on its transformation into a post-socialist world-system in the heart of Asia. It is important to point out that more than 30 other countries inhabited the same post-socialist education space at the beginning of the 1990s.

For one particular reason, the case studies on these three Central Asian education systems is central for research on policy borrowing and lending: they are *late adopters* of OBE and in that capacity borrowed OBE at a time when it had already gone global or, in some places, was already in decline. These three Central Asian educational systems were second-hand borrowers. A brief comment on the history of OBE and other neo-liberal educational reforms sailing under different names might be useful here to substantiate the point about the late arrival of such reforms in Central Asia. New Zealand revamped its public sector in the 1980s leading up to the State Sector Act of 1988 and the Public Finance Act of 1989. Emphasising outcomes-based accountability, these two acts had great repercussions for the education sector. On the opposite side of the globe, the Thatcher government pushed at the same time for a series of neo-liberal and market-driven reforms in the UK. There, the 1988 Education Act for England and Wales introduced a national curriculum, standardised testing and parental choice, all of them signposts of a new neo-liberal era in educational reform that epitomised the language of public accountability, effectiveness and market regulation.

Serving as the main reference point for the three Central Asian countries, the *New Zealand Curriculum Framework* is commonly associated with a fundamentally new approach to curriculum reform. It places the individual student and his/her learning outcomes at the centre of all teaching, and dissociates the student's learning outcomes from content taught in a specific grade. In many countries where the New Zealand reform model was adopted, OBE requires that teachers establish benchmarks for each individual student. At the end of each grade, and in some countries throughout the year, the student's performance is regularly assessed in tests to measure whether the benchmarks have been reached. In practice, the proliferation of standardised tests is but one of the impacts of OBE reform. Additionally, the benchmarks are noted in the teacher scorecards or outcomes-contracts, and teachers are held accountable for the performance of their students. Since OBE purports to measure the precise performance of a teacher as reflected in the learning outcomes of students, it has been propagated as a tool for quality enhancement in education, and aptly referred to as New Contractualism or New Accountability. Claims have been made by proponents that OBE, in opposition to content- or input-based curricula, is able to monitor the quality of education more effectively, and thereby respond to the quest for more public accountability in education.

By the time the Central Asian educational systems adopted OBE in the first years of the millennium, OBE was already beyond its peak. The metaphor of an epidemic that first starts to spread slowly, then moves into a stage of exponential growth, and finally phases out appears useful in explaining the global dissemination of OBE. During OBE's phase of slow growth in the late 1980s and early 1990s only a few educational systems adopted the reform, notably New Zealand, Australia, England and Wales, Canada and the USA. The take-off point marks the beginning of the explosive phase when numerous educational systems selectively borrowed elements of OBE. Roger Dale (2001: 498) traced the 'global career' of the New Zealand OBE model in the 1990s. The important role of international donors, notably the World Bank and regional banks, for actively disseminating and funding OBE reforms in low-income countries is not to be under-estimated.[2] By the time the Ministries of Education in Central Asian countries joined the chorus of public accountability and choice enthusiasts, ministries and teacher unions in other parts of the world were already disenchanted with OBE and had moved on to more effective curriculum or standards reform (e.g. Donnelly 2002). Incidentally, the nation-wide strike of the National Union of Teachers in the UK against excessive high-stakes exams and teaching to the test (December 2003) was concurrent with the period of greatest enthusiasm for OBE in Central Asia. Thus, the region under review in this chapter needs to be regarded as a late adopter of neo-liberal reforms. The ministries of education in Kazakhstan, Kyrgyzstan and Mongolia embraced OBE during the burnout phase of the OBE reform epidemic when other educational systems had already reached the point of weariness with similar market-driven and outcomes-based reforms. The very fact that we examine the adoption of OBE during the burnout phase of a reform epidemic implies that we in fact investigate three diverse local responses to a global reform movement. By implication, our case study analyses attempts to contribute to understanding 'policy attraction' (Phillips 2004).

OBE is Central Asia: cultural encounters with local research paradigms

The widespread criticism against any reform that is old, including OBE, made us delve into a search for reasons why OBE was so appealing to government officials in Kazakhstan, Kyrgyzstan and Mongolia. The global OBE movement has generally been part of a larger new public administration reform that emphasises data-driven or evidence-based accountability and a panoptic surveillance of system performance that is consistent with Foucault's (1991) observations of the modern state. As mentioned, the literature sometimes refers to these reforms as New Accountability or New Contractualism, or 'government by contract' (Schick 1998). According to Neave (1988), a focus on outcomes is embedded in the rise of the 'evaluative state', one that is committed to 'maintaining central control over the framing of targets whilst at the same time giving greater latitude at institutional level to choose which course is best suited to the specific institutional circumstances' (Neave 1988: 11). As detailed by many (see Smyth and Dow 1998), outcomes benchmarking and monitoring are an essential part of the new technology of scientific management over school systems.

In the context of post-socialist Central Asia, this paradigm was not really new and exactly for this reason resonated so well with the education stakeholders in the three countries. The 'command economies' of the former socialist bloc were driven by data, benchmarks, and archives piling up data sets from the monitoring departments of each ministry. Reflecting on the processes of data collection during the Soviet period, the Russian Federal Statistics Service (1996) duly observed that Soviet statistical collection was noted for its 'sufficient intensity', relying on detailed data gathered through a great number of specially organised censuses and surveys. This data-driven research was an important part of the 'Soviet insistence on planning', which was clearly reflected in five-, seven-, and ten-year plans in all areas of the economic and social development of each country. These plans entailed the setting of specific, often highly detailed, targets for the output of intermediate and finished results/products; the specification of detailed plans to achieve those targets; the allocation of capital resources, raw materials, and labour by permits and licences; and the establishment of comprehensive price schedules reflecting the planners' preferences (Noah 1986). In other words, OBE was not really new in the post-socialist context, but rather revitalised a practice that was quite common in socialist times. Among other reasons, OBE resonated so well among the post-socialist policy makers precisely because it was so similar to the planning mania and fed right into their obsession with data-driven, evidence-based research reminiscent of the socialist period.

Despite some similarities with the socialist educational planning strategies, the global OBE reform was adopted differently in each of the three Central Asian countries under review. *What* exactly was borrowed from the global OBE movement is an important question given that any major reform, including OBE, is an octopus with several arms. For example, the global OBE package extends into reforms of the curriculum, monitoring of teachers, student assessment, teacher salary schemes, public accountability with regard to the quality of schools and, in some countries, is closely associated with school choice. The question becomes, to which component are decision makers in a particular country attracted to, and why? What impact does the global reform have on existing practices, and what are the prerequisites for introducing the reform in different contexts? The following three case-studies of Kyrgyzstan, Mongolia and Kazakhstan explore local policy constellations that account for the global policy attraction and discuss how the rationales, impacts and prerequisites for introducing OBE reform varied for each context or case.

Learning from above: vertical transfer in Kyrgyzstan

The outcomes-oriented educational reform movement in Kyrgyzstan emerged in a context of pervasive corruption, particularly in higher education. Long the pride of the Soviet system, the quality of higher education had come into question in Kyrgyzstan with frequent reports of admissions bribes and grade-buying. Outcomes-based education, with its emphasis on assessment, data transparency and accountability was attractive to Kyrgyz reformers committed to eliminating corruption. While the Kyrgyz reform was originally focused on higher education, it has recently come to include wide-sweeping changes for general education. This case represents an example of vertical or intra-sectoral transfer. Put differently, the 'travelling policy' of outcomes-based education arrived in Kyrgyzstan in 2001 as a reform aimed at corruption elimination in higher education and three years later it made its way down the system to general education. The way that this vertical transfer occurred bears explanation.

An action plan for fighting corruption

The anti-corruption 'revolution' commenced with the appointment of a reform-minded Minister of Education in 2001 (IRINnews.org 2002, 12 September). Camilla Sharshekeeva, long a supporter of educational reform and a founder of the American University of Central Asia, was determined to combat corruption in higher education as the new Minister of Education. Alan DeYoung, an observer of the 2001 reform movement, writes that the new Minister of Education:

> Described what she understood as the abuses of university rectors to pocket tuition fees paid by students and to sell supposedly free slots to the highest bidding students. Combined with the alleged selling of grades that thus weakens graduate quality, Camilla Sharshekeeva from the beginning of the entire education reform agenda had university organization and university leaders in her sights (DeYoung 2004: 217).

At the request of the Kyrgyz Ministry of Education, a USAID-led group met in spring 2001 and made a list of 74 problems with the Kyrgyz education system. The list of problems was then condensed into eight topical areas:

1   minimum academic standards
2   teacher retraining
3   new technologies
4   school management
5   use of data
6   higher education rationalisation
7   higher education funding
8   structural re-organisation of the Ministry of Education and Culture (MoEC).

From the eight topical areas, four working groups were formed: School Management and Minimum Standards, Teachers Retraining and New Technologies, Higher Education Funding and Rationalization, and a group on the structure of the MoEC. The working groups met an average of twice a month between March and June 2001. In June, USAID put forth serious funding for the emerging reform effort and subcontracted John Clark, formerly of American University in Kyrgyzstan, to read the working group reports and draft an Action Plan for the reform legislation (DeYoung 2004).

The Action Plan, released six months later, had four main sections and sets of recommendations:

- General Management Reforms: develop financial accountability systems, public information systems, assure qualifications as the criteria in all hiring procedures, create school and university governance councils comprised of citizens and parents to monitor schools, initiate a standards and a merit-based national scholarship test for university scholarship allotments, create a system for identifying needy students in schools and helping them.
- Structural Reforms of the Ministry of Education and Culture: clarifying the chain of command, combine internal departments, increase departmental policy focus and strength, spin off the 'cultural' component of the Ministry, create an independent testing centre for the production of objective tests.
- School Management and Retraining: revise minimum academic standards for all subjects and grade levels, create pilot schools to test new teaching and administration styles, transition to a 12-year curriculum, develop guidelines for privatisation efforts, redevelop pre-schools, and design new ways to evaluate school performance.
- Higher Education Reforms: develop a board of trustees system to oversee rectors, create auditing capabilities for monies expenditures, revise minimum academic standards, retool curriculum to meet current social and economic needs, raise teacher salaries to reduce grade-buying, develop national university research centres, and establish a National Scholarship Test (NST) for financial aid allotment (DeYoung 2004: 217–18).

Outcomes-based education is not mentioned by name, nor is the USA, but American OBE tenants and universal OBE 'best-practices' are clearly present: revising minimum standards, instituting objective assessments to test outcomes, promoting the use of data (outcomes) to manage the educational system, a focus on community involvement for monitoring, the aligning of learned skills to current conditions and, finally, a near obsession with accountability as a means to reduce corruption and improve quality without additional financial inputs. While the Action Plan lays out reforms for all sectors of the Kyrgyz educational system, reform observers claim that all participants knew that the Kyrgyz MoEC and USAID were only serious about the higher education reforms at that point (DeYoung 2004). However, the inclusion of suggestions for system-wide changes in outcomes, transparency and accountability in the Action Plan was sure to face resistance from powerful educational stake-holders.

DeYoung (2004: 213) claims that throughout the working-group negotiations, local Kyrgyz reformers had seen the advice from the Americans as an 'external threat' and resisted many reform ideas with the reply: 'Help us obtain fiscal resources and leave your ideas at the door, we had a better system than the West before, and we just need to be able to get back to what we had.' This attitude is consistent with a post-Soviet legacy that is at times nostalgic for parts of the Soviet era, including its strong educational system. Silova (2004: 75) writes that in the post-Soviet context, 'the language of new allies has triggered major conceptual disputes about how these newly "borrowed" ideas should be understood, internalized, and implemented locally.' The Action Plan did not bring new money nor did it leave western ideas 'at the door'; as the Action Plan was light on new fiscal resources and heavy on additional forms of evaluation and accountability.

Nonetheless, the Ministry of Education and USAID pushed on with the reform package by assigning a department and a timetable to each component of the Action Plan. DeYoung

(2004: 20) writes that, 'The Action Plan, as suggested, basically called for scrapping almost the entire existing system of schooling in the Kyrgyz Republic and reinventing it with a very Western and "rational" flavor.' However, as the reform's focus on corruption in higher education had 'crossed swords' with powerful rectors and politicians, the reform legislation was eventually defeated, save the highest priority, the National Scholarship Test (NST). However, Sharshekeeva would have to push this reform from outside the ministry, as she was dismissed as Minister of Education in May 2002.

There are a variety of possible reasons why the NST survived while the rest of the Action Plan did not. Phillips (2004) theorises that in the implementation stage certain parts of reform policies are pushed faster and with more force than other parts. This was certainly the case with the higher education reforms, which DeYoung (2004: 218) claims were 'fast tracked'. It is also possible that USAID was only serious about funding the NST, as they had the Educational Testing Service (ETS) ready to consult on the test construction and American Councils for International Education: ACTR/ACCELS ready to administer it in Kyrgyzstan. It is no secret that reform proscriptions without funding and implementation capacity often go unrealised. Lastly, it is possible that the concept of testing for achievement and rewarding merit in the allotment of university scholarships resonated with legacies of socialist competition, such as Olympiads. So, while the NST struck at the heart of corruption and offered the largest area for rector-led opposition, it paradoxily survived. Its survival and eventual success had implications for the parts of the Action Plan that were left-behind.

The NST: leveraging and transferring outcomes down the system

The NST is an aptitude test similar to the SAT in the USA. In fact, the NST and its autonomous administering body, the Independent Testing Organization, are modelled after ETS in the USA. Each spring, the NST is offered to graduating seniors who want to be eligible for government-funded higher education scholarships. Explicitly aimed at equalising rural and urban educational opportunities and introducing a modern assessment culture, the NST is the only criteria used in determining the government allotment of highly valued university scholarships. This makes the NST high-stakes and highly visible. Offered in Kyrgyz, Russian and Uzbek languages, the test uses modern question construction, computerised and objective scoring, and rigorous methods aimed at fairness, transparency and accountability. Results of the exam are made public and the NST appears to be popular with school directors, parents and students. In fact, since 2002 over 100,000 students have sat for the exam (American Councils for International Education 2004, September 15).

The Independent Testing Organization lists the following successes of the NST in changing the culture of Kyrgyz education:

- Foundation of the non-profit educational NGO 'The Center for Educational Assessment and Teaching Methods'.
- Independent, objective assessment through administration of the National Scholarship Test (NST) has provided fair access to university scholarships for over 15,000 students in 2002, 2003, and 2004.
- High-level political support has been attained: Presidential and Ministerial decrees called for independent testing and allowed NGO monitoring of the university enrolment process in 2003 and 2004.

- The 2003 'Law on Education' called for the NST for university entrance.
- Results of 2004 school director surveys indicate overwhelming support for independent testing as well as increased motivation of students to learn and teachers to teach due to the introduction of the NST.
- The science of testing and educational measurement has been bolstered in the Republic – the NST assesses cognitive skills through norm-referenced aptitude testing.
- Significant investment made in training of Kyrgyzstani specialists in modern assessment methodologies – attention to test and item performance through pre-testing and post-testing item analysis, test equating and differential item functioning (American Councils for International Education 2004, September 15).

By all accounts, the NST has also changed the nature of higher education admissions. While the test has not eliminated corruption, it has introduced a culture of scientific, outcomes-based assessment as a means to improving merit identification. The popularity and visibility of the NST has also had a much larger effect on the Kyrgyz educational system: the focus on outcomes, modern assessment and public accountability has been transferred to general education. Some Kyrgyz observers claim that this connection between higher educational reform and general education reform is not surprising in a system that places great importance on what occurs in higher education. McLean, Karimov and Asankanov (2002: 4) write of the Kyrgyz reform that 'it is unlikely that parents and students who perform poorly on these exams as a result of a poor educational experience will sit still and let this continue to happen. It is likely that substantial pressure will brought to bear on school administrators, and those appointing them, when poor educational outcomes result.

Indeed, that was the hope all along. A USAID report on the NST claims, 'It is hoped that the testing format of the NST will provoke further debate and leverage reform efforts which are seeking to introduce better tools of educational measurement, *outcome oriented national standards, and even "outcome oriented" lesson planning at the classroom level*' (Drummond 2003, emphasis added).

Clearly the NST and the attack on corruption in higher education were eventually meant by reformers to translate into system-wide changes in the approach to education in Kyrgyzstan. What is not clear is how fast they thought it would happen. It turns out that they would not have to wait long; in 2004 the system-wide outcomes-based discourse of the 2001 reform gained money and momentum and was realised in new reforms.

Travelling from higher to general education

In 2004 the World Bank approved a $15.5 million Rural Education project aimed at preparing Kyrgyz children for the 'challenges of the future' (World Bank Group 2005). The OBE footprint of increased monitoring of outcomes and accountability with few new inputs is present in the new World Bank reform. According to a recent World Bank press release on the project, it will include:

An improved performance management system for teachers and principals and a related revised salary scale will be developed and applied in two pilot oblasts –

Issykul and Talas. The project will strengthen student assessment by setting up a new Assessment Unit within the Education Ministry and by arranging for student participation in the Organization for Economic Co-operation and Development's Program for International Student Assessment, or PISA. The overall sustainability of the sector will improve, since the project will strengthen the country's education strategy in ways that optimize education outcomes within prevailing resource and implementation constraints

(World Bank Group 2005)

In addition to the new World Bank money for outcome-oriented general education reforms, USAID is funding a new secondary school teacher-training programme called PEAKS (Participation, Education and Knowledge Strengthening). PEAKS seeks to reform general education by training teachers in 'international methodologies' and modern assessments based on results, as well as improve parental involvement and the training of school directors and educational managers (USAID Data Sheet 2005).

While these reforms are in their beginning stages, the discourse of neo-liberal reform and outcomes-based education has made its way from an original focus on combating corruption in higher education to programmes aimed at general educational assessment methods and educational outcomes. Silova (2004) observes that too many comparative studies of borrowing focus only on what is originally modified, omitted and accepted as a part of the transfer (p. 76). She argues that we must move beyond a focus on practices and recognise changes in discourse. Steiner-Khamsi (2000) claims that often when a reform is not implemented, a discourse is still transferred. In the case of Kyrgyzstan, a general education outcomes-oriented discourse that was started in the 2001 Action Plan is now being implemented three years later, possibly as a result of the popularity of the NST and the pressures it placed on general educational performance.

Recent outcomes-based reforms of general education in Kyrgyzstan, while not explicitly linked to the discourse of corruption elimination, must be understood in this context. A protracted and serious reform effort by USAID and the Kyrgyz MoEC in 2001–02 led to the implementation of the National Scholarship Test. The subsequent success and popularity of the test brought pressure to bear on secondary and primary schools in Kyrgyzstan. The NST's shift in focus from the inputs to outputs of education set the stage for the introduction of an outcome-orientation in Kyrgyz general education. This vertical or intra-sectoral transfer from higher education to general education has not happened on its own or without the agency of key actors. Parents and school directors have expressed their opinions, teachers have been re-trained, lawmakers have institutionalised reforms, and aid agencies have tirelessly pushed their neo-liberal 'best practices'. Highlighting the importance of individuals in 'travelling reforms', Camilla Sharshekeeva has travelled from the Ministry of Education over to the World Bank, where she is now heading up the new general education reforms.

Mongolia: banking on policy import

The outcomes-based education reform in Mongolia was part of a larger public sector reform. The Public Sector Management and Finance (PSMF) Law, approved by the Parliament of Mongolia on 27 June 2002, advocated accountability and efficiency in the areas of governance and finance. In Mongolia, finance is the engine for any reform and not surprisingly the concept of accountability, permeating each section of the 2002 law, was linked to performance agreements and performance-based bonuses.[3] The PSMF reform was funded by a $25 million loan from the Asian Development Bank (Asian Development Bank 2003). The first loan was approved in December 1999 and the second loan of $15.5 million targeting accountability and efficiency in health, education, social welfare and labour was granted in October 2003. In the late 1990s New Zealand became the magnet for policy pilgrimage. Each and every member of the Mongolian Parliament and all senior-level staff of ministries were sent on study tour to New Zealand. The policy pilgrimage from Mongolia boomed at a time when critical observers had already published and widely disseminated their doubts about whether the New Zealand-style public management reforms were applicable for developing countries (Bale and Dale 1998, Schick 1998).

Despite, or perhaps because of, Mongolia being a late adopter of the new public management reform, the various ministries carried out the reform without any further delay.[4] In 2003, the Ministry of Education published a thick 319-page white handbook on outcomes-based education with numerous examples of student benchmarks and teacher scorecards (Ministry of Education, Science and Culture 2003). By January 2005, astute commentators on OBE started to refer to the book as the Big Grey Book because readers were browsing the opaque tome in vain to find solid criteria for evaluating educational outcomes.

OBE puzzles in the Mongolian policy context

Three puzzles are striking when we examine how OBE has been implemented in practice. First, holding teachers strictly accountable for their performance is not new in Mongolia. In fact, in place was a system where teachers were not only monetarily rewarded if they performed well, but also punished if they failed to perform well. Thus, the study of the imported OBE reform in Mongolia is a good case for investigating the impact of policy import on top of already existing, similar practices. Does a policy import replace, hybridise or reinforce existing practices? We have several reasons to suggest that the OBE reform in Mongolia has merely confirmed what was already in place with regard to teacher surveillance. Nevertheless, the co-existence of several performance- and outcomes-based monitoring systems has significantly increased the bureaucratisation of the teaching profession. Drowned in paper work, teachers must submit their daily notes on students as well as monthly and semi-annual self-evaluations to the school administration.

Secondly, OBE was implemented without prior establishment of grade and subject-specific standards. On paper, the standards-based education reform was officially initiated in 1998. However, it yielded few results as the reform did not lead to the formulation of concrete and measurable standards. The curriculum, crowded with many different subjects and consequently leaving little instructional time for each of the subjects, has remained vague and abstract with regard to standards. This leapfrogging – moving directly to OBE without a prior establishment of standards – has left school administrators and teachers at a loss as to how and against which benchmarks they should evaluate outcomes. In the absence of clear and measurable criteria, school administrators and teachers have resorted to monitoring practices established in the socialist past and endured in the post-socialist present.

Thirdly, consistent with OBE reforms in many other countries of the region, the OBE reform in Mongolia did not have any budgetary implications. Against all expectations, the budget lines for salary supplements and bonuses have not been enhanced to enable merit- or performance-based salary additions. As a result of the budget ceiling, the school administration has been trapped in a zero-sum game. In order to reward a few high-performing teachers, it needs to deduct income from many other teachers at the school.

How do schools, in particular school administration and teachers, deal with these three challenges of OBE in Mongolia? This case study focuses on the first puzzle and briefly interweaves the other two. It draws on two empirical studies in which we analysed teacher salaries in Mongolia.

The first study was conducted in May 2003 in two provinces of Mongolia (Uvurkhangai and Arkhangai) and examined how teachers as parents manage to pay for the high educational cost of their university-aged children (Steiner-Khamsi *et al*. 2004). We conducted 44 interviews with teachers in four schools and gathered information on how much teachers earn in total (including base salary, salary supplements and bonuses) and how much they spend for the education of their own children. The study identified three teacher strategies – expectation of reciprocity within the family, social redistribution within the extended social network and loans – that enable teachers to bridge the sizable gap between their low income and the high educational expenses of their own children.

The second source of information is from the baseline study for the Public Expenditure Tracking Survey (PETS) funded by the World Bank and implemented by the Open Society Forum (Soros Foundation). As part of the preparation of the survey instruments and the sampling plan for the PETS study, we interviewed principals and teachers in Ulaanbaatar and in the province of Tuv in January 2005.[5]

Discipline and punish teachers

In our Teachers as Parents study (Steiner-Khamsi *et al*. 2004), we were surprised to find the elaborate systems that are in place to discipline and punish teachers for their shortcomings. These systems, of course, reflect the high status and expectations attached to the teaching profession. In provincial schools, teachers are personally held accountable by parents and the school administration, not only if students do not academically achieve in class, but also if these students do not clean the classroom, are impolite, come late to class, do not wash themselves, do not engage in useful after-school activities, do not do their homework or do not take proper notes during class. The teacher who voluntarily tutors students after school so that she does not get humiliated by parents or have her salary supplement reduced is not an extinct species in Mongolia, but rather is alive, suffering and complaining. The system of teacher accountability relies on a myriad of regulations that keep teachers in line. Before explaining the bureaucratic apparatus for disciplining and punishing teachers, it is necessary to briefly present the Mongolian performance- or outcomes-based teacher salary scheme which has been in place for the past 30 years.

The full income of Mongolian teachers has traditionally consisted of base salary, salary supplements and bonuses. The *base salary* only constitutes approximately 57 per cent of the income, and salary supplements and bonuses represent a great share of the full income. The base salary ranges from between $45 and $55 per month, depending on the rank of a teacher.[6] The promotion criteria vary slightly for the different ranks, but they all include leadership skills of the teacher (number of teachers that are mentored or trained), ethics of the teacher (in practice commonly interpreted as non-alcoholism), grades of students and awards from 'olympiads' and competitions. Of all these criteria, winning at olympiads carries the greatest weight. That is, if a teacher wins at an olympiad for a particular subject matter, all the other requirements (leadership skills, ethics, grades of students) become inconsequential. Furthermore, if she wins at a high-level olympiad (provincial or national level), she is able to skip ranks, and is directly promoted to a lead teacher or methodologist. Interestingly, the promotion and salary increase also go into effect if a student wins at an olympiad or competition; the assumption being that the teacher must have supported and promoted the award-winning student, and therefore needs to be rewarded for that student. Critics of olympiads, one of the many legacies from the socialist past, point to the detrimental effects of linking teacher salaries and bonuses to students' outcomes in olympiads. This practice encourages teachers, according to the critics, to focus on only a few promising students, coach them for olympiads, and neglect the rest of the students in a class.

It is important to bear in mind that these promotion criteria, and with them, the performance-based salary scheme, have been in place since the 1970s, long before OBE reforms were being pushed. The competitions were conducted at each administrative level – municipality, district, provincial and national – leading to a whole host of awards and insignia. Most likely, each and every citizen won a socialist competition for something: for being the best worker, the best student in mathematics or the best stamp collector – to list only a few examples. The importance of olympiads and other performance-based promotion criteria was re-affirmed in government regulations of the post-socialist era (in 1995 and 2004). A common reaction among the interviewed teachers towards OBE, and in particular towards the teacher scorecards, was that OBE is socialist competition in disguise, because the emphasis is also placed on outcomes or performance. In addition, socialist-oriented teachers viewed OBE as an egotistical version of socialist competition in that it advocates competition without any social responsibility for a group or for the collective.

The *salary supplement* constitutes regular monthly income and is given for all kinds of tasks: the salary supplement for grading student notebooks is given to all teachers, including, for example, physical education teachers. All teachers are supposed to be knowledge-centred and students are expected to take notes on what the teacher says and consolidate that knowledge in their assignments. Other sizable income is generated from teaching a class for gifted students (20 per cent supplement to the base salary), or from serving as a class teacher.

In contrast to salary supplements, *bonuses* are usually one-time awards given throughout the school year. They are supposed to be given for special accomplishments of teachers, but in practice are – in the absence of clear evaluation criteria – determined arbitrarily by the principal, the education manager (assistant principal), and the social worker,[7] who in trio constitute the school administration. The teacher scorecards, introduced in the wake of the OBE reform, fall into this category for two reasons: a high score (i.e. 60 per cent and more of all eligible points) calls for a bonus and given the vagueness of the evaluation criteria they also mean that the school administration values the teacher for reasons mysterious to all other teachers.

As common as it is to obtain a salary supplement or a bonus, it is as common to lose it or to have one's salary, supplement or bonuses deducted. Deductions are the rule and not the exception. Salary deductions are grave and are only made for teacher absences, tardiness and drunkenness.[8] In contrast, the complete withdrawal or deductions of salary supplements are very common. The school administration establishes its authority with teachers by constantly threatening to reduce their income, creating an atmosphere of intimidation and obedience in the school.

It is a striking feature of the Mongolian educational system that not only the laws and regulations are formulated meticulously, but also the sanctions for not obeying them. Apart from the host of regulations imposed by the district, provincial and central education authorities, each school also develops its own additional policies. In a school in the Bayangol city-district of Ulaanbaatar, for example, the supplement for grading student notebooks is only given if seven requirements are met, including: the full name and address of the student must be written in proper handwriting on the cover of the notebook, the student is not allowed to use pens with different colours in the note book (the teacher has a monopoly on the use of red ink), and there must be evidence that the teacher actually checked and corrected the student notebook.[9] Non-compliance with any one of these conditions leads to a supplement deduction.

Another example for the punitive system is the regulation of class teachers. In Bayangol, seven criteria must be fulfilled to receive the full supplement for class teachers. In order to receive the full supplement, 70 points must be attained, 10 per criteria.[10] The policy also clearly lays out how these points are deducted, leading either to a reduction or to an annulment of the salary supplement (Bayangol 2004b):

• For every student who is not disciplined: 5 points deduction.
• For every loss or damage of the classroom equipment and furniture: 5 points deduction.
• For not up-dating the class billboard (class newspaper, posters, etc.): 5 points deduction.
• For every student who comes late or misses class: 1 point deduction.

It was in this culture of tight surveillance of teachers and of school salaries tied to performance that OBE was introduced in school year 2003/04.

The OBE teacher scorecards

The teacher scorecards are the most visible marker of OBE, signalling a difference between what had already been in place with regard to quality monitoring and the new system of teacher surveillance. In Mongolian schools, the teacher scorecard is a sheet of paper entitled 'outcomes contract'. Each school develops its own outcomes contract, but most of the contracts between teachers and school administrations are strikingly similar. An example from a school in Zuunmod, Tuv province, illustrates the kind of outcomes listed in such contracts (Zuunmod 2004). It includes 10 outcomes that first need to be self-evaluated by the teacher and then passed on to the school administration. We list the outcomes in the following, along with a short description of how teachers and school administrators in Mongolia tend to measure them:

1   Class management: disciplining of students in class, keeping the class busy, organising extra-curricular activities for students.

2 Lesson planning: reflects the degree to which a teacher is organised, that is, whether she has a notebook in which she notes the topic for each lesson.
3 Student development: at the beginning of the school year, the teacher must formulate academic benchmarks for each student.[11] In the contract she needs to make a general statement on grade fluctuation in class.
4 Official documents and notes: refers to all documents that the teacher needs to regularly submit to the school administration, that is, cataloging teaching resources used in class, student registration and other reports for the school administration.
5 Teaching skills: although this outcome is self-assessed like all other outcomes, the teaching skills are supposed to be observed periodically by the education manager.
6 Teacher's creative work: counts how many teaching materials and booklets the teacher has developed. It has become a public concern that teachers generate additional income by forcing parents to buy these teacher products.
7 Professional development: number of courses or lectures attended and/or number of books read (called independent study).
8 Time management and task completion: indicates how often the teacher was late or absent from class and whether the teacher has carried out the tasks given by the school administration in a timely manner.
9 Teacher morality and responsibility: includes an assessment of one's own drinking habits, communication style towards students (abstaining from verbal abuse) and the school administration (obedience).
10 Maintenance of property and cleaning of classroom: addresses the condition of the classroom including the cleanliness and the condition of equipment and furniture.

Arguably, the imported OBE reform has been locally adapted or Mongolised in substantial ways. For example, indicators measuring learning and teaching outcomes have as much weight as indicators reflecting how well the teacher communicates with and responds to the school administration. The teacher must fill out the self-evaluation once a month and deposit it with the education manager (assistant principal). According to our interviewees, the education manager quickly reviews these sheets, checks them off and places them in his drawer. Very rarely are observations in class or discussions on the individual students scheduled and it is only towards the end of the semester when the school accountant informs the school administration about the savings made from school maintenance, repair, parental donations or salary and supplement deductions, that these teacher scorecards re-surface from the education manager's files. It is at this critical moment during the school year that the teacher performance on the OBE contract and other accomplishments of teachers, notably at teacher olympiads and competitions, are reviewed for bonuses. The OBE contracts are primarily seen as one of the many ways to earn more income and the teachers that we interviewed do not associate these contracts with improving the quality of teaching. For example, at the school in Zuunmod, Tuv province, the teacher scorecards are reviewed semi-annually. At the end of the fiscal year (December), the school succeeded in making considerable savings, and rewarded all those teachers with a bonus that obtained 60 per cent or more of the available points on the teacher scorecard.

As mentioned repeatedly, the system of performance-based salaries is hardly new for the Mongolian education sector. In fact, there has been an elaborate and bureaucratic mega-structure of surveillance in place underpinned with a myriad of policy documents and laws regulating, administering and legitimising that structure in minute detail. The purpose of that structure is to control teachers and to reward and punish them by means of salary supplements/bonuses and deductions, respectively. What is novel, however, is the fact that teachers now have to self-evaluate themselves. From a Foucauldian perspective, one might propose that the OBE reform institutionalised a modern technology of surveillance that demands insight, remorse, and continued self-betterment (Foucault 1995; Popkewitz 1998; Rose 1998). In practice, however, the outcomes contracts encompass a wide array of objectives, many of them matching the concerns of school administrators, with little relevance for learning outcomes. The contracts are used to control the teacher rather than to monitor the progress of the student. Furthermore, the almost complete reliance on the system of self-evaluation fuels the suspicion of teachers that the school administration uses OBE and other performance measures to legitimise the practice of patronage and favoritism in schools.

The economics of OBE

All along, dating back to the socialist past, money has been the pulse for reforms in Mongolia. Intriguingly, some of these reforms are an exact replica of what is already in place. OBE in Mongolia qualifies as such a quasi-reform that has been used as a 'flag of convenience' (Lynch 1998: 9) to access international funding. Linguistic nuances matter here. Rather than claiming that the reform was funded with the support of large loans from the Asian Development Bank, it is more accurate to state that the Ministry of Finance was given large loans *for* implementing the New Zealand management and finance system. As with other donor involvement in Mongolia, the condition of reforming the public sector was the import of a particular policy. The importance of external funding becomes apparent when we consider the large number of 'national programmes' or 'action plans' that are publicly announced but never implemented due to a lack of funding. In contrast, by using the language of OBE, funds were secured, and OBE has been fitted into a myriad of already existing accountability systems. Banking on the travelling reform of OBE does not only apply to the government level, but it also applies quite literally to the school level. Leaving aside the dubious evaluation criteria for outcomes, a well-performing teacher in a Mongolian school manages nowadays to accumulate bonuses from different accountability systems and considerably lift her low base salary. Very much to the dismay of other teachers, however, this banking of bonuses is done at the expense of those who have to blindly accept salary and salary supplement deductions made by the school administration. In the Mongolian case, OBE merely reinforced what was already in place. By adding one more monitoring policy (OBE) to the series of firmly established teacher surveillance technologies, the government was able to get loans, and some teachers, bonuses. Banking on policy import was an important reason why OBE was so appealing to government officials and school administrators.

Kazakhstan: stretching the curriculum, stretching for Europe

In Kazakhstan, the outcomes-based education (OBE) reform emerged in the context of improving educational quality, which had significantly declined after the collapse of the Soviet Union in 1991. Significant reduction in state education expenditures during the 1990s[12] resulted in a gradual reversal of the educational progress achieved during the

Soviet period, leading to decreasing enrolment rates, increasing non-attendance, and the deteriorating quality of education (Silova 2002). In particular, quality decline had been evidenced in a decreasing number of qualified teachers, reduced availability of instructional materials, outdated curricula and physical deterioration of schools (Silova 2002; Open Society Institute 2002; Chapman *et al.* 2005). As Chapman *et al.* (2005) highlighted, the challenge for Kazakhstan and other Central Asian governments has been to avoid further disintegration of their education systems and the recapturing of previous levels of education quality, while striving to build educational systems that reflect an elusive 'international standard' and prepare graduates who can be competitive for positions in more globally oriented economies. In Kazakhstan, for example, the driving force behind secondary education reform was the creation of a new education space, symbolising Kazakhstan's movement to new, European education standards. In particular, Kazakhstan's former Minister of Education, Nuraly Sultanovich Bektourganov (2002), explained that improving the quality of education was necessary in order to ensure that Kazakhstan's education system would produce 'competitive school graduates able to continue their studies in the higher educational establishments in Europe'. Furthermore, he explained that this reform would ensure that Kazakhstan would 'gradually occupy its place in the international educational space'.

Kazakhstan's 'quest for quality' (Chapman *et al.* 2005), was accompanied by two parallel, but interconnected processes, which ultimately triggered the emergence of OBE in the early part of this decade. First, higher education reform associated with the Bologna[13] and Lisbon[14] conventions emphasised the importance of reforming secondary education to ensure that school graduates are better prepared for undergraduate studies. Secondly, the extension of secondary education to 12 years was presented as an opportunity to revise Soviet-style curriculum and a necessary precondition for realigning both the primary and higher education systems towards European standards. A combination of these two education reform processes resulted in the emergence of OBE, signalling Kazakhstan's desire to join the Western alliance and increase its competitiveness in the global market. As President Nazarbayev explained, introduction of 12-year primary and secondary education and transition to four-year higher education would ensure Kazakhstan's 'competitiveness as a nation' (Kazakhstan Embassy in the USA 2004, 23 March).

Internal and external pressures for secondary education reform

Interestingly, the idea of reforming secondary education in Kazakhstan's was originally initiated by higher education administrators and academics, who complained about the ever decreasing quality of high school graduates entering universities (Silova and Kalikova 2005). Initially driven by the widespread concerns of these academics, concerns about drastically decreasing education quality were later validated by the results of the National Unified Testing (NUT). Introduced in 1999, the NUT results revealed that a large number of school graduates were poorly prepared for undergraduate studies. Since 1999, the percentage of high school graduates failing the NUT has remained unchanged, with 28–30 per cent of all potential higher education students failing the test (Ministry of Education 2004). The latest data by the Ministry of Education (2004) reveals that 24.2 per cent of all school graduates failed the test (with failure being determined by getting less than 40 of 120 points possible), while only 0.7 per cent received the highest scores (getting

101–120 points). Equipped with firm evidence of failing educational quality in schools, higher education administrators and academics began to put increasing pressure on policy makers to initiate secondary education reform, including revision of the existing curriculum.

Responding to the increasing criticism of the quality of the existing school system at the end of the 1990s, Kazakhstan's Ministry of Education announced a comprehensive school reform in 2001. The aim of the new reform was to extend the duration of secondary education to 12 years (referred to as '12-year education reform'). Among the main reasons for the envisaged change, government officials cited world education standards, particularly European education standards, as well as education reform activities underway in other former Soviet republics (including the Baltic republics, Ukraine and Russia) and Eastern and Central Europe (including Hungary and Romania). Quoting the Declaration of the Council of Europe (1992), Kazakhstan's mass media stated that 12-year education was the most widely used worldwide. For example, one of the newspapers explained that students in 160 countries study 12 or more years, while only 25 per cent of all countries study less than 12 years in basic/secondary education (Semikina 2001). Therefore, transition from 11 to 12 years of study was presented as a key to achieving recognition of Kazakhstan's secondary education certificates by universities internationally, thus 'enabling young people from Kazakhstan to continue their studies in the best universities abroad' (Draft Conception 2002).

Although government officials had readily accepted the 'travelling policy' promoting the extension of the length of the study of secondary education, local re-conceptualisation of the reform idea resulted in an amalgam of different responses among the main education stakeholders. According to one of the surveys (Komkon-2 Eurasia 2002), the majority of education administrators (62 per cent of governmental officials and 46 per cent of school directors) supported the reform, while only 15 per cent of education specialists, 19 per cent of parents, 20 per cent of high school students, and 29 per cent of teachers thought that there was a need for extending the number of years in basic/secondary education. Despite differences in opinions, however, most of the respondents were unwilling to admit weaknesses of the current curriculum inherited from the Soviet Union (i.e. usually described as centralised, rigid, inflexible and overloaded). As Semikina (2001) noted, many experts questioned the need to extend education from 11 to 12 years, given that the Soviet model was so successful – 'fundamental, substantive, and strong in tradition'. Similarly, parents were not supportive of the reform, anticipating that it would cost them more to have their children enrolled in school for an additional year. Referring to Soviet educational achievements in maths and science, one of the parents explained: 'Why should we emulate Western models when they [the West] actively cultivate our educational models and schemes?' (Semikina 2001).

Given the unfavourable environment for introducing the reform yet feeling the pressure to reach 'European standards', the first attempts at re-conceptualizing the extension of basic/secondary education to 12 years did not involve any major revision of curriculum. In fact, some of the government officials suggested leaving the existing curriculum intact (10 years), while simply adding one year at each end of the existing education structure. Some experts argued that the first (additional) year would provide opportunity for children to get better prepared for entering elementary schools, while the last (additional) year could be used either for more intensive preparation for college or for developing professional vocational skills. In other words, the initial discussion resulted in accepting the broader concept of the 'travelling policy' without implementing major changes in the inherited, Soviet-style curriculum content and process (Silova 2005b). Interestingly, the first draft of the 'Concept of Twelve-Year General Education in the Republic of Kazakhstan' (2001), which was prepared by the Ministry of Education experts, did not mention 'outcomes' or 'outcomes-based education'.

Re-defining educational quality through OBE

The draft concept was heavily criticised by many teachers and academics, as well as representatives of non-governmental organisations. In 2001, the Soros Foundation-Kazakhstan (SFK) brought together a working group of approximately 70 policy makers, academics, teachers and NGO representatives to discuss how the extension of secondary education could be used to revise the entire curriculum to address several specific education issues. Following several meetings, the group highlighted some of the weaknesses of the current secondary education system. First, the education system did not adequately reflect the new education paradigm, which emphasised individualisation and diversification and allowed upper secondary education students to make choices between academic studies and vocational paths (i.e. moving away from Soviet centralised curriculum model). Second, current educational curriculum was 'outdated' and 'overloaded', raising major concerns for the quality of education and the health of children. Third, many secondary school graduates, who did not enter higher education institutions, faced difficulties finding employment after graduation due to their lack of basic vocational skills. Finally, there was a growing concern over the quality of general secondary education, including a lack of child-centred teaching/learning methodologies and assessment systems. Combined, the working group saw the 12-year education reform as an opportunity to re-define the concept of 'education quality' in Kazakhstan.

Drawing attention to these specific education problems, the SFK addressed a variety of international experts to discuss possible alternatives for curriculum reform in Kazakhstan. From 2001–03, a 'global network of education agencies and academics was mobilized' (Seddon 2005) that included education experts from different countries, including former Soviet Union republics (Russia, Latvia and Estonia), Eastern and Central Europe (Hungary, Romania, Slovenia and Slovakia), as well as Finland, South Africa, Australia and the USA. Common to all these experts was their experience with implementation of OBE in their countries. Hannes Voolma (personal communication 2005) explained that the idea was to invite education experts from a variety of countries that had previously undertaken curricula reform aimed at the introduction of outcomes-based education. By inviting a variety of experts, the working group had an opportunity to study different strategies used by policy makers in formulating and implementing OBE in a variety of contexts.

The focus of the first meeting was on the changes required in Kazakhstan's educational system. As Seddon (2005) noted, this focus on change was a given. A key feature of the meeting was a presentation by Tom Alexander who had been Director of Education and Social Policy at the Organization for Economic Cooperation and Development (OECD) and a current General Education Sub-Board member of the Open Society Institute (OSI). Alexander's presentation highlighted features of the changing global context and argued for a specific approach to education reform in Kazakhstan. First, his presentation established a framework for policy making based on the synergies between policy areas such as education, labour markets and social issues. This framework challenged the established Kazakh view that education was about gaining more and more knowledge by arguing for connections between education, social policy and the labour market (Seddon 2005). In particular, Alexander argued that education should not be a stand-alone domain concerned with inducting young people into established knowledge traditions, but should focus on developing the kinds of capacities that enable young people to learn how to learn and how to demonstrate the kinds of literacies that support young people's labour market outcomes and enable them to address social issues. In this vision, Kazakhstan's education system was to move away from an emphasis on knowledge acquisition to an emphasis on skills, especially meta-cognitive or learning to learn skills.

Although these ideas were initially highly contested by many representatives of the working group, they laid the foundation for more focused work by a smaller group of Kazakh educators (later referred to as the 'analytical group'), which received on-going support from SFK through regular trainings, workshops and meetings with different international experts. In 2001, the analytical group prepared a policy paper, which outlined the dimensions of change in Kazakhstan's education and proposed a new, previously unarticulated solution for school reform – introduction of OBE in the context of the 12-year secondary education reform. The policy paper presented outcomes-based education as 'an approach to system wide improvement in education', which would define clear statements of expected outcomes to guide the organisation of the learning process, introduce learner-centred models, professionalise the role of teachers and increase community participation in the learning process. The analytical group continued to work together on a regular basis, organising public discussions, conferences and workshops across Kazakhstan in order to disseminate and discuss the idea of OBE with a larger group of Kazakhstan's education stakeholders.

In 2002, some members of the analytical group were included in a working group organised by the Ministry of Education, where they made key contributions to the development of the 'State Program of Education Development in the Republic of Kazakhstan for 2005–2010' (Ministry of Education 2004) and a new policy paper 'General Secondary Education Standards in the Republic of Kazakhstan: Current Situation, Exploration, Alternatives' (2003). In fact, the draft of the 'General Secondary Education Standards' officially acknowledged the importance of financial and intellectual support of SFK in the development of the draft policy document, as well as individual contribution of some members of the SFK analytical group. These two documents (i.e. the State Program and draft Standards) became the first policy instruments that institutionalised the idea of OBE in education legislation. In particular, the State Program outlined the main principles of OBE, which included a shift from 'facts-based' to 'skills-based' learning, a move from 'teacher-centred' to 'learner-centred' education models, as well as a transition from 'knowledge-acquisition' to a 'systematic understanding of the world, society, and people ... ability and desire to independently and creatively use, broaden, and deepen this understanding' (p. 28). In addition, the State Program under-scored the importance of critical thinking, reasoning and reflection as some of the main goals of the teaching/learning process. Finally, the State Program introduced the idea of national education standards 'oriented at student outcomes in a form of basic learner competencies' (p. 29). The draft 'National Standards Concept' further elaborated these ideas and defined a concrete plan for the development and implementation of OBE in Kazakhstan (e.g. the action plan includes concrete activities and budget from 2005–10).

To summarise, the emergence of OBE in Kazakhstan was accompanied by ubiquitous international references, which were de-territorialised as different OBE models were simultaneously used as exemplars for emulation in the initial stage of reform formulation. Although the main principles of Kazakhstan's OBE bore remarkable resemblance to global discourses on outcomes-based education (e.g. Spady 1994), neither the State Program nor the draft National Standards Concept made any references to specific educational practices in other geographic contexts, except for quoting the elusive 'international standards of education'. In this way, introduction of OBE played a symbolic role, presenting itself 'as a drastic break from current educational practices and as a means of providing educational success for all students' (Capper and Jamison 1993: 427). Interestingly, a simple extension of the education system to 12 years of education was not perceived as a viable option for joining the European education space. It was precisely in combination with OBE that the extension to 12 years' education was perceived as the most effective means for improving education quality, a necessary precondition for increasing Kazakhstan's competitiveness in the global market and a successful mechanism for 'entering the common world educational space' (State Program 2004: 46).

Lessons learned from late adopters

In the introductory section, we presented the epidemiological model of global reforms to draw attention to the time factor. The timing of when a global reform is adopted, that is, whether it is borrowed at an early, growth, or burn-out stage matters a great deal for the study of travelling policies. The three cases of OBE borrowing in Kyrgyzstan, Mongolia and Kazakhstan represent examples of late adoption in that OBE had already reached its peak of global dissemination and in some cases faced a decline in its popularity by the time it was implemented. By implication, we study the adoption of global reforms when we investigate late adopters. This simple statement is indeed far-reaching when we consider the lively academic debate (see Anderson-Levitt 2003; Steiner-Khamsi 2004b) on whether globalisation in education exists in reality, or is rather imagined and constructed. At face value, we side with a neo-institutionalist perspective (Meyer *et al.* 2003) on international convergence of educational reforms. In our example, the concepts and language of OBE did indeed experience a global career and the evidence of OBE adoption in these three Central Asian countries would be foolish to deny. Upon closer scrutiny, however, such a perspective applies a macro view of long-term changes and does not sufficiently examine what is happening on the ground.

Once we disaggregate our three case studies of late adopters and distinguish them contextually, additional perspectives open up. The global OBE reform was adopted so differently in each case that one wonders whether the same reform served as the exemplar of emulation. The reasons why OBE resonated in the first place, the impact that OBE had on existing practices and the prerequisites for introducing the reform varied for each context or case. In Kyrgyzstan, the OBE reform was seen as a response to corruption in education, in Mongolia it was embraced for economic reasons and in Kazakhstan it was driven by a political quest to become part of western advanced economies. The impact of these reforms also varied considerably. As mentioned in the introduction, in Mongolia, for example, OBE merely reinforced the elaborate teacher surveillance system that had already been in place for several decades, whereas in Kyrgyzstan it advocated a new public accountability and advanced standardised testing. Finally, one would assume that OBE is either a result of a comprehensive curriculum reform or at least leads to one *a posteriori*, calling into existence clear standards or outcomes for each grade level and subject matter. Again, all expectations of a clear sequence of events are shattered in our cases; all of them suggest leapfrogging in that these educational systems bypassed a comprehensive curriculum reform before introducing OBE, and whether OBE *per se* will trigger a curriculum reform in the near future is, at this time, beyond our assessment.

Having listed a few features of how OBE was locally adapted in the three contexts, the question arises as to whether 'OBE' was perhaps an unfortunate choice of terminology? The answer depends on what one establishes as a comparative framework. Compared to early adopters in New Zealand, Australia, the USA and the UK, there is indeed a very loose correspondence between neo-liberal ideology and the actual implementation of 'OBE' in the Central Asian countries of our study. But once we stop to compare the OBE of late adopters in Central Asia with the OBE of early western adopters, a different picture emerges. In an attempt to explain this loose coupling between ideology and implementation, we propose to interpret this phenomenon as one that is endemic to all global reforms, including OBE. By the time OBE went global, it did not any longer stand for a clear programme of change, but it represented an internationally shared understanding among government officials with regard to 'international standards'. This particular discourse was sufficiently vague to be embraced by many and precise enough in its label to send out a signal of internationalisation. Arguably, global reforms leave a lot of room for local implementation, especially when many countries have already adopted OBE in their own, idiosyncratic ways. How these standards are filled with meaning depends on the cultural context and as these case studies illustrated, on the local policy conflict that the act of borrowing is predisposed to resolve.

Notes

1 António Nóvoa and Martin Lawn's concept of 'education space' (2002) is closely related to Schriewer's notion of 'reference horizon' (Schriewer *et al.* 1998) in that both terms denote a cluster of societies with either a common past or a desired common future. We use these two terms, and a third – world system – interchangeably, acknowledging that there are several world systems.

2 One of the chief architects of OBE in New Zealand, Maris O'Rourke, was appointed as a senior officer at the World Bank in the mid-1990s. With her move from New Zealand to the USA in 1995, OBE moved along with her. It experienced an explosive growth in low-income countries receiving loans from the World Bank.

3 Article 47 deals with 'Assessment of Performance Agreement' and Article 49 with 'Payment of Performance Bonuses to Employees' (Parliament of Mongolia 2002).

4 The greatest delay occurred at the parliamentary level. The first draft for the Public Sector Management and Finance Law was submitted in 1997 (see Lanking 2004), but only approved in 2002. Once it was approved, the ministries were eager to adopt it, with the financial support of ADB, to their sector.

5 The baseline study was conducted in collaboration with A. Gerelmaa (Open Society Forum, Ulaanbaatar).

6 The monthly base salary ranges from 53,200 tugrik ($45) for a regular teacher to 63,840 tugrik ($55) for a teacher with the rank of an 'advisor'. According to the government regulation 42 (Offices of the Prime Minister *et al.* 2004: 274) and the regulation of the Ministry of Education (Ministry of Education and Science *et al.* 1995: 220–4), there are four ranks for teachers: regular teacher, methodologist, lead teacher and advisor. Promotion to a higher rank entails a salary increase of 5–25 per cent.

7 The social worker used to be the head of the communist pioneer organisation in the school, and was in a powerful position. Nowadays, the social worker continues to be part of the school administration and is in charge of extracurricular activities.

8 In one school in Ulaanbaatar: drunkenness calls for a 20–40 per cent salary deduction, depending on how often the teacher has shown up drunk in school in the past month.

9 The complete list of seven conditions for receiving the supplement for grading student notebooks is as follows (Bayangol 2004a): (1) Full name and address on notebook cover written in proper handwriting, (2) tidy cover of notebook (i.e. not dirty and not ripped), (3) no crossed out or corrected words, (4) legible and neat handwriting, (5) complete and correct notes on the lessons, (6) no mixing of ink in the same notebook, and (7) evidence that the teacher actually checked and corrected the student notebook.

10 The seven conditions for class teacher supplement, each carrying 10 points, are as follows (Bayangol 2004b): (1) cleanliness of classroom, (2) discipline of the class, (3) clothes and dressing of students, (4) condition of class furniture and equipment, (5) attendance of students, (6) making use of class billboard, and (7) accomplishment of given duties and responsibilities.

11 In discussion with Mongolian teachers, the argument has been made that in the absence of standardised tests (standardised tests 'only' exist for the 4th, 8th and 10th grades) the establishment of academic benchmarks at the beginning of the semester encourages grade inflation at the end of the semester.

12 Despite Kazakhstan's economic recovery at the end of the 1990s, investments in the education sector have remained considerably low compared to pre-independence levels. For example, education expenditure as a percentage of GDP has decreased from 6 per cent in 1990 to 3.4 per cent in 2001, while the overall spending on education from the state budget declined from 24.5 per cent in 1990 to 14 per cent in 2000 (State Statistical Agency of RK 2001). The share of education investment from the local budgets had also decreased from 32.3 per cent in 1997 to 17 per cent in 2000 (Asian Development Bank 2002).

13 The 1999 Bologna Declaration points out that a Europe of Knowledge is an important factor for social and human growth. The Convention follow-up – the Bologna Process – aims to establish a European Higher Education Area by 2010 in which students and staff can move with ease and have fair recognition of their qualifications. This overall goal is reflected in the main action areas defined in the Bologna Declaration: (1) adoption of a system of degrees essentially based on two cycles; (2) co-operation in quality assurance and recognition; and (3) promotion of mobility (Nyborg 2004).

14 In 1997, Kazakhstan was one of the first CIS countries, which signed the Lisbon convention 'On recognition of qualifications, referring to higher education in European region'. Ratification of this document requires positive solution of general education extension with the further recognition of higher education quality.

References

American Councils for International Education: ACTR/ACCELS (2004, September 15) *National Testing Initiative of the Kyrgyz Republic – Key Facts and Information* Bishkek, Kyrgyzstan: Author.

Anderson-Levitt, K. (ed.) (2003) *Local Meanings, Global Schooling*, New York: Palgrave Macmillan.

Asian Development Bank (2002) *Analysis of the Education Reform Process in the Republic of Kazakhstan* (Regional TA No. 5946-REG), Almaty: Asian Development Bank.

Asian Development Bank (2003) *ADB Approves Loans for Second Phase of Public Sector Reforms in Mongolia*, 14 October. Online. Available HTTP: http://www.adb.org/Documents/News/ 2003 (accessed 22 January 2005).

Bale, M. and Dale, T. (1998) 'Public sector reform in New Zealand and its relevance to developing countries', *The World Bank Research Observer*, 13: 103–21.

Bayangol (2004 a) *Bayangol duurgiin surgalt uildverleliin 'Setgemj'tsogtsolboryn angi udirdsan bagshiin nemegdel khulsiig tootsoj khulsiig tootsoj olgokh juram* [Regulation to Calculate the Salary Supplement for Class Teachers and to Evaluate the Class Teacher]. Ulaanbaatar: Bayangol City District.

Bayangol (2004b) *Bayangol duurgiin 'Setgemj'tsogtsolbor surguuliin bagsh naryn devter zasaltyg khyanaj, unelekh juram* [Regulation to Evaluate and Monitor the Notebook Correction of Teachers]. Ulaanbaatar: Bayangol City District.

Bektourganov, N. (2002) *Education in Kazakhstan: Stepping into the Twenty-first Century*. Online. Available HTTP: http://www.ibe.unesco.org/International/ICE/ministers/Kazakhstan.pdf (accessed 22 January 2005).

Capper, C. and Jamison, M. (1993) 'Outcomes-based education reexamined: from structural functionalism to poststructuralism', *Education Policy*, 7(4): 427–46.

Chapman, D.W., Weidman, J., Cohen, M. and Mercer, M. (2005) 'The search for quality: a five country study of national strategies to improve educational quality in Central Asia', *International Journal of Educational Development*, 25(5): 514–30.

Dale, R. (2001) 'Constructing a long spoon for comparative education: charting the career of the "New Zealand Model"', *Comparative Education*, 37: 493–500.

DeYoung, A. (2004) 'On the demise of the "Action Plan" for Kyrgyz education reform: a case study', in S. Heyneman and A. DeYoung (eds) *The Challenges of Education in Central Asia*, Greenwich, CT: Information Age Publishing.

Donnelly, K. (2002) *A Review of New Zealand's School Curriculum: An International Perspective*, Wellington: Education Forum.

Drummond, T. (2003) *The National Scholarship Test of the Kyrgyz Republic: A First Look*, Bishkek, Kyrgyzstan: USAID.

Foucault, M. (1991) 'Governmentality', in G. Burchill, C. Gordon and P. Miller (eds) *The Foucault Effect: Studies in Governmentality: With Two Lectures by and an Interview with Michael Foucault*, London: Harvester Wheatsheaf, 87–105.

Foucault, M. (1995) *Discipline and Punish: The Birth of the Prison*, 2nd edn, New York: Vintage.

Frank, A.G. (1992) *The Centrality of Central Asia*, Amsterdam: Centre for Asian Studies, University of Amsterdam.

Henig, J. (1994) *Rethinking School Choice: Limits of the Market Metaphor*, Princeton, NJ: Princeton University Press.

Heyneman, S. and DeYoung, A. (eds) (2004) *The Challenges of Education in Central Asia*, Greenwich, CT: Information Age Publishing.

IRINnews.org. (2002, September 12) *Kyrgyzstan: Focus on Scholarship Testing*. Online. Available HTTP: http://www.irinnews.org/report.asp?ReportID=29839&Select Region=Central_Asia& SelectCountry=KYRGYZSTAN (accessed 21 October 2004).

Kazakhstan Embassy in the United States (2004, March 23) *Kazakhstan News Bulletin*. Online. Available HTTP: http://www.kazakhembus.com (accessed 12 December 2004).

Kelly, G. (1992) 'Debates and trends in comparative education', in R.F. Arnove, G. Altbach and G. Kelly (eds) *Emergent Issues in Education: Comparative Perspectives*, Albany, NY: State University of New York Press.

Komkon-2 Eurasia (2002) *Opinions of Education Stakeholder About the Transition to Twelve Year Education*, Almaty: Soros Foundation Kazakhstan.

Lanking, R. (2004) *Don't Try This At Home? A New Zealand Approach to Public Management Reform in Mongolia*, Wellington: Graduate School of Business and Government Management (manuscript).

Luhmann, N. (1990) *Essays on Self-Reference*, New York: Columbia University Press.

Luhmann, N. and Schorr, K.E. (1979) *Reflexionsprobleme im Erziehungssystem* [Problems of Reflection in Society's System for Education], Stuttgart: Klett-Cotta.

Luschei, T. (2004) 'Timing is everything: the intersection of borrowing and lending in Brazil's adoption of *Escuela Nueva*', in G. Steiner-Khamsi (ed.) *The Global Politics of Educational Borrowing and Lending*, New York: Teachers College Press.

Lynch, J. (1998) 'The international transfer of dysfunctional paradigms', in D. Johnson, B. Smith and M. Crossley (eds) *Learning and Teaching in an International Context: Research, Theory and Practice*, Bristol: University of Bristol, Centre for International Studies in Education.

McLean, G., Karimov, M. and Asankanov, A. (2002) *The Role of Human Resources Development in Improving K-12 Educational Leadership in Kyrgyzstan*, Washington, DC: United States Agency for International Development.

Meyer, J.W., Ramirez, F.O., Schofer, E. and Drori, G.S. (eds) (2003) *Science in the Modern World Polity: Institutionalization and Globalization*, Stanford, CA: Stanford University Press.

Ministry of Education (2002) *Draft Conception of the Education Transition to 12 Years*, Astana: Ministry of Education.

Ministry of Education (2004) *Gosudarstvennaja programma razvitiia obrzovaniia v Respublike Kazakstan na 2005–2010 godi* [State program of education development in Kazakhstan for 2005–2010], Astana: Ministry of Education.

Ministry of Education, Science and Culture (2003) *A Compilation of Laws, Resolutions, Decrees and Decisions Related to the Education, Culture and Science Sector Budget and Finance*, Ulaanbaatar: Ministry of Education, Science and Culture and Second Education Development Program.

Ministry of Education and Science, Ministry of Demographics and Labor, and Ministry of Finance (1995) *Tsetserleg, surguuliin udirdakh ajiltan, bagsh, surgan khumuujuulegchded mergeshliin zereg, ur chadvariin nemegdel olgon juram* [Regulation on giving qualification- and skills-bases bonuses to administrative employees and teachers in kindergarten and in secondary schools], signed 26 December 1995, Ulaanbaatar: Ministry of Education and Science.

Neave, G. (1988) 'On the cultivation of quality, efficiency, and enterprise: an over of recent trends in higher in Western Europe 1986–88', *European Journal of Education*, 23(1): 7–23.

Noah, H. (1986) 'Education, employment, and development in communist societies', in E.B Gumbert (ed.) *Patriarchy, Party, Population, and Pedagogy*, Atlanta, GA: Georgia State University.

Nóvoa, A. and Lawn, M. (2002) *Fabricating Europe: The Formation of an Education Space*, Dordrecht: Kluwer.

Nyborg, P. (2004) *The Influence of the Bologna Process on Reform Processes in Higher Education in the Caucasus and Central Asia*. Online. Available HTTP: http://www.bologna-bergen2005.no/Docs/03-PNY/040531-0604_OSCE.pdf. (accessed on 12 January 2005).

Offices of the Prime Minister, Minister of Finance and Economy and Minister of Social Welfare and Labor (2004) *Mongol Ulsiin Zasgiin Gazriin*, 42.

Open Society Institute (2002) *Education Development in Kyrgyzstan, Tajikistan, and Uzbekistan: Challenges and Ways Forward*. Budapest: Education Support Program, Open Society Institute. Online. Available HTTP: http://www.osi-edu.net/esp/events/materials/final.doc (accessed 12 January 2005).

Parliament of Mongolia (2002, June 27) *Tosviin baiguulagyn udirdlaga, sankhuujiltiin tukhai* [Public Sector Management and Finance Act], Ulaanbbaatar: Parliament of Mongolia.

Phillips, D. (2004) 'Toward a theory of policy attraction in education', in G. Steiner-Khamsi (ed.) *The Global Politics of Educational Borrowing and Lending*, New York: Teachers College Press.

Popkewitz, T.S. (1998) *Struggling for the Soul: The Politics of Schooling and the Construction of the Teacher*, New York: Teachers College Press.

Rogers, E.M. (1992) *Diffusion of Innovations*, 4th edn, New York: Free Press.

Rose, N. (1998) *Inventing Our Selves. Psychology, Power, and Personhood*, Cambridge: Cambridge University Press.

Russian Federal State Statistics Service (1996) *Russia's State Statistics 1802–1996*. Online. Available HTTP: http://www.gks.ru/eng/history/5.asp.

Schick, A. (1998) 'Why most developing countries should not try New Zealand's reforms', *World Bank Research Observer*, 13: 123–32.

Schriewer, J. (1990) 'The method of comparison and the need for externalization: methodological criteria and sociological concepts', in J. Schriewer, in cooperation with B. Holmes (eds) *Theories and Methods in Comparative Education*, Bern: Lang.

Schriewer, J. (2000) 'World system and interrelationship networks: the internationalization of education and the role of comparative inquiry', in T.S. Popkewitz (ed.) *Educational Knowledge: Changing Relationships Between the State, Civil Society, and the Educational Community*, Albany, NY: State University of New York Press.

Schriewer, J. and Martinez, C. (2004) 'Constructions of internationality in education', in G. Steiner-Khamsi (ed.) *The Global Politics of Educational Borrowing and Lending*, New York: Teachers College Press.

Schriewer, J., Henze, J., Wichmann, J., Knost, P., Barucha, S. and Taubert, J. (1998) 'Konstruktion von Internationalität: Referenzhorizonte pädagogischen Wissens im Wandel gesellschaftlicher Systeme (Spanien, Sowjetunion/Russland, China)', in H. Kaelble and J. Schriewer (eds) *Gesellschaft im Vergleich* [Society in Comparison], Frankfurt/M: Peter Lang.

Seddon, T. (2005) *The Global Encounter: Kazakhstan*. Online. Available HTTP: http://lihini.sjp. ac.lk/careers/edreform/austr/kazak.htm (accessed 5 February 2005).

Semikina, Y. (2001) 'The twelfth floor', *Kontingent*, 15.

Silova, I. (2002) *The Right to Quality Education: Creating Child-friendly Schools in Central Asia*, Almaty: UNICEF CARK.

Silova, I. (2004) 'Adopting the language of new allies', in G. Steiner-Khamsi (ed) *The Global Politics of Educational Borrowing and Lending*, New York: Teachers College Press.

Silova, I. (2005a) *From Sites of Occupation to Symbols of Multiculturalism: Transfer of Global Discourse and the Metamorphosis of Russian Schools in Post-Soviet Latvia*, Greenwich, CT: Information Age Publishing.

Silova, I. (2005b). 'Traveling policies: hijacked in Central Asia', *European Educational Research Journal*, 4(1): 50–9.

Silova, I. and Kalikova, S. (2005) 'The emergence of outcomes-based education in Kazakhstan', unpublished manuscript.

Smyth, J. and Dow, A. (1998) 'What's wrong with outcomes? Spotter planes, action plans, and steerage of the educational workplace', *British Journal of Sociology of Education*, 19(3): 291–303.

Spady, W. (1994) *Outcomes Based Education: Critical Issues and Answers*. Arlington, Virginia: American Association of School Administration.

Spreen, C.A. (2004) 'Appropriating borrowed policies: outcomes-based education in South Africa', in G. Steiner-Khamsi (ed.) *The Global Politics of Educational Borrowing and Lending*. New York: Teachers College Press.

State Program on the Development of Education in the Republic of Kazakhstan for 2005–2010 (2004) Astana.

State Statistical Agency of the Republic of Kazakstan (2001) *Education Statistics*, Almety: SSA.

Steiner-Khamsi, G. (2000) 'Transferring education, displacing reforms', in J. Schriewer (ed.) *Discourse Formation in Comparative Education*, Frankfurt: Lang.

Steiner-Khamsi, G. (2003) 'Innovation durch Bildung nach internationalen Standards? [Innovation modeled after international standards?]', in I. Gogolin and R. Trippelt (eds) *Innovation durch Bildung*, Opladen: Leske and Budrich.

Steiner-Khamsi, G. (ed.) (2004a) *The Global Politics of Educational Borrowing and Lending*, New York: Teachers College Press.

Steiner-Khamsi, G. (2004b) 'Blazing a trail for policy theory and practice', in G. Steiner-Khamsi (ed.) *The Global Politics of Educational Borrowing and Lending*, New York: Teachers College Press.

Steiner-Khamsi, G. (2005) 'Vouchers for teacher education (non) reform in Mongolia: transitional, post-socialist, or anti-socialist explanations?', *Comparative Education Review*, 49(2): 148–72.

Steiner-Khamsi, G. and Quist, H. (2000) 'The politics of educational borrowing: reopening the case of Achimota in British Ghana', *Comparative Education Review*, 44(3): 272–99.

Steiner-Khamsi, G. and Stolpe, I. (2004) 'De- and recentralization reform in Mongolia: tracing the swing of the pendulum', *Comparative Education*, 40(1): 29–53.

Steiner-Khamsi, G., Tumendemberel, D. and Steiner, E. (2004) 'Bagsh mergejiltei etseg ekhjuud' [Teachers as Parents], *Bolovsrol Sudlal*, 18(1): 40–53; 18(2): 62–70.

Tyack, D. and Cuban, L. (1995) *Tinkering Toward Utopia*, Cambridge, MA: Harvard University Press.

USAID Data Sheet (2005) *Kyrgyzstan CBJ FY05*. Online. Available HTTP: http://www.usaid.gov/policy/budget/cbj2005/ee/pdf/116-0340.pdf (accessed 13 February 2005).

Vavrus, F. (2004) 'The referential web: externalization beyond education in Tanzania', in G. Steiner-Khamsi (ed.) *The Global Politics of Educational Borrowing and Lending*, New York: Teachers College Press.

Watts, D.J. (2003) *Six Degrees: The Science of a Connected Age*, New York: Norton.

World Bank Group (2005, February 3) *World Bank Supports Three New Projects in Kyrgyz Republic*. Online. Available HTTP: http://web.worldbank.org/WBSITE/EXTERNAL/COUNTRIES/ECAEXT/KYRGYZEXTN0,,contentMDK:20342737 ~menuPK:305766~pagePK:141137~piPK:141127~theSitePK:305761,00.html (accessed 5 February 2005).

Zuunmod (2004) *Zuunmod sumyn IV zakhirgaanaas bagsh.-tai baiguulsan 'Ur dungiin gereee'-g dugnekh khusnegt* [Outcomes Contract], Zuunmod: District School, Tuv province.

15 Marketing academic issues

To what extent does education policy steer education research in Spain?

Xavier Rambla

Introduction

In Spain the two recent more significant and controversial education reforms were passed in 1990 and 2002. The former implemented a comprehensive education system and shifted school leaving age from 14 to 16 years. The foreword of that Education Reform Act argued that 'our modernising society' had to respond to more open individual, political, cultural and productive spaces by means of more extended education and pedagogic innovation that aimed to make educational quality sure (LOGSE – *Ley Orgánica de Ordenación General del Sistema Educativo*, i.e. Organic Act on the General Framework the Educational System, 1/1990, 3 October). Some scholars, who collaborated actively to design that reform, declared that comprehensive secondary education was a common feature of European countries (Coll 1999: 21). The latter implemented tracking for 14-year-old students, because 'quality education is the obliged response to the world where we already are' (MECD 2002), and 'the whole integration of Spain into the European Union requires a higher degree of standardisation and flexibility of the educational system' (LOCE – *Ley Orgánica de Calidad Educativa*, i.e. Framework Act on Educational Quality, 10/2002, 23 December). Other scholars collaborated to design it asserting that comprehensive secondary education had eventually to implement tracking. In their view, a parallel shift could be observed towards tracking throughout the European Union (Prada 2002: 39).

Thus, for the last 15 years academic and official discourses have converged to defend opposite policy choices based in alleged empirical generalisations grounded on analogous but contradictory comparisons of European systems. Regardless of their validity, the logic of their arguments provides one of the most visible signs that education has been linked to democracy, modernisation and Europeanisation by most Spanish policy makers, researchers and, broadly speaking, citizens. Unsurprisingly, they have stretched their contentions on what education should be to all these twin notions. The implicit general assumption is that Spain has just become a modern country thanks to several social changes such as these very reforms.

International comparison is a key issue if we are to discuss the influence of the global agenda of education policy on education research in this country. For a long time both policy goals and research priorities have been embedded in the very debate on their coincidence with wider trends. Spanish intellectuals, policy makers and most people considered that they were not modern enough and had to imitate 'European' institutions, political and economic practices in order to achieve progress. This very image legitimated the reform 15 years ago. Nowadays the same assumptions hinder their own repetition, since many people conclude that the desired modernisation or Europeanisation has already taken place, but they have become very powerful rhetoric instruments nonetheless. Anybody who can blame somebody else to be traditional or old-fashioned has an advantage in political discussion. Similarly, the supporters of the last reform argued that they were not only overhauling the education system but also aligning its structure to European patterns.

If we frame this process within the current global agenda, it is necessary to ask whether there has been a connection. Roughly speaking, this modernisation agenda includes the World Bank conditioned loans, the UN Millennium Development Goals, the WTO negotiations on educational services or the EU Lisbon Declaration. Have these issues influenced the debates and analyses of policy changes in Spain? Although this is too broad a question for this chapter, it can suggest very tentatively a partial answer to one of its key implications. The global agenda has been presented as a coherent conclusion of academic research programmes on human capital, social capital, market governance, performance-based school organisation, quality and so on. So have education policy changes also responded to similar links between the academy and politics in Spain? In other countries some authors have suggested that these links may have created new mechanisms of research steering via an active promotion of certain research issues, such as research problems related to pedagogical practice (Shain and Ozga 2001) or the so-called school effects on performance (Poupeau 2003).

As to Spain, I will try to spell out some empirical indicators of a similar mechanism, focusing on the relationship between the points of view expressed in the recent debate on educational quality and the background coming from academic research on educational policy in the country. My point is that a sort of marketing strategy can be identified that favours 'quality' as a significant political and academic issue. Thus, a global concern has eventually rooted in the debate at the Spanish scale. However, contrary to France and Britain, the steering mechanism has not impinged on research production but on academic rhetoric. The fact that educational research, and consequently, research on educational policy, has a weak tradition can certainly help to explain this mechanism.

The chapter is divided into four parts. The first one sketches an historical overview, and the second one describes policy and research mechanisms. The third part provides a more detailed analysis of the debate on the 2002 Educational Quality Act. Finally, the fourth concludes that educational research steering is a kind of 'globalism' that the parties of this contention have eventually 'localised' in the Spanish academy and politics.

Educational policy and research: an historic overview

In 1970 an authoritarian government reformed the whole Spanish education system for the first time during the last 100 years. Since the early and frail Liberal constitutions in the nineteenth century, universal primary schooling had been proclaimed but never implemented. In the short Republican period between 1931 and 1939 the also frail Left-wing governments could only implement some short initiatives to build new schools (1931–33) or universalise a comprehensive system (in Catalonia for the 1936–37 and 1937–38 school years). The winners of the civil war did not show any interest in going on with educational expansion, even though the nationalisation of the whole country became their open objective so as to reinforce Spanish nationalism in front of Basque, Catalan and Galician nationalist clandestine forces. Afterwards, the Franco regime was accepted by the USA, and adopted a renewed economic policy that integrated the economy into the Western long-term cycle of growth.

In 1962 the World Bank issued its first report including specific recommendations for the Spanish government, administrative reform being one of them. In fact, the 1970 education reform was the first act that was prepared on the basis of a White Book written by technically competent staff. Its measures foresaw the extension of a new co-educational and compulsory education for 11–14-year-olds, and the creation of university-based Institutes of Education that were in charge of in-service training (Mayordomo 1999). However, these proposals were severely curtailed in the first years of implementation, and the main operational measure was merely restricted to subsidising private schools in order to universalise primary schooling. As a consequence, the school system was unable to supply places for all the children who were born during the 1960–77 demographic boom, and came close to collapse before the political transition that took place between 1978 and 1982 (Calero and Bonal 1999).

Between 1978 and 1985 many new schools were finally built, thanks to the increasing revenues that tax reform had provided to the state. Since the 1978 Constitution had also stated that education was a social right, the following governments had to design the framework acts that would define the new education system. After the defeat of the Centrist party in 1982, the Socialist party passed three foundational acts. It regulated participation and the criteria to fund private schools in 1985, the whole curriculum with the mentioned comprehensive orientation in 1990, as well as evaluation and organisation in 1995. The 1990 Education Reform Act has become the 'reform' for most teachers and families, since it included such a visible and controversial change as the integration of the former academic and vocational secondary schools. Although it explicitly required higher educational expenditure, this condition was not fully met.

When it won the 1996 election, the Conservative party became ultimately responsible for the 'reform'. However, implementation neither relied on comprehensive principles nor was concerned with higher expenditure but financial conservatism. For its first period in office the Conservative party simply issued a broad diagnosis and hinted at its intention to specify a detailed syllabus for the Humanities curriculum, but did not pass substantial legal changes. At that time the official Institute for Educational Quality, led by a prestigious scholar, actively disseminated the thesis that schools needed organisational changes to overcome some alleged shortcomings with respect to quality. After winning the 2000 election with an absolute majority, the Conservative government designed and passed the 2002 Quality Act, which opened up an intense debate between scholars and teachers. Generally speaking, its explicit philosophy was identifying quality with the 'culture of endeavour'. Its articles allowed the extension of public subsidies to private schools that supplied infant education, transformed religion into an academic subject, introduced performance-based tracking for the 15- and 16-year-olds in the two last compulsory courses, and established a final examination at the end of academic upper secondary education. Three years later, at the time of writing (March 2005), the Socialist government has been in office for one year, has already delayed some of these measures and promised an alternative legislative development.

Steering education policy and research (1996–2004)

Two processes took place during the Conservative period (1996–2004) that contextualised the debate on quality in 2002. First, educational policy highlighted this concept of quality at the same time as it cut educational expenditure. Simultaneously, the education system was fully de-centralised and some Autonomous Communities also implemented new compensatory devices. Second, like educational research, studies on educational policy showed weak institutionalisation, although its academic corpus continued to widen at a slow but persistent pace.

Between 1996 and 2000 the National Institute for Educational Quality (INCE) was reinforced within the Ministry, and José Luis García Garrido, a professor in educational science, was appointed as its director. The 1990 Act had created this institute and commissioned it to monitor and evaluate the educational system. Mostly, it produced standard examinations and many surveys of students', teachers' and parents' opinions about schools. In 1998 INCE issued a general report pointing towards a synthesis of findings and recommendations (INCE 1998). At the same time, the Ministry tried to apply the European Model for the Management of Quality (EMMQ) by means of a Yearly Improvement Plan which was explicitly deployed so that 'objective' innovation and monitoring counteracted the alleged perverse effects of child-centred pedagogies (López Rupérez 1998: 18). Paradoxically, although the EMMQ based quality management on self-monitoring, it was assumed that it could only be adopted by schools formerly exhibiting a sound culture of evaluation (López Rupérez 1998: 22). In fact, the new policy could easily play down the 1990 Act on pedagogic autonomy and curriculum development by requiring the creation of an evaluation system. Thus, official research became a very effective tool for introducing alternative issues and recommendations.

A few comments help to portray the context of that debate. On the one hand, Calero and Bonal (2004) have convincingly showed that educational expenditure never met the threshold that the 1990 Act foresaw and, even worse, that its volume stagnated in the late 1990s. As a consequence, the rhetorical emphasis on educational quality led to persistent practical shortcomings in the last judgement. On the other hand, the Ministry of Education was no longer in charge of compensatory education (Jiménez 2003). When the central government passed the Quality Act in 2002, compensatory programmes as well as the bulk of educational responsibilities became the responsibility of regional governments or Autonomous Communities. However, the Act evoked the UNESCO *Education For All* programme, and took account of the parallel concern with universal quality education, proclaiming that its aim was 'quality education for all'.

The original programme of compensatory education had been designed in the 1980s. It operated through specialised teachers who supplied complementary support to low performing children. So far, the Autonomous Communities have extended this sort of operation in several ways. Some of them have responded to the complaints of parents' associations by subsidising student textbooks according to different criteria (Jiménez 2003). Others have also implemented general plans so that compensatory initiatives can be co-ordinated between primary and secondary schools or between the Community and municipalities (Dirección General de Promoción Educativa de la Comunidad de Madrid 2001). Other plans have opened spaces for the participation of NGOs and immigrant minorities (Consejería de Educación de la Junta de Andalucía 2001); in Catalonia, several local authorities have launched local educational projects so as to broaden participation, improve co-ordination and share educational responsibilities with the Autonomous Community (Jaumeandreu and Badosa 2002). A pedagogic participatory initiative inspired by accelerated schools, the so called 'learning communities', has been experimented with in Aragón, the Basque Country and Catalonia (Comunidades de Aprendizaje 2005). Finally, the Basque government has also expanded the minimal complementary grants system in order to reinforce post-compulsory enrolment (Calero and Bonal 2004).

This description of the Quality Act policy context has to take account of a last element, namely educational social cohesion. Here, I will only provide a short report based on EUROSTAT data on early school leavers. As Table 15.1 displays, since the mid-1990s this indicator remained stable at 30 per cent of 18–24-year-olds with, at most, lower secondary education and not in further education or training. The gap with the EU 15 average has widened, because this average is lower and has experienced a visible reduction. The distance between the Spanish and the EU score was 145 in 1996, but had grown beyond 165 in 2003.

Another relevant context of the Quality Act has been the very research system, to be precise, the weak institutionalisation of education research and specifically research on education policy. Since most researchers are university lecturers and professors, their work is funded by the Spanish research and development plan, by some non-profit foundations or by specific agreements with certain departments. An important part of these research contributions is provided through PhD dissertations, or simply the individual work of scholars. In the near future, some changes could take place due to introduction of new types of contracts for academic staff in Spanish universities. These contracts require a higher profile of research activities and publications that might bring about some changes, but it is not sensible to guess their likely effect right now. Many of the first research evaluation schemes have privileged Anglo-Saxon journals and only included Spanish and Latin American ones in very marginal positions. As a consequence, the excellence standards might become almost impossible for many researchers, since they might simply disregard them. I insist that this point is such a mere conjecture that cannot provide relevant clues yet.

However, some other pieces of evidence suggest that educational research has not achieved a strong position within the Spanish research system. An overview of its role in the main institutional structures reveals that it is considered as a marginal area of knowledge. Three observations support this contention:

- To start with, there is no reference either to educational research nor to any sort of close social research in the priorities of the *Plan Nacional de Investigación Científica*,

Table 15.1: Percentage of the population aged 18–24 with at most lower secondary education and not in further education or training

	1996	1997	1999	2000	2001	2002	2003
EU 15	21,7	20,8	20,5	19,4	18,9	18,5	18
Spain	31,5	30,3	29,5	28,8	28,6	29	29,8
Spain/ EU15 Gap	145,16	145,67	143,90	148,45	151,32	156,76	165,56

Source: EUROSTAT (2003)

Desarrollo e Innovación Tecnológica 2004–07 (National Plan of Scientific Research, Development and Technological Innovation 2004–07) (MEC 2004). It is not even directly mentioned in the main areas of knowledge but listed within the sub-areas of 'social and economic science'. The other main areas are: life sciences; natural resources, food and environmental technology; space sciences; mathematics and physics; energy; chemistry; materials; industrial design and production; security and defence; information and communication technology; transport and building; and humanities.

- As to research institutes, the *Consejo Superior de Investigaciones Científicas* (High Council for Scientific Research) presents 122 research units in its website (see www.csic.es). None of them includes educational research in its title.
- The two single educational research institutes directly supported by public funding are not directly scientific units. These are the CIDE *Centro de Investigaciones y Documentación Educativa* (Centre for Educational Research and Documentation) and the INECSE *Instituto Nacional de Evaluación y Calidad del Sistema Educativo* (National Institute of Evaluation and Quality of the Educational System, the former INCE redefined by the 2002 LOCE) (see www.mec.es). Both of them are departments within the Ministry of Education. Even though CIDE funded some projects years ago, its catalogue only reports very few recent projects. INECSE and the former INCE have played a crucial role in the whole debate on quality, as has already been said and will be developed further in the next section.

While there were neither institutes nor specific funds for academic educational research, in 2002, INCE had been surveying public opinion about schools and actively disseminating its results since the mid-1990s. These data have impinged on the state of the art of this weak specialty, where most alternative research was conducted by individual scholars or small groups.

This is not to deny that educational research has improved in Spain. Full elaboration of this point is beyond the scope of this chapter, but two final observations indicate that it has become more institutionalised than in the past. First, several academic associations gather experts on recent education policy in Spain, at least in the areas of: comparative education (SEEC – *Sociedad Española de Educación Comparada*, www.sc.ehu.es/sfwseec); economics of education (AEDE – *Asociación de Economía de la Educación*, www.pagina-aede.org); pedagogy (SEP – *Sociedad Española de Pedagogía*, www.uv.es/soespe); and sociology of education (ASE – *Asociación de Sociología de la Educación*, www.ase.es). Secondly, for a long time many professional journals have been published for a broad audience but it is now possible to identify a set of academic journals where education policy is a common issue. A short and varied selection should include the following titles at least: *Bordón. Revista Española de Pedagogía* (Spanish Society of Pedagogy); *Educar* (Autonomous University of Barcelona); *Revista de Educación* (Ministry of Education); *Revista Española de Educación Comparada* (Spanish Society of Comparative Education); and *Temps d'Educació* (University of Barcelona).

Educational research and the debate on the 2002 educational quality act

The 2002 Educational Quality Act has been widely discussed by the academy and the educational community. Several journal numbers and conferences have been devoted to this issue for the last five years. In 2000 *Papeles de Economía Española* published a monograph about the linkages between educational quality and economic growth. In 2002 the former director of INCE, José Luis García Garrido, edited another monograph of the *Revista de Educación*, in which most articles were in favour of the proposed reform, and also Marchesi and Martín (2002) wrote a report on secondary education expressing alternative views. The Pedagogical Society (SEP) opened a debate in its website, and the Sociological Society (ASE) focused its annual meeting on the new Act. Finally, in 2003, *Revista de Educación* published another number on education policy, including Marchesi's and other opinions that were critical of the position of most contributors in the former year.

Many educationalists and other educational specialists also signed the Jabalquinto Declaration in favour of comprehensive and public education in 2002 (Foro de Jabalquinto 2002). Although they have only entered the debate after the Conservatives had lost the 2004 election, two more initiatives should be mentioned as a natural outcome of this collective concern. Between 2002 and 2003 *Fundació Jaume Bofill* gathered national and some international specialists and actors in the Catalan education policy network in order to produce a set of recommendations on equal opportunities (Bonal *et al.* 2004). Finally, between 2003 and 2005 the *Fòrum Social per l'Educació a Catalunya* (Social Forum for Education in Catalonia www.forumeducacio.org) was organised, and finally held in February 2005. Its assistants were mostly Catalan educators, activists and associations, but also some Latin American and European participants. Its programme discussed globalisation, the concept of education, the importance of public schooling and social education.

In this third part of the chapter I want to analyse the main arguments that were presented for and against the reform in the 2002 and 2003 academic debates. My goal is to document the research background on education policy for these debates, and to estimate the impact of INCE research on the intellectual and ideological interaction that followed both within and outside universities. Thus, the following paragraphs consist of a summary sketch of arguments presented by both sides and a partial conclusion about their connection with policy research findings.

The two main arguments for an 'Educational Quality Act' claimed for the need to bridge crucial gaps and promote the culture of endeavour.

• García Garrido (2000, 2002) asserted that he did not elaborate the Act, since he had left the government by 2000, but supported some of its tenets on the grounds that these reforms eventually put the Spanish system in the mainstream of effective education policy. Essentially, he argued that the Education Quality Act was inspired by an international consensus stating that secondary education needs some sort of tracking. He extended his point on international homologies to another measure concerning school organisation, namely external appointment of head-teachers as in most European countries. Like the Sociologist González Anleo (2002), he argued that the Act was necessary because of the low educational performance of Spanish schools. As evidence, they quoted some surveys (mostly, INCE work), OECD

Education at a Glance and the International Association for the Evaluation of Educational Achievement.

• The term 'culture of endeavour' came to summarise the main criticism that comprehensive education had received due to its alleged contradiction with academic standards. In 2001 INCE had already published a qualified assessment of child-centred and content-centred pedagogies based on a survey of primary education co-ordinators' views. The report stated that meaningful and active practices (like methodological variation, curriculum individualised adaptation or using newspapers in the classroom) could be helpful to improve performance, but other significant positive correlates required a more directed orientation (e.g. a clear sequence of content, teachers' appraisal, a constant relation between teaching and the textbook and written examinations). Interestingly, it also pointed out that public schools used these more efficient strategies less frequently than private schools (INCE 2001). The White Paper (MECD 2002) outlined a notion of quality that highlighted endeavour, assessment and teacher authority, and the Act assumed it as a principle of quality. In the latter debates several contributors supported the 'culture of endeavour' as the basis of their own teaching experience (Vinuesa 2002), their own expertise (Gervilla 2002), international literature on leadership (García Ramos 2002) or previous research on gifted students (Jiménez 2002).

Thus, besides other normative or ideological reasons, the two main arguments for the reform drew on national and international statistics, the comparative method and selected pieces of research on leadership and gifted students.

The Educational Quality Act received two main objections that attacked its alleged ideology and expressed concern with its possible effect on educational inequalities.

• Many educationalists and sociologists blamed the Act for its neoliberal and neoconservative tenets. In a very general sense, Torres (2001) had already advanced this criticism against de-regulation and de-centralisation policies, and proposed that teachers became activists. Martínez Bonafé (2002) made a similar point by spelling out the political side of textbooks. Beltrán (2002), Guerrero (2002) and Fernández Palomares (2002) also explored and criticised the neoliberal assumptions of the Act. Martínez Celorrio (2003) tried to specify what manifestations of a change in governance were visible in the Spanish Conservative project. In sum, these authors used interpretive procedures to read the implicit meanings of the Act.

• Another type of critique focused on the structural dimensions of educational problems. Many of them challenged the Ministry's assumption that international research had observed the failure of comprehensive pedagogy. On the one hand, several scholars argued that LOCE threatened to exacerbate inequality and constrain participation (Ballester *et al.* 2002; Fernández Enguita 2002; Hernández Doblon 200; Santana *et al.* 2003; Sevilla 2003). On the other hand, Gimeno (2002), Bonal (2003) and Marchesi (2003) pointed out the powerful influence of a low educational level on the academic results in a country like Spain. Marchesi's was a poignant article because it reminded that OECD PISA findings did not allow the conclusion that comprehensive education was responsible for Spain's low scores. In fact, the incumbent Conservative government had argued that the reform was a necessary response to this alleged perverse effect of comprehensive schooling. Even more, it had refused to publish the 2000 PISA report, which found that early selection is a good predictor of low scores and high inequalities (OECD-UNESCO 2003). Similarly, several educationalists and economists argued that educational expenditure also impinges on results, and the amount of funding was low in Spain (Marchesi 2000; San Segundo 2001; Calero and Bonal 2004).

Thus, critics used interpretive procedures, the comparative method and statistical data in order to challenge the official thesis that the Quality Act was an objective necessity.

In summary, the research background of the 2002 contention on quality was mostly statistical information. García Garrido (2000, 2002), Gimeno (2002) and Marchesi (2003) also used comparative analyses to underpin their points. Interpretive procedures were particularly useful for critics, and some pieces of educational research on comprehensive pedagogy, gifted students and leadership were helpful for supporters. This balance shows that INCE work was crucial not only because it supplied the bulk of the salient evidence, but also because it had become the main research effort over the period in the country.

Conclusion: a localised globalism

For the 1996–2004 period, a political and academic contention has taken place on educational quality, an issue included in the global agenda. Other authors have argued that similar movements can be seen in Britain and France, where academic research on educational power and inequalities has been under attack due to its alleged distance from practical implications (Shain and Ozga 2001; Poupeau 2003). Their common conclusions depict the emergence of a new regulation of educational research that operates at the state level. I will conclude my chapter by comparing these findings to my tentative interpretation of that controversy, and will add a more general reflection on this sort of regulation highlighting its influence at several spatial scales.

To what extent does education policy steer education research in Spain? By 2000 the supporters of the Quality Act had a big advantage within the academic field. After CIDE had reduced its funding a few years before, educational research was weaker than it used to be, and INCE had produced a huge quantitative diagnosis of the problems they claimed to solve. PISA 2000 findings could have eroded their position, but it was not difficult to limit their entry to public knowledge. Their control of *Revista de Educación* allowed them to establish the sequence of publication so that the favourable articles appeared at the same time as the Act was passed, and the critical volumes came out one year after the public discussion. They impinged on the academic debate regardless of the previous corpus of international literature on the structural factors of school performance. They did not even need to emphasise school effectiveness to present their ideas as the new modern solution. In short, their information management and marketing strategy easily introduced quality into the main academic journals at the appropriate moment.

Like in Britain and France, educational policy makers seem to have looked for (and found) new regulation mechanisms to steer educational research according to their interests. However, contrary to these other countries, in Spain they did not need to attack a previous critical research tradition, but only keep funding low and present their proposal to the academy. Although the reaction was intense in certain areas, INCE surveys were enough to meet the standards of scientific journals.

Interestingly, globalisation studies suggest a further conclusion with respect to contentious rescaling processes. Since the late 1990s some authors have argued that a crucial feature of globalisation entails the movements and mismatches of political conflicts between local, national and global scales (Jenson and Santos 2000; Jessop 2001). They have convincingly shown the new regulation procedures that are implemented at different scales where several issues are dealt with. The steering of educational research, or in a more precise sense, of research on education policy, can certainly be one of these crucial policy issues that are objects of new regulation. These authors have also seen the opportunities that rescaling can open at certain moments. The campaign for educational quality in the Spanish academy provides a significant example of both complex multi-scalar regulation and complex multi-scalar opportunities.

As to regulation, it is easy to observe that action at the state level had to be isolated from both lower and higher scales in order to be successful. On the one hand, even though the official and the favourable academic discourses repeated many international comparisons, eventually they had to omit a crucial report issued by an international organism such as the OECD. On the other hand, even though they claimed their concern with quality education for all, they also had to overlook the development of compensatory initiatives launched by Autonomous Communities. The regional education systems may not have presented such visible institutional differences as in other countries like the UK or Belgium, but they had started to experiment with more participatory, universalistic and operational devices than the culture of endeavour in Andalusia, Aragón, the Basque Country and Catalonia.

As to opportunities, once again it should be remembered that some fora emerged where national and international scholars, activists, teachers, parent associations and other civil society actors gathered. At least we can think of the two Jabalquinto Declarations (the second one was issued by Foro de Jabalquinto 2004), the seminars at the *Fundació Jaume Bofill* in Barcelona and the Social Forum for Education in Catalonia. Will these meetings be able to influence future debates? Will they make use of the complex relationships between the scales of education policy? These are open questions and opportunities.

I have borrowed B.S. Santos' expression 'localised globalism' in order to summarise the main ideas of my chapter. Global trends reflect a widening interest in steering educational research in the direction of the global agenda of educational policy. Since this agenda is controversial, its derived guidelines for research are conflictive too. Such conflict can pattern the ways in which the policy agenda and research steering take roots in a country. Several endogenous factors, such as the symbolic importance of comparative statements, the sequence of comprehensive reform and the institutional weakness of educational research, intermingled with these external factors to produce the final outcome of the debate on educational quality in 2002.

Following Santos, the widespread tension between regulation and emancipation in education policy should be remembered. First, some interest groups managed to impose their reform drawing on institutional rules that eventually constrained the space of open debate. They could follow an academic and political strategy driven by immediate objectives, and expressed in a vague neologism (namely, the culture of endeavour) and a rough comparison between the education system and alleged international trends, because they did not face a stronger and more resourceful academic educational research. They need not even draw on literature about school effectiveness, or have to blame scholarly production for impractical conclusions. But secondly, their strategy raised such contestation that it opened the possibility of engaging teachers, political parties, educational representative associations and specialists in an open discussion.

References

Ballester, Ll., Orte, C. and Oliver, J.L. (2002) 'La calidad como ideología de la contrarreforma educativa', *IX Conferencia de Sociología de la Educación*. Online. Available HTTP: http: // www.ase.es (accessed February 2005).

Beltrán, J. (2002) 'Modelos para armar o reformas a la baja: un análisis del discurso de la tríada popular (calidad, formación profesional, universidad)', *IX Conferencia de Sociología de la Educación*. Online. Available HTTP: http:// www.ase.es (accessed February 2005).

Bonal, X. (2003) 'Una evaluación de la equidad en el sistema educativo español', *Revista de Educación*, 330: 59–82.

Bonal, X., Essomba, M.A. and Ferrer, F. (2004) *Política educativa i igualtat d'oportunitats. Prioritats i propostes*, Barcelona: Editorial Mediterrània.

Calero, J. and Bonal, X. (1999) *Política educativa y gasto público en educación. Aspectos teóricos y una aplicación al caso español*, Barcelona: Ediciones Pomares-Corredor.

Calero, J. y Bonal, X. (2004). 'Financiación de la Educación en España', in V. Navarro (ed.) *El Estado del bienestar en España*, Madrid: Tecnos.

Coll, C. (1999) 'L'educació secundària obligatòria: atendre la diversitat en el marc d'un ensenyament comprensiu', *Temps d'Educació*, 21: 117–35.

Comunidades de Aprendizaje (2005) *Comunidades de Aprendizaje*. Online. Available HTTP: http:// www.comunidadesdeaprendizaje.net (accessed January 2005).

Consejería de Educación de la Junta de Andalucía (2001) *Plan para Fomentar la Igualdad de Derechos en Educació*. Online. Available HTTP: http://www.juntadeandalucia.es/ educacionyciencia (accessed December 2004).

Dirección General de Promoción Educativa de la Comunidad de Madrid (2001) *Plan General de Compensación Educativa de la Comunidad de Madrid*. Online. Available HTTP: http:// www.madrid.org (accessed December 2004).

EUROSTAT (2003) *Long-term Social Indicators*. Online. Available HTTP: http://europa.eu.int/ comm./eurostat (accessed March 2004).

Fernández Enguita, M. (2002) 'En torno al borrador de la LOCE. Los itinerarios, los abiertos y los encubiertos', *Foro de Jabalquinto*. Online. Available HTTP: http://www.leydecalidad.org (accessed March 2005).

Fernández Palomares, F. (2002) 'Reforma educativa y cambio social en la España Democrática', *IX Conferencia de Sociología de la Educación*. Online. Available HTTP: http: //www.ase.es (accessed February 2005).

Foro de Jabalquinto (2002) *La LOGSE y la contrarreforma anunciada. Foro de debate sobre la calidad de la enseñanza en el sistema educativo español*. Online. Available HTTP: http:// www.leydecalidad.org (accessed March 2005).

Foro de Jabalquinto (2004) *Debates para una ley*. Online. Available HTTP: http://www. intersindical.org/stepv/peirp/jabalquinto2.pdf (accessed March 2005).

García Garrido, J.L. (2000) 'La calidad de la educación obligatoria española en perspectiva europea', *Papeles de Economía Española*, 86: 120–35.

García Garrido, J.L. (2002) 'La nueva Ley de Calidad: reflexiones en la perspectiva internacional', *Revista de Educación*, 329: 23–38.

García Ramos, J. L. (2002) 'La calidad de las instituciones educativas y algunas de sus dimensiones básicas', *Revista de Educación*, 329: 105–25.

Gervilla, E. (2002) 'Revalorización del esfuerzo y exigencia personal', *Debate sobre la Ley de Calidad en la Educación* (organised by the Sociedad Española de Pedagogía). Online. Available HTTP: http://www.uv.es/soespe (accessed January 2005).

Gimeno Sacristán, J. (2002) 'Discutamos los problemas. Debate en torno a la Ley de Calidad', *Foro de Jabalquinto*. Online. Available HTTP: http://www.leydecalidad.org (accessed March 2002).

González Anleo, J. (2002) 'Panorama de la educación en la España de los cambios', *Revista Española de Investigaciones Sociológicas*, 100: 185–229.

Guerrero, A. (2002) 'Las directrices de la Ley de Calidad y sus repercusiones en los modelos de profesionalidad del profesorado de Educación Infantil', *IX Conferencia de Sociología de la Educación*. Online. Available HTTP: http://www.ase.es (accessed February 2005).

Hernández Doblón, F.J. (2003) 'La "extranjerización" legal y pedagógica del alumnado inmigrante', *X Conferencia de Sociología de la Educación*. Online. Available HTTP: http://www.ase.es (accessed February 2005).

Instituto Nacional de Calidad y Educación (INCE) (1998) *Instrumentos para un diagnóstico del sistema educativo español. Informe global*, Madrid: Ministerio de Educación y Cultura.

Instituto Nacional de Calidad y Educación (INCE) (2001) 'Aspectos de la práctica docente del profesorado que tienen más relación con el rendimiento de los alumnos de educación primaria', *Resumen Informativo* 22. Online. Available HTTP: http://www.mecd.es (accessed May 2002).

Jaumeandreu, G. and Badosa, J. (2002) 'Los proyectos educativos de ciudad: la experiencia de Cornellà de Llobregat', I. Blanco and R. Gomà (eds) *Gobiernos Locales y Redes Participativas*, Barcelona: Ariel.

Jenson, J. and Santos, B.S. (2000) *Globalizing Institutions. Case Studies in Regulation and Innovation*, Sydney: Ashgate.

Jessop, B. (2001) *On the Spatio-temporal Logic of Capital's Globalization and their Manifold Implications for State Power*, Lancaster: Lancaster University, Department of Sociology. Online. Available HTTP: http://www.comp.lancs.ac.uk/sociology (accessed October 2003).

Jiménez, C. (2002) 'Tercer eje de la loce o creación de un sistema de oportunidades de calidad para todos', *Debate sobre la Ley de Calidad en la Educación* (organised by the Sociedad Española de Pedagogía). Online. Available HTTP: http://www.uv.es/soespe (accessed January 2005).

Jiménez, J. (2003) 'La educación en las comunidades autónomas', *Cuadernos de Pedagogía* 323 (April): 45–75.

López Rupérez, F. (1998) 'Hacia unos centros educativos de calidad. Contexto, fundamento y políticas de calidad en la gestión escolar', *Gestión de Calidad en Educación*. Online. Available HTTP: http://www.mecd.es (accessed May 2002).

Marchesi, A. (2000) 'La evaluación de la educación secundaria obligatoria', *Papeles de Economía Española*, 86: 150–64.

Marchesi, A. (2003) 'Indicadores de la educación en España y cambio educativo', *Revista de Educación*, 330: 13–34.

Marchesi, A. and Martín, E. (2002) *Evaluación de la educación secundaria. Fotografía de una etapa polémica*, Madrid: Fundación Santa María.

Martínez Bonafé, J. (2002) *Políticas del libro de texto escolar*, Madrid: Morata.

Martínez Celorrio, X. (2003) 'Política educativa sin sociología: populismo y cierre social en las reformas conservadoras', *Sistema*, 173: 63–76.

Mayordomo, A. (1999) 'Aproximación a enfoques y tiempos de la política educativa', in A. Mayordomo (ed.) *Estudios sobre la política educativa durante el franquismo*, València: Universitat de València.

Ministerio de Educación, Cultura y Deportes (2002) *Documento de Bases para una Ley de Calidad en la Educación*. Online. Available HTTP: http://www.mecd.es (accessed 11 March 2002).

Ministerio de Educación y Ciencia – MEC (2004) *Presentación del Plan Nacional de Investigación Científica, Desarrollo e Innovación Tecnológica 2004–07*. Online. Available HTTP: http://www.mec.es/ciencia (accessed March 2005).

OECD-UNESCO (2003) *Literacy Skills for the World of Tomorrow: Further Results from PISA 2000*. Online. Available HTTP: http://www.oecd.org (accessed April 2004).

Prada, M.D. (2002) 'Diversidad y diversificación en la Educación Secundaria Obligatoria: tendencias actuales en Europa', *Revista de Educación*, 329: 39–65.

Poupeau, F. (2003) *Une sociologie d'État. L'école et ses experts en France*, Paris: Ed. Raisons d'Agir.

San Segundo, M.J. (2001) 'El impacto nacional y regional del programa de becas', *AECE Meeting Procedures*. Online. Available HTTP: http://www.pagina-aede.org (accessed January 2005).

Santana, F. and Guardia, R. (2003) 'Balance de una agenda política problemática: 1996–2003. La Evaluación Institucional "sube", la Participación Educativa "baja"', *X Conferencia de Sociología de la Educación*. Online. Available HTTP: http://www.ase.es (accessed February 2005).

Sevilla, D. (2003) 'La educación comprensiva en España: paradoja, retórica y limitaciones', *Revista de Educación*, 330: 35–7.

Shain, F. and Ozga, J. (2001) 'Identity crisis? Problems and issues in the sociology of education', *Bristish Journal of Sociology of Education*, 22(1): 109–20.

Torres, J. (2001) *Educación en tiempos de neoliberalismo*, Madrid: Morata.

16 Competition and interaction between research knowledge and state knowledge in policy steering in France

National trends and recent effects of decentralisation and globalisation

Agnès van Zanten

Introduction

It is nothing new to see knowledge used as a tool of government. Since the eighteenth century, the development of modern states and administrations monopolising government functions has encouraged top officials to appeal to science to legitimise their power (Ihl *et al.* 2004). Once states came to expand their territories and fields of intervention, they found it necessary to draw on specialist skills and learning tools. However, there are at least three reasons why using knowledge in this way now plays a more important role than it used to in the conduct of public policy. The first relates to the development of knowledge and the fact that the latter is seen as the basis of not only cultural, but also economic changes in societies. The second is that, faced with a crisis in the model of political authority based on personal status, knowledge is seen as the best way to legitimise policy choices and leaders' exhortations to change. The third is that the post-bureaucratic policies put in place by the 'managerial state' (Clarke and Newman 1997; Thrupp and Willmott 2003) are based not so much on *a priori* regulation through standards and rules laid down by political and administrative officials as on *a posteriori* regulation of the actions of those who have to reinterpret and adapt policies and be accountable for what they do, so that not only do the latter need to be better equipped than in the past in both conceptual and technical terms, but evaluation needs to be developed on a large scale.

The characteristics of the groups who develop knowledge, the types of knowledge they produce and the way this knowledge is used in the policy field nevertheless vary considerably between countries according to their intellectual traditions and the way the political and administrative system is organised. In France, perhaps more than in other countries, a contrast between two major types of knowledge producers can be seen. On the one hand, there are researchers who, with the support of government, but in a relatively independent way, develop research knowledge at universities and research centres while, on the other, there are people working within or in close interaction with policy-making bodies, who develop state knowledge. Although the two groups are separate, they have never been completely cut off from each other, at least not in the field of education. In fact, in recent times, there has been growing interpenetration of their output, as a result not only of the wider distribution of research knowledge amongst political and administrative personnel, but also the greater involvement of researchers in working out, monitoring and evaluating educational reforms. We shall tackle these various aspects in the first part of this chapter.

Furthermore, two new elements, linked to the decentralisation and globalisation of government intervention, are gradually changing the influence of both scientific and political/administrative output on the direction of education policies and could eventually lead to the disappearance of the current national model. As regards research knowledge, mention should be made of greater upstream steering of the content of research aimed at increasing its usefulness. This kind of steering is applied in particular through new methods of financing which, in France, bring in funding from decentralised bodies and supranational bodies such as the European Union in addition to public funds from ministries and agencies answerable to the central government. As regards state knowledge, alongside the models endorsed by bodies answerable to the central government, the emergence of decentralised education models promoted by local authorities can also be seen, as well as global models endorsed by representatives of supranational or international agencies such as the European Union, OECD or World Bank. We shall tackle these points in the second part of this chapter.

The complex interpenetration of education sciences and government education sciences in France

Research knowledge in education and interaction with policy

Research knowledge and state knowledge alike seek to understand a phenomenon or a set of phenomena, but differ in terms of the importance they place on another function filled by knowledge, i.e. its use for purposes of control (Duran 1999). Consequently, two ideal types of learning process can be contrasted. The first is predominantly cognitive, taking as its starting point an intellectual question that has arisen in connection with the development of a discipline or field of research. Its goal is to make reality more intelligible. The second is predominantly a cognitive/instrumental process, its starting point being a problem faced by policy makers and practitioners and its goal to come up with solutions. The investigation is pursuing not just truth but also efficiency. In other words, research is being brought into the field of policy and vice versa. There is, therefore, obviously a common core, as well as some differences in the two activities.

The distinction may, however, seem at first sight to be more relevant in France than elsewhere, if one looks at the mode of production of research knowledge that has long been dominant. Indeed, for intellectual, institutional and political reasons, there has been a long tradition of strongly speculative and theoretical, rather than empirical, research in the social sciences, which has not really encouraged taking account of the issues facing practitioners. Far from the US model of research amply funded by foundations set up by major private corporations, research in the social sciences developed in France with few resources, but in a context of greater academic independence vis-à-vis government and society. Consequently, it was able to keep a considerable distance from the conventional wisdom as well as a strongly critical bent, leading researchers to refuse demands from government and various pressure groups (Chapoulie 1991). However, although this 'radical academicism' (Layperonnie 2004) still has its champions today, the development of empirical research in social sciences over the last 30 or so years has in fact given rise to much closer links with both social and policy actors.

In the case of education, there are at least two reasons why interpenetration with social and political changes is even stronger. The first relates to the problematic status, from the scientific point of view, of the research conducted in this field. The very definition of education lies at the heart of the problem. To begin with, this field seems so familiar to most of those involved that the distinction between experts and the profane, which is central to any attempt at achieving professional and scientific autonomy (Hughes 1984), is not easy to establish, especially as many educational researchers have come from the world of teaching and this affiliation influences their choice of theoretical frameworks and research topics. Moreover, within the education sciences themselves, there is little consensus about their status as a field of basic research. This is related above all to the many disciplines involved – philosophy, psychology, didactics, history, sociology, anthropology, economics and so forth – and the differing ways they conceive of science. However, it is also due to the education sciences, in France, being absent from basic research institutions such as the national scientific research centre (Centre National de la Recherche Scientifique – CNRS) and the weakness of research, for both financial and organisational reasons, in the education science departments of universities (Prost 2001).

The second reason relates to the political importance given to the education system in France, seen as a pillar of national unity and political/administrative centralisation. Consequently, the state is always seeking control, including of the knowledge produced by that system. This explains not only the substantial development of state knowledge in the field of education that I mention in the next section, but also the attempts on the part of government to commandeer research, most recently by commissioning expert assessments. Scientific experts are chosen by political officials by reason of their scientific competence in the field concerned, but also their ability to produce knowledge of practical and political use through their links with institutions producing data, their knowledge of the professional scene and their closeness to the political biases of reformers (Tanguy 1995). We should note that the authorities may seem to exert even greater control over the work of such experts in that it is often conducted on a personal basis, encouraging the expression of an individual viewpoint rather than the collective viewpoint of the scientific community as a whole (Perret 2001).

Can we then speak of perfect synergy between the concerns of politicians and researchers, transforming education sciences and in particular the sociology of education into 'State science', as has been suggested in some recent work (e.g. Poupeau 2003)? Despite the fact that the political perspective is now incorporated to a far greater extent in scientific research, such a statement seems pretty excessive. For one thing, like those involved in the other social sciences, educational researchers who are approached by government are still considered and consider themselves as intellectuals retaining great freedom of expression. They do not bow to the political agenda, but reinterpret it in accordance with their own centres of interest. Moreover, for reasons we have studied in greater detail elsewhere (van Zanten 2005b), their real impact on policy decisions as such and on conferring legitimacy on those decisions is, in the final analysis, fairly weak.

Government sciences and the interaction with science

Government education sciences developed strongly in France when the state education system was set up. The centralised, standardised nature of the education system encouraged the emergence of a huge administration, with responsibility for budgeting, distributing resources and monitoring teachers' activity. However, although members of that administration played an essentially instrumental role, its top officials brought in scientific learning processes and sought to produce objective knowledge, especially following its expansion during the post-war period. Moreover, it was particularly easy to present the knowledge produced in this way as an intellectual contribution in that it could claim to plug gaps and compete with the limited output from the education sciences that, in some cases, had little scientific legitimacy.

Amongst producers of state knowledge in the educational field, attention should be drawn to two major producers at national level: the Department of Evaluation and Forward Planning (Direction de l'Evaluation et de la Prospective – DEP) and General Inspectorate (Inspection Générale – IGEN). The DEP, which produces predominantly statistical knowledge, has played a central role in producing not only data, but also quantitative research on pupils' achievements, teachers, the operation of schools and various education policies over the last 15 years. There are at least two reasons for this; first, quantitative research on education in France is weak, as a result not only of institutional conditions – inadequate quantitative training of future researchers, lack of resources and equipment, as well as the small number and size of research teams – but also ideological factors, especially the misgivings of more humanistic disciplines about the technical bias and objectivising nature of analysis. Secondly, some of those in charge of the Department, being close to the world of research, have acted as a bridge between research knowledge and state knowledge, by importing scientific problematics and working methods into the world of budgeting and figures (Seibel 2004).

However, the role of the DEP has also extended, in recent years, to co-ordinating and driving educational research. This government department has set up a unit to liaise with research on education and training. It has also developed private arrangements with researchers or worked with them through its involvement in commissioning and financing tenders to conduct research on topics such as territorial inequalities in education provision or dropping out. There is therefore a strong link between the DEP and the world of research, which does not preclude a degree of competition and tension around particular issues, categories, indicators or uses of knowledge, revealing that differences still exist between the predominantly cognitive rationale of researchers engaged in the pursuit of knowledge and the predominantly instrumental rationale of the DEP, whose evaluations are geared towards control (Thélot 1994).

The work of the IGEN, the other major producer of state knowledge in education, has historically developed largely in isolation from research. Its high-level officials, reporting directly to the Minister for Education, draw their professional legitimacy in the field of education from several sources. First of all, their own schooling, marked by success in prestigious competitions, making them card-carrying representatives of the educational meritocracy. Secondly, their careers, during which they have held various positions, enabling them to claim to master all or at least the majority of the issues affecting the education system. Thirdly, their position at the top of the hierarchy and within an institution which, although not comparable to a university, is sufficiently removed from the day-to-day routine of education for its members to look like 'wise men'. Fourthly, their national status, which enables them to have an overview of the whole education system. Finally, the existence of a body whose members possess knowledge and additional know-how that can be mobilised in various relevant ways depending on the questions asked.

These aspects have, for a long time, been sufficient to underpin in-house capability in respect of the teaching profession and school curricula, which has been little challenged and, for the same reason, rather introspective. Nevertheless, IGEN inspectors do now seem to be opening up towards research and the predominantly quantitative assessments of the DEP, strongly influenced by the new tasks of evaluating schools, academies, arrangements and policies that they have been asked to undertake. In fact, IGEN inspectors are increasingly using survey or evaluation protocols, indicators, statistics, service manuals, triangulation procedures and comparisons (Pons 2004). However, there is still considerable mistrust towards overly scientific or technical procedures which supposedly neglect the human factor that only a scientist with the above-mentioned skills can bring to interpretation. Furthermore, while they have weaker links with research than the DEP does, there are also tensions and forms of latent competition with researchers, especially as regards what constitutes a good qualitative perspective on educational research.

The effects of decentralisation and globalisation on the French model of linkage between research and policy

The impact on research of new local and supranational funding mechanisms

The relative independence from government of French research in the social sciences and education is due to a large extent to the funding mechanisms that predominated until the mid-1980s. During this period, it was mainly research programmes launched by the CNRS, as well as various ministries and public agencies, which supported research with relatively modest resources but, at the same time, had limited input into research problematics and methods. It is undoubtedly true that the topics covered by research programmes and calls for tender reflected a particular state perception of social problems, their causes and possible solutions, as well as a conception of the role of research in the social sciences as the provision of useful categories and analytical tools for decision making and the conduct of public policy. However, research teams were able to retain a considerable margin of professional autonomy, due to the links that often existed between researchers and those in charge of research and study within public agencies; the establishment of scientific project selection and monitoring committees; and the weight of the tradition of respect for academic freedom. This autonomy was able to find expression in the redefinition of problematics within research categories, in the conduct of research according to strictly scientific protocols and in reports in which researchers spoke their minds quite freely.

Nevertheless, while this situation still persists to some extent, the reduction in the number of grants from these centralised bodies and the newly found interest of local administrative and political officials in 'informed' steering of local options and arrangements have led to the development of research, studies and expert assessments funded by the regional or municipal authorities or by the local government adminis-trations[1] (van Zanten 1999). In the field of education, this has resulted on new calls on researchers to assess the effects of decentralisation and local educational policies. These calls emanate far less often from the local administrative arms of the Ministry of Education (Rectorates and Academic Inspectorates) than from local authorities (regions, departments or municipalities), by reason of the differences between these two types of organisation as regards knowledge of the education system. In fact, local government education authorities have long accumulated in-house capability in the matter of collecting and processing educational data and the qualitative assessment of the activity of head teachers and teachers which, in the eyes of some officials, makes it unnecessary to turn to researchers. We should point out, however, that the growing 'politicisation' of these bodies, which have not only to apply standard procedures but also, increasingly, to adapt their policy choices to the diverse needs of local areas, has begun to bring them closer to research. Conversely, having had substantial decision-making power in respect of education only since the early 1980s, the local authorities lack in-house expertise in this field (van Zanten 2004a, 2005a).

Impetus from these local authorities has led to the development of new research, especially in the richest regions, although this trend has been accompanied by a much greater gearing of research towards control and communication. In many cases, this has also brought about a substantial restriction in researchers' autonomy in designing analytical frameworks, conducting surveys – including a substantial reduction in the time allowed for completing projects – and publicising findings, which are often considered confidential and suitable for only selective dissemination. Some researchers submit to these constraints, either to increase their financial resources, or because they find this activity more useful or more likely to bring them local if not national fame quickly. However, others do resist, leading local bodies and particularly the local authorities to turn to consultancies or private polling organisations. As the latter are more likely to share local political officials' view of the purposes of survey activities and are more malleable, they lend themselves more easily to the use of findings from evaluations for the purposes of strengthening the networks of power, policy communication and media visibility (Dutercq 2000; Richard and Berthet 2002).

These trends towards the development of research that is much more directly linked to policy will, moreover, very likely be accentuated by the emergence of new supranational funding such as that from the European Union's framework research programmes. In fact, the topics covered by these programmes correspond to a political agenda which, although not entirely coherent, still seeks to bias research, as well as policy making, towards certain issues considered relevant for strengthening convergence between European countries around certain educational concepts such as competitiveness, quality, lifelong learning or European citizenship. Project selection, which is a long process involving not only independent researchers but also government officials and which includes negotiation between the latter and the research teams, logically leads to the exclusion of research that strays furthest from the above issues, while research projects are increasingly moulded from conception through to final acceptance.

In addition – and this is a vital aspect – the emphasis in these programmes is very clearly placed on funding useful research intended to provide information for supranational and national policy makers. Research teams are encouraged throughout their work and, above all, when the findings are published on completion to organise meetings and promotional events for policy makers and government officials in countries and within the European Union. They also have to produce recommendations addressed to the latter in a summary document, which is drafted under the watchful eye of the people in charge of these programmes. This politically useful research also underpins research programmes suggested by a less overtly political body, the European Science Foundation. Although its programmes, unlike those of the European Union, remain open to all kinds of research proposals, the Foundation also stresses the importance of knowledge as a tool for driving economic change and altering behaviour. In addition, it underlines the role of knowledge in resolving social problems, constructing policies, assessing the effects of these policies and, more generally, developing more effective systems of governance.

From national government sciences to local and global government sciences?

The existence of 'local government sciences' is nothing new in the French system, since the local government administrations have long had to develop methods of collecting and processing data and information in order to apply the standards and rules decreed at national level in specific areas. Moreover, the expansion of local administrations in line with the growth and diversification of the education system as of the 1970s was accompanied by a substantial growth in bureaucratic management tools, particularly involving the distribution of pupils, resources and teachers amongst schools. In recent times, however, there have been important changes related to decentralisation and the much greater pressure than in the past to adapt not just the resources of education but also its objectives to the diverse features of local areas. These developments oblige local officials to move away from predominantly bureaucratic management towards much more political management, involving choices between policy directions, the preparation of new operational and co-ordination procedures and the establishment of evaluation mechanisms (van Zanten 2004a).

However, these changes pose two new kinds of problems, the first being the legitimacy of local players on the education scene. In France, the very clear distinction between politics and administration, particularly as regards the activities of the local administrations seen as implementing rather than decision-making bodies, stands opposed to aggressive policy action by the latter and, indirectly, to any attempt to gain knowledge that could feed into genuinely local policies. The second problem relates to the availability of skills. Skills in managing the education system amongst the staff of these local government administrations have developed in a bureaucratic framework characterised by standardised, routine procedures, segmented intervention and very hierarchical decision making (Giraud and Milly 2003). Consequently, the transition from a bureaucratic management mode to a post-bureaucratic regulatory mode, based on problem analysis, globalised intervention and streamlined decision making, raises substantial new organisational challenges (van Zanten 2004c).

Despite these difficulties, policy projects showing varying degrees of ambition are beginning to emerge, particularly amongst the Rectorates. Like those developed at the Lille Rectorate, such projects are anchored in the widespread use of qualitative and quantitative evaluations and audits (Demailly *et al.* 1998). Added to this is the contribution of the local authorities to the development of local government sciences. Within the new scope for action in the field of education opened up by decentralisation, the latter are not confining themselves, as I indicated in the previous section, to using researchers to carry out expert assessments. They have also recruited specialist personnel in the field of education, often drawn from the local government administrations, in order to implement more or less ambitious local education policies. In addition, they are developing new evaluation procedures enabling them not only to get on top of what they do in the areas under their responsibility, but also to gain the necessary legitimacy in fields such as education with which until recently they had had little to do.

Apart from these developments at local level, new supranational and international government sciences are emerging. It is true that the circulation of ideas and education systems is not a new phenomenon, but its intensification with the advance of globalisation has many causes. The large-scale dissemination of particular educational policies is first of all a response to the demands of greater economic competition and worldwide circulation of capital, encouraging cuts in education expenditure, the emergence of new efficiency criteria applied to education systems and the adaptation of education to corporate strategic options. It is also the result of much faster top-down and bottom-up circulation of information and models. Finally, it is also the consequence of the appearance on the scene of bodies such as the World Bank, International Monetary Fund and OECD endorsing new international regulations. Moreover, in Europe, the growing, although indirect, influence of the European Union can be seen. This body has used the broadening of the concept of vocational training, decisions concerning student mobility and mutual recognition of diplomas, co-operation and educational exchanges and the establishment of information, evaluation and research mechanisms to develop a supranational education policy that can, de facto, evade the democratic control of nation states (Novoa 1998). However, it would be an exaggeration to suggest that there is a single, coherent neo-liberal model driven by globalisation, if only because of the 'polyphony' of the concepts with the widest currency such as decentralisation, accountability, marketisation, managerialism or professionalisation of teachers (van Zanten 2002).

It is true that France seems to be less affected by these new watchwords than other countries. There are several reasons for this: for one thing, not being dependent on external resources to finance its education system, it is much less in thrall to bodies such as the IMF or the World Bank than the emerging countries of Latin America, Asia or Africa or the transition countries in post-communist Europe. Furthermore, it defends its 'cultural exception' quite fiercely and takes little part in international bodies such as the OECD that are dominated by English-speaking countries. Finally, having set up a very elaborate system of evaluation at national level, it has been less sensitive so far to the results of international evaluations such as the latest PISA survey, particularly as the latter showed the French education system to be more efficient and fair than those of nearby countries such as Germany or Belgium. However, in the long term, by making available new data and new ways to measure the effects of national education policies, as well as by setting up competition between countries, these evaluations cannot fail to have an impact and to be used by national decision makers as policy opportunities arise. Moreover, by stressing the concept of evidence-based policy and by developing research and change scenarios alongside evaluations, the OECD is also putting itself forward as a fully fledged policy actor.

Conclusion

This analysis of the role of knowledge in the current regulation of the French education system demonstrates a degree of interaction between research knowledge and state knowledge at national level. On the one hand, researchers in education are taking more account of the real problems faced by practitioners and have no hesitation in doing assessments for the public authorities and disseminating the results of their work beyond the circle of specialists. On the other hand, it is also obvious that producers of state knowledge are increasingly using concepts, procedures and tools from the world of research. Bridges between the two groups are also developing in connection with tenders or more ad hoc operations. It can therefore be said that, in education, perhaps more than in other policy fields, an 'environment' for increasing the role of knowledge in steering decisions and policy does exist or is in the process of creation. This situation would be satisfactory if knowledge producers as a whole were to succeed, by working together, in creating a 'culture' around problems and issues faced by politicians, i.e. a space for reflection and dialogue allowing causes to be analysed, alternative solutions to be explored and the consequences for individuals and society to be assessed. Nevertheless, the emergence of such a culture comes up against several obstacles: ignorance or reciprocal discrediting of output, as well as the various forms of competition between knowledge producers, but also and more decisively the political misappropriation of knowledge, a factor that I have tackled in more depth in other papers (cf. van Zanten 2004b, 2004c).

Furthermore, as I have stressed in the second part of this chapter, this imperfect environment that has come into being at national level is weakened by the development of new links between research and policy at local and global levels. It seems highly desirable, in terms of seeking greater efficiency and equity, for the process of political decentralisation to be accompanied by the development of a larger mass of quality knowledge making it possible to adapt education to diverse local situations and to assess and compare the effects of different local policy choices. It must be emphasised, nevertheless, that the establishment of an environment in which knowledge producers likely to influence local policy can come together is currently more difficult at local than at national level. On the one hand, researchers are placed in competition with consultants from private firms and induced to adapt the problematics, methods and duration of their research to the specific requirements of policy makers who have less respect for academic freedom and are less familiar than national policy makers with research. At the same time, knowledge producers within government departments are having difficulty in getting away from predominantly bureaucratic and managerial working methods. What is more, knowledge is placed at the service of politics rather than policies due to the emphasis placed on the selective use and media hyping of certain findings.

The recent entry of international and supranational policy actors is also beginning to disrupt the former equilibrium, even though this tendency is less marked in France than in other countries. The lack of national resources for research makes researchers increasingly dependent on funding from international and supranational bodies, yet those in charge of the latter place heavy emphasis on the political usefulness of scientific knowledge and seek to mould the conduct and use of research in that image. At the same time, agencies such as the OECD are developing new models of government education sciences, posing as major producers of the comparative empirical evidence that policy makers on the world stage supposedly need to move in the right direction. While difficult at national level and very problematic at local level, the dialogue between researchers and producers of state knowledge is very weak at international level and the scientific community has little control over it. This is because there is no international educational research forum, although international associations such as the European Educational Research Association (EERA) have recently tried to set one up. Moreover, the selective use of knowledge by international and supranational organisations is beyond the control not only of the scientific community but also of the public authorities of nation states, something that is eminently problematic from a democratic standpoint.

Notes

1   Translator's note: I have used 'local government administrations (or services)' to render *'instances déconcentrées (de l'Etat)'*, for which there is no direct equivalent in England, as distinct from 'local authorities', i.e. bodies with elected councils. Cf. the following quote from the French embassy web site: ' "Deconcentration' is the internal decentralization of central government services, i.e. the State transfers some of its powers to its local representatives, so that in these spheres there is no loss of State powers.'

References

Chapoulie, J.-M. (1991) 'La seconde fondation de la sociologie française, les Etats-Unis et la classe ouvrière', *Revue française de sociologie*, 32(3): 321–64.

Clarke, J. and Newman, J. (1997) *The Managerial State*, London, Sage.

Duran, P. (1999) *Penser l'action publique*, Paris, Librarie générale de droit et de jurisprudence.

Demailly, L., Deubel Ph., Gadrey N. and Verdière J. (1998) *Evaluer les établissements scolaires. Enjeux, expériences, débats*, Paris, L'Harmattan.

Dutercq, Y. (2000) *Politiques éducatives et évaluation. Querelles de territoires*, Paris: Presses universitaires de France.

Giraud C. and Milly, B. (2003) *Les visages d'une Académie*, Lyon: Glysi-Safa.

Hughes, E. (1984) (1st edn 1958) *The Sociological Eye. Selected Papers*, Somerset, NJ: Transaction Publishers.

Ihl, O., Kaluszynski, M. and Pollet, G. (2003) *Les sciences du gouvernement*, Paris: Economica.

Layperonnie, D. (2004) 'L'académisme radical ou le monologue sociologique. Avec qui parlent les sociologues ?', *Revue française de sociologie*, 45(4): 621–51.

Novoa, A. (1998) *Histoire et comparaison. Essais sur l'éducation*, Lisbon: Educa.

Perret, B. (2001) *L'évaluation des politiques publiques*, Paris: La Découverte, coll. 'Repères'.

Pons, X. (2004) *L'évaluation des politiques éducatives, entre finalités pédagogiques et stratégies de pouvoir professionnel*, Mémoire de DEA, Paris : FNSP.

Poupeau, F. (2003) *Une sociologie d'Etat. L'école et ses experts en France*, Paris: Raisons d'agir.

Prost, A. (2001) *Pour un programme stratégique de recherche en éducation*, Paris: La documentation française.

Richard, A. and Berthet, T. (2002) 'L'expertise et l'approche territoriale. Un enjeu dans les nouvelles configurations d'acteurs', in J. Timotéo and M. Vernières (eds) *Dynamiques du local. Dix ans de recherches sur l'approche localisée de la relation formation-emploi*, Paris: CEREQ, 109–22.

Seibel, C. (2004) 'Les liens entre Pierre Bourdieu et les statisticiens, à partir de son expérience algérienne', *La liberté par la connaissance. Pierre Bourdieu (1930–2002)*, Paris: Odile Jacob.

Tanguy, L. (1995) 'Le sociologue et l'expert. Une analyse de cas', *Sociologie du travail*, 3, 457–77.

Thélot, C. (1993) *L'évaluation du système éducatif.* Paris: Nathan-Université.

Thrupp, M. and Willmott, R. (2003) *Education Management in Managerial Times.* Maidenhead: Open University Press.

van Zanten, A. (1999) 'Le savant et le politique dans les années quatre-vingt dix. Quelques problèmes éthiques de la recherche ethnographique en éducation', in I. Martinez and A. Vasquez (eds) *Recherches ethnographiques en Europe et en Amérique du Nord*, Paris: Anthropos.

van Zanten, A. (2002) 'Educational change and new cleavages between head teachers, teachers and parents: Global and local perspectives on the French case', *Journal of Education Policy*, 17: 289–304.

van Zanten, A. (2004a) *Les politiques d'éducation*, Paris: Presses Universitaires de France, coll. 'Que sais-je?'.

van Zanten, A. (2004b) 'Les sociologues de l'éducation et leurs publics', in G. Chatelanat, C. Moro and M. Saada-Robert (eds) *Unité et pluralité des sciences de l'éducation. Sondages au cœur de la recherche*, Berne: Peter Lang, 187–203.

van Zanten, A. (2004c) 'Vers une régulation territoriale des établissements d'enseignement en France? Le cas de deux départements de la région parisienne', *Recherches Sociologiques*, 35(2): 47–64.

van Zanten, A. (2005a) 'La régulation par le bas du système éducatif: Légitimité des acteurs et construction d'un nouvel ordre local', in Y. Dutercq (coord.) *La régulation des politiques d'éducation*, Rennes: Presses Universitaires de Rennes, 99–117.

van Zanten, A. (2005b) 'Le rôle de la connaissance dans la régulation du système éducatif en France: questions de la production, questions de la réception', Actes du Colloque *Le pilotage du système éducatif: enjeux, outils, perspectives*, Paris: Ministère de l'éducation, Direction de l'évaluation et de la prospective.

17 Education policy research in the People's Republic of China

Rui Yang

Since the latter part of the twentieth century, we are experiencing a duality: on one hand the way policy is made is highly contextualised and its implementation even more context-dependent, on the other policy travels globally, widespread and profound. Under such scenario, comparative research on education policy studies in various countries is growing in relevance and interest. This contribution, for the first time in the English language, investigates how education policy is researched in the People's Republic of China. It attempts to understand how Chinese education policy researchers are influenced by external forces while struggling with the local relevance of their work. Beginning with the trajectory of public and education policy research in China, it selects articles published in an influential scholarly journal in China during 2003–4 to delineate the *status quo* by looking closely at their themes, authors, perspectives and referencing. It ends up with some discussions of the tensions between the global agenda and the local context.

Introduction: public and education policy research as an emerging academic field

With the increasing presence of policy networks and the geographical and conceptual border crossing of policy elites, efforts to globalise educational institutions has meant that something of a common discourse has become apparent in educational policy. However, rather than a trans-national convergence of policy and practice in educational institutions, what occurs, when global trends are encountered in the local context, is some form of hybridisation (Well 2005). The convergence or divergence one sees in education is the product of conscious adaptation, blind imitation and pressure to conform (Stromquist 2002). Policies have been transformed many times by the time they reach local educational institutions.

If policy makers remain critical in the borrowing process, adapting the borrowed policy to their needs, the discourse will necessarily change along with its implementation (Well 2005). There is a need to remain critical throughout the policy-making process and object to the lack of reflection on discourse in education policy (Nóvoa and Lawn 2002). Policy researchers play a crucial role when they engage in discourse analysis, to deconstruct the often simplified rhetoric of globalisation, educational reform and so forth, by critically examining rhetoric or concepts that have become nearly 'universal' because of their widespread use, and by highlighting the discourse originating from global elite networks.

This chapter, for the first time in the English language, investigates how education policy is researched in the People's Republic of China. It attempts to understand how Chinese education policy researchers are influenced by external forces while struggling with their local relevance. Beginning with the trajectory of public and education policy research in China, it selects articles published in an influential scholarly journal in China during 2003–04 to delineate the *status quo* by looking closely at their themes, authors, perspectives and referencing. It ends up with some discussions of the tensions between the global agenda and the local context.

Policy science originated from societal needs during China's open-door era.[1] In line with China's reform of governance, it has grown to be an important branch of political sciences and public administration in China since the late 1970s. Its emergence and development as a new academic field is closely related to China's ongoing 'professionalisation', 'scientification' and 'democratisation' of governance (Xu 2002: 449).

During its disconnection from the West through the socialist period from the 1950s to the 1970s, the communist Chinese government had a longstanding policy research tradition. Usually initiated by the government, the research targeted some specific tasks, commonly began with investigations and experiments in selected points, and resulted in identification of problems and their solutions. Research methods and approaches were simple. Analyses were mainly confined to previous experience (Xu 2002). Research work was conducted by a handful of people, either from the Party or commissioned by the government, whose research was greatly limited not only by their knowledge structure and techniques, but especially by the then political and ideological climates.

By the early 1980s, driven by the then 'emancipation of the mind',[2] there had been many discussions over the reasons for previous policy-making failures. Academic circles began to produce research work calling for 'democratisation of policy-making' (Meng 1983). On 15 August 1986, Wan (1986), the then vice premier, articulated the tasks required to achieve 'democratisation' and 'scientification' of policy making. A number of ministries and the State Council then established research institutes respectively under their jurisdiction to conduct policy research specifically. Western works were translated into Chinese. Chinese textbooks were published (Yuan 1996). Research articles appeared in social science journals. The Chinese Association of Policy Science was founded in 1992. Policy research as a relatively independent branch and a field of inquiry was set high on the agenda of building disciplined inquiry in universities.

Nationwide, departments and institutes of public administration emerged in quick succession. Policy science/analysis became part of undergraduate and postgraduate programmes. Outside the national educational system, in accordance with the introduction of civil service, China established its national academies of administration to provide in-service training for civil servants. Policy science/analysis was listed as part of the core courses (Xu 2002: 450–1).

Looking back on the development of policy science in the past one-and-a-half decades, its close correlation with China's reform stands out. The growth of policy research and the demands for reforms of the old policy-making and administrative systems to improve policy-making efficiency and administration level have complemented each other. Such governmental 'demands' have been, and will continue to be, the dynamics for developing policy research in China, as China faces even more challenges in its social, political and economic development.

As some have emphasised, globalisation is the most fundamental challenge facing education in its history, the precise nature of the challenge, however, will not be uniform across, or even within, different countries. One major problem of the existing literature has been a tendency for arguments about globalisation to be based on sweeping generalisations and abstract theoretical assertions insufficiently connected to detailed examinations of particular historical times and geographical spaces (Yang 2002). Meanwhile, there has been a growing body of literature that discusses the increasingly intensified cross-national travelling of education policy (Seddon 2005), concerned with a process in which knowledge about policies, administrative arrangements, institutions and ideas in one political setting is used in the development of policies, administrative arrangements, institutions and ideas in another political setting (Dolowitz and Marsh 2000). Although the concept of policy borrowing is central to much of the work of comparativists (Phillips and Ochs 2003), empirical comparative studies are lacking.

Within such a context, the purpose of this chapter is to document the ways in which global policy agendas are steering education research as a means of shaping socioeconomic development in China. The strategy used here is to review a significant journal over a number of years to document the trends in China's education policy research. The journal is *China Renda Social Science Information Centre-Education*, which selects the best articles from a wide range of education journals nationwide and reprints them monthly. It has been regarded as the most authoritative collection of journal articles in education in China. In 2003, it opened a new column normally entitled 'educational policy-making and administration'. I have used this column to analyse the main dimensions of education policy research. My review covers all of the 24 issues during 2003–04.

The status quo of education policy research in China

Policy research in China covers three major domains. The first is conceptual, often called 'disciplinary building' in China. It aims at provision of university undergraduate and postgraduate programmes mainly in political sciences, public and business administration, and focuses on systematic exposition of basic concepts, principles, theories and methods in policy science and analysis. Earlier studies were heavily influenced by theories and methods of scientific socialism imported from the former Soviet Union. Since the 1990s, the USA has become a dominant source of influence. Another domain is methodological, centred on approaches and tools employed in policy research, and concentrated particularly in the 1980s. The mainstream is to borrow the methods from natural sciences, mathematics and statistics to study the 'scientificness', feasibility and optimisation of large-scale social planning and projects. The third is strategic, usually organised by various specified governmental departments to find solutions to the economic and social problems they face.

China's policy science within the past one-and-a-half decades has shown some striking features. First, it has aimed focally on how the Chinese Communist Party (CCP) and the government guide and normalise social behaviours, with emphases on the character and functions of public policies to normalise social actions, guide socio-economic development and adjust social benefits. Current university textbooks and references books listed for the entrance examination into postgraduate programmes demonstrate this clearly: most of the discussions on social and economic factors as policy contexts are brief and vague, while discussions of the nature and characteristics of public policy always stress public policy's function to normalise social behaviours and control.

For example, Zhang Jin-ma (1992: 19–20) defines public policy as 'the code of, or guidance for, individual and group conducts. It takes many forms including law, regulations, administrative decrees, and governmental written or verbal statements, instructions, action plans, and strategies'. Similarly, Chen Qing-yun (1996: 9) insists that 'public policy is the code of conduct made by the government on the basis of the specific goals under certain circumstances in the processes of selecting, synthesizing, allocating and implementing public interests'.

Research on public policy was concerned with how to better reflect the CCP's and the government's existing goals to guide and normalise social behaviours. Much less attention was paid to how policy makers' intentions, the interests of influential agencies and other stakeholders, impact on policy making.

Secondly, policy research has been classified within the boundaries of public administration, seen as a theoretical tool to upgrade policy-making level and improve policy administration efficiency. This shows partially the political demand for policy science in China. Since the 1980s, profound changes have been taking place in all aspects of Chinese society. While the government was in a situation where social issues were intricate, ever-changing and emerging constantly, the legal system was underdeveloped, civil servants were poorly trained, and the society was ruled more by 'man' than by law.

A priority is thus to reform the outdated policy-making system and methods. Chinese national leaders then identified 'scientification' and 'democratisation' of policy making as key issues of political reform, in order to upgrade government officials' policy-making level and to build up a systematic policy-making system with clearly defined procedures, support, consultation and evaluation systems to guarantee smooth reform progress (Wan 1986).

To meet such political demands, policy researchers have concentrated their attention on issues at system level and on aspects of normative choices, for example, how to optimise policy plans in policy making and raise policy implementation level. Empirical studies of the impact of various political factors in the policy process have been largely neglected. Such an orientation is in line with the training of civil servants and the Chinese government's intension to improve its policy-making level.

Thirdly, policy research serves government departments directly, providing them with policy suggestions and interpretations of existing policies. Years of reform have led to significant changes in social, economic and policy structures, especially since the 1990s. In the face of a large number of social problems, Chinese intellectuals have expressed their keenness on policy-related research. Most of their academic training backgrounds were in other fields other than policy science. They work in governmental departments or policy research institutes affiliated to governments, and have easy access to the policy information circulated only within the government. Their research targets specific policies. Research findings are in the form of specific policy analysis reports, policy plans with detailed suggestions, interpretations of specific policies and historical explanation and analyses of policies. Such research aims for governmental approval and acceptance in order to exert impact on public policy making.

These features of public policy research in China are all shared by education policy studies, to which we will now turn.

Themes

China's policy researchers rely heavily on political elites and government departments. Their research is oriented to the intentions and demands of dominant politicians and to the interests of the government departments to which they are affiliated jurisdictionally. Their choices of topics and values are inevitably influenced by political intentions and interests.

Education policy research in China is stressed by the Chinese government as the basis for rational policy making. As a consequence, it is well planned and highly organised by governmental agencies and professional bodies affiliated to governments. An organisational structure for developing research projects exists at both national and local levels. Policy guidelines for research are formulated by a central authority and research priorities are determined in light of national socioeconomic and educational development goals as well as through central and local mechanisms.

Under the general supervision of the Ministry of Education (MOE), the central mechanism for organising research projects is the National Steering Committee on Educational Research Planning (NSCERP), which is composed of high-ranking educational policy makers, prominent scholars and educational practitioners. The research structure consists of basically two parallel yet interacting systems of research organisations. One is governmental, including educational research institutes affiliated to education administrations at central and local levels. The other system is composed of professional organisations, with the Chinese Association for Educational Research being the largest. Under this scenario, research orientations, policies, priority fields, funding arrangements and macro-level evaluation are all laid down by central government agencies.

At the top of the structure is the MOE, which formulates five-year and ten-year educational development plans, upon which both educational research policies and priorities are to be based. MOE also allocates funds for educational research projects through two channels: its own departments which sponsor policy-oriented studies, and the NSCERP for 'MOE-level priority' projects. Within the MOE, the Department of Policy Studies and Legislation, and the Centre for Studies on National Educational Development, focus on macro-level educational planning and long- and medium-term development strategies. The National Institute for Educational Studies, as a research arm of the MOE, formulates research policies, coordinates research projects by local and university-based research institutes, and disseminates research findings.

Priority fields of educational research are determined according to the objectives of the national socioeconomic development programmes, based on the practical needs of educational development and reforms, and funded in light of available resources. Priority projects are generally of two types. The first, self-proposed projects by individual institutions and researchers submitted to the NSCERP, are very limited in number. The second, guided projects proposed by the NSCERP, are for nationwide bidding. Applications for priority projects need to be first approved by the administrative heads of the institution where the applicant is employed, screened by the MOE, and then reviewed by the NSCERP for approval. Projects are financed according to their levels of priority, overwhelmingly by governments at different levels.

Superficially, there is a division between various research institutions: university-based research tends to follow along disciplinary lines, while research units within governmental agencies mainly conduct policy-oriented studies for overall planning and macro-level development strategy and management. A closer look reveals the powerful dominance of the government. First, the reputation and amount of funding depend on the level of the funding by government. Researchers try desperately to win funding from the government, with little time, energy and interest left for self-chosen topics.

Secondly, publication of research outputs in China depends on whether or not they meet the prevailing ideo-political needs. Those meeting the criteria are reprinted by nationally leading journals such as the professional *Renda* Social Science Information Centre or more generally by *Xinghua Digest*. Authors of these selected articles would obtain greater professional recognition and further financial gains. By acknowledging research and researchers in this way, individual policy researchers' topics are often very similar to state priorities and aspirations.

For example, of the 114 articles reprinted by *China Renda Social Science Information Centre-Education* in 2003–04, 25 (21.9 per cent) were on educational reforms; 18 (16 per cent) on theoretical studies of educational policy; 12 (10.5 per cent) on *minban* (private) education including privatisation; 11 (9.6 per cent) on educational legislation and legal issues of school activities; 9 (7.9 per cent) on regional disparities, rural education and educational development in China's far west; 7 (6.1 per cent) respectively on educational investment and school effectiveness including principalship; 5 (4.4 per cent) on commercialisation of education; 4 (3.5 per cent) respectively on curriculum, equity, teacher education, basic education, and China's collaboration with international organisations including especially the WTO. These topics are precisely in line with the priorities identified by the central government. They also parallel international agendas, showing Chinese policy researchers are sharing global policy experience to resolve their local problems.

Researchers

Mao Zedong once said metaphorically that China's intellectuals are like hair, which must attach itself to the skin of the ruling class. Dating back to the Spring and Autumn Period (770–475 BC) and the Warring States Period (475–221 BC), the Chinese ancient scholar-gentry were a tool in the service to the ruling class. Rulers commonly attracted a large group of scholars for their own purposes. This was part and parcel of their art of ruling.

With this tradition, Chinese intellectuals have always been aligned with official ideologies (Wang 1996; Misra 1998). Their academic life has, since 1950, been tightly controlled in terms of academic growth and development, research focuses and intellectual and ideological directions. Although there have been increasing opportunities for them to avoid being directly involved in politics within the ongoing reform process, very few have taken advantage of this.

Intellectuals refer to a group of educated people who maintain a sense of distance from, and remain critical towards, the mainstream society. The Chinese equivalent term for intellectual is *zhishi fenzi*. The first two characters mean cognition, thus *zhishi fenzi* are those who have knowledge of the world and themselves. Barmé (1996) questioned the difference between Chinese ancient scholar-gentry and today's intellectuals. While a defining feature of the Western concept of intellectual is its critical spirit, the primary characteristic of China's ancient scholar-gentry was that they were would-be officials who are willing to die for a ruler who appreciated them. There was a powerful emotional hold that the rulers had over the scholar-gentry class.

Policy researchers in China are today's Chinese intellectuals. They have carried forward some of the traditions of their predecessor-Chinese ancient scholar-gentry. Just as Mao Zedong satirised, Chinese intellectuals have no alternative but to attach themselves to the new 'skin' – the CCP and the government it controls. In a deeply politicised society with a high degree of surveillance and monitoring, most of them are essentially 'hired scribblers'. Like their predecessors, their role has been to integrate people into the existing society, rather than to critique that society. Chinese policy researchers are servants of the national elite. They are, to borrow Bourdieu's pithy aphorism, the 'dominated faction of the dominant class', the elaborators of cultural capital, the shape of which is given to them but which they do not for the most part create.

The nineteenth century saw the diffusion of the European model of the university throughout much of the world, under conditions of imperialism and colonialism. With the establishment of China's first modern university (Hayhoe 1996), Western intellectual concept and practice were slowly introduced into China. Such an ideal, however, has always been fragile. Chinese policy researchers are facing a similar trend towards an eroding public position of intellectuals, as in Western societies: new forms of political and economic domination in which expert knowledge is increasingly the domain of technicians not 'thinkers', and in which political decisions are made and political morality framed without reference to the intellectuals who were once the source of the important ideas in the public domain (Posner 2001). With the death of ideology, the ideologues become redundant, and the traditional role of intellectuals, as the voice of integrity and courage to speak out against those in power (Said 1994), is disappearing.

Among the 129 authors of the 114 selected articles, 3 were working in schools, 19 worked in policy research institutes under direct jurisdiction of the central and provincial governments, and 107 were based at universities studying education policy. For these university-based researchers, the professionalisation of intellectual life has shaded into careerism. Being an academic is little different from any other civil service job (Bauman 1987). In this context, the knowledge that has been produced within the formal higher learning system is highly professionalised but less critical. Organic intellectuals, as defined by Gramsci (1999), are becoming rare. Many Chinese policy researchers as intellectuals have retreated from the public sphere and focused on their specialised fields. Their sense of calling is being replaced by a sense of vocation.

Such lack of independent, critical thinking is evidenced by the fact that none of the total 114 reprinted articles specifically on educational policy offered any real criticism of the government. On the contrary, many sang the praises of government policies, while others strove to be the first to express their support. These articles, as research outputs, also show that China's education policy researchers are carefully avoiding highly detailed evaluation of the actual effects of existing policies.

Policy transfer is not an independent process but is part of the wider policy process and shaped by such a process. While policy transfer involves primarily the state, as well as international organisations, with key actors being bureaucrats and politicians, the above profile of Chinese policy researchers demonstrates their involvement in the import of ideas as well.

Perspective

Research perspective illustrates an important part of the present situation of China's education policy studies:[3] how Chinese researchers justify their choice and the particular use of methodology and methods. Based on their research outputs, an overwhelming majority of them hold an objectivist view. This perspective is also in line with the official stance. They believe that understandings and values are objectified in the people who are studying. Academic publications and official policy texts have demonstrated this belief clearly: if they go in the right way, they can discover the objective truth.

This stance began to influence educational research in China in the twentieth century and gradually occupied a dominant position (Shi 2004). By the late 1990s, objectivism had been deeply rooted in China's educational research circle, embedded in every aspect of daily work, including researchers' beliefs, their research goals and the way they conduct research.

The following summary by Ding (2004) serves as a good example:

> Major methods in educational research have long been literature review and logical reasoning. With the integration of other disciplines in natural and social sciences and the speed of world process of globalisation, we must conform to international practice and methods, advocate scientifically-based research, normalise our methods and behaviours, improve our research quality in order to achieve scientification of our educational research and serve our educational practice and policy-making.

According to most Chinese policy researchers, the social sciences have historically fallen behind natural sciences in their value orientations and methods. This explains their low efficacy in solving practical problems and in promoting social progress. The emergence of modern natural sciences exposed such flaws and urged people to reform social sciences. They further believe that Marxism accomplished the scientification of social research. Karl Marx is indisputably regarded as the most prominent figure in modern history of social sciences.

However, with a different research tradition for thousands of years, and especially after decades of tight control of the state, the reality of China's education policy research is a mix of traditional Confucian ethical sermon, Chinese interpretation of Marxism and policy explanation and/or justification in line with governments. China's education policy research relies overwhelmingly on the traditional Chinese way of argumentation. Their findings are often bogged down in a quagmire of empty remarks. Some Chinese policy researchers are dissatisfied with this situation and turn to Western theoretical constructions, treating the Western as 'the universal' and gold standard without really understanding them (Xu 2002: 450).

Based on research methods, among the 114 scholarly articles on China's education policy carried by *China Renda Social Science Information Centre-Education* during 2003–04, there were 78 commentaries; 15 personal assertions; 5 literature reviews; 4 descriptive, quantitative (statistical), and comparative respectively; 2 case studies, 1 historical; and 1 project report based on empirical work. It is evident that the overwhelming majority were personal reflections, lacking theoretical contribution and short of tight logical reasoning. This echoes, yet is even worse than, the general situation of China's educational research (Yang 2005). Many Chinese education policy studies are like fast-food: they can still be welcomed for their suitability to the ideo-political occasions and for most influential social groups, although they are superficial and far-fetched.

What China's education policy research circle has demonstrated is similar to what Mazrui (1975: 330) cautioned African countries against many years ago, that is, to adopt a second Western derived orthodox, Marxism-Leninism. The difference in China's case is that the patterns to be reformed were not imposed by former colonisers, but invited by the Chinese themselves. Interestingly, Mazrui suggested that African countries should develop their indigenous languages and culture in a domestication of the colonial heritage, and should diversify the sources of knowledge they brought into the university drawing upon scholarship from China and other regions.

Internationally, preponderance to positivism and inadequate conceptualisation of the role of subjective perception and judgement has been recognised as a shortfall in the literature (Dolowitz and Marsh 1996). People are becoming dissatisfied with the inability of Western science to describe all that occurs in people's experience of the world. Some have launched passionate attacks on the 'paradigmatic tyranny' of the natural sciences (Rahnema 2001), turning their thoughts to indigenisation. As a movement of self-reflection, indigenisation is a response to the long-term Western domination of social studies (Yeh 1994), and integrates one's reflections on the local into her/his approaches.

The calls for indigenisation have been heard for decades in the greater China region (Yang and Wen 1982, Wang 1996), and recently from a few mainland Chinese education researchers (Lu 2001). While this provides China's social scientists with a unique opportunity, China's education policy studies have displayed a positivist picture, demonstrating that Chinese researchers are attempting to emulate the Western objectivist epistemology. Most of them would agree with Parsons' (1977: 61) view that 'There is not "natural" or "cultural" science; there is only science or non-science and all empirical knowledge is scientific in so far as it is valid.'

The shortage of a critical indigenous perspective is common in mainland China's education policy research today. Indigenous Chinese wisdom and the imported Western knowledge have never been on an equal footing in China's education policy research. It is the Western experience that has always been dominant. The introduction of Western theories and methods was, is and will be seen as China's real need. The imported knowledge, however, is always highly contextualised (Wallerstein 1996), and needs to be substantially modified when applied in China. It is here that China's practice has fallen short.

While going much further, the Chinese situation confirms Popkewitz and Lindblad's (2000) criticism towards the literature in general that education policy research tends to accept the discourses of policy as the governing structures for research, and becomes bound to the policy makers' definition of the problem, taking the categories and problem definitions derived from governmental policies as the problems of research without any serious intellectual scrutiny.

Referencing

Referencing further illustrates the *status quo* of China's education policy studies, since it is crucial for Chinese education policy researchers to have a thorough knowledge of the subject matter and the ability to understand the intent of previous writers in their fields. Original research reviews the existing literature and adds a new dimension to an ongoing debate. The researcher must have the ability to see through a vast accumulation of factual data and expressed opinion in order to determine the central points of debate. Moreover, referencing demonstrates Chinese policy researchers' knowledge of the local and the global.

This, however, is not the case in China. According to Fan (2000: 42), among the publications of 395 surveyed 'core social science journals' in 1995, only 36.44 per cent (2,500 out of 6,823) listed references. In education, 165 publications included references with a percentage of 26.7. Fan (2000: 55–8) went on to show that 24.4 per cent of the referenced literature in educational research were newspaper articles, 32.11 per cent translated works (of which an overwhelming proportion were works by Karl Marx, Friedrich Engels and Vladimir Lenin), 27.34 per cent Chinese classics and reference books, and 2.75 per cent government documents, archives and degree theses. From 1978 to 1995, the number of cited foreign literature did not change much. Over the 18 years, their percentages ranged from 0 to 1.85 of the total references with only one year when there was more than 2 per cent (2.12).

In educational research in 1995, 74.31 per cent of the cited sources were originally in Chinese, 10.83 per cent translated foreign literature, 4.22 per cent in foreign languages and 10.64 per cent were unclear in terms of the original language. It remains rare for mainland Chinese educational researchers to publish internationally, even more so in foreign languages.[4] Few publications produced by Chinese social scientists appear in internationally reputable journals. International publications by mainland China's social scientists increased from 80 in 1985 to 202 in 1996, despite that Chinese governments and universities having taken initiatives in encouraging international publications in social sciences (Fan 2000: 60–2).

The situation of education policy research is very similar. The 114 articles carried by *China Renda Social Science Information Centre-Education* during 2003–04 listed 803 references. On average, each article contained 7.1 references. The most cited were Chinese books (273 in total or 33.99 per cent), and the second were Chinese journal articles (206 in total or 25.65 per cent). There were 165 (20.54 per cent) translated works, among them 159 were from English originally. The references in foreign languages numbered 71 (8.84 per cent), among them 67 were in English. The numbers of cited newspaper articles, policy documents, website resources, Marxist works and Chinese ancient writings were respectively 38 (4.72 per cent), 24 (2.98 per cent), 16 (1.99 per cent), 13 (1.61 per cent), and 4 (0.49 per cent).

Compared with Fan's (2000) findings, there had been a considerable increase of references cited in each article. Yet, 15 articles did not list any references. The increase of foreign language references was dramatic. Here, the authors were divided. While many did not cite any foreign literature, an increasing number were relying on foreign resources almost exclusively. One article by a returnee included 32 references, all in English. It is also evident that different writers have a striking variety of sources to cite, and different fields of studies have different pools of literature resources. For example, while many rarely cited newspapers references, one author, who did not have any foreign languages, listed 8 out of 13 and 12 out of 22 respectively in his two articles on rural education. Other features included declining citation of Marxist classics and dramatic increase of citation of website resources.

Together with the growing use of Westernised theories illustrated in the above section, the increasing use of English language sources has also resulted from the fact that international organisations, *inter alia* the World Bank, advocate and even enforce similar policies in China, despite China's strong state. This further shows that Chinese policy makers and researchers now look to other political systems for knowledge and ideas about institutions and policies and about how they work in other jurisdictions.

Conclusions: dilemmas and directions

Driven by practical problems, China's policy research is in an active state. It has, however, maintained a low theoretical level. Since the 1980s, it has borrowed theories and methods directly from other disciplines and from the West. Many researchers come from scientific socialism, attracted by the rise of policy science. They have brought in the theories and methods from scientific socialism, and applied the philosophical, especially dialectical materialist, theories indiscriminately to interpret policy phenomena, policy-making process and their relations with socioeconomic contexts. Due to theoretical emptiness and dogmas, their approaches can hardly offer any effective theoretical guidance to China's education policy studies.

The other source is Western (mainly American) policy research and theoretical constructions. Western theories and methods of policy studies flooded into China especially in the 1990s. They have propelled China's policy research forward. Meanwhile, problems are looming large. A clear shortage of comprehensive, systematic study of the imported Western theories and methods has led to superficial, fragmentary understandings of them. In practice, the application of these seemingly 'advanced' theories and methods often ends up with a blunder (Chen 2000). Without deep knowledge of their localities, indiscriminate use of Western theories and methods has failed to help China define, recognise and formulate policy problems, let alone providing effective solutions (Hu 2000). The identification of wrong problems could be a fatal mistake in policy analysis (Dunn 1988; Dryzek and Ripley 1988).

Education policy research in China lacks academic norms. Research outputs are full of subjective and random judgements, without sufficient reflection on the actuality of policy phenomena and their processes. Policy research endeavour is directly controlled by political ideologies and value orientation (Xu 2002). Here, China has much to learn from the Western policy research norms and the spirit of 'speaking truth to power' (Wildavsky 1979; Weimer and Vining 2005).

To extricate itself from such predicaments, China's policy research needs to understand both the strengths and the limitations of Western theories and methods, resulting from their specific times and spaces, when they are used in the Chinese context, and move towards indigenisation. Instead of making remarks as outsiders, Chinese policy researchers need to develop their unique perspectives and values based on rich local experience. This is an awareness of their local society and culture. Such a sense of locality would allow Chinese policy researchers to seize the initiative in identifying the real needs of their local societies and in setting up their own research agendas and targets.

Following the identification of local needs and research targets, there is a need for a large amount of empirical studies of local policy practice. Due to the uniqueness of Chinese culture and China's different social structure, international mainstream policy theories and methods, which are based almost entirely on longstanding empirical researches in the West, cannot be simply applied in analysing China's education policies.

A major task ahead is to search for locally effective theories and methods. A great quantity of empirical studies of local education policies will pave the way for the development of China's education policy research.

Our turbulent and unpredictable times are also ideal for localised struggles to create new forms of knowledge and power, free from the tyranny of massive and totalising ideologies (Sieber 1981, Hogwood and Peters 1985, Kothari 1987, Brenkman 1987). The above analysis shows that Chinese education policy researchers are far from responding to this momentous challenge. The majority have taken the rationality and progressiveness of science as an obvious fact. Although well positioned by the wealth of unique cultural heritages and the huge demographic and geographical size with sufficient centre of gravity to operate with relative autonomy, the practice of China's education policy studies shows that Chinese social researchers are losing their opportunities to contribute more substantially to nurturing an international knowledge order that reflects and supports the rich diversity in access to knowledge around the world, and that counteracts the tendency towards homogeneity and standardisation fuelled by the interests of technology, communication and commerce.

With absorption of Western knowledge as the pressing matter of the moment, China's real effort is to 'upgrade' academic programmes based on Western experience. Despite the conventional posture on Chinese culture and society as both a starting-point and the final settling place, the wealth of educational knowledge and experience in Chinese rich civilisation is often missing in education policy studies. Indigenous Chinese knowledge has been given little opportunity to influence the ideas and practices of policy research. They are seldom presented as established and coherent sets of beliefs, and are largely devalued and even ignored as processes or coherent methods of learning and teaching. Fundamental assumptions of Chinese indigenous knowledge have been excluded by the very nature of the dominant Western paradigm to a surprising extent, despite the enormous potential for a melding of values from Western academic traditions with aspects of the Chinese traditional scholarship (Hayhoe 2001).

Lacking a focus on the local policy context (Steiner-Khamsi 2005), and with a research steering from the global/West, Chinese policy researchers are taking on the Western science rather than negotiating it in relation to their own local customs and tradition. They have actively, and relatively uncritically, engaged with cross-national policy borrowing. I would offer a caution and suggest closer and more critical examination of the trajectories of education policy in China. There is a need to continually – and critically – navigate 'the local' within 'the global' as policies evolve. This last point about the importance of context-specific differences returns me to my introductory discussion about hybridisation, which allows for a combination of elements to make up the final programme package for policy transfer. A best policy practice does not qualify as best practice under changed constellations. The substantive elements of one programme, although successful in one location, may require a fundamentally different delivery mechanism for it to be effective in another. This 'missing piece' can be copied or emulated from a second location.

Notes

1 After being closed to international intercourse for decades, China adopted its policy of opening to the outside world at the Third Plenary Session of the Eleventh Central Committee of the Communist Party of China held in December 1978.

2 Emancipating the mind has been closely related to the initiation of China's reform and opening programme. In 1978 when the Cultural Revolution had just ended, the national economy was on the brink of collapse. Chinese people were expecting that everything distorted and disordered during the Cultural Revolution would be set to rights. However, some individual central leaders stuck to their leftist stand under the banner of the 'two whatevers' (whatever decision Chairman Mao made should be resolutely safeguarded; whatever instructions Chairman Mao gave should be unswervingly carried out), which actually meant to safeguard the mistakes of Mao Zedong in his later years and the erroneous 'Cultural Revolution'. A philosopher at Nanjing University published an article and concluded that the 'two whatevers' were essentially characterised by idealist empiricism, negating the basic Marxist viewpoint that practice is the criterion for judging truth. The article evoked repercussions nationwide, while people clinging to the 'two whatevers' tried to stifle the discussion. At this critical juncture, Deng Xiao-ping, strongly supported the discussion and delivered a speech titled Emancipating the Mind, Seeking Truth from Facts and Uniting as One in Advancing Forward at the Central Working Conference held before the Third Plenary Session of the Eleventh Central Committee of the Communist Party of China. The speech served both as the best summary of the nationwide debates over the criterion for truth, and as the theme report to the Third Plenary Session of the Eleventh Central Committee of the Communist Party of China, which became a turning point in modern China's historical development, for it advocating foci on economic development and instituting the reform and opening programme. Indeed, the discussion marked the beginning of modern China's emancipation of the mind.

3 I tend to use terms such as 'perspective' and 'tradition' instead of 'paradigm'. This is because when Kuhn introduced 'paradigm' into the philosophy of science, he used the term in relation to natural sciences. Kuhn's philosophy and his definition of paradigm originated from his observation of the relation between natural and social sciences. He noted the differences between the debates among social scientists and those among natural scientists (Giddens 1996).

4 By the time, it had become much less rare, however, for some of them to publish in Chinese in Hong Kong, Macau, Taiwan and Singapore.

References

Barmé, G.R. (1996) *Shades of Mao: The Posthumous Cult of the Great Leader*, Armonk, NY: M. E. Sharpe.

Bauman, Z. (1987) *Legislators and Interpreters: On Modernity, Post-modernity and Intellectuals*, Ithaca, NY: Cornell University.

Brenkman, J. (1987) *Culture and Domination*, Ithaca, NY: Cornell University Press.

Chen, Qing-yun (1996) *Gonggong Zhengce Fenxi* (Public Policy Analysis), Beijing: China Economy Press (in Chinese).

Chen, Zhen-ming (2000) 'Ershiyi shiji zhongguo zhengce kexue de yanjiu fangxiang (Research trends of China's policy science in the twenty-first century)', *Journal of Beijing Academy of Administration*, 1: 9–10 (in Chinese).

Ding, Jie (2004) 'Understanding problems in educational research and promoting educational development)'. Online. Available HTTP: http://www.cnier.ac.cn/wendang/2003122401.htm (accessed on 24 February 2004 in Chinese).

Dolowitz, D.P. and Marsh, D. (1996) 'Who learns from whom: a review of the policy transfer literature', *Political Studies*, 44(2): 343–57.

Dolowitz, D.P. and Marsh, D. (2000) 'Learning from abroad: the role of policy transfer in contemporary policy-making', *Governance*, 13(1): 5–23.

Dryzek, J.S. and Ripley, B. (1988) 'The ambitions of policy design', *Policy Studies Journal*, 7(4): 705–19.

Dunn, W.N. (1988) 'Methods of the second type: coping with the wilderness of conventional policy analysis', *Policy Studies Journal*, 7(4): 720–37.

Fan, Bing-si (2000) *Dangdai Zhongguo Shehuikexue Baokan Wenxian Fenxi: 1978–1995* (An Analysis of Contemporary China Journal and Newspaper Social Science Literature: 1978–1995), Shanghai: East China Normal University Press (in Chinese).

Giddens, A. (1996) *In Defence of Sociology: Essays, Interpretations and Rejoinders*, Cambridge: Polity Press.

Gramsci, A. (1999) *Selections from the Prison Notebooks*, New York: International Publishers.

Hayhoe, R. (1996) *China's Universities 1895–1995: A Century of Cultural Conflict*, New York: Garland.

Hayhoe, R. (2001) 'Lessons from the Chinese academy', in R. Hayhoe and J. Pan (eds) *Knowledge Across Cultures: A Contribution to Dialogue among Civilizations*, Hong Kong: Comparative Education Research Centre, University of Hong Kong.

Hogwood, B.W. and Peters, B.G. (1985) *The Pathology of Public Policy*, Oxford: Clarendon Press.

Hu, Xiang-ming (2000) 'Zhengce kexue de zhongguohua yu lilun chuangxing (Sinocisation and theoretical innovations of policy science), *Journal of Beijing Academy of Administration*, 1: 10–11 (in Chinese).

Kothari, R. (1987) 'On human governance', *Alternatives*, 12(8): 277–90.

Lu, Jie (2001) 'On the indigenousness of Chinese pedagogy', in R. Hayhoe and J. Pan (eds) *Knowledge Across Cultures: A Contribution to Dialogue among Civilizations*, Hong Kong: Comparative Education Research Centre, University of Hong Kong.

Mazrui, A. (1975) 'The African university as a multinational corporation', *Harvard Education Review*, 45(2): 191–210.

Meng, Fan-sen (1983) 'Xuyao jianli yimen yanjiu dan he guojia shengming de kexue – zhengcexue (There is a need to build up policy science to study the life of our Party and our nation)', *Lilun Tantao* (Theoretical Enquiry) 7: 17–21 (in Chinese).

Misra, K. (1998) *From Post-Maoism to Post-Maxism: The Erosion of Official Ideology in Deng's China*, New York and London: Routledge.

Nóvoa, A. and Lawn, M. (2002) *Fabricating Europe: The Formation of an Education Space*, Dordrecht: Kluwer.

Parsons, T. (1977) 'Value-freedom and objectivity', in F.R. Dallmayr and T.A. McCarthy (eds) *Understanding and Social Inquiry*, Notre Dame: University of Notre Dame Press.

Phillips, D. and Ochs, K. (2003) 'Processes of policy borrowing in education: some explanatory and analytical devices', *Comparative Education*, 39(4): 451–61.

Popkewitz, T. and Lindblad, S. (2000) 'Educational governance and social inclusion and exclusion: some conceptual difficulties and problematics in policy and research', *Discourse*, 21(1): 5–44.

Posner, R. (2001) *Public Intellectuals: A Study of Decline*, Cambridge, MA: Harvard University Press.

Rahnema, M. (2001) 'Science, universities and subjugated knowledges: a "Third World" perspective', in R. Hayhoe and J. Pan (eds) *Knowledge Across Cultures: A Contribution to Dialogue among Civilizations*, Hong Kong: Comparative Education Research Centre, University of Hong Kong.

Said, E.W. (1994) *Representations of the Intellectuals: The 1993 Reith Lectures*, New York: Pantheon Books.

Seddon, T. (2005) 'Travelling policy in post-socialist education', *European Educational Research Journal*, 4(1): 1–4.

Shi, Zhong-ying (2004) 'Essentialism, anti-essentialism and pedagogical studies in China', *Educational Research*, 25(1): 11–20 (in Chinese).

Sieber, S.D. (1981) *Fatal Remedies*, New York: Plenum.

Steiner-Khamsi, G. (2005) 'Non-travelling "best practice" for a travelling population: the case of nomadic education in Mongolia', *European Educational Research Journal*, 4(1): 22–35.

Stromquist, N.P. (2002) *Education in a Globalised World: The Connectivity of Economic Power, Technology, and Knowledge*, Lanham, MD: Rowman and Littlefield.

Wallerstein, I. *et al.* (1996) *Open the Social Sciences: Report of the Gulbenkian Commission on the Restructuring of the Social Sciences*, Stanford, CA: Stanford University Press.

Wan, Li (1986) 'Juece minzhuhua he kexuehua shi zhengzhi tizhi gaige de yige zhongyao keti (The democratisation and scientification of policy-making is an important task for political reform)', *Renmin Ribao* (People's Daily), 15 August: 1.

Wang, Jing (1996) *Higher Culture Fever: Politics, Aesthetics, and Ideology in Deng's China*, Berkeley, CA: University of California Press.

Weimer, D.L. and Vining, A.R. (2005) *Policy Analysis: Concepts and Practice*, Upper Saddle River, NJ: Pearson Prentice Hall.

Well, T. (2005) 'Educational policy networks and their role in policy discourse, action, and implementation', *Comparative Education Review*, 49(1): 109–17.

Wildavsky, A.B. (1979) *Speaking Truth to Power: The Art and Craft of Policy Analysis*, Boston, MA: Little, Brown.

Xu, Xiang-lin (2002) 'Zhengce kexue de lilun kunjing yu bentuhua (Theoretical dilemmas and indigenisation of policy science)', in 'Beida Forum' Editorial Committee (ed.) *Ershiyi Shiji: Renwen Yu Shehui* (The Twenty-first Century: Humanity and Society), Beijing: Peking University Press (in Chinese).

Yang, Kuo-shu and Wen, Chung-I (eds) (1982) *The Sinicisation of Social and Behavioural Science Research in China*, Taipei: Institute of Ethnology, Academia Sinica (in Chinese).

Yang, Rui (2002) *Third Delight: The Internationalisation of Higher Education in China*, London and New York: Routledge.

Yang, Rui (2005) 'Internationalisation, indigenisation and educational research in China', *Australian Journal of Education*, 49(1): 66–88.

Yeh, Chi-jeng (1994) 'A sociological analysis of indigenisation in social research', *Hong Kong Journal of Social Sciences* 3(Spring): 52–78 (in Chinese).

Yuan, Zheng-guo (1996) *Jiaoyu Zhengce Xue* (Educational Policy), Nanjing: Jiangshu Education Press (in Chinese).

Zhang, Jin-ma (1992) *Zhengce Kexue Daolun* (Introduction to Policy Science), Beijing: China People's University Press (in Chinese).

Part III

Global–local politics of
educational research

18 Knowledge beyond the knowledge economy

Merely cultural? Merely commercial?
Merely civilizing? [1]

*Johannah Fahey, Jane Kenway,
Elizabeth Bullen and Simon Robb*

Introduction

Every presence defines an absence. When knowledge economy policies define worthwhile knowledges, they leave out those knowledges deemed marginal to current economic growth. They legitimise particular kinds of knowledge whilst ignoring and thus diminishing others. Further, knowledge economy policies seek to determine and control the flow of knowledge and the manner in which it is communicated (Kenway *et al.* 2004; Bullen *et al.* 2004a). Typically, cultural economies and the aesthetic, and by implication arts and humanities disciplines and other knowledges associated with them, are a major absence. They are regarded as incommensurable with the dominant techno-economic paradigm.

Policy conceptualisations of the global knowledge economy have led to the channelling of much research funding into the priority areas of science and technology (Kenway *et al.* 2004a). This policy steering by global policy agencies and diverse national governments around the world raises questions about the future foci, directions and indeed survival of humanities and creative arts faculties and fields in universities – particularly as they have traditionally been conceived. How these faculties and the different disciplines within them might best respond to knowledge economy policies is therefore a question of importance, although one that is yet to be adequately answered. This chapter seeks primarily to contribute to the discussion and debates (see further Kenway *et al.* 2004) and secondly to suggest some implications of this debate for educational research and thereby to assist educational researchers to consider similar isssues.

In the first part of this chapter we will show how one university arts faculty actively engages with and contests the manner in which knowledge economy policies are typically theorised, particularly with regard to innovation. We suggest that this faculty's approach is a significant advance on conventional 'culture free' notions of the knowledge economy. However, drawing on Jean-François Lyotard's critique of knowledge in contemporary society, in the second part of the chapter, we raise some questions about the approach developed by this particular faculty and by implication other similar approaches. In the final section, we seek to advance discussions about the role and value of the humanities and creative arts by drawing on Lyotard's notion of the 'libidinal economy'. In the libidinal economy the radical potential of aesthetic knowledges can be understood as valuable creative forces operating against the techno-economic limits placed on knowledge by policy. We conclude by drawing out some of the implications of this line of analysis for educational research. To pursue our overall argument we draw on interdisciplinary research conducted under the rubric of aesthetic knowledge. Overall, this chapter highlights some ways to enrich understandings of the role of the humanities and creative arts in theorisations of the knowledge economy.

Merely cultural?

The Organization for Economic Cooperation and Development's (OECD) land mark document on the knowledge economy argues that 'in the long run, knowledge, especially technological knowledge, is the main source of economic growth and improvements in quality of life' (OECD 1996: 13). Culture is seen to have little or no connection to economy. Such views are evident in 'Backing Australia's Ability', the Australian government's major innovation policy ensemble introduced in 2001. *Backing Australia's Ability – Building our Future through Science and Innovation* is the most recent Australian science and innovation package totalling a commitment of $5.3 billion over seven years from 2004–05. This package builds on the initial 2001 *Backing Australia's Ability: An Innovation Action Plan for the Future* investment of $3 billion over five years to 2005–06. Together these packages constitute a 10-year, $8.3 billion funding commitment stretching from 2001–02 to 2010–11. *Backing Australia's Ability* represents a commitment to pursue excellence in research, science and technology, through three key themes: the generation of new ideas (R&D); the commercial application of ideas; and developing and retaining skills (Commonwealth of Australia 2004). This innovation agenda privileges techno-scientific orientations to research.

In Australia, this set of policies provoked considerable disquiet amongst the arts, humanities and social sciences communities. For example, in her National Press Club address of 2001, Dr Margaret Seares (Chair of the Australia Council) spoke of the 'benign neglect' (2001: 1) of the arts in Australian public policy, stating:

> We should take note that there is no reflection in the 'Backing Australia's Ability' document – the major innovation policy statement – of the close interconnection that exists between culture, creativity, and innovation. And, in all the discussion that has followed there has been no reference to the potential role of the cultural industries in developing and enhancing Australia's innovation effort.
>
> (Seares 2001: 3)

Seares contrasts this 'neglect' of the arts in Australian public policy with the British Labour Government's Green Paper of 2001, *Culture and Creativity: The Next 10 years* which acknowledges the significant role played by culture and creativity in innovation.[2] It looks:

> forward to a future in which individual creative talent is given the support it needs from childhood to flourish; in which artists and cultural institutions are freed from bureaucratic controls; and in which freedom to explore and enjoy creativity and culture is available to all.
>
> (DCMS 2001, online)

The Green Paper, she says, demonstrates the British government's recognition of the arts as a contributing factor in economic growth. Further, in the Foreword to the Green Paper, Blair proposes that the arts matter 'because they can enrich all our lives' (DCMS 2001). Seares contrasts this to the Australian government's 'neglect' of the arts demonstrated by its inability to incorporate 'culture and creativity into its national innovation agenda' (Seares 2001: 4).

While acknowledging the benefits for universities of increased funding for research and innovation, many from within the academy also believe the government's national innovation agenda is too restricted and that it needs to be opened out to allow it to properly attend to matters of culture, creativity and society. Academics from such fields have thus resisted on a range of fronts, in relation to diverse issues and in a range of ways (see the papers in Kenway *et al.* 2004). For example, the learned academies of the humanities and the social sciences lobbied the Australian government on the issue, and managed to ensure that the National Research Priorities were broadened somewhat. Other academics are reforming their curriculum and research directions within their own institutions so that they might better connect with certain knowledge economy imperatives, but at the same time speak to matters of culture and creativity.

Let us take the case of Cunningham and Hartley (Centre Director of the Creative Industries Research Applications Centre (CIRAC) at Queensland University of Technology (QUT), and Dean of the Creative Industries Faculty at QUT). They maintain 'there's a "commonsense" here that "creativity" means "scientists thinking creatively about innovation"' (Cunningham and Hartley 2001: 7). Cunningham proposes an alternative to this techno-scientific model of innovation, saying 'our sector', which he refers to as 'the applied social and creative disciplines':

> needs to learn to see ourselves as part of the knowledge-based economy and as an integral and arguably central part of any decent innovation/R&D agenda, and to begin to win some degree of recognition for this association.
>
> (Cunningham and Hartley 2001: 7)

In this report, Cunningham not only re-defines 'innovation' by positioning the applied social and creative disciplines as central to this definition, he also re-defines the role of the applied social and creative disciplines within the knowledge-based economy. The worth of the social and creative disciplines is no longer established by their cultural or social function. Where 'their value derives solely from public good arguments' (Hartley *et al.* 2002: 5). Rather, the value of these disciplines is now determined according to their commercial potential, Cunningham says:

> 'creativity' needs to be reconceptualised in line with the realities of contemporary commercial democracies. 'Art' needs to be understood as something *intrinsic*, not *opposed*, to the productive capacities of the contemporary global, mediated, technology-supported economy.
>
> (Cunningham 2001: 3, original emphases)

As innovation and R&D in the applied social and creative disciplines (such as business, education, leisure and entertainment, media and communications) is viewed as being as important to economic growth as innovation and R&D in science and technology, the 'interconnection that exists between culture, creativity, and innovation', which Seares refers to in her address to the Australian National Press Club, is extended to include a commercial dimension. 'We can no longer afford to understand the social and creative disciplines as commercially irrelevant, *merely "civilising"* activities. Instead they must be recognized as one of the vanguards of the new economy' says Cunningham (2002: 9, emphasis added).

In the most comprehensive analysis of the creative industries in Queensland, the Brisbane's Creative Industries 2003 report identified four characteristics that combine to define activity within the creative industries in Australia. The creative industries:

- involve activities which have their origin in individual creativity, skill and talent;
- have the potential for wealth and job creation through generation and exploitation of intellectual property;
- have creative intangible inputs which add more economic and social value than is added by manufacturing;
- encompass and link the traditional cultural industries (such as the performing arts) with the new economy 'info-intensive communication and cultural industries (such as computer game design)' (Cox *et al.* 2003: 6)

In keeping with these criterion, the Creative Industries Faculty at QUT 'is dedicated to the creative aspects of the new economy and the content industries – looking at the development of content and creative technology applications' (QUT 2003: 3).[3] As 'the convergence of broadcasting, telecommunications, and computer communications has reached a stage where technical infrastructure, connectivity and market capitalization ... are well advanced' (QUT 2004, online).

The Creative Industries Faculty at QUT combines teaching and research in creative arts subjects including Communication Design, Creative Writing, Dance, Drama, Fashion Design, Film and Television, Journalism, Media Communication, Music and Sound, and Visual Arts. The faculty represents a move towards reconceptualising the old-school arts and humanities disciplines in terms of the knowledge-based economy as the creative arts subjects offered in this faculty are applied to business and information technologies. And content creation in 'knowledge consumption services' (such as entertainment, education, government, health information and business) becomes the means to realise commercial potential. The Creative Industries Faculty at QUT acknowledges the important economic function of creativity by providing a curriculum where 'creativity' is viewed as 'an enterprise sector' and 'creative industries emerge as the commercial, or commercializable, applications of creativity' (Cunningham and Hartley 2001: 4). For example, the Bachelor of Creative Industries, which 'prepares you to work as an entrepreneur in the global knowledge economy', entices prospective students by maintaining it is at 'the forefront of entrepreneurial, cultural, commercial and creative developments' (QUT 2004, online).

Cunnningham and Hartley contribute to the debate on the future of the arts and humanities in the current policy environment by using the language of knowledge economy policy to re-define the science and technology led innovation/R&D agenda and incorporate the applied social and creative disciplines:

This thinking broadly suggests that the future of the new economy does not lie solely in the development of scientific or knowledge silos but in the creation and integration of content to develop sustainable interactive environments. It allies individual artistic, design, writing and production talent with the broad social and commercial reach of information technology, media and entertainment.

(Hartley *et al.* 2002: 6)

For Cunningham and Hartley the issue is not simply about recognising 'creativity' as 'an enterprise sector' in the creative industries. It is also about responding to technological change within the knowledge economy; disconnecting technology from science and re-applying it to the creative industries to position these industries as drivers of new technologies. QUT's Cooperative Research Centre (CRC) for Interactive Design, which is part of the Creative Industries Faculty, is the first arts faculty to receive funding for a CRC. The Centre draws on creative, social and technological disciplines with a focused commercial intent: freeing 'new technologies from old ways of thinking' and transforming 'concepts and curiosities into exciting applications and commercial outcomes' (QUT 2004, online). It 'provides one example of how research in the social and creative disciplines can be meaningfully hybridized with basic research in technology, to create new commercial opportunities' (Hartley *et al.* 2002: 1). Research areas include human-computer interaction, user interface design, network capacity and new content production. The research that is pursued considers 'the combination of all these elements as being interaction', an understanding where commercialisation depends on a 'whole product value proposition' (Hartley *et al.* 2002: 8). The emphasis on research in the 'content industries' and interest in human computer interaction means the Interactive Design Centre focuses more on 'knowledge consumption services' than the knowledge production (of science and technology R&D initiatives), understanding that new commercial applications of knowledge are required for the knowledge economy, and recognising that this new economy is consumption driven ('60–70% of GDP' [Hartley *et al.* 2002: 1]).

The hybridisation of the creative industries and technology, in order to realise commercial potentials, explicitly addresses the new model of the knowledge economy that 'is driven by convergence, globalisation and digitisation' (Hartley *et al.* 2002: 5). Furthermore, the interest in 'the complexities of human desire' (Hartley *et al.* 2002: 8) and how users are affected by their interaction with new media content and new technologies acknowledges the role of consumption in the new knowledge economy.

Merely commercial?

The QUT agenda has the important benefit of challenging the reduction of the national innovation system in Australia to science and technology and, in this sense, it has made a major contribution to research policy. However, it also involves a somewhat uncritical acceptance of the notions that technology is the driver of economic growth and that R&D should be primarily steered towards enhancing commercial applications. We grant that the objectives of the Creative Industries Faculty at QUT challenge the techno-*scientific* orientation of innovation in the knowledge economy by acknowledging the role played by the arts and creative disciplines within the innovation process. As Hearn (Research Development Coordinator in the Creative Industries Faculty) argues 'we need to think of innovation in other terms apart from bio-tech' (2002: 3). However, QUTs aesthetic objectives nonetheless conform 'with some variable of performativity' (Bain 1995: 7) as 'the commercialisation agenda ... is a dominant agenda in the faculty' (Hearn 2002: 4). In other words, the creative arts are repackaged under the banner of industry. Grierson elaborates the point:

> Creativity and innovation as fundamental practices of the arts are repositioned via the alignment of creative innovation with an economic model of enterprise.... Whereas the arts as imaginative practice are fed by powers of uncertainty that prevail through creative processes, the arts as industries are driven by the assumed certainty of a teleological end-point of productive worth and economic value.
>
> (Grierson 2003: 5)

Such views, in a sense, exemplify the remarks Lyotard made about knowledge in *The Postmodern Condition: A Report on Knowledge* (1984) where he implicitly but accurately predicts knowledge economy policies. This report was commissioned by the Council of Universities (Provincial Government of Quebec, Canada) in 1979 and discusses the status and function of knowledge in the world's most privileged societies in the final quarter of the twentieth century. In the report, Lyotard discusses the ways in which different ways of knowing about and dealing with the world (science, technology, law, the university system, etc) are understood and valued in contemporary society. He says:

> Knowledge in the form of an informational commodity indispensable to productive power is already, and will continue to be, a major – perhaps *the* major – stake in the worldwide competition for power.
>
> (Lyotard 1984: 5)

In *The Postmodern Condition* Lyotard reflects on some of the defining features and dominant themes of postmodernity: in particular 'the relation between the social fragmentation of contemporary society and the global interconnection of media and markets' (Williams 1998: 1). For Lyotard, rapid developments in science and technology and the global spread of capitalism since the Second World War have put an end to grand narratives. He states 'the project of modernity ... has not been forsaken or forgotten, but destroyed, "liquidated"' (1992: 18). Lyotard believes capitalism is driven by efficiency: as production and consumption are continuously made cheaper and quicker so as to maximise the potential for profit (see further Bullen *et al.* 2004). Knowledge, research and development in contemporary societies are driven by capitalism. Lyotard states:

> Capitalism has been able to subordinate to itself the infinite desire for knowledge that animates the sciences and to submit its achievements to its own criterion of technicity: the rules of performance that requires the endless optimization of the cost/benefit ratio.
>
> (Lyotard 1993b: 25)

While this link between performativity and capitalism is increasingly evident, knowledge economy policies position technology as the catalyst of revolutionary change and tend to locate technology outside of society and culture. In other words, as May says, they stress 'the independence of technology from social forces' (2002: 26). And, as Bimber

(1995: 84) explains, there is an assumption that 'technological developments occur according to some naturally given logic, which is not culturally or socially determined, and that these developments force social adaptation and changes'. Elam (1994) identifies a further consequence of the focus on technology. He argues that, within the neo-Schumpeterian perspective:

> Tangible but impersonal technologies have always been given precedence over the less palpable forces shaping economy and society. Even within the techno-economic sphere itself, the realm of *embodied* technology has continually dominated over that of *disembodied* technology which can now all too easily fall into a catch-all socio-institutional context.
>
> (Elam 1994: 46–7, original emphases)

These forces also drive knowledge economy policies. Techno-scientific knowledge and social and creative knowledge are valuable only if they produce commercial results. Within this rationale all knowledge must have a practical use and produce tangible outcomes; as opposed to being 'merely civilising', providing critical commentary, stimulating public debate or representing not intellectual property but intellectual freedom. Within this system, the logic of performance 'neccessarily involves a certain level of terror: [knowledge must] be operational (that is, commensurable) or disappear' says Lyotard (1984: xxiv). Any kind of knowledge and innovation that cannot be measured by capitalism's standards (based on techno-efficiency and geared towards profit) remains neglected within this system: as 'knowledge is and will be produced in order to be sold, it is and will be consumed in order to be valorized in a new production: in both cases, the goal is exchange' (Lyotard 1984: 4).

As we have argued elsewhere (Bullen *et al.* 2004a, 2004b), research and learning in the arts and humanities are not a luxury (Bigelow 1998). Some of the benefits of humanities research Bigelow (1998: 37) identifies include:

- the vital role it plays in intellectual freedom;
- the indispensable service it provides through critical analysis;
- the provision of a sense of place in history and the world;
- its function as a key player in public culture;
- the preservation and transmission of traditions from one generation to the next;
- the questioning and maintenance of ethical values; and
- thinking constructively about what the future may hold.

However, these things are also largely intangible, certainly not technology-driven, and are problematic in terms of producing measurable economic outcomes – and '*embodied* technologies' (Elam 1994). The benefits of aesthetic knowledges are difficult to measure quantitatively. And this places pressure on university faculties to justify their existence within the techno-economic understandings of the knowledge economy via the rhetoric of technologisation and commercialisation, innovation and hybrisation. Foregrounding the imperative to commercialise, Gillies (2001: 42) iterates some of the particular difficulties commercialisation poses for the humanities and social sciences, but concludes that these disciplines 'risk deeper penury and even depiction as the Luddites of the twenty-first century, unless they can embrace the commercialising spirit'.

Lyotard maintains the postindustrial and postmodern age alters the status of knowledge. Technological transformations, the 'convergence, globalisation and digitisation' referred to by Hartley *et al.*, now dictate the form that knowledge must take. And, according to knowledge economy policies, knowledge must be translatable into marketable and computerised information to be considered valuable: 'the creation and integration of content to develop sustainable interactive environments' promoted by Cunningham and Hartley. Lyotard predicts that as a result:

> Anything in the constituted body of knowledge that is not translatable in this way will be abandoned and that the direction of new research will be dictated by the possibility of its eventual results being translatable into computer language.
>
> (Lyotard 1984: 4)

We do not suggest that the commercial and vocational orientation of the creative industries at QUT is inevitably problematic. Work in the arts and humanities has long existed 'within larger psycho-political-economic-cultural frameworks' (Wilson 2002: 6). What we do suggest however, is that, insofar as the creative industries project responds to the knowledge economy policy paradigm, the knowledge that it counts becomes highly circumscribed. The knowledge that matters in a knowledge-based economy is technological knowledge. The ultimate test of its worth, however, is its commercial value. This leaves some important questions unanswered. Indeed, as arts and humanities faculties like QUT change to meet the demands of these times, new questions arise. How are critical and disciplinary values to be reconciled with market values, the notion of the public intellectual with the entrepreneur, intellectual freedom with intellectual property? What will be the long-term effect of subsuming the traditional disciplines within programmes that are more transparently compatible with the aims, priorities, and rhetoric of knowledge economy policy?

Merely civilising?

According to Williams:

> Lyotard's philosophy rejects the argument that claims that the greatest performance and hence the greatest well-being can be achieved in capitalist systems. Instead, he draws our attention to the necessary injustice of systems dependent on a criterion of performance that cannot be sensitive to radically different ways of living.
>
> (Williams 1998: 4)

Lyotard's *Économie Libidinale* (1993b [1974]) precedes *The Postmodern Condition: A Report on Knowledge* and 'there are many of the characteristic hallmarks of postmodernism [in the text] – the disdain for tradition and its grand narratives, the refusal to enter into debate with one's perceived opponents, the overwhelming sense of scepticism about current cultural values' (Sim 1996: 18). In *Économie Libidinale*, Lyotard moves away from the 'grand narratives' of the Enlightenment project, with its focus on the mind and its privileging of rationality, and towards the postmodern body as a site for the play of libidinal forces and the discharge of energy. Lyotard's philosophy is concerned with the materialist enactment of desire, as he believes it contains the possibility for transformation and the means for critical engagement.[4] Lyotard's philosophy is a synthesis and repudiation of his earlier links with Marx's political economies and Freud's libido theory. Lyotard's perspective is 'not a familiar commonsense view of society … [rather, he] stretches the definition of society to include in it a much stranger underlying matter' (Williams 1998: 12), namely the 'libidinal'. Lyotard 'calls the world "libidinal economic" where society is defined as an economy exploiting and releasing desires and feelings – a fit description of a capitalist society' (Williams 1998: 10).

Lyotard's definition of society as 'libidinal economic' 'involves the description of systems as economies [or "dispositions"] *regulating* the flow of feelings and desires' (Williams 1998: 19, emphasis added). In this context, the 'innovation agenda' in the knowledge economy, consisting 'of the flows and relationships among industry, government and academia' (OECD 1996: 7), is the 'disposition' that 'control[s] feelings and desires … [giving] account of the "proper" use of a feeling or the "proper" way to exploit and satisfy desires' (Williams 1998: 48). 'Innovation' is defined as 'a specific … activity carried out in the economic sphere with a commercial purpose' (Fagerberg 2002: 9). And the production of knowledge, is not simply seen as the generation of new ideas, but rather the generation of new ideas that lead to new products. Overall, this means all 'intensities' are reduced to a desire for profit or a desire to consume.

However, 'although the libidinal economy exploits intensities, it never fully understands or controls them' (Williams 1998: 40). In Lyotard's libidinal economy 'energy is [also] highly unstable. That is, libidinal intensities – feelings and desires – emerge in an *unpredictable* manner' (Williams 1998: 40, emphasis added). Therefore, although capitalism specialises in systematising desire through 'the power of comparison', as desire is by nature excessive, the capitalist system also contains disruptive energy: the 'libidinal excess over and above exchange [which entails] an incommensurability – not an equivalence' (Cooper and Murphy 1999: 231). This libidinal force disturbs consensus from within, and makes possible the emergence of new forms and new voices. In this respect, the libidinal economy is a way to 'explain the paradoxical relation between feelings, affects and desires and the dispositions at the basis of any account of these intensities' (Williams 1998: 50). It is understood as 'the state which calls into question all efforts at "grand narrative closure"' (Sim 1996: 25). There is 'no system without libidinal desires and feelings; no feelings and desires without systems' (Williams 1998: 3). Lyotard's libidinal economy is an economy where different possibilities for knowledge and action exist within a system determined by techno-economic concerns. In Lyotard's libidinal economy the radical political potential of art, and more specifically, the philosophical category called aesthetics,[5] are both valuable creative forces operating against the controls placed on knowledge and power by governments, corporations and the global market.

Let us now consider an example of libidinal energies within a university research setting that might defy the libidinal closure of knowledge economy policies. SymbioticA and its Tissue Culture & Art (TC&A) Project is an initiative in which aesthetic objects provide the means for critique in ways that engage with some of the pressing issues of these times. SymbioticA operates within the Department of Anatomy and Human Biology at the University of Western Australia. However, this is not a science research programme – although it involves tissue engineering – nor is it conducted by scientists. 'SymbioticA is a research laboratory dedicated to the exploration of scientific knowledge in general, and biological technologies in particular, from an artistic and humanistic perspective'

(University of Western Australia 2004, online). Intitiated by Oran Catts, the TC&A Project 'explore[s] questions arising from the use of living tissue to create/grow semi-living objects/sculptures and to research the technologies involved in such a task' (Catts and Zurr 2002: 365).

In Lyotard's discussions of aesthetics, 'it is art's potential to challenge established ideas and systems that remains the point of focus' says Malpas (2003: 89). In the libidinal economy, artistic expression is a force that is irreducible to rational thought and resistant to closure. This form of desire 'belongs to no-one. [It] cannot be assumed, accepted, understood [or] locked up in names' (Lyotard 1993b: 20). It is a force that we can only experience.

The Pigs Wings Installation, which is part of the TC&A Project, uses the adage 'pigs might fly', a common expression describing an event that is extremely unlikely to occur, to highlight the fact that these wing shaped objects, grown using living pig tissue and animated using living muscle, are nascent half-natured, half-cultured organisms belonging to an as yet unrealised future. By creating partial life art organisms the project calls into question new knowledge and raises debate about the direction of biotechnology. This art does not offer direct answers to political and philosophical problems. Rather, it generates questions that challenge set ways of thinking and discourses that attempt to provide all-encompassing explanations and systems. As Lyotard suggests, 'if we are to testify to difference and fragmentation, then we must do so in art' (Williams 1998: 1).

It has been suggested that artists can be a key to innovation and creativity in industry and science because of their ability to 'see things differently' (Australia Council 1999: 1).

> Artists are not only embracing all aspects of computers and telecommunications, but also concepts and artifacts of a wide range of biological and physical sciences and technology. Many are already working collaboratively and successfully with science and technology ... These projects are changing the concept of 'what an artist is' and, more importantly, 'what an artist can do'.
>
> (Australia Council 1999: 2)

Rather than conforming to the rules established by the knowledge economy: where creative endeavour must be reduced to commercial imperatives to be considered valuable, as demonstrated by the Creative Industries Faculty at QUT, the artists working on the TC&A Project 'return us to more fundamental sensations that have become hidden under elaborate forms of thought' (Williams 1998: 6). They achieve this effect by creating partial life entities that are the embodiment of the cultural fears and anxieties generated by developments in biotechnology. As scientific knowledge is explored from an artistic and humanistic perspective the political and critical role of aesthetic experiences and creativity is revealed. Catts says:

> We're not here to make money and I would say that if you put making money as the bottom line of what ever process you are [involved in then] you lose quite a lot of the innovation aspect of it because you are obviously narrowing yourself too much to something that might be sold ... we really see our work as more subversive in the sense that we are suggesting alternatives to biomedical research and also the ways it's being commercialised.
>
> (Catts 2002: 3)

Intentionally contentious and culturally and ethically ambiguous, the ambivalence that tissue culture art provokes in the viewer is designed to draw attention to 'our lack of cultural understanding in dealing with new knowledge and control over nature' (Catts and Zurr 2002: 370). As Catts (2002) explains:

> Developments in technology are actualized possibilities, not necessarily the only ways knowledge can be utilized ... The exploration of contestable possibilities is important to the understanding of the ways technology may develop. By fostering artistic critical engagements with biological research, SymbioticA provides a 'greenhouse' for developing alternatives to the commercial mainstream.
>
> (Catts 2002)

Conclusion

Throughout this chapter we have pointed to some of the limitations of knowledge economy policies. We have indicated that in privileging a techno-economic rationale and a commercial agenda such policies have some major blind spots with regard to cultural and creative economies; these are understood as merely cultural. We have also pointed to some of the ways in which the key edicts of knowledge economy policies have been, and indeed can be, contested by those who work within universities. Such contestations take various shapes and challenge various aspects of knowledge economy policies. We have implied that one of the reasons that those challenges rooted in notions of the cultural or the creative economy are able to achieve momentum is that they draw these economies into alignment with the key commercialising and technologising imperatives of knowledge economy policies. The aesthetic and the libidinal are, as Lyotard makes clear, harnessed in the interests of capitalism's latest inflection. The benefit here is that the relevant fields of arts and humanities knowledge not only survive but thrive. However, no longer understood as merely cultural they run the risk of becoming merely commercial. As we said at the outset, 'every presence defines an absence' and the absence that emerges here is the civil function and public good of the aesthetic knowledges associated with cultural economies. The knowledges generated by arts and humanities disciplines that have a 'merely civilising' critical, not commercial, value have, as a result of this double manoeuvre become further marginalised and diminished. Nonetheless, as we indicated drawing on Lyotard, a feature of libidinal economies is that the libidinal energies of art and aesthetics cannot be readily constrained and contained; they have a radical potential that emerges in unexpected places and forms. The striking irony of the Tissue Culture Project is that it deploys art and science to point very directly to some 'contestable possibilities' that exist in relation to the knowledge economy policies. And in so doing it points to some of the risks that techno science poses for humanity.

There are many questions that the above narratives pose for education as a field of research. The first and most obvious is how is educational research understood in knowledge economy terms? Is it seen as producing or being able to produce the sorts of exploitable knowledge that is so valued by the knowledge economy? Or, is it seen as incommensurable; as merely cultural or social? If so, is it not a paradox that knowledge can be understood as economic and education as cultural. Secondly, to what extent has educational research adopted the techno-economic rationale and commercial agenda that is so privileged by knowledge economy research policies? Is educational research adopting similar survival strategies to those adopted by certain creative industry faculties; is it becoming 'merely commercial'? Is it 'growing' those aspects of itself that allow it to be seen as commensurable and shrinking those that are 'merely civilising'? If so, is it not also a paradox that 'the endless optimisation of the cost/benefit ratio' (Lyotard 1993b: 25) now applies to education and that educational research can relinquish its civilising purposes under the name of knowledge? Is educational research simply 'libidinal economic' when it comes to the knowledge economy? Have education's 'intensities' been reduced to a desire for performativity or does some disruptive energy, some 'libidinal exceso, remain to interrupt consensus from within, and makes possible the surfacing of new forms and new voices? Does educational research still have leaky libidinal energies? If so, are they as deliberately contentious and culturally and ethically ambiguous as SymbioticA? If education were to have its own SymbioticA what might it look like?

Notes

1   This chapter arises from the Australian Research Council Discovery grant, *Knowledge/ economy/society: a sociological study of an education policy discourse in Australia in globalising circumstances,* 2002–5. It is also the basis for a chapter of our forthcoming book called *Haunting the Knowledge Economy* to be published by Routledge in its International Library of Sociology Series edited by John Urry.

2   This paper is part of an ongoing policy commitment to the aims outlined in the initial *Creative Industries Mapping Document* of 1998. The UK is generally considered as demonstrating the prototype of contemporary creative industries policy frameworks and initiatives. The Blair government established a Creative Industries Task Force after its election in Britain in 1997. The newly created Department of Culture, Media and Sport (DCMS) prepared the *Creative Industries Mapping Document* in 1998. In the document creative industries were defined as 'those activities which have their origin in individual creativity, skill and talent and which have the potential for wealth and job creation through the generation and exploitation of intellectual property' (DCMS 1998, online). It mapped Advertising, Architecture, Arts and Antique Markets, Crafts, Design, Designer Fashion, Film, Interactive Leisure Software, Music, Television and Radio, Performing Arts, Publishing and Software into the creative industries sector. In *Creative Britain*, Chris Smith, the Minister for Culture and Heritage, also emphasised the centrality of the 'creative economy' – defined generically as 'that cluster of individuals, enterprises and organisations that depends for the generation of value on creative skill and talent and on the intellectual property that it produces' (1998: 15). By moving the creative industries 'from the fringes to the mainstream' (Smith 1998: 9) the Creative Industries Task Force identified an emerging global trend where the creative industries sector was recognised as the fastest growing sector of the global knowledge-based economy (see OECD 1996; Jeremy Rifkin *The Age of Access* 2000 and John Howkins *The Creative Economy* 2001). The most recent UK Creative Industries initiative is the *Creative Industries Forum on Intellectual Property* which brings together key players to discuss how to best meet the opportunities and threats that rapid technological developments are generating for the UK's Creative Industries sector. The Forum will address key issues, such as: strategies for maximising the opportunities for the Creative Industries in a digital environment; business models; education and awareness raising; and challenges such as file-sharing and piracy (DCMS 2004, online).

3   Cunningham is both the senior consultant on the Creative Industries report and the Director of the Creative Industries Research and Applications Centre (CIRAC) at QUT. Content is defined as information disseminated via the internet, radio, television, advertising and the print media, and 'content growth areas' are identified as 'online education, interactive television, multi-platform entertainment, computer games, and web design for business-to-consumer applications' (Cunningham 2002: 3).

4 Lyotard's 'libidinal economy' was inspired by Georges Bataille's perspective on economic structure and his conception of a 'general economy' outlined in *The Accursed Share* (1988–91). In contrast to the notion of scarcity and capitalist restraint driving economic activity in classical economics, Bataille proposes a law of surplus where economic movement is viewed as a flow of energy in abundance or excess.

5 Aesthetics has two meanings in philosophy. The restricted sense is that it is the study of beauty in art and nature. More generally, it refers to the whole process of human perception and sensation: those feelings of pleasure and pain that are not reducible to clearly defined intellectual concepts.

References

Australia Council (1999) *Submission to the National Innovation Summit.*

Bain, W. (1995) 'The loss of innocence: Lyotard, Foucault, and the challenge of postmodern education, in M. Peters (ed.) *Education and the Postmodern Condition*, Westport, CT: Greenwood Publishing, 1–20.

Bataille G. (1988–91) *The Accursed Share: An Essay on General Economy*, New York: Zone Books.

Bigelow, J. (1998) 'Valuing humanities research', in A. Low *et al.* (eds) *Knowing Ourselves and Others: The Humanities in Australia into the 21st Century*, vol. 3, Canberra: Commonwealth of Australia, 37–58.

Bimber, B. (1995) 'The three faces of technological determinism, in M.R. Smith and L. Marx (eds) *Does Technology Drive History: The Dilemma of Technological Determinism*, Cambridge, MA: MIT Press, 79–100.

Bullen, E., Robb, S. and Kenway, J. (2004a) ' "Creative destruction": knowledge economy policy and the future of the arts and humanities in the academy', *Journal of Education Policy*, 19(1): 3–22.

Bullen, E., Kenway, J. and Robb, S. (2004b) 'Can the arts and humanities survive the knowledge economy? A beginner's guide to the issues', in J. Kenway, E. Bullen and S. Robb (eds) *Innovation and Tradition: The Arts, Humanities, and the Knowledge Economy* 'Eruptions: New Thinking across the Disciplines', Series Editor: Erica McWilliam, New York: Peter Lang.

Catts, O. and Zurr, I. (2002) 'Growing semi-living sculptures: the Tissue Culture & Art Project. *Leonardo*, 35(4): 365–70.

Catts, O. (2002) Interview with Elizabeth Bullen. Personal communication, Western Australia: 1–20.

Commonwealth of Australia (2004). *Backing Australia's Ability – Building our Future through Science and Innovation*, Canberra: Commonwealth of Australia.

Commonwealth of Australia (2001). *Backing Australia's Ability: An Innovation Action Plan for the Future*, Canberra: Commonwealth of Australia.

Cooper, B.P. and Murphy M.S. (1999) 'Libidinal economies: Lyotard and accounting for the unaccountable', in M. Woodmansee and M. Osteen (eds) *New Economic Criticism: Studies at the Intersection of Literature and Economics*, London: Routledge, 229–42.

Cox, S., Ninan, A. and Keane, M. (2003) *Brisbane's Creative Industries 2003*, Queensland, Australia: Brisbane City Council, 1–50.

Cunningham, S. (2001) 'From cultural to creative industries: theory, industry and policy implications, in C. Mercer (ed.) *Culturelink Review*, Zagreb: Institute for International Relations, 1–13.

Cunningham, S. (2002) 'Culture, services, knowledge or is content king, or are we just drama queens?', *Communications Research Forum*, Canberra: Australia.

Cunningham, S. and Hartley, J. (2001) 'Creative industries – from blue poles to fat pipes', *National Humanities and Social Sciences Summit*, Canberra: Australia, National Museum.

Department for Culture, Media and Sport (2001) *Culture and Creativity: The Next Ten Years*. Online. Available HTTP: http://www.culture.gov.uk/global/publications/archive_2001/ Culture_Creativity10yrs.htm (accessed 23 July 2004).

Department for Culture, Media and Sport (1998) *Creative Industries Mapping Document*. Online. Available HTTP: http://www.culture.gov.uk/global/publications/archive_1998/ Creative_Industries_Mapping_Document_1998.htm (accessed 23 July 2004).

Department for Culture, Media and Sport (2004) *Creative Industries Forum on Intellectual Property*. Online. Available HTTP: http://www.culture.gov.uk/global/press_notices/ archive_2004/dcms089_04.htm (accessed 10 August 2004).

Elam, M. (1994) 'Puzzling out the post-Fordist debate: technology, markets, institutions', in A. Amin (ed.) *Post-Fordism: A Reader*, Oxford: Blackwell, 43–70.

Fagerberg, J. (2002) 'A layman's guide to evolutionary economics', *Industrial R&D and Innovation Policy Learning*, Leengkollen: Asker. Online. Available HTTP: http:// folk,uio.no.janf/downloadp/02fagerberg-evolution.pdf.

Gillies, M. (ed.) (2001) 'Commercialization and globalization, in Department of Education, Training and Youth Affairs', *National Humanities and Social Science Summit*, Position Papers, August, Canberra: Commonwealth of Australia, 41–8.

Grierson, E. M. (2003) 'The arts and creative industries: new alliances in the humanities', *Hawaii International Conference on Arts and Humanities*, February, Hawaii: Waikiki Hotel.

Hartley, J., Cunningham, S., Hearn, G. and Jones, J. (2002) 'Response to the Queensland R&D Strategy Issues Paper', Queensland, Australia: Creative Industries Faculty, Queensland University of Technology, 1–10.

Hearn, G. (2002) Interview with Elizabeth Bullen. Personal communication, Brisbane, Australia, 1–17.

Howkins, J. (2001) *The Creative Economy: How People Make Money from Ideas*, London: Penguin.

Kenway, J., Bullen, E. and Robb. S. (eds) (2004) *Innovation and Tradition: The Arts, Humanities, and the Knowledge Economy*, 'Eruptions: New Thinking across the Disciplines', Series Editor: Erica McWilliam, New York: Peter Lang.

Kenway, J., Bullen, E. and Robb, S. (2004a) 'The knowledge economy, the technopreneur and the problematic future of the university', in *Policy Futures in Education*, Special Issue on University Futures (ed. M. Marginson and M. Peters) 2(2): 333–51.

Kenway, J., Bullen, E. and Robb, S. (2004b) 'Global knowledge politics and exploitable knowledge', in J. Kenway, E. Bullen and S. Robb (eds) *Innovation and Tradition: The Arts, Humanities, and the Knowledge Economy*, 'Eruptions: New Thinking across the Disciplines', Series Editor: Erica McWilliam, New York: Peter Lang.

Lyotard, J.-F. (1984) *The Postmodern Condition: A Report on Knowledge*, trans. G. Bennington and B. Massumi. Manchester: Manchester University Press.

Lyotard, J.-F. (1992) *The Postmodern Explained: Correspondence 1982–1985*, ed. J. Pefanis and M. Thomas; trans. D. Barry, B. Mather, J. Pefanis, V. Spate and M. Thomas, Minneapolis, MN: University of Minnesota Press.

Lyotard, J-.F. (1993a) *Political Writings*, trans. B. Hutchings and K. Paul Geiman, London: University College London Press.

Lyotard, J.-F. (1993b [1974]) *Libidinal Economy*, trans. I. Hamilton Grant, Bloomington, IN: Indiana University Press.

Malpas, S. (2003) *Jean-François Lyotard*, London: Routledge.

May, C. (2002) *The Information Society: A Sceptical View*, Cambridge: Polity Press.

OECD (Organization for Economic Co-Operation and Development) (1996) *The Knowledge-based Economy*, Paris: OECD.

QUT (Queensland University of Technology) (2003) *Postgraduate Prospectus: Creative Industries*, Brisbane: QUT, 1–48.

QUT (Queensland University of Technology) (2004) *Creative Industries.* Brisbane: QUT. Online. Available HTTP: http://www.creativeindustries.qut.com/studyopt/creativeindu/ (accessed 10 August 2004).

Rifkin, J. (2000) *The Age of Access: The New Culture of Hypercapitalism where All of Life is a Paid-for Experience*, New York: Putnam Publishing Group.

Seares, M. (2001) *National Press Club Address*, Canberra: National Press Club, 1–9.

Sim, S. (1996) *Jean-François Lyotard*, New York: Prentice Hall/Harvester Wheatsheaf.

Smith, C. (1998) *Creative Britain*, London: Faber & Faber.

University of Western Australia (2004) *Tissue Culture & Art Project.* Online. Avaliable HTTP: http://www.tca.uwa.edu.au (accessed 23 July 2004).

Williams, J. (1998) *Lyotard: Towards a Postmodern Philosophy*, Cambridge: Polity Press.

Wilson, S. (2002) *Information Arts: Intersections of Art, Science and Technology*, Cambridge, MA: MIT Press.

19 After methodolatry

Epistemological challenges for 'risky' educational research

Erica McWilliam

Introduction

The chapter explores the relationship between educational research and risk as a 'moral climate of politics' (Giddens 2002: 29) impacting powerfully on educational policy and processes. In exploring this question, the chapter mounts a cautious argument that the epistemological challenges attending such new global imperatives as risk are yet to be taken up in any substantial way in mainstream educational research. This is so despite the flurry of activity around diversifying social scientific inquiry, and the growing numbers of people who now engage in research activity within and outside universities. It is contended that this is due in no small part to the failure of educational researchers to *think about thinking about* research and to take this thinking forward to the consideration of questions of methodology.

The word *methodolatry*, with its implicit critique of the sanctification of Method-as-Technique, has been with us for over a decade now. While there seems to be some disagreement about who first coined the term, with some scholars attributing it to Mary Daly and others to Gordon Allport, the advent of the word itself tells us something about the crisis of legitimacy for scientific method that has been born out of a more general crisis of legitimacy for social hierarchies and mechanisms of power and control, a crisis that became palpable in the sixties and seventies. Put bluntly, 'hard science' is no longer near to Godliness.

Despite the decades that have passed since Karl Popper's first attack on non-critical rationality, and Paul Feyerabend's championing of an 'ever more imaginative and wild' irrationality (Bernstein 1988: 4), newcomers to research methodology are still discovering that debates about the sanctity or otherwise of Method are well and truly part of conceptual architecture for thinking and doing research. Such new career researchers may well be either excited or daunted – or both – by the tilt against methodological 'purity' and what it implies about research methodology as a 'game of truth and error' (Foucault 1985: 6), rather than Truth itself.

Meanwhile, some of their colleagues have continued to express concerns about the new climate of methodological permissiveness, blaming it for a perceived loss of intellectual rigour and a rise in self-interested – even narcissistic – inquiry. Paul Filmer's account of and advocacy for, the centrality of 'disinterestedness' in the modern university (Filmer 1997) is a case in point. For Filmer, the ethos of disinterestedness, i.e. of 'detachment ... from automatic reduction to conditions of instrumental functionality', ought always to be *the* driving logic of research (p. 57). In other words, research that is only focused on solving a particular problem for a particular stakeholder group in a particular time and place, is research whose potential for lack of objectivity may put science and the university at risk. The risk is that stakeholder interests and timetables may come to drive methodology, with systematic curiosity giving way to the quick fix. And there is mounting evidence that this is indeed an issue for social scientific research, as short-term methods that promise 'results now' come to be preferred over longitudinal and other forms of 'patient' research. In Australia, with the current policy imperative to 'timely completion',[1] no doctoral supervisor would rush to give carte blanche to a candidate's proposal for a longitudinal study or a long-term ethnographic engagement with a remote social community. Put another way, Margaret Mead would be unlikely in the current policy environment to do her doctorate on or in Samoa.[2]

Paul Filmer is much less interested in the ethical problems of intercultural research than he is in reclaiming the idea of a university that is beyond bias. If, as he claims, the role of the modern university ought to be 'to promote disinterested research for its own sake' (p. 57), then *interested* research, i.e. research that is designed to work in the interests of a particular group or community located in a particular time and place, is tainted by bias, not as pre-judgement (Gadamer 1975) but as prejudice of one sort or another. In other words, Filmer does not accept Gadamer's proposition that all researchers come to the research project with cultural and other baggage that needs to be brought forward for scrutiny. So Filmer would not see the foregrounding of pre-judgment as a crucial one for methodology. For Filmer, scrupulous detachment is a disposition that precedes methodology, not a myth to be exploded as part of the work of methodology.

Filmer's concerns about the risk of interestedness are not new: they have antecedents within the very work of those who first challenged the idea of a pure scientific rationality. Karl Popper himself was less than sanguine about what he perceived as the sudden and alarming collapse of his cautious invitation to a more critical rationality into what he saw as a potentially flabby subjectivism and relativism. Moreover, this sort of concern continues to be reflected in the writing of those like David Silverman (2000) who demand that qualitative methods transcend the logic of 'Sez you!'

My interest here is not to revisit questions around the appropriateness or otherwise of 'irrationality-as-subjectivism-and-relativism' in the conduct of research, but rather to explore educational research as a site in which new permissions, old orthodoxies *and* their contestation are now doing particular sorts of work in framing educational priorities, policy and practice at a time when much is shifty and uncertain in the world. What are we doing now at a time when we are supposed to be working after and beyond invitations to depart from, or remain true to, epistemological orthodoxies?

My exploration of epistemological challenges will proceed from the Foucauldian logic that *what enables also constrains*. That means that I am not seeking to develop columns of pluses and minuses that, taken together, serve as a map of the current global-local politics of educational research. Rather, I am interested to flesh out how certain performances of educational research produce truth claims and counter-claims, and thus, new 'truth' effects. To do so, I want to 'read' educational method in the context of one powerful global imperative, namely *risk-consciousness*. I choose risk-consciousness not because it is the only global imperative worth investigating (sustainability, digitalisation, self-stylisation, international relations might be equally compelling), but because it has a special piquancy after the events of September 11, 2001. Post-September 11 has seen, among other things, a greater suspicion and timidity in social and cultural life in the West, and its political corollary, a preference for aggressive mono-cultural, even fundamentalist, responses to complex global political problems.

My interest is how educational research has engaged with risk as a 'moral climate of politics' (Giddens 2002: 29) impacting powerfully on educational policy and processes. In exploring this question, I seek to mount a cautious argument that the epistemological challenges that attend such new global imperatives as risk are yet to be taken up in any substantial way in mainstream educational research. This is so despite the flurry of activity around diversifying social scientific inquiry, and the growing numbers of people who now engage in research activity within and outside universities.

Risk as a moral climate

As Anthony Giddens (2002) reminds us, the idea of risk – of 'hazards that are actively assessed in relation to future possibilities' (p. 22) – is quite recent historically, and a very important idea for a society that 'lives after the end of nature' (p. 27), i.e. after magic, cosmology and the fates gave way to scientific calculation and/as insurance. Thus the notion of *performance* in a risk society is very much focused on danger – the danger of failing to perform in ways that are morally and politically, as well as organisationally, acceptable. Ulrich Beck (1992) concurs with Giddens, arguing that risk society is characterised by negative logic, a shift away from the management and distribution of material/industrial *goods* to the management and distribution of *bads*, i.e. the control of knowledge about danger, about what might go wrong and about the systems needed to guard against such a possibility. If we are to accept this reasoning, then September 11 did not usher in a newly risk-conscious logic in organisational life, but gave added impetus to what was already a driving rationality towards risk minimisation.

Mary Douglas's (1966, 1970, 1985, 1990) anthropological research is underpinned by a similar understanding of risk as shifting from a positive to a negative logic. Her analyses of social and cultural life show how risk society shifts attention from risk as the probability of losses and gains, to the idea that, in contemporary times, risk simply means *danger*. She states:

> The modern risk concept, parsed now as danger, is invoked to protect individuals against encroachments of others. It is part of the system of thought that upholds the type of individualist culture which sustains an expanding industrial system.
>
> (Douglas 1990: 7)

Following Douglas, 'risk-as-danger', is generally understood by cultural theorists to serve the 'forensic needs' of a new and expanding global culture in 'politicizing and moralizing the links between dangers and approved behaviours' (Pidgeon *et al.* 1992: 113). 'Good' behaviour is conduct that mobilises the eradication or minimisation of risk – in the case of publicly funded academic institutions, the risk of waste of resources, of low standards, of student failure and so on.

This politicising and moralising work has its own constitutive logic. As Giddens understands it, risk gives rise to 'a new moral climate ... marked by *a push and pull* between accusations of scaremongering on the one hand, and of cover-ups on the other' (p. 29, emphasis added). The push-and-pull dynamic of risk is evident both within and outside domains of social and organisational life, in the form of claims and counter-claims that, when taken together, constitute certain matters as more or less 'risky' or certain people as more or less 'at risk'. Amid the rising crescendo, according to Giddens, we cannot know beforehand 'when we are actually scaremongering and when we are not' (p. 30). Statistics may well materialise that 'confirm' both the accusations of scaremongering *and* of cover-up. Anecdotal evidence may be piled on top to support or refute claim and counter-claim. This is a key mechanism through which risk-consciousness does its moral/political work as a climate for thinking risk and for inquiring into social practices and social identities.

Risk as a policy climate

The recent imperative to audit research is a marker of this risk-consciousness being applied by governments to universities. Following the UK's introduction of the Research Assessment Exercise for assessing the quality and impact of research in that country, both New Zealand and now Australia have been moving to a similar audit of research activity in publicly funded institutions. While the auditing of research comes with the friendliest of epithets (i.e. as identifying and rewarding 'quality'), the logic is doubly negative – *to prevent the possibility of things going wrong.*

This logic is not new. In Australia, for example, concerns about the capacities of Australian universities to self-manage around risk – its identification and its eradication – have been a theme of both state and federal governments in recent times. In 2000, Government bureaucrat Michael Gallagher (2000) pointed to 'a number of failures' (p. 38) that he linked to the 'trial and error dimension' of university management practice to date. According to Gallagher, the lack of uniformity of practice within universities has been fundamental in producing failure. 'The next phase of development', Gallagher concluded '... [will be] more formalized and professionally risk managed' (p. 38). This logic echoed the Higher Education Management Review Committee in Australia (Hoare, Stanley, Kirkby and Coaldrake 1995) and the Dearing Report (1997) in the UK, both of which foregrounded the failure of universities to develop the sort of management culture necessary to self-regulation in relation to organisational performance.

Current policy shifts to audit research 'quality', then, are part of a more long-term government demand for waste identification and eradication, given the cost of higher education in general and research in particular. Alan Lawson (1999) understands the negative logic thus:

> Because higher education is valued, it is potentially a commodity. But it is only a commodity worth paying for if it can be made to seem scarce. Once it is scarce it can be competed for, accounted for, and subjected to audits that will inevitably disclose how those scarce resources are being wasted ... higher degree education ... has been redefined as a 'scarce' commodity which we can ill-afford to 'waste' (p. 11).

Lawson goes on to argue that, in higher degree research in Australia, conflations of postgraduate student data relating to attrition and completion rates render the field vulnerable to accusations of waste. Importantly, he demonstrates how such accusations, once made, continue to be fed by dubious claims about the irrelevance of much higher degree study and employer dissatisfaction with higher degree graduates (p. 11). So the issue of what counts as evidence of research 'quality' (or the lack of it) and the issue of who should be the arbiters of 'quality', become nodes around which academics and government bureaucrats have come to push and pull in the struggle to articulate the version of quality research that comes to count as true.

Risk, policy and epistemology

The 'push-and-pull' of rationalities of risk, with its double imperative to claim and counter-claim, produces cleavages not only for governments and publicly funded organisations, but for social and community groups. It mobilises some to advocate a particular course of action on the basis of what has been identified as harmful, and others to reject the claims of such advocates on the grounds that they are alarmist and/or dismissive of sound evidence to the contrary. This sort of push-and-pull has profound consequences for social policy makers and for those who implement social policy. Like their counterparts in the private sector, governments and their agencies are well aware of the reputational damage that can be done by public accusations of dangerous practice and cover-up. It is therefore in their interests for such claims to be refuted, and this can best be done by apparently 'disinterested' research that finds 'contrary' evidence or little evidence.

Notwithstanding the burgeoning of 'interested' research in recent times, 'disinterested' research remains a most powerful weapon for waging a war against the claims of any individual or organisation. Put another way, despite the folkloric wisdom of 'lies, damned lies and statistics', the claim to 'objective findings' is the one that translates into real political clout. It is also true, however, that *interested* research – 'real' cases involving 'real' people that demonstrate the success of a programme in moving a vulnerable individual from victimhood to victory – has become increasingly important in the allocation of funds to particular social programmes (see Morgan 2001). Salvation narratives are grist to the political mill. The combination of both objective and subjective evidence is a winning combination, and this may explain a growing preference for multi-method research in investigating 'risky' social problems.

With so much riding on making and refuting allegations of risk, it is unsurprising that we are seeing such a flurry of activity around identifying, detecting and eliminating risk from educational settings. As social organisations with responsibilities for a populations identified as most vulnerable, schools and childcare agencies have become targets of a burgeoning number of 'safety' policies containing rules and regulations for minimising risk to children in educational settings (Scott *et al.* 2000, McWilliam and Jones 2005). An effect of this, according to Jennifer Nias (1999), has been an expansion of the parameters of a properly enacted ethic of pedagogical care, so that it now includes an unprecedented array of issues for which teachers can and do hold themselves responsible. In the domain of early childhood, this expanded duty of care produces a further effect – one that Joanne Wallace (1997) has called 'child panic' – that frames the provision of child care as increasingly untenable, particularly for men (Johnson 2000).

This climate of suspicion, characterised in part by sensational media revelations of priestly and teacherly impropriety, is very much focused on the potential of a care-giving adult to abuse children sexually and psychologically (McWilliam 2003; Singh and McWilliam 2005).

Concomitant with the flurry of policy activity around harm minimisation, there has been a flurry of research activity focused on identifying new dangers or the persistence of old dangers in educational practice and the human services more generally. There is a particularly interesting effect of this – that *we are more likely to see evidence of risk everywhere*. Jo Tobin's (1997) study of American and Irish teachers' responses to fictive critical incidents is a useful example of this phenomenon in action. In Tobin's study, American teachers 'saw' evidence of child abuse where Irish teachers did not. Tobin concluded it was not that one cultural group was right and the other wrong – the stories they read in the focus groups were after all fictional – but that American teachers had come to see certain behaviour as indicative of risk in a way that Irish teachers did not. What Tobin's study demonstrates is how our capacity to 'see' or 'not see' danger is culturally enabled and constrained, and this has profound implications when we sally forth into the field to find the truth about what's out there.

This propensity to see risk everywhere may account, at least in part, for the rise of *bullying* as an object of research scrutiny in the interests of harm minimisation (with its various new characterisations, e.g. cyber-bullying, relational bullying and so on), and as a 'finding' of educational research. A search of the social scientific research literature on bullying shows that the term has risen dramatically in usage, from 14 in 1993 to 160 a decade later.[3] My point here is that it is too easy to make the assumption that we are at last beginning to uncover the *true* dimensions of bullying in our schools and workplaces. To accept this premise is to fail to understand how 'bullying research' is actively producing – and produced by – a world in which more behaviours come to *count* as bullying and more educators and policy makers are able to 'see' the danger of bullying in organisational and social life.

As a corollary of this, we have also seen greater attention being paid to 'anti-bullying' policies and practices, and the rise of research that explores 'best practice' in overcoming the harm that attaches to bullying. One antidote to bullying, i.e. the personal psychological quality of *resilience*, is thus also becoming a 'hot topic' of social scientific inquiry. Evidence of the take-up of resilience/resiliency in social scientific literature, as well as everyday language, confirms a similar burgeoning interest in 'resilience' as a potential solution to a range of interpersonal, organisational and community problems, with 280 references to the term 'resilience' in 2003 compared with only 85 a decade earlier. As with the term 'bullying', the new literature is not unified in its use of the term. It is evoked variously by developmental psychopathologists, psychologists, sociologists, anthropologists and others as psychological 'buoyancy and adaptation' (Pulley and Wakefield 2001), a calculable 'adversity quotient (AQ)' (Stolz 1997), a 'key (personal) skill' (Pulley 2004), 'an attitude of self-employment' (Brown 1996), and/or 'a capacity to satisfy customer needs on the spot' (Siebert 2002).

What risk-consciousness does, then, as a logic produced out of a political and moral climate of risk-as-danger, is to organise researchers into those who continue to find more and different sorts of harm (bullying or abuse, or mental illness or social dysfunction or …) and those who investigate or develop 'best practice' for minimising that harm. This is not to say that bullying, abuse, etc. is all imagined or fictive, but rather to argue that we come to *see* certain harmful phenomena as ubiquitous and we become complicit, for better and worse, in filling the world with the problem and its solution.

In 'Filling the world with self-esteem: a social history of truth-making' (1996), Steven Ward explains how this process occurred in relation to *self-esteem* – how we came to see its presence and its absence in just about everyone just about everywhere. Ward argues that, while William James's work was important as an historical precursor, the term self-esteem was first legitimated in clinical and experimental studies in psychology in the 1940s and 1950s, particularly through the work of Abraham Maslow (1942). He argues that it was during the middle and late 1950s that the term was taken up by others working from different perspectives within counselling psychology, particularly the client-centred therapy associated with Carl Rogers. As Ward sees it, the period 1940–70 was crucial because it was during this time that 'self-esteem became a central concept in experimental and survey studies in psychology and social psychology' (p. 9), being adopted in studies of ethnocentrism, social class, stress, delinquency, failure, motivation and so on (p. 10). Crucially for its magnification, the large-scale empirical study of Morris Rosenberg published in 1965 concluded that parenting and educational tactics were two of the most important factors impacting on adolescent self-esteem. It was this conclusion, and the work which it spawned in the years that followed,[4] which allowed the idea to be taken up so quickly in educational literature and in policy matters related to education, and it was also this idea which gave psychology such a privileged position when it came to remediating 'indiscipline' in the classroom.

Educational research, then, invents and then discovers knowledge objects and disseminates these as 'findings'. And this is true whether the research methodology is quantitative or qualitative or both. The game we play is to shore up our claims by pointing to meticulous methods for data collection and analysis. This has come to include a passion for backing up quantitative research (a survey or similar technique showing it's really 'out there' in some form or other), with qualitative research involving 'cases' with their own peculiarities and commonalities. Since the advent of Nu*dist, Nvivo and the like, we have come to rely on utilising such software for organising data into categories that can name what we have found. In other words, we have developed a preference for 'mixed methods' that can show statistically how much is really happening as we identify more and more 'cases' of the phenomenon under scrutiny, requiring more and more research dollars to flow to future projects that can find and eliminate or at least minimise the harms that we identify as associated with such 'cases'.

Contradiction as epistemology

Again, this is not to say that nothing is actually happening in the world or that we should not try to categorise what we understand to be happening. Rather, it is to argue that educational research can too easily become blinkered by simplistic epistemological assumptions that only one proposition, or its obverse, is true. And this constitutes a failure of imagination – the capacity to imagine that *both and neither of the contrary propositions we might want to argue are necessary and true*. Put another way, we need to develop a greater capacity for *irony* in our thinking about research. In the case of risk, the tendency is to come down on the side of 'claim' (look how much more bullying or abuse is really our there) or 'counterclaim' (look at how 'child panic' makes teachers victims) rather than being able to hold together the push and pull rationality in the design of risk-related research itself.

If we are unable to hold contrary imperatives together, then, in Beck's (2004) terms, what we end up with are 'zombie categories' (p. 146). Such categories render simplistic the complexities of new social relationships and cultural forms. They are a hallmark of the failure to make what Patti Lather (1996) has called the 'double move' of *thinking about thinking about* the phenomenon under scrutiny. For Beck, they are the hallmark of the failure of research to take up the challenge of a 'methodological cosmopolitanism' (Beck 2004: 148) that can connect us with a different account of the social, one that integrates 'culture, politics, values, religion, technological developments, global risk dynamics and so on' (p. 155). This would include, among other things, the study of processes of what Beck calls 'individualisation', that is 'how legal and educational institutions are producing individualised life-forms through basic political civil and social rights, most of which are centred on the individual' (p. 156).

One way of making this move in 'risk-focused' research is to treat risk as a logic for *thinking* individual and social good, a 'regime of truth' (Foucault 1980: 131) that constitutes proper (i.e. risk-conscious) social and organisational conduct. In Michel Foucault's (1985) terms, it means that risk works as a 'game of truth and error' rather than as Truth itself (p. 6). Such a moral climate constitutes 'risk-consciousness' as an ideal – a 'prescriptive text ... that elaborate[s] rules, opinions and advice as to how to behave as one should' (p. 12), allowing individuals to 'question their own conduct, to watch over and give shape to it, and to shape themselves as ethical subjects' (p. 13). In terms of contemporary working life, risk as a moral climate offers new ways for educators to be *properly professional*, one of which is alertness to potential dangers and greater attention to the work of minimising the possibility of something going (morally, politically) wrong.

As social scientific inquiry identifies more and more risks that pertain to social life, so risk management-as-risk-minimisation becomes a higher priority in all Western organisations, including schools. It is a system into which the local, disciplinary-specific or 'craft' knowledge of teachers, administrators and auxiliary others must be plugged in order to count as the proper knowledge of the truly professional worker. It is not that local knowledge is being displaced altogether. Rather it is being made over as 'professional expertise' through a process that Ericson and Haggerty (1997) describe in the following way:

> [P]rofessionals obviously have 'know-how', [but] their 'know-how' does not become expertise until it is plugged into an institutional communication system. It is through such systems that expert knowledge becomes standardized and robust enough to use in routine diagnosis, classification, and treatment decisions by professionals (p. 104).

The idea that schooling is being made the subject of 'routine diagnosis, classification, and treatment decisions' may well be viewed as an Orwellian development in education. However, I am not seeking in this chapter to make any moral or ideological judgment of this type. What I am seeking to point to is the way in which educational research is both enabled and constrained simultaneously by the logic of the times we inhabit and the methods we use. As researchers, we cannot be 'outside' this logic, and we see it evidenced across the entire spectrum of educational life. It does not surprise that the largest teacher employer body in my home State of Queensland makes the following declaration on its website: 'All staff members ... including contract staff are responsible for managing risks'.[5] Nor does it surprise that risk management in practice is understood by that same body as originating with the questions: 'What can go wrong? How can it go wrong? What will it cost if it goes wrong?'[6] The call to recognise potential dangers and to ensure that such dangers are minimised is instantly recognisable as a ubiquitous imperative of modern living. Put bluntly, risk management is now everyone's business, and educational research plays its part in ensuring that this continues to be so, for better *and* worse.

The ubiquity of the claim threat of risk ensures that any public service that is dependent either directly or indirectly on taxpayer funding now has a risk management strategy in place to demonstrate organisational commitment to risk minimisation. This is especially true for schools, with their added burden of a high duty of care for their clients as legal minors. So while schools need to show themselves to be more accountable (i.e. more risk responsive), the individuals within schools are also having to cope with effects – both intended and unintended – of risk as a system of management and surveillance, including self-surveillance (Meadmore 1999; Sachs 2003).

A special problem now arising for teachers is that the logic of risk management as a 'push' towards *risk minimising* is a logic that runs counter to the *risk-taking* logic that underpins robust and insightful learning (Taylor 1999). The paradox here is that *risk minimising becomes good for schools at the same time that it is bad for learning*. Schools leaders are 'at risk' pedagogically if and when they manage their work and identity in ways that have them hunkered down at the low risk end of a risk management continuum, and they are at risk in managerial terms if they are taking risks. This paradox, produced as it is by push-and-pull in the present moral climate of 'risk-as-danger', needs to be addressed in its entirety, and this can only be done through an epistemological framework that works to accommodate paradox. In epistemological terms, if we are to hold contrary imperatives together within the design of the research itself, we want to be able to ask how schools take risks and minimise them simultaneously, without a ready-made conspiracy theory to serve as a response.

To hold together contrary imperatives within the one set of epistemological assumptions is to work against the logic of *either* push *or* pull. In Richard Rorty's (1989) terms, it means working to develop a *re-descriptive* project that refuses a final vocabulary of explanation (p. 73). Ironic scholarship refuses to tidy up by way of providing the vision splendid, by advocating or condemning or redeeming. In expressing this view, I am not suggesting that Martin Luther King got it all wrong – that the mountaintop ought to be supplanted by a more mundane landscape of scepticism and doubt. Rather, I am arguing with writers like Donna Haraway the importance of a place for ironic texts alongside advocacy in order to 'keep the faith' in a liberal humanist order of thought. As Haraway (1991) puts it, irony is faithful to a liberal social order in the same way that blasphemy is faithful to a wider church:

> Blasphemy protects one from the moral majority within, while still insisting on the need for community. Blasphemy is not apostasy. Irony is about contradictions that do not resolve into larger wholes, even dialectically, about the tension of holding incompatible things together because both or all are necessary and true.
>
> (Haraway 1991: 149)

In educational research, ironic or blasphemous texts are those that do not produce formulae and visions and truths for making ourselves into 'quality professionals', or 'nurturing caregivers', or 'excellent teachers' or 'reflective practitioners' or 'facilitators of learning' or 'critical pedagogues' or even 'good citizens'. The sort of knowledge produced by ironic research is 'self-referential' knowledge (Baert 1998), that is, knowledge which cuts across traditional consensus to create distance from our most familiar categories, treating them as contingent and strange. Used in this way, self-referential knowledge is not specifically knowledge which informs one about *oneself* (eg, critical self-reflection), but rather asks about those taken for granted knowledges through which we *produce* a body of scholarship we call educational research.

Teaching research methods

So what are the implications of all this for teaching research methods? Certainly we have known for some time (i.e. time *after methodolatory*) that the qualitative/quantitative binary is problematic as a starting point. Bringing in the quantitative experts (if there are any still remaining in faculties of education) followed by the qualitative experts (with the attendant problem of disciplinary 'coverage' and/or representation) is still a common practice in research methods pedagogy but this approach seems to confuse rather than enable postgraduate students as the array of possible methodological options expands. The unfortunate imperative that tends to arise out of this sort of pedagogy is a decision to work backwards from a set of research techniques to a do-able problem. An approach that has been taken in some quarters to avoid this conundrum has been to develop expertise in one singular approach (e.g. action research or case study) and ensure that the students are experts in using the relevant techniques. There are worse options than this.

However, what this chapter seeks to pre-empt is the usefulness of the study of knowledge as a starting point for teaching research methods. While I am aware that many of my colleagues share this view, I am less sanguine about the attempts that have been made in the social and human sciences to do the pedagogical work necessary to making epistemology accessible to the uninitiated. The tendency has been, unfortunately, to think epistemology means 'high theory' as a starting point and that this in turn means Popper and Feyerabend and any number of other bigwigs in the Method debate. I suggest that a more useful introduction to epistemology would be to make it evident through reading research itself as a social and cultural practice. I do not mean by this that students should read a wide range (or even a narrow range) of research reports and papers, but that they should be engaged with tasks that make research itself a problem worth thinking about.

To illustrate, I return to the statistics about bullying given earlier. If it is true that there were 14 mentions of the term 'bullying' in research conducted in 1993, and 160 a decade later, what might this connote? In simple tick-the-box test terms, does it mean that:

(a) there is *more bullying going on* than there was in the 1990s; or
(b) that *we are more aware* of bullying in post-millennial times; or
(c) that there is more public concern about bullying so *more funds to research* bullying; or

(d) that the *expense of litigation* drives public institutions to minimise the risk of bullying claims?

Importantly, we need to add to this somewhat predictable list of options:

(e) that *more behaviours have come to count as bullying*; or
(f) that *more social researchers are engaged in 'redemptive research'*; and so
(g) researchers and policy makers are *filling the world with bullying*?

What might it mean to argue that *all* these explanations are necessary and true? Can we hold them all together in our thinking? Do we need to? Does any one claim refute any other? What is worth researching, then, in terms of 'bullying' as a site of knowledge production and distribution? What do 'experts' have to say about this (as distinct from hearing about their own specialisms)?

This sort of activity does not require the novice researcher to be expert in understanding the traditions of mainstream philosophies of Western science. It can, however, raise questions about the practice of research as fieldwork, as headwork and as textwork (McWilliam, Lather and Morgan 1996), rather than as a choice between competing paradigms. In pedagogical terms, it gives access to complex ideas rather than requiring mastery of theory as an opening gambit. And importantly, it points to thoughtfulness about how knowledge works as a starting point for considerations of method. To understand 'the rise of bullying' as a complex and multi-faceted set of cultural practices is to begin to see how one's own research is part of an attentional and material economy, *for better and worse*. It might also stave off the unseemly rush to the field that is so characteristic of researchers who already know what's 'out there'.

Beyond blaming

It is always tempting, of course, to lay blame somewhere, and preferably far from ourselves. Whether we blame a pernicious state or rampant consumerism or a welfare mentality or a colonial past or individual dysfunction, we can quickly find real explanatory power slipping from our grasp, either because we have eliminated the possibility of finding otherwise, or because we have attempted to 'fix' the fluidity of modern social life and the shiftiness of social practices. Zigmunt Bauman (2004) makes a powerful argument against such epistemological fixity. He speaks of the new set of social conditions that he terms 'the liquid-modern setting of the social' (2004: 21), as a setting in which adjustment, adaptation and habituation – the capacity to learn and reproduce appropriate social behaviours – is itself no longer the key to success. Instead of opening up possibilities, such learning may be unhelpful because it assumes a fixed or predictable social world. Bauman elaborates:

> Just as long-term commitments threaten to mortgage the future, habits too tightly embraced burden the present; learning may in the long run disempower as it empowers in the short .... 'Your skills and know-how are as good as their last application'.
>
> (Bauman 2004: 22)

In this liquid social setting, *forgetting* (or what Bauman calls 'de-learning'), becomes as important as learning. For Bauman, it is 'the interplay of learning and de-learning' (p. 22) that is crucial here.

There are profound implications for our learning about the conduct of research in what Bauman in arguing. Among the 'habits too tightly embraced' in educational research, we might well include both the defence of disinterestedness and also the idea that a declaration of strong moral-ethical commitment is a sufficient case for arguing the validity of method. Neither 'detachment' nor 'advocacy' of themselves have any special merit in terms of epistemology if and when the social ground is shifting so dramatically as to call into question the very idea at the centre of educational thought – that learning is the key to power and success. When the predominant value that attaches to learning itself is destabilised, then much is thrown into disarray. In failing to de-learn the routines of educational research, including the routine arguments we continue to make for or against one Method or another, we may well find ourselves paying attention to questions that do not *tell* in other contexts, and are increasingly tired in our own. But finally, the most significant casualty is genuine explanatory power.

Notes

1 The Federal Government's Research Training Scheme limits the funding period of higher degree research to a period of no more than 4 years full-time.
2 While some might want to draw attention to the cultural problems of Mead's work and argue against the cultural value of Mead's work, there is no doubting its on-going usefulness for intercultural debate.
3 Databases searched include the Science Citation Index Expanded (SCI-EXPANDED), the Social Sciences Citation Index (SSCI) and the Arts & Humanities Citation Index (A&HCI).
4 Importantly, this work often provided quite precise means for 'measuring' self-esteem, including The Twenty Statements, Sherwood's Self-Concept Inventory, The Tennessee Self-Concept Scale, The Self-Esteem Scale, Social Self-Esteem Scale and so on (see Ward 1996: 10).
5 See http://education.qld.gov.au/strategic/policy/quideleines/risk/integrated.html.
6 Ibid.

References

Baert, P. (1998) 'Foucault's history of the present as self-referential knowledge acquisition', *Philosophy and Social Criticism*, 24(6): 111–26.

Bauman, Z. (2004) 'Zigmunt Bauman: liquid sociality', in N. Gane (ed.) *The Future of Social Theory*, London: Continuum, 17–46.

Beck, U. (1992) *Risk Society: Towards a New Modernity*, London: Sage.

Beck, U. (2004) 'The cosmopolitan turn', in N. Gane (ed.) *The Future of Social Theory*, London: Continuum, 143–67.

Bernstein, R.J. (1988) *Beyond Objectivism and Relativism: Science, Hermeneutics and Praxis*, Philadelphia, PA: University of Pennsylvania Press.

Brown, B.L. (1996) 'Career resilience', ERIC Clearinghouse on Adult, Career, and Vocational Educational (ERIC Document Reproduction Service No. EDE 402474). Retrieved 11 September 2004 from http://www.ericacve.org/docs/dig178.htm.

Dearing, R. (1997) *Higher Education in the Learning Society. The National Committee of Inquiry into Higher Education* (The Dearing Report), London: HMSO.

Douglas, M. (1966) *Purity and Danger: Concepts of Pollution and Taboo*, London: Routledge and Kegan Paul.

Douglas, M. (1970) *Natural Symbols: Explorations in Cosmology*, New York: Pantheon.

Douglas, M. (1985) *Risk Acceptability According to the Social Sciences*, New York: Russell Sage Foundation.

Douglas, M. (1990) *Risk and Blame: Essays in Cultural Theory*, London: Sage.

Ericson, R.V. and Haggerty, K.D. (1997) *Policing the Risk Society*, Toronto: University of Toronto Press.

Filmer, P. (1997) 'Disinterestedness and the modern university', in A. Smith and F. Webster (eds) *The Postmodern University: Contested Visions of Higher Education*, Maidenhead: Open University Press.

Foucault, M. (1980) *The History of Sexuality, vol. 1: An Introduction*, Trans. Robert Hurley, New York: Pantheon.

Foucault, M. (1985) *The Use of Pleasure: The History of Sexuality, vol. 2*, Trans. Robert Hurley, London: Penguin.

Gadamer, H. (1975) *Truth and Method*, Trans and ed. G. Barden and J. Cumming, New York: Seabury Press.

Gallagher, M. (2000) 'The emergence of the entrepreneurial public universities in Australia', Paper presented at the IMHE General Conference of the OECD Paris, September, Occasional Paper Series 00/E, Commonwealth of Australia, DETYA.

Gane, N. (Ed.) *The Future of Social Theory*, Continuum: London.

Giddens, A. (2002) *Runaway World: How Globalisation is Reshaping our Lives*, London: Profile Books.

Haraway, D. (1991) *Simians, Cyborgs and Women: The Reinvention of Nature*, London: Free Association Books.

Hoare, D., Stanley, K., and Coaldrake, P., (1995) *Higher Education Management Review: The Report of the Committee of Inquiry*, Canberra: AGPS.

Johnson, R. (2000) *Hands Off! Erasure of Touch in the Care of Children*, New York: Peter Lang.

Lather, P. (1996) 'Methodology as subversive repetition: practices towards a feminist double science', Paper presented at the American Educational Research Association Annual Meeting. New York, April.

Lawson, A. (1999) 'From West to waste through dirty data', *Campus Review*, 7–13 April: 11.

Maslow, A.H. (1942) 'Self-esteem (dominance feeling) and sexuality in women', *Journal of Social Psychology* 16, 259–94.

McWilliam, E. (2003) 'The vulnerable child as a pedagogical subject', *Journal of Curriculum Theorizing*, 19(2): 35–44.

McWilliam, E. and Jones, A. (2005) 'The risk of being a teacher', *British Journal of Educational Research*, 31(1), in press.

McWilliam, E., Lather, P. and Morgan, W. (1996) *Field Work, Head Work, Text Work: A Textshop in New Feminist Research* (video, 50 mins with workbook), Brisbane: Centre for Policy and Leadership Studies, QUT.

Meadmore, D. (1999) 'Keeping up to the mark: testing as surveillance', in C. Symes and D. Meadmore (eds) *The Extra-ordinary School: Parergonality and Pedagogy*, New York: Peter Lang, 149–61.

Morgan, T. (2001) 'Villains, victims, heroes: the social production of "problem" youth', in P. Singh and E. McWilliam (eds) *Designing Educational Research: Theories, Methods and Practices*, Flaxton: PostPressed, 209–20.

Nias, J. (1999) 'Primary teaching as a culture of care', in J. Prosser (ed.) *School Culture*, London: Sage, 66–81.

Pidgeon, N., Hood, C.C., Jons, D., Turner, B. and Gibson, R. (1992) 'Risk perception', in N. Pidgeon (ed.) *Risk Analysis, Perception and Management: Report of a Royal Society Study Group*, London: The Royal Society, 89–134.

Pulley, M. L. (2004) 'Effective leaders can "go with their gut"', *Centre for Creative Leadership Newsletter*, September.

Pulley, M.L. and Wakefield, M. (2001) *Building Resiliency: How to Thrive in Times of Change*, Greensboro, NC: CCL Press.

Rorty, R. (1989) *Contingency, Irony, and Solidarity*, New York: Cambridge University Press.

Sachs, J. (2003) *The Activist Teaching Profession*, Buckingham: Open University Press.

Scott, S., Jackson, S. and Backett-Milburn, K. (2000) 'Swings and roundabouts: risk anxiety and the everyday worlds of children', *Sociology*, 32(4): 59–73.

Siebert, J. (2002) 'Modes of thought and meaning making: the aftermath of trauma', *Journal of Humanistic Psychology*, 44(3): 299–319.

Silverman, D. (2000) *Doing Qualitative Research: A Practical Handbook*, London: Sage.

Singh, P. and McWilliam, E. (2005, in press) 'Pedagogic imaginings: negotiating pedagogies of care/protection in a risk society', *Asia-Pacific Journal of Teacher Education*, 33(2).

Stolz, P.G. (1997) *Adversity Quotient: Turning Obstacles into Opportunities*, New York: John Wiley and Sons.

Taylor, P.G. (1999) *Making Sense of Academic Life: Academics, Universities and Change*, Buckingham: SRIIE and Open University Press.

Tobin, J. (ed.) (1997) *Making a Place for Pleasure in Early Childhood Education*, New Haven, CT and London: Yale University Press.

Wallace, J. (1997) 'Technologies of "the child": towards a theory of the child-subject', *Textual Practice*, 9(2): 285–302.

Ward, S. (1996) 'Filling the world with self-esteem: a social history of truth making', *Canadian Journal of Sociology*, 2(1): 1–23.

20 Policy scholarship against de-politicisation

Patricia Thomson

In his later years Pierre Bourdieu became active in campaigns 'against globalisation' (Bourdieu 1998, 2003). He argued that globalisation was in itself a policy agenda through which ideas of freedom were mobilised via new networks to grant new liberties to 'economic determinisms'. Speaking in support of the struggles of French workers, farmers and small business owners, he derided the notion that nation states were powerless. He argued that 'globalisation' was in and of itself a policy agenda which persuaded nation states to divest themselves of the powers to control economic forces, and to surrender to 'the most powerful concentration of capital – economic, political, military, cultural, scientific and technological – as the foundation of a symbolic determination without precedent, wielded in particular via a stranglehold of the media' (2003: 39).

While political activity had always been international, what was now different, according to Bourdieu, was that the scale, forums and ways in which political struggles could be waged were changed to become more fragmented, self-organised, symbolic and media savvy, oriented towards local issues and everyday life, internationalist and solidaristic. He advocated an engaged and political scholarship in which the 'routines and presuppositions associated with membership in universes governed by different laws and logics' (2000: 47) are re-built. This he suggested constituted a refusal of, and a resistance to, depoliticisation. He proposed that political hope lay in new social movements which required not only activism but also *long-term theoretical elaboration*.

In this chapter I consider what Bourdieu's urging for elaborated theoretical work might mean for education policy scholars. I suggest that it consists of at least four steps:

1 a problematisation of the very idea of globalisation;
2 discussion of alternative possibilities;
3 investigation of new policy 'spaces'; and
4 critically working with/against universities and research policy while making connections with messy counter realpolitik(s).

It is important to note at the outset that this chapter is not a take-up of Bourdieu's methodology or sociology. Rather, it grapples with what I take to be Bourdieu's embodiment of, and argument for, a particular kind of scholarly habitus, that of a public intellectual who does both academic and political work.

Therefore, I begin with a brief discussion of the idea of an engaged scholarship, and it is here that I do turn to Bourdieu.

Thinking against the grain

Bourdieu wrote frequently about social science. Through works such as *Homo Academicus* (1988), *In Other Words* (1990), *Academic Discourse* (Bourdieu, Passeron and de Saint Martin 1995), and *Science of Science and Reflexivity* (2004) he argued that academic work is not neutral. Scholarship serves particular interests. It is produced within a hierarchically organised social space (which Bourdieu called a 'field') whose purpose is the neutral production of ideas and ways of being a scholar and doing scholarship. This is not a socially neutral activity because it not only advantages those already in positions of institutional authority and those with significant academic reputations, but it also reinforces and perpetuates particular 'truths' about academic work, scholars and disciplines. Bourdieu's writings documented how scholarship, far from being the 'objective' pursuit it claimed, generally supported the maintenance of the broader status quo, and often worked particularly in the interests of those in powerful positions in other areas (e.g. the political or economic fields).

Bourdieu suggested that the political counter to this partial scholarship was to take up what the academy said it supported, but actually did not do, namely, a profoundly sceptical stance and a rigorous approach to inquiry. Bourdieu was a strong advocate of detailed empirical work from which theories could be built on a situated case-by-case basis. He argued that a meticulous social science, utilising a broad range of methods, was required. However, this thorough questioning, and methodical approach was not simply to be applied to the object of research, but also to the researcher and her/his positioning within the academic field. Researchers thus had to regard with suspicion and interrogate their own categories, interests and self-construction.

Thus, when Bourdieu called for long-term theoretical elaboration, and an engaged scholarship, he was not proposing contract research for Greenpeace. Perhaps paradoxically, and possibly counter to a commonsense interpretation, Bourdieu was referring to the importance of the allegedly traditional disposition of researchers, that of 'objective' knowledge producers whose precision and 'disinterest' works in the public interest. He suggested (Bourdieu 2004) that researchers must:

1 'objectivate' themselves, and their social, religious, cultural position and trajectory in order to problematise taken for granted assumptions;
2 objectify their position in the space-time of their discipline in order to bring to the surface the shared beliefs, assumptions, silences and censorship of themselves as 'academic'; and
3 objectivate the scholarly universe, and in particular the 'illusion of the absence of illusion' (p. 94).

In order to do such work, methodological and epistemological/ontological rigour was required (I return to this point again later in the chapter). The reflexive intellectual practice Bourdieu promoted, a practice of interrogating not only social phenomena but also the production of knowledge about them, may now be absolutely critical to work on – and against – what he referred to as the depoliticising globalisation agenda.

Following Bourdieu it is critical therefore when considering how to do policy work in globalising times, to take up at the outset the category that underpins the question and frames the response. This is not in order to produce a commentary on existing texts.

Rather, it is to move towards a more nuanced set of contingent, intellectual resources that also indicate how it is that scholarship might be implicated in the production of the very thing it seeks to deconstruct.

Globalisation – the very idea

There are burgeoning popular and academic literatures on globalisation. In response to the search term 'globalisation', the search engine ScholarGoogle produced 68,000 references and 142,000 in response to 'globalisation' (undertaken 4 February 2005). Another web search located 19 journals with either the words globalisation or global in their titles: these included *The Journal of Global Ethics, Global Networks, Global Governance, Global Society* and *Globalisation, Society and Education.*[1] The web bookseller, Amazon (UK) produced 676 titles in response to the word globalisation entered as a book title word (4 February 2005). There are university courses and awards which incorporate globalisation in their title, and many universities, including my own, have globalisation as one of their key interdisciplinary research themes.

Some of these literatures take globalisation as a 'fact'. For example, Anthony Giddens' Reith lectures (1999) were entitled *Runaway World. How Globalisation is Reshaping our Lives*. Sashi Tharoor (2004), celebrated novelist and senior United Nations policy officer, writes:

> The defining features of today's world are the relentless forces of globalisation, the ease of communications and travel, the shrinking of boundaries, the flow of people of all nationalities and colours across the world, the swift pulsing of financial transactions with the press of a button.
>
> (Tharoor 2004)

But many scholars seek to investigate, theorise and challenge this globalisation. Most use definitions of globalisation which refer both to the apparent compression (time-space convergence) of the world and an increased consciousness of the world as a whole (e.g. Robertson 1992). Within education, much of the work on globalisation has emanated from policy scholars. It has by definition tended to focus on the activities of policy makers, namely nation states, and has often taken a highly critical stance of their determinist 'globalisation made me do it' (Kuehn 1998) rhetoric. Avis (2002), for example, in an analysis of English training policies writes:

> In recent years it has become axiomatic that education systems are required to develop human, social and cultural capital so as to render the national economy competitive, with this being built upon value-added labour processes. Underpinning such notions is the idea that economic globalisation stands as some sort of juggernaut that forces nations to respond in particular ways and that those who develop alternative strategies that stand against its logic will become uncompetitive with consequent harm to the social formation. There is no choice but to adapt to the stringencies forced upon the social formation by global economic relations. This notion lies at the centre of New Labour thinking.
>
> (Avis 2002: 77)

This critique of government policy, and its uncritical adoption of globalisation as the rationale for its actions, generally encompasses the following phenomena which are narrativised as:

(1) The continuing concentration of capital, and movement of corporate activities to locations where labour, materials and markets are in ready supply, and the creation of 'rust belt and sunbelt' localities. This has produced a new poverty borne of de-industrialisation which geographically maps together with on-going poverty to (re)produce gendered educational geographies of 'failure' (Anyon 1997; Thomson 2002).
(2) New forms of organisation often referred to as fast capitalism. New forms of post-Fordist flexible organisation yoke not simply the labour of workers to the company, but also their ideas and identities; and there are new forms of management and leadership in which on-going concerns with quality, efficiency and effectiveness are dealt with as questions of strategy, scenarios and soul. These ideas are translated in education policy as a fixation on leadership, standards, teams, and learning networks (Gunter 2001; Thrupp and Wilmott 2003).
(3) A changed nation state which has ceded powers and is now beholden to international policy bodies such as the OECD, World Bank, World Trade Organisation and European Union. These bodies work to homogenise policy agendas across nation states:[2] for example in education the focus on international league tables and tests which drives internal policy reforms (Henry *et al.* 2001, Novoa and Lawn 2002).
(4) The adoption by nation states of neoliberal policy agendas of corporatisation, marketisation and privatisation. In the public sector and in education this is manifest in modernist/modernising New Public Management with its pantechnicon of audit, performativity and impression management technologies (Blackmore and Sachs in press; Robertson 2000). The rhetoric of leadership, individualism and choice mask the ongoing classed practices of dis/advantage (Ball *et al.* 2000; Power *et al.* 2002). Nation states appear to 'borrow' these policies from each other.

At the same time, however, globalisation is also recognised by education policy scholars as dependent on:

(5) The development of high speed information and communication technologies which make possible the operation of 24-hour financial markets; the instantaneous transmission and reception of data, images and narratives around the world and the development of sophisticated networked systems of information storage and retrieval, audit and surveillance. Policies are able to 'travel' by virtue of their online availability to policy-advising bureaucrats.

All together these are the basis for:

(6) a new knowledge economy, in which profitability, productivity and national prosperity are deemed to derive from research and development, innovation and entrepreneurialism in predominantly techno-scientific arenas. New funding for science research has been directed towards universities who are seen as key resources

for national and regional economic development (Marginson and Considine 2000, Peters 2003), rather than as sites for the exercise of reason and the production of national cultures (Readings 1996). The arts and humanities are given token recognition, and despite the rhetoric of life-long learning, further education concentrates not on general adult education but on basic skills and/or competencies seen to be the key to a 'trained' peripheral workforce attractive to transient industries (Coffield 1998; Selwyn *et al.* 2001; Taylor and Henry 1994).

Given this analysis of globalisation and how it plays out in and as education policy, it is not surprising that the literatures show a number of case studies of local manifestations and hybridisations and some work on international policy making and effects in various sites. There are also some arenas of disagreement.

Angus (2004), for example, says that globalisation is a descriptive rather than an explanatory category – it fails to come to grips with the question – Why is this happening and in this way? He is also worried that analyses which foreground international policy elites overstate their role compared to the unexplored activities occurring over capital which remain in a methodological blind spot. Both Lawn (2001) and Hargreaves and Moore (2000) take Smyth and colleagues (Smyth and Dow 1998; Smyth *et al.* 2000) to task for constructing a grand narrative of globalisation in which power operates ruthlessly from top to bottom in a seamless trajectory, rather than discussing local specificity, which Lingard (2000) has described as 'vernacular globalisation'.

However, I propose in the remainder of this chapter that more than this kind of critique is required. In keeping with Bourdieu's urging to see this as a 'policy agenda' as well as taking up the directions already established in educational policy research, I want to ask some critical questions of globalisation as a policy.

Critical scholars are accustomed to generating questions to ask of policy. These include – Where did this policy come from? In whose interests does it work? How might it be different? These are the questions with which educational policy scholars are already engaged. Here I propose some others.

If this policy agenda is a problematisation (Bacchi 1999) then:

- How robust is this problematisation?
- What are its 'blank and blind' (Wagner 1993) spots?
- What possibilities are thus available for reconstruction and/or resistance?

These questions form the basis for the next two sections of this chapter. Throughout I begin to elaborate a series of questions and issues pertinent to educational policy researchers and to educators more generally.

In asking these questions, I am attempting to move beyond the idea of globalisation as an agenda to be critiqued, refuted and researched and towards a position of seeing it as a discourse, a regime of truth or, in Bourdieu's terms, a doxic category. My move therefore is deconstructive in order to partially reconstruct.

Globalisation as problematic

The basic premise here is that even in critiquing globalisation, the category itself remains and indeed may be strengthened even by use which is critical. Therefore, it is imperative that in addition to critique, the problematisation represented by the category is interrogated.

To begin to address the problematisation, it is essential to move outside the confines of education as a disciplinary field. Within the social sciences, the idea of 'globalisation' is seen by some as:

(1) An empirically inadequate category

Hirst and Thompson (1996) suggest that the notion of globalisation is substantively overstated, dehistoricised and based on a 'tendency casually to cite examples of internationalisation of sectors and processes as if they were evidence of the growth of an economy dominated by autonomous market forces' (p. 2). Given that imperialism, migration and international trade are ongoing practices, they suggest that more careful historical work is required to establish what material, cultural and political shifts have actually taken place, where and for what reasons and with what effects. Feminist geographers Gibson-Graham (1996) argue that the notion of capitalism as ever-concentrating and totalising, is an essentialised and masculinist grand narrative which ignores the everyday realities of most people's lives and the simultaneous presence of other subaltern economies. They cite the existence of family and community-based economies, cooperatives and collectives, practices which constitute discursive resources for thinking of alternative arrangements.

(2) An homogenising category

The suggestion appears to be that all nation states are the same under globalisation. This fails to recognise the unevenness of the phenomena in question. In particular, it imposes a description of what is happening in Western nation states on all nations and, in refusing to deal with the power imbalances across the globe, actually works to maintain the invisibility of imperialist relations and the domination and machinations of American-Anglo corporations seeking further advantage via free trade agreements of various kinds. It further glosses over the different responses of nation states. New Public Management, for example, is not imposed in all 'advanced capitalist' countries, and is not automatically associated with neoliberalism in the states in which it is adopted (Hood 1995, 1998).

(3) A myopic category

The dominant metaphor used of globalisation is as a series of nested Russian dolls with the large one dictating the activities of all of the smaller ones within. The alternative is to recognise that globalisation always occurs somewhere particular, that it concerns not only questions of scale but also the ongoing histories, cultures and politics of distinctive national, regional and local places. There are various attempts to name this specificity – the 'glocal' (Robertson 1992) being one of the most well known.

Another critique is that globalisation cannot capture the simultaneous interconnectedness, fluidity and lacunae, conflicts and shifts of what is happening. Appadurai (1996) argued the benefits of 'scapes', Castells (1996, 1997, 1998) the idea of 'flows', Giddens (1990) the notion of time-space compression, while Massey (1993, 1999) developed the notion of power-geometries and thinking of the local as embedded in 'stretched out relations'. Massey, along with other geographers, is highly critical of the notion of 'flows' in particular, because of the implied metaphor of space as an a-temporal empty container through which culture travels.

(4) A dangerous category

Many scholars simply find the category and its narratives unhelpful or unappealing. Thrift (1996) has worked on understanding what he calls the 'phantom state', a network of money, information and communication flows and state institutions, as an alternative to the idea of deterritorialisation embodied in the term 'globalisation'. He argues instead for reterritorialisations. James (1996) wants to redeem the importance of the nation state. According to him, there is still no viable alternative in sight that can be held responsible for the redistribution of resources and for the production and maintenance of civic order. Robbins (1999) argues that the idea of internationalism should be revived since it carries with it a significant history of ethical-political action.

These are only a sample of the arguments that are currently in play in the social sciences. However, they do serve to illustrate the possibility of alternative approaches within educational policy research. Rather than simply using globalisation as a government policy agenda to contextualise a study, to critique and/or to connect to findings, there are alternative ways of both framing and theorising policy 'contexts, texts and effects' (Taylor 1997) which neither simply accept/reject the representation offered.

I now explore this option further by taking up the second and third of my questions related to blank and blind spots. I sketch three other phenomena taken as globalisation, and briefly indicate some opportunities for educational policy research.

Globalisation – blank and blind spots

My purpose in this section is to sketch out an argument and to show possibilities. Here, I turn not only to other disciplines but also to other areas of education inquiry with which policy researchers might fruitfully converse. In particular, I point to a disconnect between curriculum and policy researchers. This is particularly alarming in those countries like England in which the national curriculum is only discussed in official policy texts as a technical matter – a question of 'effective' learning and teaching and the management of time, sorting and grouping, and testing – rather than also as the sum of substantive decisions about which and whose knowledges are important and to what ends (Young 1998).

Globalisation can also be understood as:

(1) A deepening environmental crisis which produces unpredictable weather, water and food catastrophes, a loose social 'green' movement organised as networks of opposition, and the refusal/inability of nation states to regulate environmentally damaging corporate activities.

There are curriculum implications here for educators, not only about subject matter but about the ethical underpinnings of the curriculum (Gough 1999). There are also strong imperatives for self-managing schools, most of whom do not connect local responsibility for budgets with questions of sustainability and civic responsibility. There is scope here for policy work which might prove influential in raising awareness of these issues.

(2) Increased movement of people around the world, as refugees and immigrant workers (Barndt 2002; Brah *et al.* 1999) on the one hand, and elite 'knowledge-workers' and well-heeled tourists (Judd *et al.* 1999) on the other. As a result there is deepening diversity in large and small population centres and heightened connections and familiarity with places far away from 'home'. The development of sequestered communities (Davis 1992), and tribalisms and internecine fundamentalisms (Giddens 1991; Maffesoli 1995) is concurrent with moves to 'world cities' (Sassen 1994). This is accompanied by escalating intervention by the USA and associated allies in the affairs of 'other' nations by means of tied loans, aid and war; and deepening inequity between and within nation states (Allen and Hamnett 1995,; Bauman 1998; Lovering 1998). Issues of whether to assimilate, integrate or reject 'strangers' is constructed in part by transnational patterns/structures (Dale 1999) and it presents ethical–political dilemmas that are shared by many nation states – even if their solutions are not the same.

Educational policy specifically concerned with social justice and the theoretical debates around recognition and redistribution cannot afford to ignore the transnational dimensions of justice and focus only on the specific policies of single nation states. These are inextricably connected with wider movements, and in the case of Commonwealth countries like Canada, Australia, New Zealand and South Africa, it is utterly impossible to move far into discussion of equity, diversity and difference without considering the vexed practices of reconciliation with traditional land owners (the legacy of earlier periods of international imperialism). However, as noted earlier, individual national policy responses to the division and sharing of social space vary. It is perhaps surprising that the limited notions of citizenship enshrined in the national curricula of nation states have not been more strongly critiqued by policy scholars interested in 'globalisation', that there is not more attention paid to the bifurcation of the public spaces of cities via urban planning policies and the connections with school 'choice', and that the quandaries around inclusion of faith schools in public education systems and the very varied policy options adopted by different nation states are not debated more strenuously.[3]

(3) Recognisable cultural shifts which bring the aestheticisation of everyday life, a shift to bespoke cultural consumption and proliferating commercialised and oppositional subcultures (Andrews 1997; Nayak 2003) are accompanied, some suggest, by a general 'McDonaldisation' of lifeworlds (Ritzer 1993, 1998), hyper-reality (Baudrillard 1994), 'risk' (Beck 1992) and the growth of 'non-places' (Auge 1995). New identities and new 'places' are constructed in the interstices and tangles of these phenomena (Featherstone 1995, King 1997, Short and Kim 1999). Media is increasingly the arena through which politics and policy are played out.

Some educational policy attention[4] is now beginning to be paid to the imbrication of media and policy. Politics is now irrevocably conducted in and through media. The practices of politicians and policy actors now explicitly include attention to language and image (Fairclough 2000). Governments attempt to steer media: they orchestrate their policy making via continuous polling, press releases and the granting of strategic exclusive stories to favoured journalists, well-timed broadcasts and even insertion of key government initiatives into popular television soaps. They employ staff dedicated specifically to write policy and to develop the bite-sized media 'definitions' which encapsulate policy initiatives. A recent book by a former adviser to UK prime minister Tony Blair, *One out of Ten* (Hyman 2005), is explicit about the strategies employed by New Labour to counter what Hyman describes as a cynical and unsupportive media. He not only confesses to being the originator of the damaging phrase 'bog standard comprehensive' but also acknowledges and details the problems produced for schools by the government's continued need to be seen to be launching policy initiatives on the basis of improvement (movement toward 'targets').

The rhetoric of policy, and the images of education conveyed in media and popular film and fiction are fruitful areas for policy work. Of course, the relationship between media, politics and policy is complex: each field has considerable influence on the other. However, it is a critical and relatively undeveloped arena for policy inquiry, since media discourses (re)produce both public and everyday life (Blackman and Walkerdine 2001).

These were just three examples of how a focus on the blank and blind spots created by the idea of globalisation might yield particular opportunities for policy scholars. There are of course many more. In the next section of this chapter I move on to consider what flows from the kind of deconstruction and inter and intra-disciplinary work I have been advocating.

Resistance and reconstruction

I have argued that education policy research might benefit from stronger connections with other academic work that interrogates 'globalisation'. Here, I suggest that similar benefits might accrue from more systematic connections with more general sociological literatures on the times in which we live. I particularly look here to the various presentations of late modernity/high modernity/late capitalism/risk society/postmodernity combined with work from sociology, anthropology, cultural studies and political philosophy which attempts to develop (re)generative theoretical resources.

There are now interesting opportunities for such hybridised policy work. The move to post/modernist national curriculum frames in Quebec, Canada and Tasmania and Queensland Australia, are of international interest and significance; they attempt to marry an analysis of changing times with the need for new knowledges; they move into knowledge domains rather than traditional disciplines; and the two Australian versions offer collectives of teachers the opportunity to act as professional knowledge producers. In order to make sense of how these curriculum policies came into being, a complex set of macro, meso and micro policy analyses would be required.

Another area of policy interest is concerned with what might be seen as the increasing pedagogicisation of everyday life effected on the one hand via media and the changing role of cultural institutions and digitised knowledge 'archives', and on the other through the continued intrusion of schooling into family lives and training into work/ underemployment/unemployment. While the latter of these is the subject of considerable educational policy activity, the connections and tensions between the two are not often noted. A strong theorisation of the production of the subject within knowledge capitalism would be only one aspect of such a research project.

A concrete example of the kind of policy scholarship I am arguing for can be found in recent work by Kenway, Bullen and Robb (Bullen *et al.* 2004; Kenway *et al.* 2004, 2005). They have taken one of the key planks of the globalisation, the knowledge economy, interrogated it and illustrated the absence of the Arts and Humanities. They then propose a retheorisation of an approach to knowledge capitalism, utilising Lash and Urry's (1987) notion of 'disorganised capitalism' and Beck's argument for reflexivity, which builds on the traditions of critical creativity within the arts. They then document examples of the ways in which this theory is made practical by describing two projects, one in the Creative Industries, and the other an interdisciplinary science-arts endeavour. This scholarship points to the benefits of more work on knowledge production itself as a means of reviving educational research.

Taking account of the existing debates about the validity or otherwise of practitioner and professional knowledge, thinking about the production of a well-educated society and interrogating the idea of 'lifelong learning', there is scope here for moving educational research into new terrains. In the light of economist definitions of knowledge economies, we need to engage more strenuously with questions of the production of knowledge,[5] as opposed to research on 'teaching and learning', which largely obliterates important questions about the nature, interests, communities, purposes and landscapes of knowledge itself.

Finally, and possibly counter to the arguments made so far in this chapter, there is also gain to be had from continuing to work with the idea of globalisation, but as a term whose meaning is, as Derrida (1978) suggests, open to endless play. Buenfil-Buergos (2000: 6) proposes that globalisation should be seen as an open sign in which political work can be done.

> The association of globalization with a neoliberal, postmodern, and postsocialist global capitalist society ... can be superseded by progressive anticapitalist global perspectives: in this enterprise Rationalism and Habermas's non-distorted communicative action would play a key role ... we can have bad capitalist globalization as a necessary condition for the emergence of a good global village.
>
> (Buenfil-Buergos 2000: 6)

In arguing for seeing globalisation as coming from above and below, in suggesting that the notions of anti-imperialist politics and decolonising theory ought to be brought into the policy research ambit, in positing a new cosmopolitanism, in putting the body and its labour together with the internationalisation of capital, scholars are reappropriating globalisation and marrying it with alternative formulations of the social phenomena in play.

The incomplete list of critiques and alternative proposals I have provided are reason to consider carefully the ways in which the notion of globalisation is used as a contextualisation for analysis, or as an explanation of findings. The even more under-theorised idea of 'policy borrowing', dubbed a 'stumpy little offshoot' by Lawn (2001: 436) in connection with work on teachers, is even more of a concern.

However, in conclusion, and rather than attempt further deconstruction, I conclude by considering briefly, as Bourdieu would argue must be the case, how it is possible to do this work within the current university/ies.

Problematic places from which to speak about policy

Scholarship is of course not outside this 'globalisation' nor its de and reconstruction. Universities now: operate as businesses competing for international students; seek to advance their status in world as well as national and local league tables; and advertise internationally for staff. Academics now routinely travel to other countries for conferences and sabbaticals, conduct joint international projects, publish in journals with 'international standing' and readership, and benefit from opportunities to move from one country to another. Academic work is produced in contexts which are increasingly subject to modernist management and audit regimes, and the push for 'performativity' is a recognisable transnational concern.

However, as argued, academic work is not simply produced by this kind of academic 'globalisation', the social sciences in particular are also responsible for producing the theorisations of globalisation, new times, late and high modernity and so on. Since this scholarship is not neutral, describing a world 'out there' and a detached 'truth', but it is both productive and reproductive of the social economic and political world, the questions of how and what we, as social scientists do/think/write is of importance. I have argued that policy researchers need to become more deconstructive and also more inter- and intra-disciplinary in their orientation.

This kind of inter and transdisciplinary knowledge production is explained, within the academic community, as a characteristic of the time in which we live, namely traditional boundaries of all descriptions, including those around knowledge, are breaking down. But, in another example of the mutually (re)productive nature of academic work, universities and research funding councils are also engaged in actively promoting interdisciplinarity, opening numerous new research centres which bring together scholars from various schools and departments. Even though it is generally not the theoretical work within the academy that is used to legitimate the new interdisciplinary centres, but more often government policy rhetoric about 'knowledge-based economies/societies or information economies/societies' the end result is the same – interdisciplinarity is favoured over strictly bounded disciplinary activity. This is of course a classic illustration of Bourdieu's thesis of academic distinction: 'homo academicus' is both a product of, and produces the structure, culture and relations of the institution (Bourdieu 1988, Bourdieu *et al.* 1995).

However, at the same time, in education in particular, there is active policy encouragement of particular forms of knowledge production – randomised trials, large-scale quantitative studies, a focus on 'what works'. I do not intend to reproduce the debates here, but it is important to note the particularity of demands made on educational research and the rhetorical contradiction with other research policy that promotes interdisciplinary work and knowledge production in new professional spaces. That we have not yet come to terms with these kinds of policy demands, and continue to be engaged in 'mono-disciplinary' activities points to a possible failure to take up the opprotunities on offer. We have not yet agreed as a scholarly community on what might constitute the rules of good research. Discussions about methodological standards that are not standardising of methodololies (cf. Burbules and Philips 2000) in combination with the adoption of an ontological/epistemological stance that is self-critical are yet to achieve consensus.

Bourdieu provides something of a lead here, although not one that is complete, since there is no getting outside of social practice. As outlined, he argues for principled scholarly activity that refuses to be commandeered by partisan interests, a reflexive stance – which is these times is more akin to schizophrenic dialogue between identities – and connections with broader social movements to which the knowledge produced is of practical use. Bourdieu's 'sociology as a martial art' saw him writing for a range of audiences, particularly as a journalist in *Le Monde* and other 'quality' media. He made himself available for private consultations with leaders of progressive political organisations and, when asked, spoke in public. He also saw his teaching as a key activity. Edward Said had much the same repertoire and argument.

It is not the case that all of us can do this. There are not enough media outlets, not all social movements are receptive, some of us inhabit profoundly anti-intellectual spaces, and in some cases, speaking out may well be a very risky business. It is clear from the examples of the great public intellectuals that while one can be ontologically and politically committed to a cause and the basis for scholarship clearly epistemologically situated in a (post)critical theory, the methodological approach taken must be, in order to be both academic and potentially useful, as close to the rhetoric of tough minded, thorough and objective scholarship as far as possible. To recapitulate my argument, this means treating all propositions with suspicion, especially those we hold dearest. Globalisation as a category must be held as potentially dangerous while being both a simultaneously helpful and unavoidable category. We must continue to ask how we are benefiting from its use.

This kind of scholarship, Bourdieu suggests, is paradoxically profoundly political.

Notes

1 The additional 14 journals were: *International Journal of Technology and Globalisation*; *Yale Global Online*; *Journal of Global History*; *Global Society*; *Journal of Global Awareness*; *Globalisation Journal*; *The Global Economy Journal*; *Indiana Journal of Global Legal Studies*; *Journal of Global Bhuddism*; *Globalization*; *Global Public Health*; *Global Media and Communications*; *Journal of Ethics and Globalisation* and *The Global Policy Journal*. Search conducted 4 February 2005 using Scholar Google.
2 See, for example, the special issue of *European Educational Research Journal* (2005) 4(1) on 'travelling policy' in post-socialist education.
3 There are of course exceptions: on citizenship, for example, see Kennedy (1997), Hall *et al.* (1999) and Davies *et al.* (2005); on choice, cities and public space, see Pacione (1997) on Glasgow, and Kozol (1991) and Anyon (1997) on urban USA for partial explications; and on religious and private schools and the erosion of 'the public' see, for example, Harrison and Kachur (1999) on Alberta and Reid and Thomson (2003) on Australia.
4 See, for example, the special issue of *Journal of Education Policy* 19(3).
5 For example, there is much debate to be had around the ideas of Gibbons *et al.* (1994) which are confined largely to discussions of professional doctorates.

References

Allen, J. and Hamnett, C. (eds) (1995) *A Shrinking World? Global Unevenness and Inequality*, Oxford and New York: Oxford University Press.
Andrews, D. (1997) 'The (trans) National Basketball Association: American commodity – sign culture and global-local conjuncturalism', in A. Cvetkovich and D. Kellner (eds) *Articulating*

the Global and the Local. Globalisation and Cultural Studies, Boulder, CO: Westview Press, 72–101.

Angus, L. (2004) 'Globalization and educational change: bringing about the reshaping and renorming of practice', *Journal of Education Policy*, 19(1): 23–41.

Anyon, J. (1997) *Ghetto Schooling. A Political Economy of Urban Educational Reform*, New York and London: Teachers College Press.

Appadurai, A. (1996) *Modernity at Large. Cultural Dimensions of Globalisation*, Minneapolis, MN and London: University of Minnesota Press.

Auge, M. (1995) *Non-places. Introduction to an Anthropology of Supermodernity* (trans. J. Howe), London and New York: Verso.

Avis, J. (2002) 'Imaginary friends: managerialism, globalisation and post-compulsory education and training in England', *Discourse*, 23(1): 75–90.

Bacchi, C.L. (1999) *Women, Policy and Politics. The Construction of Policy Problems*, London, Thousand Oaks, CA and New Delhi: Sage.

Ball, S., Maguire, M. and Macrae, S. (2000) *Choice, Pathways and Transitions Post-16. New Youth, New Economies in the Global City*, London: Falmer.

Barndt, D. (2002) *Tangled Routes. Women, Work and Globalisation on the Tomato Trail*, Lanham, MD: Rowman and Littlefield.

Baudrillard, J. (1994) *Simulacra and simulation* (trans. S. F. Glaser), Ann Arbor, MI: University of Michigan Press.

Bauman, Z. (1998) *Globalisation. The Human Consequences*, New York: Columbia University Press.

Beck, U. (1992) *Risk Society. Towards a New Modernity*, London: Sage.

Blackman, L. and Walkerdine, V. (2001) *Mass Hysteria. Critical Psychology and Media Studies*, Basingstoke and New York: Palgrave.

Blackmore, J. and Sachs, J. (in press) *Performing and Reforming Leaders: Gender, Educational Restructuring and Organisational Change*, New York: SUNY.

Bourdieu, P. (1988) *Homo Academicus* (trans. P. Collier), Stanford, CA: Stanford University Press.

Bourdieu, P. (1990) *In Other Words. Essays Towards a Reflexive Sociology*. Stanford, CA: Stanford University Press.

Bourdieu, P. (1998) *Acts of Resistance. Against the New Myths of our Time*, Cambridge: Polity Press.

Bourdieu, P. (2000) *Pascalian Meditations*, Cambridge: Polity Press.

Bourdieu, P. (2003) *Firing Back. Against the Tyranny of the Market 2* (trans. L. Wacquant), New York: The New Press.

Bourdieu, P. (2004). *Science of Science and Reflexivity* (trans. R. Nice), Cambridge: Polity Press.

Bourdieu, P., Passeron, J.-C. and de Saint Martin, M. (1995) *Academic Discourse* (trans. R. Teese. Original edn 1965), Stanford, CA: Stanford University Press.

Brah, A., Hickman, M. and Mac An Ghaill, M. (eds) (1999) *Global Futures. Migration, Environment and Globalisation*, London and New York: St Martins Press.

Buenfil-Buergos, R. N. (2000) 'Globalization, education and discourse political analysis: ambiguity and accountability in research', *Qualitative Studies in Education*, 13(1): 1–24.

Bullen, E., Robb, S. and Kenway, J. (2004) ' "Creative destruction": knowledge economy policy and the future of the arts and humanities in the academy', *Journal of Education Policy*, 19(1): 3–22.

Burbules, N. and Philips, D. (2000) *Postpostivism and Educational Research*, Lanham, MD: Rowman and Littlefield.

Castells, M. (1996) *The Information Age: Economy, Society and Culture. The Rise of the Network Society*, Oxford: Blackwell.

Castells, M. (1997) *The Information Age: Economy, Society and Culture. The Power of Identity*, Oxford: Blackwell.

Castells, M. (1998) *The Information Age: Economy, Society and Culture. End of the Millenium*, Oxford: Blackwell.

Coffield, F. (1998) 'A tale of three little pigs: building the learning society with straw', *Evaluation and Research in Education*, 12(1): 44–58.

Dale, R. (1999) 'Specifying global effects on national policy: a focus on the mechanisms', *Journal of Education Policy*, 14(1): 1–14.

Davies, I., Evans, M., and Reid, A. (2005) 'Globalising citizenship education? A critique of "global education" and "citizenship education"', *British Journal of Educational Studies*, 53(1): 66–89.

Davis, M. (1992) *City of Quartz. Excavating the Future in Los Angeles*, London: Vintage.

Derrida, J. (1978) *Writing and Difference* (trans. A. Bass, 1995 edn), London: Routledge.

Fairclough, N. (2000) *New Labour, New Language*, London: Routledge.

Featherstone, M. (1995) *Undoing Culture. Globalisation, Postmodernism and Identity*, London, Thousand Oaks, CA and New Delhi: Sage.

Gibbons, M., Limoges, C., Nowotny, H., Schwartzman, S., Scott, P. and Trow, M. (1994) *The New Production of Knowledge: The Dynamics of Science and Research*, London: Sage.

Gibson-Graham, J.K. (1996) *The End of Capitalism (as we knew it). A Feminist Critique of Political Economy*, Oxford: Blackwell.

Giddens, A. (1990) *The Consequences of Modernity*, Cambridge: Polity Press.

Giddens, A. (1991) *Modernity and Self-identity*, Stanford, CA: Stanford University Press.

Giddens, A. (1999) *Runaway World. How Globalisation is Reshaping our Lives*, London: Profile Books.

Gough, N. (1999) 'Globalisation and school curriculum change: locating a transnational imaginary', *Journal of Education Policy*, 14(1): 73–84.

Gunter, H. (2001) *Leaders and Leadership in Education*, London: Paul Chapman Publishing.

Hall, T., Coffey, A. and Williamson, H. (1999) 'Self, space and place: youth identities and citizenship', *British Journal of Sociology of Education*, 20(4): 501–13.

Hargreaves, A. and Moore, S. (2000) 'Educational outcomes, modern and postmodern interpretations: response to Smyth and Dow', *British Journal of Sociology of Education*, 21(1): 27–42.

Harrison, T. and Kachur, J. (eds) (1999) *Contested Classrooms. Education, Globalisation and Democracy in Alberta*, Edmonton: University of Alberta Press.

Henry, M., Lingard, B., Rizvi, F. and Taylor, S. (2001) *The OECD, Globalisation, and Education Policy*, Oxford: Pergamon Press.

Hirst, P. and Thompson, G. (1996) *Globalisation in Question: The International Economy and the Possibility of Governance*, Cambridge: Polity Press.

Hood, C. (1995) 'The "New Public Management" in the 1980s: variations on a theme', *Accounting, Organisations and Society*, 20(2/3): 93–109.

Hood, C. (1998) *The Art of the State. Culture, Rhetoric and Public Management*, Oxford: Clarendon Press.

Hyman, P. (2005) *1 out of 10. From Downing Street Vision to Classroom Reality*, London: Vintage.

James, P. (ed) (1996) *The State in Question. Transformations of the Australian State*, Sydney: Allen and Unwin.

Judd, Dennis, B. and Fainstein, S. (eds) (1999) *The Tourist City*, New Haven, CT: Yale University Press.

Kennedy, K. (ed.) (1997) *Citizenship Education and the Modern State*, London: Falmer Press.

Kenway, J., Bullen, E. and Robb, S. (2004) 'The knowledge economy, the techno-preneur and the problematic future of the university', *Policy Futures in Education* 2(2), 330–49.

Kenway, J., Bullen, E. and Robb, S. (2005) *Innovation and Tradition. The Arts, Humanities and the Knowledge Economy*, New York: Peter Lang.

King, A. (ed) (1997) *Culture, Globalisation, and the World System: Contemporary Conditions for the Representation of Identity*, Minneapolis, MN: University of Minnesota Press.

Kozol, J. (1991) *Savage Inequalities: Children in America's Schools*, New York: Harper Perennial.

Kuehn, L. (1998, August 20) 'Globalisation made me do it', Paper presented at the VETNet conference: Changing Work, Changing Society, Adelaide.

Lash, S. and Urry, J. (1987) *The End of Organised Capitalism*, Oxford: Blackwell.

Lawn, M. (2001) Extended review of Smyth, Dow, Hattam and Reid (2000) 'Teachers' work in a globalizing economy', *British Journal of Sociology of Education*, 22(3): 435–39.

Lingard, B. (2000) 'It is and it isn't: vernacular globalisation, educational policy and restructuring', in N. Burbules and C. Torres (eds) *Globalisation and Education. Critical Perspectives*, New York: Routledge, 79–108.

Lovering, J. (1998) 'Globalisation, unemployment and "social exclusion" in Europe: three perspectives on the current policy debate', *International Planning Studies*, 3(1): 35–56.

Maffesoli, M. (1995) *The Time of the Tribes: The Decline of Individualism in Mass Societies* (trans. D. Smith), London and Thousand Oaks, CA: Sage.

Marginson, S. and Considine, M. (2000) *The Enterprise University: Power, Governance and Reinvention in Australia*, Cambridge: Cambridge University Press.

Massey, D. (1993) 'Power-geometry and a progressive sense of place', in J. Bird, B. Curtis, T. Putnam, G. Robertson and L. Tickner (eds) *Mapping the Futures. Local Cultures, Global Change*, London: Routledge, 59–69.

Massey, D. (1999) 'Imagining globalisation: power-geometries of time-space', in A. Brah, M. Hickman and M. Mac An Ghaill (eds) *Global Futures, Migration, Environment and Globalisation*, London: Macmillan, 27–44.

Nayak, A. (2003) *Race, Place and Globalisation. Youth Cultures in a Changing World*, Oxford: Berg.

Novoa, A. and Lawn, M. (eds) (2002) *Fabricating Europe: The Formation of an Education Space*, Dordrecht: Kluwer.

Pacione, M. (1997) 'The geography of educational disadvantage in Glasgow', *Applied Geography*, 17(3): 169–92.

Peters, M. (2003) *Building Knowledge Cultures: Education in an Age of Knowledge Capitalism*, Lanham, MD: Rowman and Littlefield.

Power, S., Edwards, T., Whitty, G. and Wigfall, V. (2002) *Education and the Middle Classes*, Buckingham: Open University Press.

Readings, B. (1996) *The University in Ruins*, Cambridge, MA: Harvard University Press.

Reid, A. and Thomson, P. (eds) (2003) *Rethinking Public Education: Towards a Public Curriculum*, Brisbane: Postpressed.

Ritzer, G. (1993) *The McDonaldisation of Society*, Thousand Oaks, CA: Pine Forge Press.

Ritzer, G. (1998) *The McDonaldisation Thesis*, London, Thousand Oaks, CA and New Delhi: Sage.

Robbins, B. (1999) *Feeling Global. Internationalism in Distress*, New York: New York University Press.

Robertson, R. (1992) *Globalisation, Social Theory and Global Culture*, London: Sage.

Robertson, S. (2000) *A Class Act: Changing Teachers' Work, the State and Globalisation*, London: Falmer.

Sassen, S. (1994) *Cities in a World Economy*, Thousand Oaks, CA: Pine Forge Press.

Selwyn, N., Gorard, S. and Williams, J. (2001) 'The role of the "technical fix" in UK lifelong learning policy', *International Journal of Lifelong Education*, 20(4): 255–71.

Short, J.R. and Kim, Y.-H. (1999) *Globalisation and the City*, Essex: Longman.

Smyth, J. and Dow, A. (1998) 'What's wrong with outcomes? Spotter planes, action plans and steerage of the educational workplace', *British Journal of Sociology of Education*, 19(3): 291–304.

Smyth, J., Dow, A., Hattam, R., Reid , A. and Shacklock, G. (2000) *Teachers' Work in a Globalizing Economy*, London: Falmer.

Taylor, S. (1997) 'Critical policy analysis: exploring contexts, texts and consequences', *Discourse*, 23(13): 23–35.

Taylor, S. and Henry, M. (1994) 'Equity and the new post-compulsory education and training policies in Australia: a progressive or regressive agenda?', *Journal of Education Policy*, 9(2): 105–27.

Tharoor, S. (2004) 'Globalisation and the human imagination', *World Policy Journal* (summer). Online. Available HTTP: http://www.sashitharoor.com/articles/WPJ-sum04.htm (accessed 28 February 2005).

Thomson, P. (2002) *Schooling the Rustbelt Kids. Making the Difference in Changing Times*, Sydney: Allen & Unwin (Trentham Books UK).

Thrift, N. (1996) *Spatial Formations*, London: Sage.

Thrupp, M. and Wilmott, R. (2003) *Educational Management in Managerialist Times: Beyond the Textual Apologists*, Buckingham: Open University Press.

Wagner, J. (1993) 'Ignorance in educational research: or, how can you not know that?', *Educational Researcher*, 22(5): 15–23.

Young, M. (1998) *The Curriculum of the Future: From the New Sociology of Education to a Critical Theory of Learning*, London: RoutledgeFalmer.

Index